Empowering Low-Resource Languages With NLP Solutions

Partha Pakray
National Institute of Technology, Silchar, India

Pankaj Dadure
University of Petroleum and Energy Studies, India

Sivaji Bandyopadhyay
Jadavpur University, India

A volume in the Advances in Computational Intelligence and Robotics (ACIR) Book Series

IGI Global
PUBLISHER of TIMELY KNOWLEDGE

Published in the United States of America by
IGI Global
Engineering Science Reference (an imprint of IGI Global)
701 E. Chocolate Avenue
Hershey PA, USA 17033
Tel: 717-533-8845
Fax: 717-533-8661
E-mail: cust@igi-global.com
Web site: http://www.igi-global.com

Library of Congress Cataloging-in-Publication Data

Names: Pakray, Partha, 1982- editor. | Dadure, Pankaj, 1994- editor. | Bandyopadhyay, Sivaji, 1963- editor.
Title: Empowering low-resource languages with NLP solutions / edited by: Partha Pakray, Pankaj Dadure, Sivaji Bandyopadhyay.
Description: Hershey PA : Engineering Science Reference, [2024] | Includes bibliographical references. | Summary: "The book aims to fill the gap in the existing literature and shed light on the unique challenges, opportunities, and potential solutions for applying NLP techniques to low-resource languages"-- Provided by publisher.
Identifiers: LCCN 2023049085 (print) | LCCN 2023049086 (ebook) | ISBN 9798369307281 (hardcover) | ISBN 9798369307298 (ebook)
Subjects: LCSH: Computational linguistics. | Natural language processing (Computer science) | Low-resource languages.
Classification: LCC P98 .E47 2024 (print) | LCC P98 (ebook) | DDC 006.3/5--dc23/eng/20240409
LC record available at https://lccn.loc.gov/2023049085
LC ebook record available at https://lccn.loc.gov/2023049086

This book is published in the IGI Global book series Advances in Computational Intelligence and Robotics (ACIR) (ISSN: 2327-0411; eISSN: 2327-042X)

British Cataloguing in Publication Data
A Cataloguing in Publication record for this book is available from the British Library.

Advances in Computational Intelligence and Robotics (ACIR) Book Series

Ivan Giannoccaro
University of Salento, Italy

ISSN:2327-0411
EISSN:2327-042X

MISSION

While intelligence is traditionally a term applied to humans and human cognition, technology has progressed in such a way to allow for the development of intelligent systems able to simulate many human traits. With this new era of simulated and artificial intelligence, much research is needed in order to continue to advance the field and also to evaluate the ethical and societal concerns of the existence of artificial life and machine learning.

The **Advances in Computational Intelligence and Robotics (ACIR) Book Series** encourages scholarly discourse on all topics pertaining to evolutionary computing, artificial life, computational intelligence, machine learning, and robotics. ACIR presents the latest research being conducted on diverse topics in intelligence technologies with the goal of advancing knowledge and applications in this rapidly evolving field.

COVERAGE

- Intelligent Control
- Artificial Life
- Evolutionary Computing
- Pattern Recognition
- Computational Logic
- Agent technologies
- Robotics
- Brain Simulation
- Artificial Intelligence
- Synthetic Emotions

IGI Global is currently accepting manuscripts for publication within this series. To submit a proposal for a volume in this series, please contact our Acquisition Editors at Acquisitions@igi-global.com or visit: http://www.igi-global.com/publish/.

The Advances in Computational Intelligence and Robotics (ACIR) Book Series (ISSN 2327-0411) is published by IGI Global, 701 E. Chocolate Avenue, Hershey, PA 17033-1240, USA, www.igi-global.com. This series is composed of titles available for purchase individually; each title is edited to be contextually exclusive from any other title within the series. For pricing and ordering information please visit http://www.igi-global.com/book-series/advances-computational-intelligence-robotics/73674. Postmaster: Send all address changes to above address.

Titles in this Series

For a list of additional titles in this series, please visit: http://www.igi-global.com/book-series/

Principles and Applications of Adaptive Artificial Intelligence
Zhihan Lv (Uppsala University, Sweden)
Engineering Science Reference • © 2024 • 300pp • H/C (ISBN: 9798369302309) • US $325.00

AI and Blockchain Applications in Industrial Robotics
Rajashekhar C. Biradar (Reva University, India) Geetha D. (Reva University, India) Nikhath Tabassum (Reva University, India) Nayana Hegde (Reva University, India) and Mihai Lazarescu (Politecnico di Torino, Italy)
Engineering Science Reference • © 2024 • 414pp • H/C (ISBN: 9798369306598) • US $300.00

Emerging Advancements in AI and Big Data Technologies in Business and Society
Jingyuan Zhao (University of Toronto, Canada) Joseph Richards (California State University, Sacramento, USA) and V. Vinoth Kumar (Vellore Institute of Technology, India)
Engineering Science Reference • © 2024 • 320pp • H/C (ISBN: 9798369306833) • US $270.00

Advanced Applications of Generative AI and Natural Language Processing Models
Ahmed J. Obaid (University of Kufa, Iraq) Bharat Bhushan (School of Engineering and Technology, Sharda University, India) Muthmainnah S. (Universitas Al Asyariah Mandar, Indonesia) and S. Suman Rajest (Dhaanish Ahmed College of Engineering, India)
Engineering Science Reference • © 2024 • 481pp • H/C (ISBN: 9798369305027) • US $270.00

Artificial Intelligence in the Age of Nanotechnology
Wassim Jaber (ESPCI Paris - PSL, France)
Engineering Science Reference • © 2024 • 299pp • H/C (ISBN: 9798369303689) • US $300.00

IGI Global
PUBLISHER of TIMELY KNOWLEDGE

701 East Chocolate Avenue, Hershey, PA 17033, USA
Tel: 717-533-8845 x100 • Fax: 717-533-8661
E-Mail: cust@igi-global.com • www.igi-global.com

Table of Contents

Preface xiv

Chapter 1
Datraw, Advancing Collaborative Data Collection, and Recognition Models for Low Resource Languages in the Research Community 1
Bandaru Sugandhi, MathWorks, India

Chapter 2
Language Resource Acquisition for Low-Resource Languages in Digital Discourses 11
Kathiravan Pannerselvam, Central University of Tamil Nadu, India
Saranya Rajiakodi, Central University of Tamil Nadu, India
Bharathi Raja Chakravarthi, University of Galway, Ireland

Chapter 3
Linguistic Analyzers of the Arabic Language: Linguistic Engineering Basis..... 25
Ali Boulaalam, Moulay Ismail University, Meknes, Morocco
Nisrine El Hannach, Poly-Disciplinary Faculty of Nador, Mohammed 1st University, Oujda, Morocco

Chapter 4
A Case Study on Tools and Techniques of Machine Translation of Indian Low Resource Languages 51
Anuraj Bose, Vellore Institute of Technology, India
Goutam Majumder, Vellore Institute of Technology, India

Chapter 5
Systematic Review of Morphological and Semantic Analysis in a Low Resource Language: Tamil 86
P. Matan, College of Engineering Guindy, Anna University, Chennai, India
P. Velvizhy, College of Engineering Guindy, Anna University, Chennai, India

Chapter 6
Machine Learning Approach for Kashmiri Word Sense Disambiguation 113
Aadil Ahmad Lawaye, Baba Ghulam Shah Badshah University, India
Tawseef Ahmad Mir, Alliance University, India
Mahmood Hussain Mir, Alliance University, India
Ghayas Ahmed, Baba Ghulam Shah Badshah University, India

Chapter 7
Implementation and Analysis of Shallow Parsing Techniques in Khasi Language 137
Eusebius Lawai Lyngdoh, North-Eastern Hill University, India
Aiom Minnette Mitri, North-Eastern Hill University, India
Goutam Saha, North-Eastern Hill University, India
Arnab Kumar Maji, North-Eastern Hill University, India

Chapter 8
Named Entity Recognition (NER) in Low Resource Languages of Ho 157
Satya Ranjan Dash, KIIT University, India
Bikram Biruli, KISS University, India
Yasobanta Das, KISS University, India
Prosper Abel Mgimwa, Real Hope Secondary School, Mafinga, Tanzania
Muhammed Abdur Rahmaan Kamaldeen, KIIT University, India
Aloka Fernando, University of Moratuwa, Sri Lanka

Chapter 9
Cross-Lingual Transfer Learning for Bambara Leveraging Resources From Other Languages 183
Ousmane Daou, KIIT University, India
Satya Ranjan Dash, KIIT University, India
Shantipriya Parida, SILO AI, Finland

Chapter 10
Twitter Sentiment Analyser Using NLP Techniques 198
Swarup Kumar Shaw, St. Xavier's College, Kolkata, India
Vinayak Jaiswal, St. Xavier's College, Kolkata, India
Sun Ghosh, St. Xavier's College, Kolkata, India
Anal Acharya, St. Xavier's College, Kolkata, India
Debabrata Datta, St. Xavier's College, Kolkata, India

Chapter 11
Transformer-Based Memes Generation Using Text and Image........................233
Dhirendra Kumar Sharma, University of Petroleum and Energy Studies, India
Rishab Jain, University of Petroleum and Energy Studies, India
Anshika Saini, University of Petroleum and Energy Studies, India

Chapter 12
Cyberbullying in the Digital Age: Consequences and Countermeasures 247
Ayushi Malik, University of Petroleum and Energy Studies, India
Pankaj Dadure, University of Petroleum and Energy Studies, India

Compilation of References 274

About the Contributors 307

Index 312

Detailed Table of Contents

Preface.. xiv

Chapter 1
Datraw, Advancing Collaborative Data Collection, and Recognition Models for Low Resource Languages in the Research Community.................................. 1
Bandaru Sugandhi, MathWorks, India

There is a significant need for a platform for all that promotes collaborative data collecting and supports community-driven advances in task recognition in the current era of increasing low resource data-driven research. "Datraw," a groundbreaking platform meant to connect researchers with the larger research community, serves as a centralized hub, empowering researchers to upload sample data with labels, while inviting linguists, common individuals, and fellow researchers to contribute by drawing data, whether in the form of characters or complete works and build rich and expansive dataset for low resource language and offers the opportunity to leverage the amassed datasets for training basic classification models. Through comprehensive validation and review methods, the platform assures data integrity and quality, ensuring that the obtained data stays correct and relevant for recognition tasks.

Chapter 2
Language Resource Acquisition for Low-Resource Languages in Digital Discourses.. 11
Kathiravan Pannerselvam, Central University of Tamil Nadu, India
Saranya Rajiakodi, Central University of Tamil Nadu, India
Bharathi Raja Chakravarthi, University of Galway, Ireland

This chapter explores the acquisition of language resources for low-resource languages in digital discourse, focusing on code-mixed content in social media posts and comments. Comprehensive language resources enhance our understanding of language usage patterns in online discussions. The methodology includes data collection, annotation, and automated tools, resulting in a practical framework. Challenges addressed in the chapter include data diversity, annotation complexity, linguistic variability, limited annotated data, and ethical considerations. Solutions proposed range from robust data preprocessing techniques to contextual analysis approaches, ensuring acquired quality and ethical use of resources. The chapter also discusses future directions, paving the way for further research and technology development in natural language processing and sociolinguistics. This chapter equips researchers and practitioners with essential knowledge and tools for advancing linguistic analysis and technological applications in the evolving digital landscape.

Chapter 3
Linguistic Analyzers of the Arabic Language: Linguistic Engineering Basis.....25
Ali Boulaalam, Moulay Ismail University, Meknes, Morocco
Nisrine El Hannach, Poly-Disciplinary Faculty of Nador, Mohammed 1st University, Oujda, Morocco

This scientific initiative aims to formulate a number of hypotheses in order to prepare linguistic analyzers for the Arabic language based on the theoretical foundations and methodological frameworks of platform linguistics, which are the appropriate framework for building linguistic resources that can be invested in the field of automatic processing of natural languages. In this context, the theory of the syntactic lexicon was adopted, as it is the solid nucleus of dependency grammar that has proven to be effective in the field of describing natural languages, and thus being able to simulate and computerize them and crystallize linguistic algorithms that can be automated by using the open source unitex platform, which is based mainly on final state automata, final graphs, and transducers.

Chapter 4
A Case Study on Tools and Techniques of Machine Translation of Indian Low Resource Languages 51
Anuraj Bose, Vellore Institute of Technology, India
Goutam Majumder, Vellore Institute of Technology, India

India, celebrated for its vast linguistic diversity with 1,599 languages (including 122 prominent ones), exemplifies the richness of language variation. Indo-Aryan languages, spoken by 70% of the population, and Dravidian languages, used by 19%, create this diverse linguistic tapestry. Effective communication in this interconnected society is crucial, and machine translation plays a pivotal role in bridging language gaps. Speech is a cost-effective mode of interaction, particularly important in a globalized world. Machine translation, a part of natural language processing (NLP), aids in overcoming language barriers. This chapter presents enlightening case studies and valuable best practices, inspiring meaningful translation efforts for low-resource language communities. Together, we can break linguistic barriers, fostering a world of boundless communication and enduring cultural treasures. Challenges like limited linguistic resources, technological deficiencies, and community engagement issues persist.

Chapter 5
Systematic Review of Morphological and Semantic Analysis in a Low Resource Language: Tamil 86
P. Matan, College of Engineering Guindy, Anna University, Chennai, India
P. Velvizhy, College of Engineering Guindy, Anna University, Chennai, India

Natural language processing discusses the applications of computational technique analysis and synthesis of natural languages. Semantic and morphological analysis are the two basic percepts in the natural language processing domain. Semantic analysis is the process of analyzing the lexical, grammatical, and syntactical parts of the words. The study of words known as morphology focuses on the meaning and structure of words. In this chapter, the authors focus on various morphological analyzers developed for Tamil language. Developing a highly accurate and adaptable morphological analyser is a challenging task. Morphological analyser basically identifies the morphemes and parts of speech for tagging. The atomic version of a word that retains the original meaning is called a morpheme. Morphological analyzer type includes phrase level and word level analyzers. Universal networking language (UNL) is a declarative kind used to express the natural language text using a semantic network. The major applications of UNL are information retrieval system, machine translation system, and UNL-based search engine.

Chapter 6
Machine Learning Approach for Kashmiri Word Sense Disambiguation 113
Aadil Ahmad Lawaye, Baba Ghulam Shah Badshah University, India
Tawseef Ahmad Mir, Alliance University, India
Mahmood Hussain Mir, Alliance University, India
Ghayas Ahmed, Baba Ghulam Shah Badshah University, India

Studying the senses of words in a given data is crucial for analysing and understanding natural languages. The meaning of an ambiguous word varies based on the context of usage and identifying its correct meaning in the given situation is a famous problem known as word sense disambiguation (WSD) in natural language processing (NLP). In this chapter, the authors discuss the important WSD research works carried out in the context of different languages using different techniques. They also explore a supervised approach based on the hidden Markov model (HMM) to address the WSD problem in the Kashmiri language, which lacks research in the NLP domain. The performance of the proposed approach is also examined in detail along with future improvement directions. The average results produced by the proposed system are accuracy=72.29%, precision=0.70, recall= 0.70, and F1-measure=0.70.

Chapter 7
Implementation and Analysis of Shallow Parsing Techniques in Khasi Language 137
Eusebius Lawai Lyngdoh, North-Eastern Hill University, India
Aiom Minnette Mitri, North-Eastern Hill University, India
Goutam Saha, North-Eastern Hill University, India
Arnab Kumar Maji, North-Eastern Hill University, India

In the realm of natural language processing (NLP), after part-of-speech (POS) tagging, the subsequent crucial step is shallow parsing. In this endeavour, the authors have undertaken the development of a shallow parser for the Khasi language. The work explores an array of techniques from both traditional machine learning (ML) and modern deep learning (DL) methodologies. They have employed a variety of ML algorithms, including decision trees, logistic regression, support vector machines, random forest, and multinomial naive bayes. Additionally, they have harnessed the power of DL with models such as the vanilla recurrent neural network, long short-term memory network, gated recurrent units, and bidirectional LSTM, all geared towards achieving the shallow parsing objective. The crux of the effort lies in the meticulous comparative analysis of these techniques. The chapter delves into a comprehensive discussion of their individual performances.

Chapter 8
Named Entity Recognition (NER) in Low Resource Languages of Ho 157
Satya Ranjan Dash, KIIT University, India
Bikram Biruli, KISS University, India
Yasobanta Das, KISS University, India
Prosper Abel Mgimwa, Real Hope Secondary School, Mafinga, Tanzania
Muhammed Abdur Rahmaan Kamaldeen, KIIT University, India
Aloka Fernando, University of Moratuwa, Sri Lanka

The Ho tribe is an indigenous community that primarily inhabits the Indian states of Odisha, Jharkhand, West Bengal, Assam, and Chhattisgarh. The Ho language, which belongs to the Austroasiatic language of Munda family, is their primary means of communication. Warang Chiti is the script for writing Ho language. Creating user-friendly tools, applications, and resources that support Ho language users in various aspects, such as typing, spell-checking, dictionary lookup, text conversion between UNICODE and 8-bit encodings, speech-to-text, and text-to-speech translation, this chapter discusses data augmentation techniques, transfer learning methods, domain adaptation strategies, and the importance of resource creation. It also emphasizes the need for collaborative efforts and community-driven initiatives to advance NER research in low resource language settings.

Chapter 9
Cross-Lingual Transfer Learning for Bambara Leveraging Resources From Other Languages 183
Ousmane Daou, KIIT University, India
Satya Ranjan Dash, KIIT University, India
Shantipriya Parida, SILO AI, Finland

Bambara, a language spoken primarily in West Africa, faces resource limitations that hinder the development of natural language processing (NLP) applications. This chapter presents a comprehensive cross-lingual transfer learning (CTL) approach to harness knowledge from other languages and substantially improve the performance of Bambara NLP tasks. The authors meticulously outline the methodology, including the creation of a Bambara corpus, training a CTL classifier, evaluating its performance across different languages, conducting a rigorous comparative analysis against baseline methods, and providing insights into future research directions. The results indicate that CTL is a promising and feasible approach to elevate the effectiveness of NLP tasks in Bambara.

Chapter 10
Twitter Sentiment Analyser Using NLP Techniques 198
Swarup Kumar Shaw, St. Xavier's College, Kolkata, India
Vinayak Jaiswal, St. Xavier's College, Kolkata, India
Sun Ghosh, St. Xavier's College, Kolkata, India
Anal Acharya, St. Xavier's College, Kolkata, India
Debabrata Datta, St. Xavier's College, Kolkata, India

Twitter is a popular platform where users express their opinions on various topics, including social, political, and economic issues. By monitoring the sentiment of tweets related to a particular topic, companies or governments can identify potential problems before they escalate into full-blown crises, allowing them to take appropriate action in a timely manner. The chapter typically involves collecting a large dataset of tweets, cleaning and pre-processing the data, and then using natural language processing (NLP) and machine learning techniques to classify the sentiment of each tweet.

Chapter 11
Transformer-Based Memes Generation Using Text and Image......................... 233
Dhirendra Kumar Sharma, University of Petroleum and Energy Studies, India
Rishab Jain, University of Petroleum and Energy Studies, India
Anshika Saini, University of Petroleum and Energy Studies, India

Memes are gaining popularity day by day to convey humor, news, social commentary, etc., but they can spread hatred and offence in the society. In this chapter, the authors create an automatic meme generator that generates relevant memes. In this chapter, Memebotics tool takes input as image or text and uses multiple pre-trained models of GPT to make memes more creative and quicker. Memebotics uses sentiment analysis to verify that created memes are relevant and do not hurt the sentiment of any society. The authors use VADAR, SVM techniques to identify the best model for sentiment analysis. They tested the model with different versions of EleutherAI GPT-Neo to find the model that can work on low configuration and saves time and money. As a result, they have created a model that generates memes that are relevant to all culture, language, and religion.

Chapter 12
Cyberbullying in the Digital Age: Consequences and Countermeasures 247
Ayushi Malik, University of Petroleum and Energy Studies, India
Pankaj Dadure, University of Petroleum and Energy Studies, India

This chapter delves into the pervasive issue of cyberbullying, an alarming phenomenon that has emerged with the advent of digital communication platforms. While the digital age has brought numerous benefits, it has also introduced drawbacks, with cyberbullying significantly affecting the emotional and psychological well-being of individuals, particularly adolescents. The chapter reviews existing approaches to address cyberbullying, including technological interventions, policy measures, and educational initiatives. The chapter also highlights the importance of maintaining an updated and accessible database of cyberbullying incidents to facilitate research, policymaking, and intervention development. Moreover, this chapter underscores the potentially severe consequences of cyberbullying on victims, ranging from anxiety and depression to even self-harm.

Compilation of References 274

About the Contributors 307

Index 312

Preface

In the rapidly evolving landscape of technological advancements, this book stands as a testament to our commitment to inclusivity and linguistic diversity. At its core, the narrative revolves around the application of Natural Language Processing (NLP) to address the digital challenges faced by low-resource languages. The journey commences by introducing Datraw, a methodology designed to advance collaborative data collection and recognition models tailored specifically for low-resource languages within the research community. Subsequent chapters navigate through the intricate processes of Language Resource Acquisition, linguistic engineering foundations for the Arabic language, and case studies on machine translation of Indian low-resource languages. Systematic reviews unfold in chapters dedicated to morphological and semantic analyses in languages like Tamil, showcasing the adaptability of NLP solutions across diverse linguistic landscapes. Practical applications continue to unfold with a focus on machine learning approaches for tasks such as Kashmiri Word Sense Disambiguation, implementation and analysis of shallow parsing techniques in the Khasi language, and Named Entity Recognition (NER) in low-resource languages like Ho.

The book also explores cross-lingual transfer learning, leveraging resources from other languages to enhance languages such as Bambara. Beyond language-specific applications, it addresses the broader spectrum of sentiment analysis on Twitter, transformer-based meme generation using text and image, and the critical issue of cyberbullying in the digital age. This compilation is more than a collection of chapters; it is a collective effort to empower, uplift, and provide visibility to languages that have historically been marginalized in the digital landscape. As you delve into the nuanced discussions within each section, we invite you to contemplate the intersection of technological innovation and linguistic diversity, and the profound impact it has on our global community.

Partha Pakray
National Institute of Technology, Silchar, India

Pankaj Dadure
University of Petroleum and Energy Studies, India

Sivaji Bandyopadhyay
Jadavpur University, India

Chapter 1
Datraw, Advancing Collaborative Data Collection, and Recognition Models for Low Resource Languages in the Research Community

Bandaru Sugandhi
MathWorks, India

ABSTRACT

There is a significant need for a platform for all that promotes collaborative data collecting and supports community-driven advances in task recognition in the current era of increasing low resource data-driven research. "Datraw," a groundbreaking platform meant to connect researchers with the larger research community, serves as a centralized hub, empowering researchers to upload sample data with labels, while inviting linguists, common individuals, and fellow researchers to contribute by drawing data, whether in the form of characters or complete works and build rich and expansive dataset for low resource language and offers the opportunity to leverage the amassed datasets for training basic classification models. Through comprehensive validation and review methods, the platform assures data integrity and quality, ensuring that the obtained data stays correct and relevant for recognition tasks.

DOI: 10.4018/979-8-3693-0728-1.ch001

1. INTRODUCTION

Natural Language Processing (NLP) (Nadkarni et al., 2011) is a sub field of artificial intelligence (AI) that focuses on the interaction between computers and humans through natural language. It seeks to enable computers to understand, interpret, and generate human language in a way that is both meaningful and useful. NLP is a multidisciplinary field that draws from computer science, linguistics, and cognitive psychology, among others, to develop algorithms and models that facilitate this interaction. NLP faces several challenges, including. NLP models require large amounts of annotated data for training, which can be challenging to obtain for less commonly spoken languages or specialized domains.

Low-resource languages (LRL) (King, 2015), also known as under-resourced languages, refer to languages for which there is limited availability of linguistic resources, such as annotated text data, language models, or NLP tools. Key challenges for LRL includes Lack of Data. There's a limited amount of text data available in these languages, which makes it difficult to train accurate language models and perform supervised learning effectively. Due to the scarcity of data and resources, developing NLP systems for LRL is complex and demanding.

Data serves as the foundation upon which NLP models are built and refined. It empowers these models to understand, generate, and manipulate human language effectively, making them valuable tools in a wide range of applications, from chat bots and sentiment analysis to language translation and information retrieval. The quality, quantity, and diversity of data directly impact the capabilities and limitations of NLP systems. Low-resource languages, which lack abundant linguistic resources, can benefit from data collection efforts. NLP researchers and practitioners often work on methods to collect and use data efficiently for these languages.

Data collaboration in Natural Language Processing (NLP) refers to the practice of multiple individuals or organizations working together to collect, annotate, share, and use linguistic data for NLP-related tasks. This collaboration is essential because NLP models, such as those powered by machine learning and deep learning, heavily rely on large and diverse datasets to achieve high levels of accuracy and generalization. Optical Character

Recognition (OCR) (Mithe et al., 2013) is a technology used to convert scanned documents, images, or handwritten text into machine-readable and editable text. It is an essential component of Natural Language Processing (NLP) when dealing with text data that exists in physical or image form, rather than digital text formats. OCR plays a crucial role in making printed or handwritten text accessible and usable for various NLP tasks.

Low-resource languages, which lack abundant linguistic resources, can benefit from data collection efforts. NLP researchers and practitioners often work on methods to collect and use data efficiently for these languages. In the rapidly evolving landscape of linguistic research, the pivotal role of online frameworks in advancing collaborative data collection and recognition models for lowresource languages cannot be overstated. These frameworks bridge geographical and linguistic barriers, enabling researchers and experts from around the globe to collectively contribute to language preservation, documentation, and analysis. The advent of such frameworks marks a significant leap forward in democratizing linguistic research, fostering collaboration, and accelerating the development of innovative recognition models tailored to the unique linguistic nuances of low-resource language. Hence, In the current era of expanding low-resource data-driven research, there is an enormous need for a tool that is accessible to all encourages collaborative data collection and supports community-driven achievements in task recognition. To address the above need, a framework "Datraw" has been designed, serves as a centralized hub, allowing researchers to upload sample data with labels while inviting linguists, common people, and fellow researchers to contribute by drawing data, whether in the form of characters or complete works, and building a rich and expansive dataset for low resource languages, as well as the opportunity to leverage the amassed datasets for training basic classification models.

This introduction has provided an encompassing preview of the subsequent sections. Section 2 critically examines relevant papers, forming the foundation for the research. Following that, the section is delineated, accompanied by comprehensive technical insights, including model specifications. This leads into the Section 3, which demonstrates the practical implementation of the framework through a detailed demo. As we proceed, Section 4 of the system's performance will be assessed, followed by a thorough exploration of its limitations in Section 5. The chapter collectively set the stage for a comprehensive exploration of the research's intricacies and findings.

2. LITERATURE REVIEW

Rabby et al. (2018) highlights the significance of machine learning and deep learning research in recent years, with a particular focus on handwritten recognition. The paper emphasizes the challenges posed by the lack of datasets and the difficulties associated with collecting handwritten data. The research introduces a comprehensive approach to collecting and processing handwritten data for the development of Handwritten Recognition (HWR) algorithms for various languages. The method involves writing characters on paper, scanning them into JPEG format, and addressing issues related to data collection, form creation, methodology, and software tools. The authors discuss their own efforts to create a handwritten database for the Bangla language and showcase a Graphical User Interface (GUI) capable of processing 100 scanned images per minute, each containing 120 characters. The paper underscores the critical need for large databases in training and testing handwritten recognition systems and acknowledges the challenges in data accumulation from diverse sources. Du et al. (2020) address Optical Character Recognition (OCR) systems and their diverse applications, including office automation, factory automation, online education, and map production. The paper acknowledges OCR as a challenging task due to the variability in text appearances and the demand for computational efficiency, particularly in the context of processing massive image datasets. The paper(conclusion) underscores the significance of PP-OCR as a practical solution for lightweight OCR systems and the availability of valuable datasets and models for research and application development.

Krishnan et al. (2014) examines the state of Optical Character Recognition (OCR) systems for Indic scripts, highlighting the challenges they face. The existing OCR systems are deemed insufficient for recognizing a wide range of printed documents due to several reasons, including a lack of resources, insufficient examples with natural variations, and limited documentation on font and style variations. Additionally, these systems rely on hard segmentation of word images, followed by isolated symbol recognition, which poses limitations. Variations among scripts, UNICODE conversion rules, nonstandard fonts/styles, and substantial degradation further contribute to the lack of robust solutions. It underscores the need for more annotated data and resources to enhance OCR performance.

Gong and Yao (2021) discusses the advancements and challenges in Optical Character Recognition (OCR) technology, particularly in the context of handwritten text recognition and mathematical expression recognition. The paper introduces a deep learning-based framework consisting of three components: the Detection & Classification Network (DCN) for identifying and classifying text and mathematical expressions, text recognition and mathematical expression recognition models, and a merging component to consolidate the outputs. Traditional OCR systems relied on hand-crafted features and classification models, which were time-consuming and costly. Deep learning, with models like SSD and attention-based encoder-decoder models, has significantly improved OCR accuracy. The paper highlights the specific challenges of recognizing mathematical expressions due to their structural complexity and proposes a unified framework to address these issues. The work contributes a robust approach to detecting and recognizing printed and handwritten text and mathematical expressions, with potential applications in various industries and education scenarios.

The paper presents a comprehensive Optical Character Recognition (OCR) system for uppercase English alphabets of various fonts and sizes, aiming to address applications in the Banking, Corporate, Legal, and other industries. The OCR system comprises pre processing, segmentation, feature extraction, and recognition modules.

In today's data-driven world, the need to manage and process printed documents efficiently has become increasingly critical. OCR technology automates tasks related to document retrieval, archiving, updating, and distribution by converting printed text into machine-readable ASCII characters. However, recognizing printed characters presents challenges due to variations in fonts, noise, image shapes, and sizes. A robust OCR system requires effective pre processing, feature extraction, and recognition techniques to eliminate noise, extract meaningful features, train the system, and classify patterns accurately.

Lucas (1995) presents the application of a syntactic neural network (SNN) to hand-written digit recognition, emphasizing the system's high classification speed and accuracy. The SNN approach is motivated by the need for high-performance optical character recognition (OCR) in both offline and online applications. The method converts handwritten characters into chain-coded bitmaps, treating each character class as a language and training SNNs as recognizer for these languages. The results demonstrate the system's capability to process over two thousand characters per second during training and about two hundred per second in recognition mode, significantly outperforming other OCR techniques in terms of speed while maintaining high accuracy levels. The paper states that obtaining a sufficiently large and diverse dataset for training OCR systems can be challenging. The authors rely on datasets like ESSEX and CEDAR, which provide the necessary data for their experiments. However, data collection and creation remain a potential challenge, especially when addressing specific applications.

3. SYSTEM OVERVIEW

"Datraw" has been designed to serve as a centralized platform, allowing researchers to share data samples with labels while welcoming language experts, regular individuals, and fellow scholars to participate by drawing data, whether in the form of characters or complete works and creating a rich and expansive dataset for low resource languages, as well as the chance to employ the collected datasets for training essential models of classification.

To upload sample data or get shared datasets, a first-time user has to register and an existing user has to log in to the application from home page as shown in Figures 1, 2 and 3. On logging in, the user lands on home page from where use can now go to upload page from menu on top right to upload a CSV file which contains a column with labels/id assigned to a sample character data and another column with a link directing to sample data of characters, probably an image in any language as shown in Figure 4. On uploading the CSV file user will be directed to the page shown in Figure 5 providing a link, which helps the user to share with colleagues, friends and known ones. The one with the link, can enter the system and contribute to dataset collection by drawing character sample data shown on the top side of the page. A whiteboard can be found on the bottom of the same page, where the user or contributor can draw the given character data on the top as shown in Figure 6. This collected data will be made available for the user who uploaded the respective character sample data and the user can access or download the CSV file of these datasets by going to the “View Submission” option on the bottom of the page that user landed after uploading data.

An user can also make their dataset public, by accepting the consent received during uploading character sample data through CSV file. Hence, users can also leverage shared datasets from “Data store” menu item at the top of the page as shown in Figure 8. At the same time, a user will be prompted to allow everyone to contribute for drawing characters in the sample data they uploaded. Now users can also contribute to public character sample date uploaded by some other user, by going to the “Contribute” menu item at the top of a page.

Figure 1. Home page

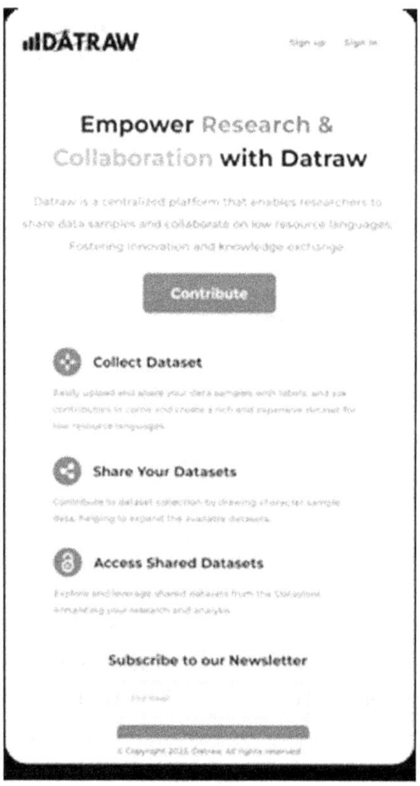

Figure 2. Sign up page

Figure 3. Sign in page

Figure 4. Generate page

4. ADEQUACY

The "Datraw" framework offers a range of benefits to researchers, language experts, individuals, and scholars interested in low resource languages and data collection. It provides a centralized platform for researchers to share data samples along with labels. This centralization streamlines the process of accessing and sharing data, making it easier for researchers to collaborate and access valuable resources. The framework welcomes participation from a diverse group of individuals, including language experts, regular people, and scholars. This inclusively ensures that data collection efforts are not limited to a select group but are open to anyone interested in contributing to the project. Our system encourages the collection of diverse data, ranging from individual characters to complete works. This diversity in data types enriches the dataset and makes it more comprehensive, allowing for a broader range of research applications.Low resource languages often lack sufficient linguistic data. It addresses this gap by creating a platform for the collection of data in these languages. This, in turn, contributes to the enrichment and preservation of linguistic diversity.

Figure 5. Dash menu

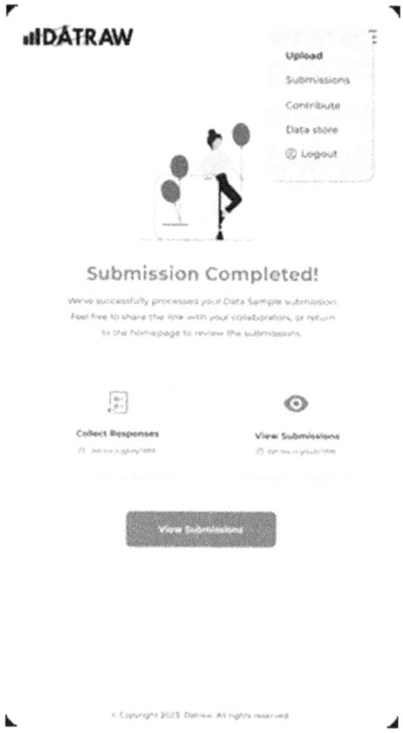

Figure 6. Contribute page

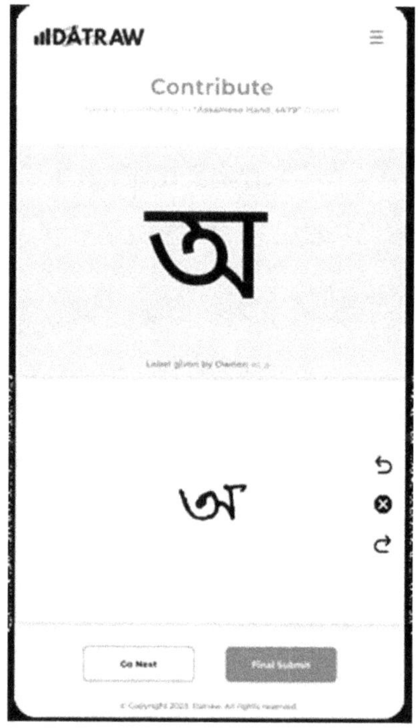

The collected datasets on "Datraw" can be used for training essential classification models. Researchers can leverage these datasets to develop and refine models for various natural language processing tasks, such as text classification, sentiment analysis, and machine translation. By providing a centralized platform, it makes data and resources more accessible to a wider audience. This accessibility promotes knowledge sharing and accelerates research progress in the field of low resource languages. The framework empowers individuals and communities to actively participate in language data collection. It democratizes the process and allows people from various backgrounds to contribute to linguistic research. Our framework contributes to the advancement of research in low resource languages by providing researchers with the necessary tools and datasets. This, in turn, leads to more robust and accurate models and applications for these languages.The datasets and resources created through this framework have the potential for long-term impact. They can serve as foundational resources for future research, enabling ongoing studies and applications in low resource languages.

Figure 7. Submission page

Figure 8. Data store

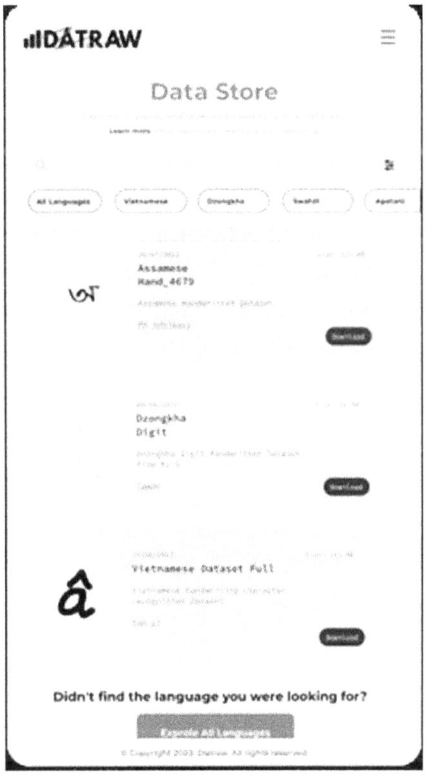

5. LIMITATIONS

Ensuring the quality of the collected data can be challenging when the platform welcomes contributions from a wide range of participants. There may be variations in data accuracy, relevance, and reliability, which can impact the overall quality of the dataset. “Datraw” requires robust technical infrastructure to support data storage, access, and collaboration. Ensuring the platform’s scalability and reliability can be a challenge, especially as the user base and dataset size grow. Encouraging active participation from a diverse user base, including language experts and regular individuals, may require effective engagement strategies. Ensuring sustained interest and contributions can be an ongoing challenge. Maintaining and curating the collected datasets over time can be resource-intensive. Ensuring the longevity of the platform and continued data quality may require ongoing efforts and resources. Data collected from different sources may come in various formats and lack standardization. Integrating and preprocessing such diverse data can be time-consuming and require significant effort.

6. CONCLUSION

In summary, "Datraw" offers a collaborative and inclusive platform that facilitates data collection, promotes diversity in datasets, and empowers individuals and researchers to contribute to the advancement of low resource language research. It has the potential to significantly impact the field by addressing data scarcity and fostering collaboration within the research community. "Datraw" addresses important aspects of data collection and collaboration in low resource languages. However, it must grapple with challenges related to data quality, privacy, bias, volume, diversity, collaboration, maintenance, standardization, infrastructure, and user engagement to fulfill its objectives effectively.

REFERENCES

Du, Y., Li, C., Guo, R., Yin, X., Liu, W., Zhou, J., Bai, Y., Yu, Z., Yang, Y., Dang, Q., & Wang, H. 2020. Ppocr: A practical ultra lightweight ocr system. *ArXiv*, abs/2009.09941.

Krishnan, P., Sankaran, N., Singh, A. K., & Jawahar, C. V. 2014. Towards a robust ocr system for indic scripts. *2014 11th IAPR International Workshop on Document Analysis Systems*, 141–145. 10.1109/DAS.2014.74

Lucas, S. M. 1995. High performance ocr with syntactic neural networks. In *1995 Fourth International Conference on Artificial Neural Networks* (pp. 133–138). IET. 10.1049/cp:19950542

Mithe, Indalkar, & Divekar. (2013). Optical character recognition. *International Journal of Recent Technology and Engineering*, *2*(1), 72–75.

Prakash, M. (2011). Natural language processing: An introduction. *Journal of the American Medical Informatics Association*, *18*(5), 544–551. doi:10.1136/amiajnl-2011-000464 PMID:21846786

Shahariar Azad Rabby, A. K. M. (2018). A universal way to collect and process handwritten data for any language. *Procedia Computer Science*, *143*, 502–509. doi:10.1016/j.procs.2018.10.423

Chapter 2
Language Resource Acquisition for Low-Resource Languages in Digital Discourses

Kathiravan Pannerselvam
https://orcid.org/0000-0002-9249-8293
Central University of Tamil Nadu, India

Saranya Rajiakodi
Central University of Tamil Nadu, India

Bharathi Raja Chakravarthi
https://orcid.org/0000-0002-4575-7934
University of Galway, Ireland

ABSTRACT

This chapter explores the acquisition of language resources for low-resource languages in digital discourse, focusing on code-mixed content in social media posts and comments. Comprehensive language resources enhance our understanding of language usage patterns in online discussions. The methodology includes data collection, annotation, and automated tools, resulting in a practical framework. Challenges addressed in the chapter include data diversity, annotation complexity, linguistic variability, limited annotated data, and ethical considerations. Solutions proposed range from robust data preprocessing techniques to contextual analysis approaches, ensuring acquired quality and ethical use of resources. The chapter also discusses future directions, paving the way for further research and technology development in natural language processing and sociolinguistics. This chapter equips researchers and practitioners with essential knowledge and tools for advancing linguistic analysis and technological applications in the evolving digital landscape.

DOI: 10.4018/979-8-3693-0728-1.ch002

INTRODUCTION

In today's digital age, communication predominantly occurs on the Internet, primarily due to the widespread popularity of social media platforms. Among the most extensively used social networking services are Facebook, YouTube, WhatsApp, Instagram, Twitter, and Reddit. Facebook, boasting nearly three billion monthly users, is a remarkable achievement in Information and Communication Technology (ICT). It is a powerful tool for connecting people online, enabling the sharing of personal information, photos, videos, and messages, and consuming various content, including news. Users express their opinions, emotions, and thoughts in their respective languages, leading to a continuous rise in users on platforms like Facebook, Twitter, and other social networking services each year (Mahmud et al., 2023).

As social interactions migrate to online platforms, a new layer of linguistic complexity emerges – one that weaves together languages and dialects in a phenomenon known as code-mixing. Within this evolving landscape, acquiring language resources for low-resource languages gains significance, with a particular focus on acquiring and annotating code-mixed content within social media posts, online discourses, and their accompanying comments (*Code-Switching | Linguistic Benefits & Challenges | Britannica*, n.d.). The primary emphasis in current NLP research is placed on just 20 out of the approximately 7,000 languages spoken globally, resulting in a situation where most languages receive limited attention in study and investigation (Magueresse et al., 2020).

Low-Resource Languages

With a population of 1.4 billion people conversing in 447 languages and over 10,000 dialects, India ranks as the country with the fourth-largest linguistic diversity globally. Nevertheless, Indian languages face significant underrepresentation on the Internet, and the development of Natural Language Processing (NLP) systems tailored to Indian languages is still in its early stages. Even the most advanced multilingual NLP systems struggle to deliver optimal performance when applied to Indian languages (Kumar et al., 2022). For example, Tamil, a Dravidian language predominantly spoken in India, Sri Lanka, Malaysia, and Singapore, is characterized by its agglutinative nature and intricate morphological structure, as highlighted in reference. The Tamil language has 247 characters, encompassing 12 vowels, 18 consonants, 216 composite letters formed by combining each consonant with each vowel, and a unique character known as "Ayutha eluththu" (Kumaresan et al., 2021).

Code-Mixed and Code-Switched

People from India and other non-English-speaking regions often opt not to rely solely on one language in their social media messages. Instead, they employ transliteration and randomly incorporate English words or phrases through code-mixing, demonstrating their linguistic versatility in diverse language combinations, such as Tamil-English or Arabic-English. Code-mixing (CM) represents a dynamically evolving field of study within text mining (Thara & Poornachandran, 2018). Code-mixing is prevalent in various forms of communication among multilingual speakers, encompassing both spoken and text-based interactions. It pertains to how bilingual or multilingual individuals seamlessly integrate elements of one language into their utterances in another language. It is worth noting that most language pairs lack adequate resources for code-mixing tasks (Chakravarthi et al., 2022). Nowadays, social media communications, blogs, and reviews teem with inventive and clever code-mixed messages.

Applications

Despite their limited linguistic resources and smaller user bases, low-resource languages find versatile applications in various domains. They can be harnessed for sentiment analysis (Kannan et al., 2021) to gauge public opinion and political sentiment, detecting hate speech and offensive content to promote online safety (Kohli et al., 2021; Mahmud et al., 2023), predicting fake news to combat misinformation (Kumari et al., 2021), classifying memes for cultural preservation and effective communication (Ghanghor et al., 2021), enabling speech-to-speech translation for cross-cultural understanding, detecting signs of depression to support mental health, developing recommendation systems for personalized content suggestions, and identifying idiomatic expressions to bridge language and cultural gaps, ultimately fostering inclusivity and enhancing technology's accessibility for diverse linguistic communities.

This proposed book chapter describes a compelling journey that navigates the outlines of low-resource languages and their encounters with code-mixing in digital spaces. This chapter explores the challenges and opportunities of low-resource languages from the ever-expanding realm of online communication. In embarking upon this exploration, we embrace a dual role: linguistic detectives, unraveling the complexities of code-mixing within the digital footprint of low-resource languages, and technological pioneers, charting pathways to harness and analyze these resources effectively. This chapter unveils the potential implications of code-mixed language resource acquisition – not just for linguistic research but for applications spanning natural language processing, sentiment analysis, and sociolinguistics. This comprehensive analysis aims to provide practical insights and guidance to linguists, researchers, and technologists in acquiring, annotating, and utilizing code-mixed language resources. The following RQs are formulated by this chapter's objective and addressed in the remaining sections.

Research Questions

RQ1. How can language resource acquisition strategies be optimized and tailored to address the distinct challenges of low-resource languages, explicitly focusing on code-mixed content in social media posts, online discourses, and comments?

A multifaceted approach is essential to optimize language resource acquisition strategies for addressing the unique challenges of low-resource languages, especially when dealing with code-mixed content in social media posts, online discussions, and comments. This approach includes collecting and curating data from various online platforms, engaging native speakers and crowdsourcing initiatives, employing data augmentation and generation techniques, utilizing active learning and semi-supervised methods, implementing cross-lingual transfer learning, fostering community partnerships, upholding ethical data collection practices, refining annotation and evaluation processes, considering multimodal data sources, and promoting resource sharing and collaboration. By tailoring these strategies to the specific needs of low-resource languages and code-mixed content, researchers and organizations can enhance the development of more inclusive and effective language technologies for diverse linguistic communities.

RQ2. What methodologies and collaborative approaches can linguists, researchers, and technologists employ to ensure efficient and accurate acquisition and annotation of code-mixed language resources from online platforms?

Through collaboration, linguists, researchers, and technologists can enhance the efficient and accurate acquisition and annotation of code-mixed language resources from online platforms. This involves employing web scraping tools, crowdsourcing initiatives, and partnerships with social media platforms to gather data systematically. Machine learning and cross-lingual transfer learning methods can automate the collection, while active learning and semi-supervised techniques can prioritize and annotate valuable data. Collaboration with communities and experts, adherence to ethical guidelines, data diversity, and multimodal approaches ensure comprehensive and representative resources. Continuous evaluation and sharing of resources within the research community further refine the datasets, ultimately advancing the development of robust language technologies for code-mixed languages.

RQ3. How does acquiring comprehensive language resources for low-resource languages, explicitly focusing on code-mixed content, enhance our ability to analyze and understand language usage patterns within social media and online discussions?

Acquiring comprehensive language resources for low-resource languages, specifically emphasizing code-mixed content, greatly enhances our capacity to analyze and comprehend language usage patterns in social media and online discussions. This endeavor ensures a better representation of linguistic diversity, provides deeper insights into language dynamics, cultural context, and societal nuances, tracks language evolution, improves sentiment analysis and language technologies, aids in policy enforcement and content moderation, supports language preservation efforts for endangered languages, facilitates cross-linguistic research, and serves as essential training data for Natural Language Processing (NLP) models. It broadens our understanding of online communication while fostering inclusivity and linguistic diversity.

DATA ACQUISITION

Data acquisition involves collecting and capturing data from various sources, instruments, or sensors for analysis, storage, or further processing. It is a crucial step in data management and analysis, commonly used in science, engineering, research, and business intelligence. Data acquisition systems often involve using specialized hardware and software to gather and record data, ensuring accuracy and reliability in the data collection process (Thavareesan & Mahesan, 2020).

Social Network Platforms

We can acquire data for low-resource languages from social media platforms such as Twitter, Facebook, Reddit, Instagram, YouTube, and messaging apps like WhatsApp and Telegram (Pannerselvam et al., 2023). These platforms offer diverse text and content in multiple languages, making them valuable sources for linguistic data collection. Additionally, exploring online forums, language-specific apps, blogs, and local news websites in regions where the low-resource language is spoken can further enrich our dataset. However, it is essential to adhere to ethical and privacy guidelines, respect user privacy, and consider data availability and collection methods when using social media for data acquisition (Kalaivani et al., 2021; Khanam, 2016; Ravikiran & Annamalai, 2021). Table 1 is an example of the low-resourced language dataset and its detailed illustration.

Table 1. List of low-resourced language datasets, sources, and applications

Name	Languages	Source	Applications
Offenseval Dravidian (Chakravarthi et al., 2021)	English-Tamil, English-Malayalam, English - Kannada	YouTube	Offensive language detection
FIRE 2020 Dravidian Code Mixed (Chakravarthi et al., 2021)	Tamil, Malayalam	YouTube	Sentiment Analysis
TamilMemes (Suryawanshi et al., 2020)	Tamil	WhatsApp, Facebook, Instagram, and Pinterest	Meme Classification
FIRE 2013-16 Tasks (Banerjee et al., 2020)	English, Hindi, Tamil, Telugu,	Tweets, Facebook,	Transliterated Search, Question Answering
Stance Detection (Srinidhi Skanda et al., 2017)	English – Kannada	Facebook	Stance detection

DATA PREPARATION

Data Annotation: To Enhancing Data Clarity and Quality the manual curation and labeling of data, making it an essential component of data preparation that demands expert knowledge. When it comes to annotating text data, particularly in the context of low-resource languages, linguistic experts play a crucial role. In social media, users often deviate from strict grammatical rules, resorting to acronyms, extra punctuation, and special symbols that are comprehensible to humans but can pose challenges for machines. Therefore, rectifying such linguistic nuances during the data annotation process is imperative to ensure data clarity and accuracy (Palomino, 2018; Tsapatsoulis & Djouvas, 2017).

Data augmentation, a transformative practice in data science and machine learning, is reshaping how we harness data for model development. This technique expands and enriches datasets by creating synthetic data points through diverse transformations or modifications. Widely applied in computer vision, its applications extend across domains, including natural language processing and speech recognition. Data augmentation enhances model performance, mitigates overfitting, bolsters robustness, and often preserves privacy. Its versatility ranges from augmenting images in computer vision to generating variations in text for natural language processing, and its value is pivotal in realizing the potential of machine learning in diverse applications (Shorten et al., 2021).

Data Preprocessing

In the realm of Natural Language Processing (NLP), effective data preprocessing is a cornerstone for enhancing the accuracy and efficiency of text analysis. For the Tamil language, a Dravidian language spoken primarily in Sri Lanka, India, Malaysia, and Singapore, the preprocessing pipeline involves several key steps, including stop word removal, stemming, lemmatization, and Part-of-Speech (POS) tagging (Kumaresan et al., 2021). These are the crucial components and their significance in preparing Tamil text data for NLP applications.

Stop Word Removal: In Tamil, stop words are common words such as articles, pronouns, and prepositions that appear frequently but carry limited semantic meaning. Removing these stop words reduces noise in the text data and enhances the efficiency of downstream NLP tasks like sentiment analysis and text classification (Kathiravan & Haridoss, 2018; Rajkumar et al., 2020).

Stemming: This process aims to reduce words to their base or root form. In Tamil, stemming is particularly valuable due to the language's rich morphological structure. By reducing inflected and derived forms to their root, stemming helps achieve text normalization and simplification, ultimately improving information retrieval and search relevance. In the early 2000s, significant strides were made in developing language-specific stemmers and morphology analyzers for various Indian languages. Shambhavi et al. (Shambhavi et al., 2011) introduced a Kannada morphology analyzer and generator, leveraging a tire-based approach. Authors (Ramanathan & Rao, 2003) crafted a lightweight stemmer tailored for Hindi, focusing on suffix removal to enhance information retrieval. Authors proposed the Porter stemming algorithm (Willett, 2006) and found application in electronic libraries and information systems (Thangarasu & Manavalan, 2013).

Building on these foundational works, recent developments in stemmer technology have continued to advance the field. In recent years, researchers have explored machine learning-based approaches to stemmers, leveraging deep learning techniques and neural networks to create more context-aware and accurate stemmers. These advancements have improved information retrieval and enabled a more comprehensive range of applications in machine translation, sentiment analysis, and chatbot development, contributing to the evolution of language processing in diverse linguistic contexts.

Lemmatization: While stemming focuses on reducing words to their base form, lemmatization goes further by considering the context and morphological analysis. In Tamil, a language with a complex inflectional system, lemmatization accurately identifies and extracts the dictionary form of words. This ensures precise analysis, especially in machine translation and speech recognition applications (Ezhilarasi & Maheswari, 2021).

Part-of-Speech (POS) Tagging: POS tagging involves assigning grammatical categories (nouns, verbs, adjectives, etc.) to words in a sentence. In Tamil, POS tagging helps in syntactic and semantic analysis, enabling the extraction of grammatical structures and relationships within the text. It is invaluable for tasks like named entity recognition and grammar checking. Accurate identification of the lexical category or Part of Speech (POS) of words plays a pivotal role in developing Natural Language Processing (NLP) systems. However, existing POS taggers for Tamil present certain challenges, including limited availability, accuracy issues, and non-standard POS tagsets. This research paper introduces ThamizhiPOSt, a cutting-edge contextual neural POS tagger specifically designed for Tamil. ThamizhiPOSt proficiently assigns POS tags to words within a sentence, employing the widely recognized Universal Part of Speech tagset. Its tagging decisions are contextually driven, considering the word's role within the sentence structure.

Furthermore, ThamizhiPOSt seamlessly integrates a tokenizer and a sentence segmenter, enabling it to handle raw Tamil text effectively. In our evaluation, ThamizhiPOSt demonstrates an impressive accuracy rate of 93.27% for unseen data, surpassing the performance of publicly available Tamil POS taggers. To foster collaboration and development in the NLP community, we have made ThamizhiPOSt and its associated resources accessible to the public. Additionally, ThamizhiPOSt has been published as a Python library, inviting others to leverage and build upon this valuable tool for advancing Tamil language processing applications (Sarveswaran & Dias, 2021).

NLP practitioners and researchers can refine and optimize text data by implementing these data preprocessing steps tailored to the Tamil language, making it more amenable to various applications. Whether it is sentiment analysis of Tamil social media content, machine translation, or enhancing search capabilities, the careful preprocessing of Tamil text data is essential for unlocking the full potential of NLP in this linguistically rich and culturally diverse language.

WORD EMBEDDING

Word embeddings are a type of numerical representation of words in natural language processing (NLP) and machine learning. They convert words or phrases into numerical vectors, allowing machines to understand and work with textual data effectively. Word embeddings capture the semantic and syntactic relationships between words by mapping them to points in a high-dimensional vector space. The key idea behind word embeddings is that words with similar meanings or contextual usage should have similar vector representations. This means that words that often appear together in similar contexts will be closer to each other in the vector space.

Word embeddings are typically learned from large text corpora using techniques like Word2Vec, GloVe, or FastText (Thavareesan & Mahesan, 2020). Once learned, these embeddings can be used in various NLP tasks, such as text classification, sentiment analysis, machine translation, and more. They help improve the performance of NLP models by providing a more meaningful and compact representation of words, reducing the dimensionality of the input data, and capturing semantic relationships. Word embeddings have become a fundamental component of NLP and have significantly advanced the field by enabling machines to understand and process human language more effectively.

(Saurav et al., 2021) employed various techniques to create word embeddings for 14 different languages. For Word2Vec embeddings, with dimensions ranging from 50 to 300, they utilized both skip-gram and Continuous Bag of Words (CBOW) architectures, implementing them with the gensim library. Words occurring less than twice in the corpus were treated as out-of-vocabulary words. FastText embeddings, following the skip-gram architecture and dimensions of 50 to 300, were also generated using gensim. Then they applied the same frequency-based criteria for out-of-vocabulary words. GloVe embeddings, with dimensions of 50 to 300, were created, and words with an occurrence frequency below 2 were excluded. MUSE cross-lingual embeddings were developed for all language pairs, resulting in 196 models, and ELMo embeddings were trained for each language with 512 dimensions. They have made all these models available in our repository, recognizing the lack of pre-trained word embeddings for these languages in official repositories.

CHALLENGES AND SOLUTION

Natural Language Processing (NLP) is a dynamic field with immense potential, but it also presents several challenges that researchers and practitioners must address. Here, we discuss some of the prominent challenges in NLP and propose potential solutions:

Navigating these challenges is essential for the continued progress of NLP. Researchers and practitioners must collaborate to develop innovative solutions, leverage advanced techniques, and prioritize ethical considerations to create more effective and responsible NLP systems.

Table 2. Challenges and their solutions in the low-resourced language

Challenges	Solutions
Data Noisiness and Diversity	Preprocessing techniques, such as data cleaning and normalization, can help mitigate noise. Additionally, using large and diverse datasets for training can improve model robustness.
Annotation Consistency and Complexity	Implement clear annotation guidelines and provide annotator training. Regular inter-annotator agreement checks and refinement of guidelines can improve consistency.
Linguistic Variability and Context Sensitivity	Contextual embeddings (e.g., BERT, GPT) and deep learning models can help capture context sensitivity. Fine-tuning on domain-specific data can also enhance performance.
Limited Availability of Annotated Data	Active learning strategies can reduce annotation efforts by focusing on the most informative data. Data augmentation and transfer learning from larger, related datasets can also help when labeled data is scarce.
Ethical Considerations and User Privacy	Implement strict data anonymization and aggregation techniques to protect user privacy. Develop clear ethical frameworks for NLP research and applications, with transparency and user consent as core principles.

FUTURE DIRECTIONS

Several exciting future directions are emerging in the evolving landscape of low resource language data acquisition. Collaborative approaches, including crowdsourcing and community engagement, will play a pivotal role in collecting and enriching language data while respecting cultural nuances and ethical considerations. Active learning strategies and data augmentation techniques will maximize the utility of limited annotated data, ensuring efficient resource utilization. Transfer learning, zero-shot learning, and few-shot learning methods are poised to empower low-resource languages by leveraging models trained on high-resource languages and adapting them with minimal labeled examples. Ethical data collection and privacy safeguards will remain a top priority, ensuring that data acquisition respects the rights and consent of language communities. Preservation efforts for endangered languages through digital archives and multimodal data collection (combining text, audio, image, and video data) will advance language documentation and revitalization initiatives. Collaboration between organizations, governments, academia, and industry stakeholders will foster resource sharing and accelerate progress. Developing machine translation systems and cross-lingual applications tailored to low-resource languages will also bridge communication gaps and enhance accessibility. In contrast, benchmark datasets and evaluation metrics specific to these languages will drive innovation and benchmarking efforts, ultimately facilitating a deeper understanding and preservation of linguistic diversity worldwide.

CONCLUSION

In conclusion, the landscape of low-resource language data acquisition is on the brink of transformative change. The challenges posed by limited linguistic resources are being met with innovative solutions driven by collaborative efforts, advanced technologies, and a commitment to ethical data practices. The future holds promise in community involvement, active learning, transfer learning, and preserving endangered languages. Multimodal data collection and interdisciplinary collaborations are expanding our understanding of language diversity. Moreover, the development of machine translation systems and cross-lingual applications is poised to enhance communication and accessibility for speakers of low-resource languages. The commitment to ethical data collection and respect for linguistic communities will remain paramount as we progress. By addressing these challenges and embracing these opportunities, we are advancing the field of natural language processing and enriching our collective appreciation of the richness and diversity of human language. The journey to empower low-resource languages transcends technology; it is a testament to our commitment to inclusivity, cultural preservation, and celebrating linguistic heritage on a global scale.

REFERENCES

Banerjee, S., Choudhury, M., Chakma, K., Naskar, S. K., Das, A., Bandyopadhyay, S., & Rosso, P. (2020). MSIR@FIRE: A Comprehensive Report from 2013 to 2016. *SN Computer Science*, *1*(1), 55. Advance online publication. doi:10.1007/s42979-019-0058-0

Chakravarthi, B. R., Priyadharshini, R., Muralidaran, V., Jose, N., Suryawanshi, S., Sherly, E., & McCrae, J. P. (2022). DravidianCodeMix: Sentiment analysis and offensive language identification dataset for Dravidian languages in code-mixed text. *Language Resources and Evaluation*, *56*(3), 765–806. doi:10.1007/s10579-022-09583-7 PMID:35996566

Chakravarthi, B. R., Priyadharshini, R., Thavareesan, S., Chinnappa, D., Thenmozhi, D., Sherly, E., McCrae, J. P., Hande, A., Ponnusamy, R., Banerjee, S., & Vasantharajan, C. (2021). Findings of the Sentiment Analysis of Dravidian Languages in Code-Mixed Text. *CEUR Workshop Proceedings*, *3159*, 872–886.

Code-switching | Linguistic Benefits & Challenges | Britannica. (n.d.). Retrieved September 16, 2023, from https://www.britannica.com/topic/code-switching

Ezhilarasi, S., & Maheswari, P. U. (2021). Depicting a neural model for lemmatization and POS tagging of words from palaeographic stone inscriptions. *Proceedings - 5th International Conference on Intelligent Computing and Control Systems, ICICCS 2021*, 1879–1884. 10.1109/ICICCS51141.2021.9432315

Ghanghor, N. K., Krishnamurthy, P., Thavareesan, S., Priyadarshini, R., & Chakravarthi, B. R. (2021). IIITK@DravidianLangTech-EACL2021: Offensive Language Identification and Meme Classification in Tamil, Malayalam and Kannada. *Proceedings of the 1st Workshop on Speech and Language Technologies for Dravidian Languages, DravidianLangTech 2021 at 16th Conference of the European Chapter of the Association for Computational Linguistics, EACL 2021*, 222–229.

Kalaivani, A., Thenmozhi, D., & Aravindan, C. (2021). TOLD: Tamil Offensive Language Detection in Code-Mixed Social Media Comments using MBERT with Features based Selection. *CEUR Workshop Proceedings*, *3159*, 667–679.

Kannan, R. R., Rajalakshmi, R., & Kumar, L. (2021). IndicBERT based approach for Sentiment Analysis on Code-Mixed Tamil Tweets. *CEUR Workshop Proceedings*, *3159*, 729–736.

Kathiravan, P., & Haridoss, N. (2018). Preprocessing for Mining the Textual data-A Review. *International Journal of Scientific Research in Computer Science Applications and Management Studies IJSRCSAMS*, *7*(5). www.ijsrcsams.com

Khanam, M. H. (2016). *Named Entity Recognition using Machine Learning Techniques for Telugu language*. Academic Press.

Kohli, G., Kaur, P., & Bedi, J. (2021). ARGUABLY at ComMA@ICON: Detection of Multilingual Aggressive, Gender Biased, and Communally Charged Tweets Using Ensemble and Fine-Tuned IndicBERT. *Proceedings of the 18th International Conference on Natural Language Processing: Shared Task on Multilingual Gender Biased and Communal Language Identification*, 46–52. https://aclanthology.org/2021.icon-multigen.7

Kumar, G. K., Gehlot, A. S., Mullappilly, S. S., & Nandakumar, K. (2022). MuCoT: Multilingual Contrastive Training for Question-Answering in Low-resource Languages. *DravidianLangTech 2022 - 2nd Workshop on Speech and Language Technologies for Dravidian Languages, Proceedings of the Workshop, 1*, 15–24. 10.18653/v1/2022.dravidianlangtech-1.3

Kumaresan, P. K., Premjith, Sakuntharaj, R., Thavareesan, S., Navaneethakrishnan, S., Madasamy, A. K., Chakravarthi, B. R., & McCrae, J. P. (2021). Findings of Shared Task on Offensive Language Identification in Tamil and Malayalam. *ACM International Conference Proceeding Series*, 16–18. 10.1145/3503162.3503179

Kumari, R., Ashok, N., Ghosal, T., & Ekbal, A. (2021). Misinformation detection using multitask learning with mutual learning for novelty detection and emotion recognition. *Information Processing & Management, 58*(5), 102631. doi:10.1016/j.ipm.2021.102631

MagueresseA.CarlesV.HeetderksE. (2020). *Low-resource Languages: A Review of Past Work and Future Challenges.* http://arxiv.org/abs/2006.07264

Mahmud, T., Ptaszynski, M., Eronen, J., & Masui, F. (2023). Cyberbullying detection for low-resource languages and dialects: Review of the state of the art. *Information Processing & Management, 60*(5), 103454. doi:10.1016/j.ipm.2023.103454

Palomino, N. (2018). The Role of Approximate Negators in Modeling the Automatic Detection of Negation in Tweets. *ProQuest Dissertations and Theses, May,* 203. https://search.proquest.com/docview/2065161701?accountid=49007%0Ahttp://www.yidu.edu.cn/educhina/educhina.do?artifact=&svalue=The+Role+of+Approximate+Negators+in+Modeling+the+Automatic+Detection+of+Negation+in+Tweets&stype=2&s=on%0Ahttp://sfx.cceu.org.cn doi:10.1201/9781003319887-8

Pannerselvam, K., Rajiakodi, S., & Pichai, S. (2023). Intelligent Named Entity-Based Cybercrime Recognition System for Social Media Network Platforms. *Cybersecurity for Decision Makers,* 111–126. doi:10.1201/9781003319887-8

Rajkumar, N., Subashini, T. S., Rajan, K., & Ramalingam, V. (2020). Tamil Stopword Removal Based on Term Frequency. In K. S. Raju, R. Senkerik, S. P. Lanka, & V. Rajagopal (Eds.), *Data Engineering and Communication Technology* (pp. 21–30). Springer Singapore. doi:10.1007/978-981-15-1097-7_3

Ramanathan, A., & Rao, D. D. (2003). A lightweight stemmer for Hindi. *The Proceedings of EACL.*

Ravikiran, M., & Annamalai, S. (2021). DOSA: Dravidian Code-Mixed Offensive Span Identification Dataset. *Proceedings of the 1st Workshop on Speech and Language Technologies for Dravidian Languages, DravidianLangTech 2021 at 16th Conference of the European Chapter of the Association for Computational Linguistics, EACL 2021,* 10–17.

Sarveswaran, K., & Dias, G. (2021). Building a Part of Speech tagger for the Tamil Language. *2021 International Conference on Asian Language Processing, IALP 2021,* 286–291. 10.1109/IALP54817.2021.9675195

SauravK.SaunackK.KanojiaD.BhattacharyyaP. (2021). *"A Passage to India": Pre-trained Word Embeddings for Indian Languages.* http://arxiv.org/abs/2112.13800

Shambhavi, B. R., Kumar, P. R., Srividya, K., Jyothi, B. J., Kundargi, S., & Shastri, G. V. (2011). Kannada morphological analyser and generator using trie. *International Journal of Computer Science and Network Security, 11*(1).

Shorten, C., Khoshgoftaar, T. M., & Furht, B. (2021). Text Data Augmentation for Deep Learning. In Journal of Big Data (Vol. 8, Issue 1). Springer International Publishing. doi:10.1186/s40537-021-00492-0

Srinidhi Skanda, V., Anand Kumar, M., & Soman, K. P. (2017). Detecting stance in kannada social media code-mixed text using sentence embedding. *2017 International Conference on Advances in Computing, Communications and Informatics, ICACCI 2017,* 964–969. 10.1109/ICACCI.2017.8125966

Suryawanshi, S., Chakravarthi, B. R., Verma, P., Arcan, M., McCrae, J. P., & Buitelaar, P. (2020). A Dataset for Troll Classification of TamilMemes. *Proceedings of the WILDRE5– 5th Workshop on Indian Language Data: Resources and Evaluation, 1*(May), 7–13. https://www.aclweb.org/anthology/2020.wildre-1.2

ThangarasuM.ManavalanR. (2013). *A Literature Review: Stemming Algorithms for Indian Languages. 4*(8), 2582–2584. http://arxiv.org/abs/1308.5423

Thara, S., & Poornachandran, P. (2018). Code-Mixing: A Brief Survey. *2018 International Conference on Advances in Computing, Communications and Informatics, ICACCI 2018*, 2382–2388. 10.1109/ICACCI.2018.8554413

Thavareesan, S., & Mahesan, S. (2020). Sentiment Lexicon Expansion using Word2vec and fastText for Sentiment Prediction in Tamil texts. *MERCon 2020 - 6th International Multidisciplinary Moratuwa Engineering Research Conference, Proceedings*, 272–276. 10.1109/MERCon50084.2020.9185369

Tsapatsoulis, N., & Djouvas, C. (2017). Feature extraction for tweet classification: Do the humans perform better? *Proceedings - 12th International Workshop on Semantic and Social Media Adaptation and Personalization, SMAP 2017*, 53–58. 10.1109/SMAP.2017.8022667

Willett, P. (2006). The Porter stemming algorithm: Then and now. *Program, 40*(3), 219–223. doi:10.1108/00330330610681295

Chapter 3
Linguistic Analyzers of the Arabic Language:
Linguistic Engineering Basis

Ali Boulaalam
https://orcid.org/0000-0002-0465-1914
Moulay Ismail University, Meknes, Morocco

Nisrine El Hannach
https://orcid.org/0000-0001-9794-9842
Poly-Disciplinary Faculty of Nador, Mohammed 1st University, Oujda, Morocco

ABSTRACT

This scientific initiative aims to formulate a number of hypotheses in order to prepare linguistic analyzers for the Arabic language based on the theoretical foundations and methodological frameworks of platform linguistics, which are the appropriate framework for building linguistic resources that can be invested in the field of automatic processing of natural languages. In this context, the theory of the syntactic lexicon was adopted, as it is the solid nucleus of dependency grammar that has proven to be effective in the field of describing natural languages, and thus being able to simulate and computerize them and crystallize linguistic algorithms that can be automated by using the open source unitex platform, which is based mainly on final state automata, final graphs, and transducers.

DOI: 10.4018/979-8-3693-0728-1.ch003

1. INTRODUCTION

This research falls within the framework of Dependency Grammar Systems such as the theory of the syntactic lexicon, which is considered as Theoretical and methodological fulcrum of platform linguistics, or as it is termed fourth-generation linguistics. It proved useful in developing research on the linguistic architecture of various natural languages, through its reliance on the techniques of electronic dictionaries and the local grammar based on several automates and transducers. This system enabled the achievement of an accumulation of knowledge whose level differed from one language to another, despite the early scholars' efforts in this regard, the Arabic language still occupied a weak place. This fact is due to the absence of institutional structures incubating full-fledged scientific projects, as most of the attempts remained Scattered, individual initiatives governed by academic goals in general. All these initiatives did not go beyond the morphological aspects, and thus the focus on building a synthetic analyzer for the Arabic language, along with the rest of the other linguistic analyzers, becomes an urgent need in order to complete the construction process of comprehensive linguistic resources for the Arabic language.

With this in mind, this scientific participation seeks to achieve the following objectives:

- Platform linguistic and knowledge society
- Linguistic analyzers and Arabic language engineering
- Determining methods for building a syntax analyzer for the Arabic language through the technique of syntactic lexicon tables.
- Demonstrating techniques for converting synthetic tables into parametric graphs.
- Defining the technical procedures for the elaboration of patron graphs through applications in the Arabic language.
- Processing technologies through the "unitex"
- Summaries, conclusions, and prospects.

2. PLATFORM LINGUISTICS AND KNOWLEDGE SOCIETY

Contemporary linguistics has developed from viewing language as finite structural frameworks upon which linguistic codes are built, to perceiving language as an infinite and algorithmic formal system inherent to human competencies, namely, natural language. Despite the temporal distance and epistemological divergence between these two perspectives, they share a commonality in their utilization of descriptive language rooted in the humanities, such as logic and psychology, including cognitive sciences, all falling within the same domain albeit with variations in semantic content. Each perspective has formulated a lexicon of linguistic concepts that defines the language it investigates, all emerging from the core of its theoretical concerns and requirements.

After presenting the theoretical frameworks of the linguistic journey in its two main traditional directions, in light of the technological advancements witnessed in natural language processing research, it becomes apparent that the adoption of either perspective, or even both together, is insufficient for the development of sound computer applications. Thus, we have constructed a new theory that integrates elements from both directions, which we refer to as "Lexicon-Grammar."

In this context, Arabic linguistics has gone through four successive chronological stages. We can explain this transition from one generation to another through the evolution of scientific discoveries. Human knowledge evolves based on what it discovers within the realm of word's phenomena. It's not just because scientists desire cognitive development; rather, each scientific era has its own scientific tools for describing natural phenomena. As humans realize that the tools, they have developed for scientific research are no longer capable of achieving their cognitive aspirations, they create new tools that enable them to explore the world and describe its phenomena.

Therefore, the transition from one linguistic generation to another aligns with the general cognitive evolution witnessed in scientific research. It's not a flaw for cognitive models to move from one stage to another; the flaw lies in persisting in research with intellectually sterile tools. Unfortunately, this has been the reality for many linguists in Arabic-speaking universities to this day. Hence, we introduce the gradual division of linguistic generations, emphasizing that the concept of a generation does not refer to the number of years but rather signifies the development of scientific knowledge related to the treatment of the Arabic language system:

> **The first generation**: Initially, traditional Arabic grammar, in all its various directions, constituted the standard framework. After a comprehensive theoretical linguistic model had been established for Arabic, encompassing all major issues in the field of linguistics, it delved into endless details. This led to differences in viewpoints among grammarians, some of which were of a personal nature, while others were influenced by religious or doctrinal beliefs. This situation prompted some philosophers who closely observed the tools of linguistic sciences to refer to them as "speculative sciences."

The Arabic linguistic model was then applied to other domains such as jurisprudence and interpretation. These tools worked effectively on the Arabic language system, addressing both its formal and content-related aspects. However, as their procedural tools were exhausted, they began to repeat themselves. This repetition took the form of texts, commentaries on texts, and commentaries on commentaries, eventually leading to a cessation of innovation and introducing a certain cognitive stagnation in linguistic studies.

> **The second generation**: In a later period, precisely during the Renaissance era, philological and comparative studies between Indo-European languages, especially Sanskrit, emerged. This was in addition to studies that revitalized linguistic jurisprudence from a new perspective. In the Arab world, individuals began to apply this approach to the Arabic language. Research teams were formed to investigate the roots of the Arabic language and compare it with its Semitic counterparts, much like comparative studies in many other countries, especially in Asian countries. However, these studies did not leave behind a scientific model that subsequent generations could widely adopt, unlike ancient Arabic studies. This was due to the depletion of the reference framework on which they were based.

Despite this theoretical depletion, some Arab countries still have faculties and departments of "Language Origins," and some of these "academic" institutions continue to produce researchers in this field, while incorporating elements of the classic Arabic model that still thrives in these institutions, resisting any new scientific developments that could challenge the prevailing scientific perspective.

During this period, the Arab world did not witness studies that connected language with its speakers from different social strata, as Europeans did. Instead, Arab scholars turned their attention to the accumulation of handwritten texts in Arabic and global libraries, dedicating themselves to editing and annotating these texts. Research teams of specialized scholars were formed to investigate the field of linguistic jurisprudence, which differed from philology as it was known in the West and as some Arab researchers represented it.

> **The third generation**: At the beginning of the 20th century, linguistic studies emerged in their descriptive sense, what is now known as the structuralist approach. This approach was based on a new philosophy aimed at describing natural phenomena in terms of form and presenting them as they are without interpretation. This included language, which was treated as a subject isolated from external influences. The term "linguistics" came to represent the study of the linguistic system, separated from external influences, including the language speakers themselves.

Many of our researchers embraced the structuralist model applied to the Arabic language. This led to the production of a substantial body of work, some of which was valuable, while much of it did not significantly contribute to the description of Arabic linguistic phenomena. Eventually, there was a surplus of literature in this direction, which extended to literature and led many to analyze texts structurally, extracting tools from their scientific context and applying them to Arabic texts, making them less readable. This trend did not stop at structural studies but expanded into semiotic, semiotic, and discursive studies, all of which were products of the stage in which this type of approach thrived in the Western world.

As for whether our researchers fully embraced the roles of structuralists, that is a question we leave for others to answer. However, what we emphasize is that the structuralist stage, in all its branches, is no longer capable of providing substantial contributions due to the exhaustion of its procedural tools and its limited cognitive returns for our young researchers seeking new knowledge built on rational thinking.

In response to the stagnation of the structuralist model in dealing with natural languages and its complete inability to interpret linguistic phenomena, transformationalists paved a new path, establishing the foundations for an interpretive approach to language. They shifted the discourse from performance, which couldn't go beyond the possibilities of description, to the interpretation of linguistic phenomena in general by investigating the structural foundations of language competence. This approach gave rise to new linguistic models that mimic human creativity in language use.

This direction evolved through linguistic models that began in 1957 and concluded in the late 1980s. However, its light dimmed, and its cognitive spring dried up because its procedural tools stopped being effective. These tools, which had been relied upon to propel linguistic work forward, were unable, contrary to their initial promise, to keep pace with the digital evolution aimed at creating a computational model capable of transferring the mechanisms of linguistic competence to the digital realm, especially in its advanced programming form.

As a result, this linguistic approach had to cease its scientific contributions and succumb to the reality, despite the significant efforts made by Moroccan researchers in building a new Arab linguistics framework. It had to make way for the fourth generation of linguistic research, which explores language from another perspective, aligning with present and future cognitive developments.

The Fourth Generation: If experts in the hard sciences agree that linguistics is the most experimental of experimental sciences itself, as it is based on formal principles that combine theory and practice, and if computer experts have achieved cognitive self-sufficiency that has shifted the computer from learning to teaching, where it has become a source of knowledge in all its forms, then

> this description is essentially the basis for building a new Arabic linguistic model called "Fourth-Generation Linguistics." This model is primarily the foundation for a knowledge society, which cannot be bypassed without the language channel. Here, we mean the Arabic language, which is one of the most responsive languages to computation since it is based on well-defined formal algorithms in both generative and analytical directions. This facilitates the construction of a mathematical model for this language.

Since research in natural languages has now shifted towards the approach taken by scientific knowledge in the new technology, that is digitization, any research in language, especially Arabic, that operates outside this framework will be of no use, if not futile. Therefore, we firmly believe that any research in the Arabic language must be based on a deep understanding of the principles of digitization, which views language as a system of algorithms, automation, and gradient equations that produce linguistic sequences and framed meanings for knowledge. Research in language, or language engineering, should contribute to the development of computer programs that digitally describe language to meet machine requirements. Language, essentially, is a system of mathematical programs stored in the competence, not a random storage from which performance is drawn. Therefore, it has become essential for today's linguist, who is the linguist of the digital future, to be proficient in mathematical and computer principles, especially in its programming aspect, in order to make language effectively fulfill its role in producing and transferring knowledge to future generations that will no longer deal with traditional methods.

To clarify the concept of language engineering and move from theoretical discourse to practical framework, it is worth mentioning some achievements in Arabic language engineering that have been realized to date[1] (شانحلا, 2013).

From this perspective, platform linguistics has contributed to the production of new knowledge by accompanying new digital theories in their original knowledge domain, both theoretically and methodologically. It operates in the same area as industrial artificial intelligence experts in various fields of application in human life, especially in the industrial sector, which relies on natural language in its construction according to the requirements of new digital technology. It also collaborates with artificial intelligence in its work within the knowledge domain represented by NBIC2 (Nano, Bio, Info, and Cognitive Science).

As these fields evolve, humanity is still striving to overcome the stage of weak artificial intelligence (WEAK IA), which is preoccupied with deep (Heudin, 2016)[3] learning technology. It awaits the completion of precise data description and collection, according to the requirements of Fourth-Generation Linguistics, to achieve what is known as Full Data. This will enable the transition to strong artificial intelligence (STRONG IA), a milestone set for 2030, when scientists will begin developing the third generation of artificial intelligence, known as the individualistic generation4. Experts in artificial intelligence have outlined a program with execution extending to the year 2045, which will result in the complete transition of the development program from humans to machines (Alexandre, 2017)[5]. At that time, we do not know what the future holds for the fully hybridized human, as envisioned by experts in strong artificial intelligence (Eagleman, 2016)[6]. At all these stages, Fourth-Generation Linguistics contributes to shaping the new concepts that describe this cognitive transition. Without it, technical work will remain absent from circulation (Kahane, 2001)[7].

3. NOOJ PLATFORM AND ARABIC LANGUAGE ENGINEERING

The exponential growth observed in computer technology, especially in natural language engineering, which relies on artificial intelligence applications, both strong and weak, and its cognitive branches such as deep learning and machine learning, has led to the emergence of a highly precise and rigorous terminology (Gaston,2012). This terminology has become essential for adjustment and the unpacking of its compressed meanings, facilitating its use in various expected applications in the Arabic language. In response to this technological development, the fourth generation of linguistics has produced a new system of linguistic rules for redefining the structure of natural languages (Gross,1975). These rules are derived from a new cognitive foundation that had been absent from traditional linguistic research in its previous three generations.

To shed light on this linguistic-engineering interaction that has given rise to this new field of natural language processing, we will provide a brief overview of the achievements made by fourth-generation linguistics (Silberztein, 2016). These achievements have shifted the research from understanding natural languages as they exist in human cognition towards a formalized representation (Silberztein, 1993). Furthermore, we will present some essential terminology models to build a lexicon of terms in natural language engineering. We will focus on the Nooj platform, which employs artificial intelligence mechanisms to develop various applications based on electronic dictionaries and local grammatical rules (Mesfar, 2008).

We will conclude this research by applying these concepts to a recent scientific article on the application of machine learning technology to the Arabic language. It will be shown that 70% of these concepts are shared by two integrated fields in this technology: computational linguistics and artificial intelligence[8] (مالعلوب, 2018).

Thus, new linguistics have emerged that utilize hybrid knowledge, combining linguistic understanding of language with the engineering understanding that forms the basis of linguistic data representation (Gross & Helmy, 2002). This fusion of cognitive foundations has given rise to a new direction known as "platform linguistics," which is a generation of data representation within a computational platform using various aspects of artificial intelligence technologies. This approach has allowed us to build encrypted electronic dictionaries that serve as the foundation for developing versatile applications and constructing symbolic frameworks composed of neurons, axons, dendrites, and transducers, simulating the neural pathways in the human brain responsible for producing linguistic data (Buvet & Crezka, 2009). In this way, the concept of syntax has become a machine that simulates the natural brain, but it cannot function outside the framework of the engineering platform that supports it. We emphasize that we use the Nooj platform, which is built on the principles of the structural lexicon theory, as the linguistic interface for the computational platform (El Hannach, 1990). This highlights the level of collaboration between linguists and computer scientists in the development of a new linguistic engineering.

Based on these data, it has been possible to establish the architecture of Arabic engineering in accordance with the following requirements: the computation of linguistic levels is linked to the construction of an electronic lexicon for Arabic vocabulary within a reference computational framework, embodied in a platform that is capable of dealing with the Arabic system at all levels (Gross, 1981). Among these platforms, Nooj stands out as an excellent linguistic engineering tool. It is a textual tool that offers mechanisms for developing linguistic analyzers used in numerous academic and service applications, starting from interactive textual research. One of the features of this platform is the adoption of a cascade principle between levels, allowing the automatic vocabulary of the language to be used simultaneously in the development of morphological, syntactic, and semantic analyzers (Gross, 1986). This is because the platform is primarily directed towards linguistic analysis of all languages supported by the global Unicode standard. Moreover, this platform is characterized by linguistic flexibility; it does not adhere to the requirements of a single linguistic theory. It naturally incorporates mechanisms from multiple linguistic theories, benefiting from the evolution of linguistic descriptions of natural languages. It does not favor any particular theory, setting it apart from other computer platforms aimed at engineering natural language systems9.

For reference, the results of work on this platform include the development of linguistic analyzers in more than one language, machine translation, and ontology. However, its most prominent feature is its interactive language teaching capabilities. All these applications are produced sequentially, with each application being interconnected and dependent on the others. There is no separation between these applications because the tools employed in the platform are flexible and adaptable to all of these applications. They are inherently derived from artificial intelligence technology. In this research, we will focus on how this platform deals with all of these applications as a whole.

a. Arabic Morphological Analyzer

Based on the aforementioned, we aim to digitally process the lexicographic/morphological aspects of the Arabic language using self-learning machine learning technology. This technology is a cornerstone of the Nooj platform, which originates from the structural lexicon theory. The starting point for this work will be the fusion between the root and pattern components that form the basis of the Arabic language system. This is unlike the Latin agglutinative language system, which is based on the concept of lemma (Gross, 1989).

As a result of this work, an electronic lexicon will be created, encompassing a comprehensive description of the morpho-syntactic data of the Arabic language. It will be complemented by local structures in the form of finite state automata (état finis automata) that enable automatic recognition of structured data in both directions: generation and analysis for all lexicographic entries found in lengthy or short arbitrary linguistic texts. It also allows for the construction of grammatically correct Arabic sentences based on a strict formal framework (Guillet, 1986).

The lexicon relies on a formal description of all Arabic linguistic entries without exception, where the descriptions are more critical than the entries themselves. This is because the computer reads symbolic representations before data, as the latter is generated and analyzed computationally through symbols. These symbols are usually fewer in number than the data itself, as each symbol corresponds to a significant number of linguistic materials in terms of generation and analysis (Zellig, 1971). Since Arabic is based on an inflectional system, it cannot be described based on the stem concept used in agglutinative languages. Arabic allows for the abbreviation of descriptive symbols because its lexicographic entries are based on the root and pattern components, which interact algorithmically. This interaction produces a linguistic structure consisting of:

Figure 1. Roots and patterns

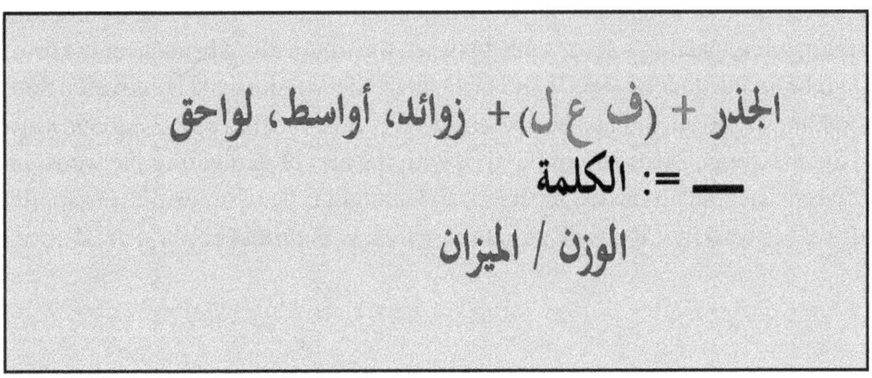

In this manner, the Arabic parts of speech are configured as follows: nouns, verbs, derivatives, and roots. As for the letters, this analysis does not apply to them due to their limited number in the Arabic linguistic system. Linguistic utterances have been computationally divided based on the distribution of weights with linguistic roots. There are approximately 12,600 roots, ranging from trilateral to quadrilateral, and a total of 413 patterns, collectively generating all Arabic language vocabulary (LECLER, 1990).

All Arabic words are morphologically and lexically encoded using three obligatory letters in the following order (Mejri, 2011): (1) ف, (2) ع, (3) ل. This order signifies the word's affiliation with the Arabic system. Any deviation from this order results in the word being considered foreign or uninflected (الحاج شا,1985). This order is exploited to activate the trilateral roots, where each letter in the root corresponds to one of the preceding three symbols. The pattern is responsible for distributing short and long vowels among the root components, allowing the generation of parts of speech that differ not in their root but in the application of the pattern. From a single root, all four linguistic utterances can be generated (الحاج شا,1992). For example, for the root ب ر ض (d-r-b), we can apply the verb pattern to get بَرَضَ (daraba), the noun pattern to get بَرَضٌ(darabun), the derivative pattern to get بارض (dārib), and the source pattern to get برَض (ḍarb).

It's important to note that the vowel placement is not determined by the root; instead, it follows the pattern system (بوعلام2017). The pattern system only controls the first and second vowels, while the third vowel adheres to the structural system, which we will discuss later. This system remains consistent for quadrilateral roots as well, where a fourth letter is added at the end of the preceding trilateral sequence in the form of ل (l), and the same principles that apply to trilateral roots are applied to quadrilateral roots. The number of quadrilateral roots does not exceed 1,800 root units, compared to the much higher number of trilateral roots.

The following table provides statistics about Arabic roots along with their associated patterns, represented by the symbolic components[10].

The root represents the linguistic input in the language program. Initially, the user selects the desired root, whether it's trilateral or quadrilateral. Then, the program starts applying matching algorithms between the linguistic substance of the root and the symbolic substance (ف.ع.ل). In a later stage, the weight/scale is activated through embedding algorithms that insert additions (prefixes, suffixes, infixes, and vowels) into the theoretical structure of the root with the aim of generating the word. In the analysis phase, the process is reversed, and another type of algorithms is applied to analyze the word into its basic structure, which is the root (العماري, 2004).

Table 1.

العتاد اللغوي للمعجم الإلكتروني: المفردة=: جذر X وزن			
الجذور الثلاثية	الجذور الر عية	المقولة اللغوية	العدد
9652	1800	الأسماء	160
		الأفعال	60
		المشتقات	73
		المصادر	136

الشكل (6–أ) إحصائيات معجم العرفان الإلكتروني

- For each inflectional form, there is a corresponding semantic component stored in the program. This inflectional semantic component is what ensures the connection between the inflectional level, lexicon, and semantics. The phenomenon of inflectional fusion, unique to the Arabic language, allows words within a sentence to move freely. The relationship between inflection and phonetic levels doesn't require explicit evidence, especially when it comes to irregular roots. Given that each inflectional form is associated with a specific meaning, organized as semantic fields, inflection has taken a significant portion of the semantic domain.
- Trilateral roots are characterized by considerable flexibility within the linguistic structure, in contrast to quadrilateral and pentagonal roots.

b. Arabic Structural Analyst

The Arabic structural analyst operates on two integrated processes:

1. Developing a linguistic system for symbolic algorithms responsible for generation. This involves branching the tree structure for each basic input in the Arabic language system. The confined roots represent the total number of inflectional inputs in the Arabic language, requiring the initiation of inflectional processing that employs phonological components, especially those related to assimilation, substitution, inversion, strengthening, hamza, and assimilation. The linguistic program should also encompass inflectional rules for various types of additions that can affect the root. These rules should follow a fixed

and controlled system to generate lexically sound data. These data are the same as those produced by the linguistic component in the human brain using the same symbolic linguistic algorithms. Thus, the work involves simulating the function of the capacity, which relies on a well-structured program (يرهفـلا يسافـلا, 1985).

2. The analytical software system, which starts from a random point among the multiple outputs in generation. This can occur at the inflectional level, where it can start from any generated inflectional form, or at the structural level, where it can start from any grammatically correct sentence generated through previous generation processes. The aim here is to trace it back to its input, which is achieved by reversing the process from generation to input (سيروم, 1989.)

Based on the above, it can be said that the structural composition is based on the assumption that the verb is a function (Fonction), while the rest of the elements are variables, as follows: P = V (n1, n2 … nx)

The electronic lexicon for Arabic language structures is built on this basis. Given the algebraic nature of the Arabic language system, represented by the linguistic algorithm system that combines different components of the system, linking these levels is highly complex and can only be achieved by providing the machine with symbolic linguistic rules, both generative and analytical (لالهل& يزاغ, 2009)

The variety of verb types in the language system, including regular, defective, and assimilated verbs, inevitably leads to a diversity of acceptable linguistic structures. These structures are derived from basic syntactic categories defined as follows:

A. The number of original structures is relatively limited, equivalent to the number of verbs in the Arabic language. Statistical studies have stopped at around 20,000 commonly used verbs in the Arabic language system. These are organized into basic syntactic categories, not exceeding thirty-five primary categories. These are determined according to a system of distributional rules that define the general structural framework for each primary syntactic category. In most cases, these structures have real semantics, while figurative semantics arise from distributional replacements between the components of the basic verb. This is based on the assumption that the basic verb represents the function that controls the variables, and not the other way around.

B. The number of transformed structures in the Arabic language system is subject to generative transformation algorithms applied regularly to the original structures, following rules of insertion, deletion, transfer, and all operations leading to the production of correct structural forms. This means that for each primary syntactic category, there is an undefined number of transformed syntactic categories. This increases the number of grammatical forms in the electronic lexicon.

Each primary syntactic category corresponds to a set of transformational operations, although this is weaker in some categories. Through field research on Arabic language structures, it has become evident that verbs (basic structures) exhibit similarities but not exact identities. Finding a verb in the database of original verbs (structures) in the Arabic language system that is entirely identical to another verb in all aspects at all levels is impossible. This reinforces the principle that any computer program must operate on the principles of constants and variables in the enumeration of language structures in both the distributional and transformational levels.

Building on this duality of constants and variables, the process of classifying Arabic language structures is carried out by constructing grammatical forms to test the structural data in both the distributional and transformational levels. These are then placed in a calendar of structural characteristics for each syntactic category separately based on structural inputs. This organization forces us to divide these grammatical forms into smaller groups, each containing a set of characteristics defining the structure of each syntactic category. The model presented in this study is an excerpt from the basic verb structure category: F s0 (=:مغ) s1 (سنإ), which branched into the following:

- Passivation (بلق)
- Adjectivation (فيصوت)
- Nominalization (ميسوت)
- Restructuration (إعادة البناء).

It is evident from this that generating data at the inflectional and structural levels cannot be done individually but through a system of algorithms applied in a classified manner. A single algorithm system can generate a large number of linguistic data that fall within its linguistic scope. For instance, an inflectional algorithm of type "Musa" cannot be applied to all entries in the Arabic lexicon. Similarly, algorithm "S" cannot be applied to algorithm "Musa." Each type of algorithm has its specific generative domain within the defined linguistic category. The same applies at the structural level, where it is impossible to apply algorithm "Mutaawil" to algorithm normalization for each one of them has its domain of application within the specific linguistic category. Each linguistic category forms the practical domain for applying its respective algorithm and nothing else.

Implementing this new cognitive framework in linguistic research, the verb becomes a simple sentence[11] because it controls all the elements associated with it. It branches into three sections:

1. Regular verbs, which control all components of the sentence.
2. Irregular verbs, which are only classified by root and pattern, with the verbal function weakening through the mentioned normalization operation.
3. The third type of verb is the idiomatic sentence (Idioms). The latter is a type of linguistic expression that remained elusive in the realm of linguistic analysis due to its resistance to open semantic composition. They exhibit non-compositionality and opacity resulting from the fusion of linguistic components among themselves. This takes them out of the scope of traditional lexicographic analysis, which is primarily based on individual meaning units before they are integrated into a compressed structural composition.

When searching for obstacles hindering the completion of this application, it became clear that several issues needed resolution before building a comprehensive linguistic engineering model for the Arabic language system, encompassing all its ascending levels, from individual sounds to structural composition. New studies, focusing more on visual experiences than linguistic ones, were carried out.

A machine-readable lexicon was constructed for these expressions, initially numbering around thirty thousand idiomatic structures, most of which are commonly used in today's functional Arabic language. After structuring these expressions and placing them into grammatical forms, it became possible to computationally process them using the latest platforms of new linguistic-engineering research.

In this case, the NOOJ platform was the most suitable, as it provides a specific platform for the Arabic language[12] (علي بوعلام, 2018) Based on syntactic structures, automatons can be prepared1[3] as finite state automata primarily designed for lexicon processing, to generate and analyze text vocabulary written in a platform-specific language. They represent logical relationships between the input and its outputs, in the case of generation. The relationship between output and input is ensured in the case of analysis. The connecting lines between logical components capture all the logical possibilities that either generate or analyze the input. It is a logical link between the components of the input. Below is a model of the syntax specific to resources in the Arabic language, representing the logical connection between the four morphological elements: verbs, roots, derivatives, and nouns, in the following form[14] (الحناش, 2017):

Figure 2. Logical automatons logically connecting Arabic statements

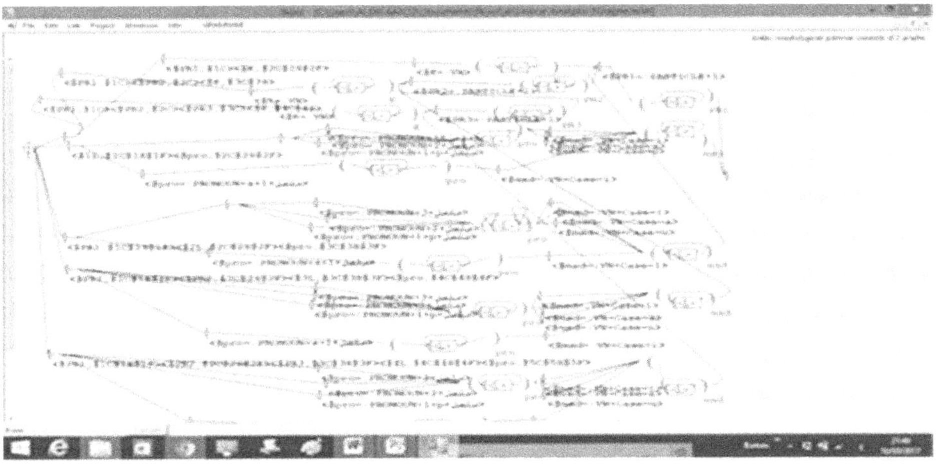

4. DETERMINING THE METHODS OF BUILDING THE ARABIC LANGUAGE'S SYNTACTIC ANALYZER THROUGH THE SYNTACTIC LEXICON TABLES' TECHNIQUE

Generally, Structural analysis falls within two main methodologies, which derive their reference from two different theoretical frameworks. Through them, a classification of contemporary linguistic theories was developed, as there are theories that depend, in their syntactic approach, on construction grammar such as the generative-transformational theory, and other ones that are structurally based on dependency grammars, such as syntactic lexicon theory and the theory of text meaning. However, this difference in the theoretical benchmark did not constitute a dividing line for the interaction between the two methodologies. Instead, many links still exist in the visual aspect that facilitates the process of moving between the grammar of constituents and the grammar of dependency within the framework of what is termed as "interactive grammar", which has become a methodological necessity for the automatic processing of natural languages.

Thus, there is no longer a fundamental difference between the two cited types of grammar. Rather, it is possible to move from one dependent tree to a Head-bearing composite structure by integrating the obtained components through the transversal process of the dependency relationship. Moreover, in return, it is possible to move from a syntax tree with lexicon predicate to a dependent tree without component representation by directly linking a specific compound factor to the head of this component (Kahane, 2001)[15].

5. DEMONSTRATING TECHNIQUES FOR CONVERTING SYNTACTIC TABLES INTO PARAMETRIC GRAPHS

It is possible to talk about the Arabic language's automatic syntactic lexicon by monitoring some of the scientific projects accomplished in this field, which are generally characterized by their scarcity compared to the abundant scientific production that has been achieved in the morphological field. The scientific work that has been accomplished in the scope of the syntactic lexicon theory is considered an essential entry point in talking about the main determinants of building the Arabic language's automatic syntactic lexicon. Especially if we know that some linguistic platforms have been engineered according to the theoretical foundations and methodological procedures of the compositional grammar system, as it is an associative grammar that has the elements of interaction with other linguistic theories.

Figure 3. Syntactic table

التوسيمات																		الفاعل						
																		المصدر المؤول						
جلب سالقص ل من 1	أضفى من0فعص على من 1	أعطى من0النقص في ل من 1	بعث من0النقص في من 1	حرك من فعص في من 1	حرك من0النقص في من 1	أحدث من0 فصل من 1	أحدث من0 الفصل من 1	أدخل من0فعص على من 1	أدخل من 0 النقص على من 1	خلق من0النقص ل من 1	خلق من0 النقص ل من 1	قرّ من 0 فعص في من 1	قرّ من 0 النقص في من 1	قرّ من 0 فعص في من 1	سبب من0 فعص من 1	سبب من 0الأقص ل من 1	سبب من 0فعص ل من 1	من0=: فعص من ق	من0=: كون ج	من0=: أن ج	من0=: أنّ ج	من0=: من غم	من0=: من أفعل	الفعل
+	-	-	+	-	+	-	-	-	-	-	+	-	-	-	-	+	-	+	+	+	+	+	+	أذى
+	-	+	+	+	+	+	-	+	+	+	-	-	-	-	+	+	+	+	+	+	+	+	+	ألم
+	+	-	+	-	+	-	+	-	+	-	+	+	+	+	-	-	-	+	+	+	+	+	+	أسف
+	-	+	-	-	-	+	-	-	-	-	-	-	-	-	-	-	-	+	+	+	+	+	-	أبطأ
+	+	+	+	-	+	+	+	+	+	-	-	-	+	+	+	+	+	+	+	+	+	+	+	أبهج
+	-	-	-	-	-	+	+	+	+	-	+	-	-	-	-	+	+	+	+	+	+	+	+	أتعب
-	-	-	-	-	-	+	-	-	-	-	-	-	-	-	+	-	-	+	-	+	+	+	-	أثلج
-	-	-	-	-	-	+	-	-	-	-	-	-	-	-	+	-	+	+	-	+	+	+	-	أثمل
+	-	+	+	+	-	+	-	-	-	-	-	+	-	+	+	+	-	+	+	+	+	+	-	أجج
+	-	+	-	-	+	+	-	-	-	-	+	-	-	-	-	+	+	+	+	+	+	+	-	أجهد
+	-	-	+	-	-	+	+	-	-	-	-	-	-	-	+	+	+	+	+	+	+	+	+	أحرج
-	-	-	-	-	-	+	-	-	-	-	-	-	-	-	-	-	+	+	+	+	+	+	-	أحرق
+	+	-	+	+	+	+	+	+	+	+	+	+	+	+	+	+	+	+	+	+	+	+	+	أحزن
+	-	-	+	+	+	+	+	-	-	+	+		+	-	+	-	+	+	+	+	+	+	+	أحنق
+	+	+	+	-	+	+	-	-	-	-	-	-	-	-	-	-	-	+	+	+	+	+	-	أحيي
-	-	-	-	-	-	+	-	-	-	+	+	-	-	-	+	-	-	+	-	+	+	+	-	أخذ
+	-	-	+	-	+	+	-	-	-	-	+	-	-	-	+	-	+	+	+	+	+	+	+	أخاف
+	+	-	+	-	+	-	+	-	-	-	-	-	-	+	+	-	+	+	+	+	+	+	+	أخجل
-	-	-	-	-	-	-	-	-	-	-	-	-	-	-	+	-	-	+	-	+	+	+	+	أخرس

The syntactic tables, which form in their depth associative-semantic trees, are the methodology used to build the automated syntactic lexicon within the framework of the compositional grammar theory. Where the simple sentence is considered as the minimum unit of analysis, which consists of a predicate and subjects, and the verb constitutes the lexical entry of the synthetic table, which includes within its predicative scheme its distributional and transformative/derivational characteristics. This is done through the process of labeling the entries according to the binary negative (-) and positive (+) in which the columns containing the entries intersect with the lines carrying the characteristics, according to the grammatical system, as shown in the following figure[16] (شاحان, 1985):

The syntactic tables that have been completed within the framework of the syntactic lexicon theory, which constitute a huge scientific achievement that enabled the preparation of comprehensive databases of linguistic characteristics in the levels of lexical competence for various natural languages. These tables need to be reconstructed in a way that makes its linguistic resources compatible with the advanced systems adopted in the field of automatic processing of natural languages. Thus, it can be used to feed the lexical databases of the automated syntax analyzers (Sagot &Tolone, 2010)[17].

In this regard, a number of scientific attempts have emerged in several languages, including the French language. They were able to develop the system of syntactic tables by completing them and transforming them into organizational structures that can be used in a syntactic analyzer. It was restructured into a version organized in the form of "XML" and called "Iglex" (Sagot &Tolone, 2010)[18], which in turn made it possible to convert it into a dictionary of Arabized forms of the French language "Lefff", which is a comprehensive syntax dictionary for the French language that includes all the specifications required to build syntactic analyzers. Such as the "FRMG"[19] analyzer that relies on dependent tree grammar "TAG" based on the "Dyalog" system in the download process.

From this point of view, some research was based on studying the possibility of converting syntactic tables into local grammar through the technique of parametric graphs, where a building of the possible structures graphs, that refers to the columns of the syntactic tables through the variables; and then the process of generating a copy of the graphs for each line in the table is carried out, through which the variables are replaced with the content of the cells located at the intersection point of similar columns and the processed line. If the cell is positive, the variable parallel to it is replaced with "E", and if it is negative, the domain containing the variable is deleted, as follows:

Figure 4. Variables table

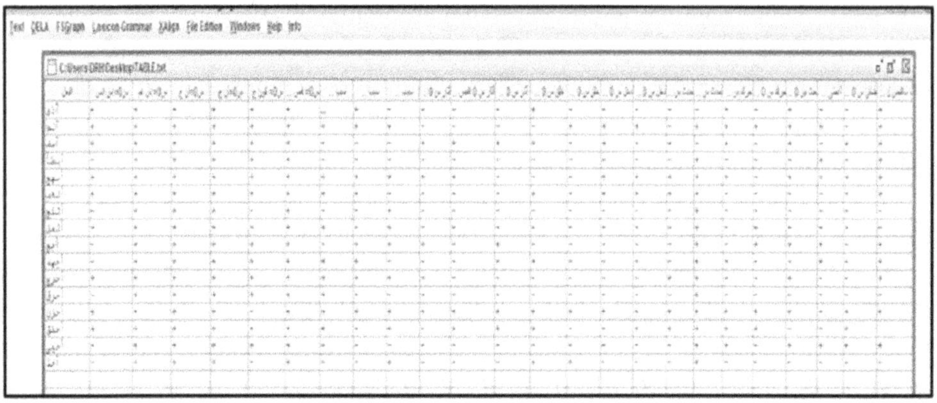

6. DETERMINING THE TECHNICAL PROCEDURES FOR COMPILING MEDIA GRAPHICS IN THE FORM OF MASTER GRAPHICS

Automated Processing Techniques Through the "Unitex" Platform

The Unitex platform consists of a set of programs that enable the processing of texts in various natural languages, through the use of linguistic resources in the form of automatic dictionaries, syntax grammars, and syntactic tables. This process is based on standardized slicing mechanisms subject to precise intervals, calibration of ambiguous linguistic forms, and application procedures based on lexicons[20].

- **Converting synthetic tables into Unitex graphics:** The process of converting Lexicon-Grammar Tables into graphics at the level of the Unitex platform is subject to the following stag**es:**

Table 2.

-	+	cacher	-	-	+	-	-	-	-	-	-	-	-	-	-	
-	+	**caler**	-	-	+	-	-	+	+	-	+	-	-	-	-	

Figure 5. Parametric graphs

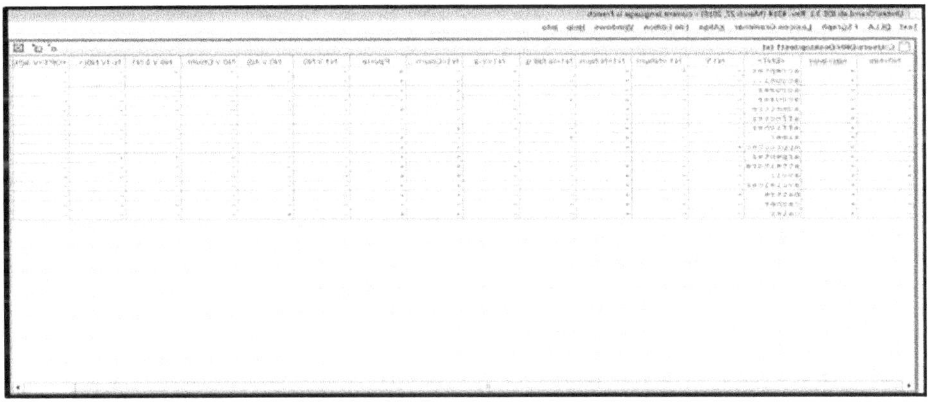

- Converting syntactic tables into csv format, using the EXEL program
- Creating parametric graphs

Figure 6. Parametric graphs

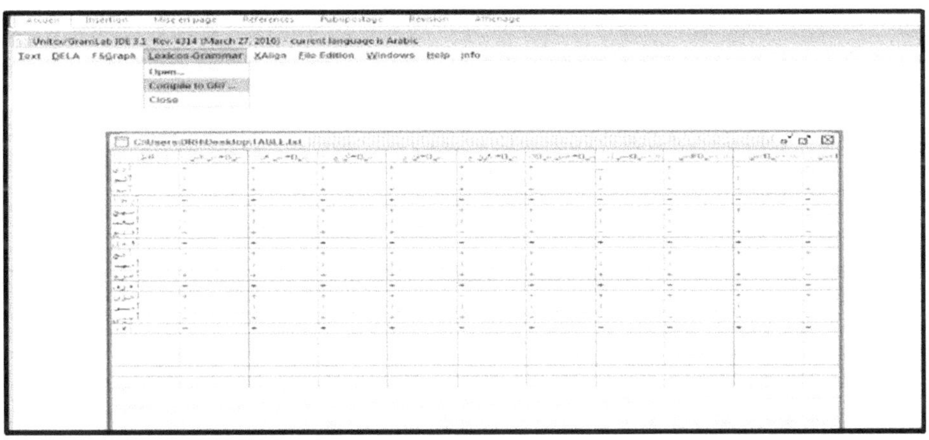

- Click on the "lexique-grammaire" icon, then on "Compile to GRF", as shown in the figure below:
- Through these applications, we get the following
- In the field above, "Reference Graph (in GRF format"), we put the title of the parametric graph, while in the "Resulting grf grammar", then we fix the title of Name of produced subgraphs, where we can specify the names of the generated graphs. After that, click on the "Compile" icon.

Figure 7. Text graphs

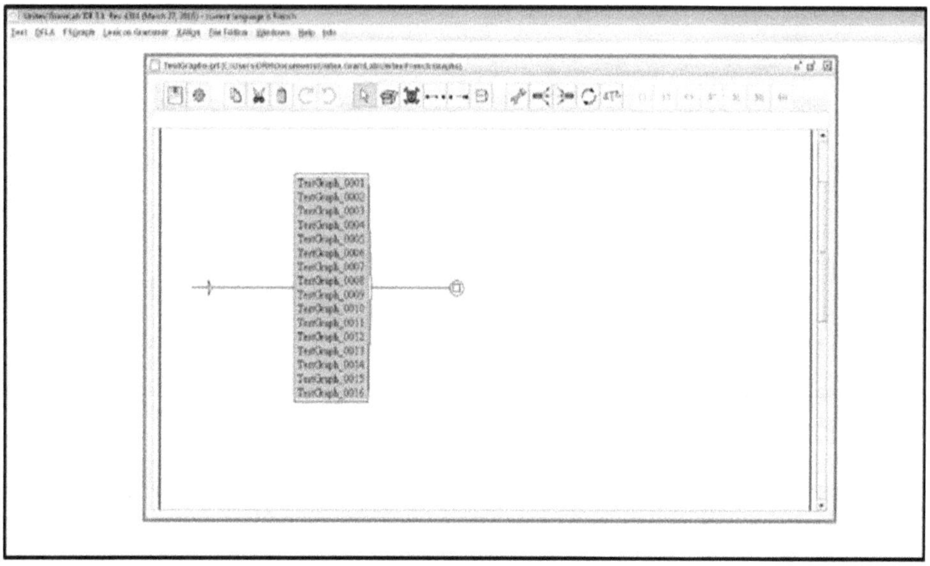

- Where we get a graph of the syntactic table:

Figure 8. Syntactic table

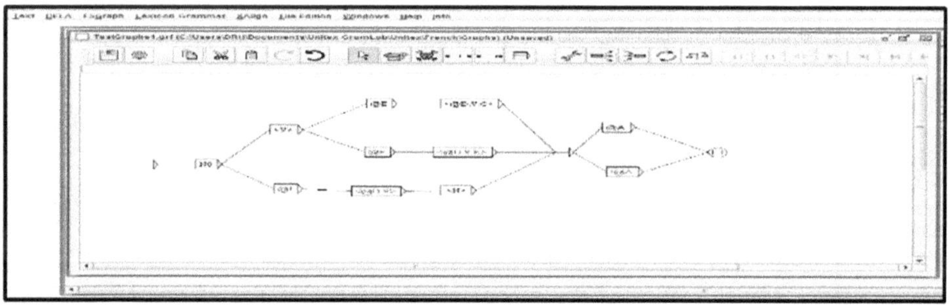

The result of the graphs on a text:

Figure 9. Graph results

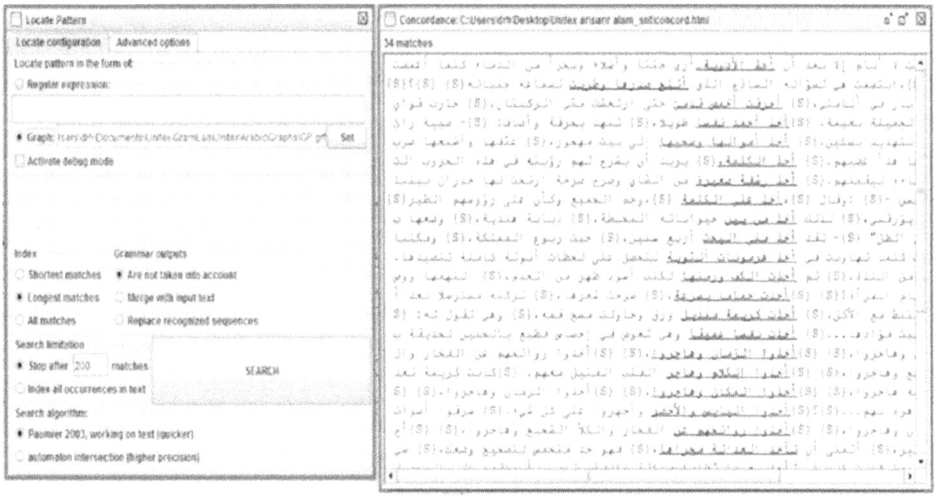

7. CONCLUSION AND DISCUSSION

This study provided a comprehensive overview of the evolution that natural language processing has undergone in its application to the Arabic language. It highlighted the most important applications that have emerged as programs, which cannot be utilized in serious service fields, primarily because most of them rely on computer expertise without linguistic expertise. They introduced some theoretical approaches referred to as abstraction, which contradict both methodologically and theoretically with the aspirations of natural language processing. This has resulted in formalistic applications that do not delve into the depth of the linguistic system in its both morphological and syntactic aspects, let alone its semantic and pragmatic dimensions.

To overcome this deficiency in the existing knowledge, an innovative linguistic framework called the "Structural Lexicon" was adopted, which serves as the foundation for the NooJ platform. This platform has gained global recognition as the only platform in the field of natural language processing based on a linguistic theoretical framework backed by cognitive principles drawn from the natural sciences. These principles are also common to most engineering and computer science applications.

The adoption of this reference framework based on the principle of extension in building the linguistic database enabled the development of the "Knowledge Electronic Lexicon," upon which various computer applications have been built. These applications employ machine learning techniques that allow for the development of practical applications related to various research fields in the Arabic language, particularly research on large linguistic corpora, which encompass legal, literary, and philosophical texts, among others.

This framework also allows educators to develop interactive educational applications to enhance critical thinking skills among learners. Additionally, journalists, who often need to collect data from websites for analytical articles, can benefit from the developed lexicon. Moreover, experts in economics and social sciences, as well as decision-makers, can rely on the advanced lexicon to improve the efficiency of their tasks, ultimately saving them time, a crucial factor in building knowledge, which has become a commodity in today's knowledge-based society.

The theory of the structural lexicon is built on classification tables, and it relies on verbs as inputs to produce outputs in the form of basic, transformed/derived sentences that are both structurally and semantically acceptable. This framework provides a suitable foundation for automated natural language processing, enabling the creation of formal mathematical models using tools such as Unitex and NooJ, which are based on finite-state automata for both generation and analysis, allowing for automated recognition in its generative and analytical components.

If the theory of the syntactic lexicon is based on taxonomic tables, Verbs depend on their inputs in order to produce outputs in the form of basic and transformative/derived sentences that are syntactically and semantically acceptable, then it provides the appropriate ground for the automatic processing of natural languages that enables Prepared simulated mathematical models according to the Unitex and NOOJ platforms, which are based on the end-state automation technology for automatic identification in both its obstetric and analytical parts.

Overall, this scientific paper attempted to establish a theoretical and methodological system for building Arabic language's linguistic analyzers, especially those related to the syntactic side, whereby it was possible to crystallize schematic predicative of the syntactic structures in the form of tables integrating the distributional and transformational characteristics, which enabled them to be invested within the scope of the unitex platform, through Graphics techniques, as well as practical applications on texts and blogs, yielded effective results.

Limitations

Despite the achieved results, the work needs additional efforts to integrate all linguistic phenomena, especially the multiple-word expressions, which will constitute a horizon for future research to overcome the shortcomings that may afflict the description process with a comprehensive dimension.

Ethics Statement

This chapter follows all the ethical principles that a relevant and responsible scientific project must abide by. First of all, it contributes to the well-being of humanity by making technology link people belonging to different cultures and speaking different languages through machine translation. Second, it fosters public awareness and understanding of computing-related technologies, by making different educational communities aware of the importance of technology-based scientific innovations. Thirdly, this project tries to uphold and revalorize the Arabic language by making it follow technological advancement and be part of this new world in which computers play a leading role. And finally, this article seeks to achieve high quality, by preparing and implementing an automated syntactic lexicon capable to fill up the existing gap in the language's database.

REFERENCES

Alexandre, L. (2017). *La guerre des intelligences: Intelligence artificielle versus Intelligence humaine*. JCLattès.

Buvet, A. P., & Crezka, A. (2009). Les dictionnaires électroniques du modèle de classes d'objets. *Langages*, 176.

Eaglman, D. (2016). *Les vies secrètes de cerveau.* Academic Press.

El Hannach, M. (1990). Esquisse d'une théorie informatico-linguistique de construction des dictionnaires électroniques de l'arabe. *Linguistica – communicatio, 2*(2), 1990.

Gross, G. (2012). *Manuel d'analyse linguistique: approche sémantico-syntaxique du lexique*. Presses universitaires.

Gross, M. (1975). *Méthodes en syntaxe: Régimes des constructions complétives.* Hermann.

Gross, M. (1981). Les bases empiriques de la notion de prédicat sémantique. *Langages*, 63.

Gross, M. (1986). Grammaire transformationnelle du Français: syntaxe du verbe cantilène. Academic Press.

Gross, M. (1989). La construction de dictionnaires électroniques. *Télécommunication, 44*(1-2).

Guillet, A. (1986). Représentation des distributions dans un lexique–grammaire. *Langue française, 69.*

Harris, Z. S. (1971). *Structures mathématiques du langage*. Dunod.

Ibrahim, A. H., & Gross, M. (2002). Une refondation de la linguistique au crible de l'analyse automatique. Taln 2002, Nancy.

Kahane, S. (2001). Grammaires de dépendance formelles et théorie Sens-Texte. TALN 2001, Tours.

. Leclere, C. (1990). Organisation du lexique-grammaire des verbes Français. *Langue française*, 87.

Mejri, S. (2011). *Constructions à verbes supports, collocations et locutions verbales*. Academic Press.

Mesfar, S. (2008). *Analyse morpho-syntaxique automatique et reconnaissance des entités nommées en arabe standard* [Thèse de doctorat]. Université de Franche-Comté, France.

Sagot, B., & Tolone, E. (2010). *Exploitation des tables du Lexique-Grammaire pour l'analyse syntaxique automatique.* Paris-Rocquencourt / Paris 7, Université Paris-Est.

Silberztein, M. (1993). *Dictionnaires électroniques et analyse automatique des textes, le système INTEX*. Masson Paris.

Silberztein, M. (2016). *La formalisation des langues, l'approche de NooJ*. Hermann.

ENDNOTES

1 محمد الحناش: مجلة التواصل اللساني، مقدمة المجلد 15 / 2013.

2 N : Nano technology, B : Bio technology, I : Informatics, & C : Cognition

3 Comprendre le Deep Learning, Jean Claude Heudin, Science e-Book, 2016

4 Recently (in 2013) at King Saud University, a scientific chair was established called the "Chair of Individuality and Third Vision," where artificial intelligence technologies are applied. The research team working in this chair has published several scientific research papers that connect the structure of natural languages and artificial intelligence, using terminologies from fourth-generation linguistics.

5 Laurent Alexandre, La guerre des intelligences : Intelligence artificielle versus Intelligence humaine, JCLattès, 2017.

6 Les vies secrètes de cerveau, Davis Eaglman, 2016.

7 Sylvain Kahane : Grammaires de dépendance formelles et théorie Sens-Texte, TALN 2001, Tours, 2-5 juillet 2001,p :4.

8 علي بوعلام: لسانيات المنصات واللغة العربية، تطبيقات حاسوبية من خلال استخدام منصة نوج، ص: 7.

9 There are many computer platforms, such as Google, which are comprehensive. They enable users to translate, and search for vocabulary, images, and more, making it more of a search engine than a platform specialized in natural languages. There are platforms dedicated to natural languages like INTEX, but they remain limited in processing interactive texts. Moreover, they do not produce linguistic analyzers at the morphology, syntax, and semantics levels, as is the case with the platform NOOJ, which we adopt.

10 محمد الحناش: اللغة العربية والحوسبة، تطبيق منصة Nooj على معجم "العرفان"، ص: 13.

11 We distinguish between structure and sentence. Structure is a general formal framework that generates a large number of linguistic materials, such as morphology, which generates a large number of vocabulary items. On the other hand, a sentence is a practical application of the structure, and it does not generate anything other than itself.

12 علي بوعلام، لسانيات المنصات، 2018.

13 It is a machine that generates the linguistic data described in the previous electronic lexicon. It takes the form of human brain components in terms of dendrites and axons, connected by transducer-shaped nodes. These are the points where nerves converge before branching into sub-branches. The input unit represents the basic linguistic unit from which a set of sub-linguistic sequences is generated, such as root + pattern =: from which the input, for example, "kataba," is generated, leading to a set of sub-entries: "katib," "maktub," "kitab," etc. The generation process is performed by applying a set of algorithms to the input, resulting in a new sub-input that includes all the morphological, semantic, and lexical specifications described.

14 محمد الحناش: معجم العرفان، ص 36.

15 Sylvain Kahane : Grammaires de dépendance formelles et théorie Sens-Texte, TALN 2001, Tours, 2-5 juillet
2001,p :4.
محمد الحناش: النحو التاليفي مدخل نظري، مجلة أدبية ولسانية العدد 1 السنة الأولى ص: 16

17 Benoît Sagot, Elsa Tolone : Exploitation des tables du Lexique-Grammaire pour l'analyse syntaxique automatique Paris-Rocquencourt / Paris 7, Université Paris-Est, p : 4.

18 Benoît Sagot, Elsa Tolone : Exploitation des tables du Lexique-Grammaire pour l'analyse syntaxique automatique Paris-Rocquencourt / Paris 7, Université Paris-Est, p : 5.

19 French MetaGrammar

20 Paumier S., (2009)., Unitex2.0, user manual, Université Paris-Est Marne-la Vallée

Chapter 4
A Case Study on Tools and Techniques of Machine Translation of Indian Low Resource Languages

Anuraj Bose
https://orcid.org/0009-0000-4644-6639
Vellore Institute of Technology, India

Goutam Majumder
https://orcid.org/0000-0002-9892-4628
Vellore Institute of Technology, India

ABSTRACT

India, celebrated for its vast linguistic diversity with 1,599 languages (including 122 prominent ones), exemplifies the richness of language variation. Indo-Aryan languages, spoken by 70% of the population, and Dravidian languages, used by 19%, create this diverse linguistic tapestry. Effective communication in this interconnected society is crucial, and machine translation plays a pivotal role in bridging language gaps. Speech is a cost-effective mode of interaction, particularly important in a globalized world. Machine translation, a part of natural language processing (NLP), aids in overcoming language barriers. This chapter presents enlightening case studies and valuable best practices, inspiring meaningful translation efforts for low-resource language communities. Together, we can break linguistic barriers, fostering a world of boundless communication and enduring cultural treasures. Challenges like limited linguistic resources, technological deficiencies, and community engagement issues persist.

DOI: 10.4018/979-8-3693-0728-1.ch004

1. INTRODUCTION

India has 1600 more languages as well as the 23 officially recognized by the Constitution in 2011[1]. In this era of digitalization, communication technology for Indian languages is essential in various business fields. A major number of languages are "low resourced," making establishing language-based interfaces for the Indian market an important challenge (Miao et al., 2021). Before identifying the first machine translation system, it's worth noting that the "translation memorandum" guided by 'Warren Weaver' alongside IBM word for word translation mechanism on 1954 gave rise to one of the earliest applications seen as being solved by computers: machine translation (Hutchins, 1997).

A low-resource challenge for NLP could emerge mostly because of a result of the low-resource status of the languages or domains that are being evaluated (Hedderich et al., 2020). By examining many criteria, including the total count of first language speakers around number at accessible datasets, researchers have tried to identify low-resource languages (LRLs). In a broader perspective, a language is classified as low resource when it exhibits one or more of the subsequent characteristics (Lu et al., 2013). Such as:

- Limited function of speech, text, or transcribed data.
- Insufficient linguistics are knowledge in a specific language.
- Absence of a comprehensive pronunciation dictionary.

Any MT model anticipates data and related transcripts as inputs to understand the pattern and structure of any language. Even though there is a substantial amount of free raw speech for Indian languages available (Khan et al., 2017), getting the associated transcription is a difficult and expensive procedure. Consequently, throughout the previous decade, virtually little effort has been made by many researchers (Kandimalla et al., 2022). One of the efforts is noted as the syllable pronunciation dictionary was created using a simple rule-based parser since Indian languages are syllabic (Prahallad et al., 2012; Baby et al., 2016; Ramani et al., 2013; Pandey et al., 2017).

In order to increase machine efficiency in jobs involving high-resource languages, efforts have been undertaken to address low resource languages since the commencement of the digital India mission in 2015 (Edunov et al., 2018). Unfortunately, research on machine translation for the Indian language is hampered by the absence of publicly available models and baselines; one prominent example of this is the Indian language corpora initiative corpus (Jha, 2010).

This chapter highlighted the potential technological and community-driven solutions, that can enhance the translation process and make it more sustainable.

Provide insights on recommendations for policymakers, researchers, and practitioners to promote and support translation initiatives for low-resource Indian languages.

2. BACKGROUND OF LOW RESOURCE LANGUAGE (LRL)

2.1 Present State-of-the-Art of Indian LRLs

Indian languages are broadly classified into two forms as: (a) Low Resource Language (LRL); (b) Higher Resource Language (HRL)[2]. In India the oldest and most linguistically diverse types of regional languages are found, where every few kilometres the dialect or language varies (Diwan et al., 2021). The majority of the Indian languages are categorized into a variety of language families or genealogical kinds[3], such as, (a) Austro-Asiatic; (b) Dravidian; (c) Indo-Aryan; (d) Tibeto-Burman; (e) Tai-Kadai; (f) Andamanese (Heitzman & Worden, 1995).

Language families in India share numerous linguistic traits, resulting in a rich tapestry of acoustic and linguistic diversity. Out of 29 Indian-based languages, 22 are designated as official languages among all the Indian LRLs[4] (Sailor & Hain, 2020). LRRs are used in real-world scenarios like healthcare information dissemination and automated voice messages in rural areas. Automated Speech Recognition (ASR) can benefit these communities by using special traits and parallels across languages, potentially aiding in the development of multilingual and code-switching ASR systems (Datta et al., 2020). Techniques that take use of special traits and parallels across the Indian languages might aid in the development of multilingual and code-switching ASR systems.

Cui et al. (2015) conducted a study on low-resource languages (LRLs) and their use in machine learning (ML) representations. They found that multilingual ASR techniques can improve performance by utilizing codeswitching characteristics of source language speech. However, the study also highlighted the need for proper language choice for better performance. A multilingual MT system based on Hindi, Marathi, and Odiya is anticipated to be beneficial.

2.2 Empowering Marginalised Communities

The Indian Languages Corpora Initiative (ILCI) is led by the Department of Technology Development in Indian Languages (TDIL). It aims to advance Natural Language Processing (NLP) by making data publicly available, building multilingual systems, and developing assessment standards. (Doddapaneni et al., 2023). AI4Bharat, a non-profit open-source community, is involved in these initiatives. The National Language Translation Mission (NLTM), also known as "Bhashini," was introduced in the 2021 budget to overcome language barriers and ensure digital empowerment in India. (Sridhar et al., 2020).

3. CHALLENGES OF LOW RESOURCE INDIAN LANGUAGES (LRLS)

The challenges associated with low-resource Indian languages for machine translation are multifaceted and encompass several key areas. In this Section, first we have reported challenges facing by the MT community due to structural changes in Indian state languages.

3.1 Demographic and Structural View of the Indian State Languages

Out of 42 percent of Indians are native speakers of Hindi, the language that is most often spoken there. However, 5% of people speak more than thirty distinct languages, including classical ones like Tamil, Sanskrit, Malayalam, Odia, and Telugu. There are four categories of Indian language proficiency: Indo-Aryan, Sino-Tibetan, Dravidian, and Afro-Asiatic. The Bangla language, which is spoken in Bangladesh, West Bengal, Tripura, and Assam, lacks natural language processing (NLP) technologies (Patra et al., 2015; Das & Bandyopadhyay, 2010).

Tamil is a highly developed Dravidian language spoken by 15 million people in South-East India, primarily in Tamil Nadu and internationally in Sri Lanka. Its vast vocabulary, logical understanding, and precise grammar allow for refined expression of thoughts and ideas. Tamil's numerous honorifics reflect its decadent culture.

Malayalam is used as a language by people in Kerala, a few communities in Karnataka as well as Tamil Nadu. Approximately 35 million people throughout the country speak this language. It employs a nominative-accusative gender marking scheme and the SOV writing style. It has been written in left-to-right Malayalam script. Sentence like സീതയ്ക്ക്ചിത്തരചന ഇഷ്ട മാണ് which, English became "Sita loves drawing". Here the word സീതയ്ക്ക് (Sita, Subject), ഇഷ്ടമാണ് (loves, Verb) and ചിത്തര ചന (drawing, Object).

The 45 million individuals that call Gujarat home speak Gujarati, an Indo-Aryan language. It is written in Gujarati script through SOV, writing in style and is written from left to right. Examples include in the phrase તે આઈસ્ક્રીમ ખાય છે, becomes "He is eating ice cream" in English. In this sentence તે represents the subject, આઈસ્ક્રીમ is an object and verb is ખાય છે.

Kannada, which is extensively spoken in other parts of India, serves as the primary tongue of Karnataka. Kannada is a language that thirty-six million individuals in India speak and write. Despite Kannada is a Dravidian language with a large body of historical writing, there aren't many computerized linguistic tools available for it, which makes it difficult to examine the language's literature owing to its semantic and syntactic complexity. It also follows the SOV structure and is quite agglutinative, written in a left-to-right direction. For instance ರಾಮ ಶಾಲೆಗೆ ಹೋದ(SOV) is in English is "Rama went to school". Here, ರಾಮ(Rama, Subject), ಶಾಲೆ(school, object), and ಹೋದರು(went, verb).

Andhra Pradesh and Telangana, two southern Indian states, both have Telugu as their official language. The Telugu-speaking immigrant populations in the United States, Canada, and the United Kingdom also speak it. Telugu has a subject-object verb pattern that reads from left to right. A Telegu sentence ఆమె నన్ను కొట్టింది is equivalent to the English sentence "She beat me", where ఆమె represents 'she' as subject, నన్ను represents 'me' as object and కొట్టింది as 'beat' as verb. Table 1, summarize the structural form along with scripts used to write for Indian LRLs.

Table 1. Various statistics related to Indian low-resource languages, scripts, and structures used for communication purposes

Language	Script	Word Order	Family	Number of Speakers (in Millions)	Writing Direction
Urdu	Urdu	SOV	Indo-European	170	Right to left
Tamil	Tamil	SOV	Dravidian	81	Left to right
Nepali	Devanagari	SOV	Indo-Aryan	24	Left to right
Sinhala	Sinhala	SOV	Indo-European	17	Left to right
Sindhi	Devanagari Perso -Arabic	SOV	Indo-European	25	Left to right Right to left
Telugu	Telugu	SOV	Dravidian	93	Left to right
Punjabi	Perso-Arabic, Gurmukhi	SOV	Indo-European	125	right to left left to right
Oriya	Oriya	SOV	Indo-European	38	Left to right
Assamese	Bengali	SOV	Indo-European	15	Left to right
Malayalam	Malayalam	SOV	Dravidian	38	Left to right
Bengali	Bengali	SOV	Indo-European	265	Left to right
Marathi	Devanagari	SOV	Indo-European	95	Left to right
Gujarati	Gujarati	SOV	Indo-European	60	Left to right
Kannada	Kannada	SOV	Dravidian	36	Left to right
Hindi	Devanagari	SOV	Indo-European	615	Left to right

3.2 Global LRLs and MT Scenario

Since multilingual methods tend to be trained on larger amounts of data than single models, (Arivazhagan et al. 2019) demonstrate that multidisciplinary models can enhance the translated effectiveness for midrange and low resources languages. Thereby, in conjunction with low-resource multilingual data throughout instruction, it is also use high-low resources coupled data, which includes English→Occitan. Transfer of expertise may occur when students are trained on both high- and low-resource language pairs (Zoph et al., 2016), particularly if each of the languages are related linguistically.

Even though machine translation (MT) has been shown to be a valuable aid in the work process of qualified translators, it remains uncommon for Irish translators working as freelancers or for translation agencies at the moment. Irish has limited access to modern technology that has been demonstrated to be successful for majority languages since it is a minority language with less resources (European Language Resource Coordination, 2020)[5].

Scholars are exploring methods for translating into morphologically rich languages, including discriminative lexicon models, two-tiered approaches, unsupervised morphology learning, and adding per-word linguistic information. The Dagstuhl conference aimed to discover new methods, while Automatic Post-Editing (APE) aims to improve output quality and reduce posting work for expert translators[6] of Machine Translation (MT).

The most popular technique is statistical phrase-based post-editing, which creates a parallel corpus using human post-edited data and the MT output. Additional methods include rule-based methods, hybrid word alignment methods, and a basic rule-based method for English to Irish machine translation (Dowling, et, al. 2016).

As a number of people have noted, MT systems adoption in Europe has proceeded far more slowly than anticipated; markets are few and dispersed, and experienced translators continue to be antagonistic.

Although there is a lot of promise, it is not yet fully used. Multinational corporations including major translators are the main users of MT systems. Smaller companies choose translations workbenches, which can occasionally be networked to share terminology databases and translating memory. Freelance translations are also starting to think about getting workstations of their own. The less expensive PC-based solutions are still not being bought on the same scale as in North America or the nation of Japan, and are usually only of use to individuals with sporadic translation need (Hutchins et. al., 1996).

200 thousand papers are utilized annually by the European Commission thanks to its increasing usage of Systran. The main consumers were non-linguistic staff members who needed versions for publications in languages other than their native

tongue as well as interpretations for informative (brief and/or repetitive) documents. The increased use is due to improved accessibility features and interfaces. The main course of study for translation is EURAMIS[7].

The Verbmobil project, supported by the German Ministry of Research and Technology, is a language instruction system developed to facilitate commercial talks between Japanese and German executives. The system uses English as the common discussion language and disambiguated visualizations, utilizing specialist databases or speech act data. The study of discourse in this area has gained significant attention[8].

Since Eurotra's demise, European Union research grants have been awarded on a broad range of initiatives in the expansive subject of language engineering, including translation support in a variety of settings and multilingual tools of many types. Sensible throughout, the importance of general-purpose and reusable goods is emphasized, along with execution and cooperation with industry partners (Hutchins et al., 1996).

It is impossible to include every project that incorporates translation and multilingualism. Just a select handful are emphasized. The goal of the ALEP project has been to provide a platform that would enable various technological and scientific endeavors pertaining to natural language processing. These endeavors include the creation of a text handling system and an all-encompassing formalism and rule interpreter.

There is naturally a great deal of worry with legitimate and acceptable assessment methodologies as the focus on the user experience of multinational and translation systems grows in European. The EAGLES study group, which Elizabeth King published on in AMTA-94, is a crucial instrument for developing standards for review and evaluation of language engineering tools. It hasn't examined MT as of yet; instead, it has focused on authoring tools and grammatical checkers (Kugler et al., 2013).

3.3 Challenges and Approaches used for Indian LRLs

In the 1990s, machine learning experienced a significant transformation from rules-based to statistically based approaches in processing natural languages tools. (Banane & Erraissi, 2022). Since then, around of 20 languages out of the 7000 spoken languages have seen many developments, considered English as a primary international language Around 20 languages, including English, have seen significant developments, but low-resource languages require extensive research and are susceptible to challenges, requiring further research.:

- The projection approach, a commonly used annotation method, can be challenging to apply across high-resource languages due to structural differences and lack of guidance. (Magueresse et al., 2020).
- Each mapping approach of one language to another, requires the creation of a dataset, bag of words, and raw text collection for LRLs (Magueresse et al., 2020).
- The most critical resource of a language is its lexicon, which NLP activities mostly depends. However, LRLs lack sufficient textual data, making it difficult to create an effective lexicon (Elkateb et al., 2006).
- LRLs have continuously changing morphology, which poses a challenge in providing a complete framework for identifying morphological patterns.
- NLP applications such as question-answer systems, sentiment analysis, image-to-text mapping, machine translation, and named entity recognition-based systems are exceedingly challenging to carry out in low-resource languages (Guellil et al., 2021).
- Essential NLP tasks such as stop-word detection and elimination, tokenization, part-of-speech tagging, sentence parsing, lemmatization, stemming, etc., are also challenging in low-resource languages (Guellil et al., 2021; Patra et al., 2015).

4. PRESENT CASE STUDIES OF NLP

George University and IBM developed the first machine translation application in 1954, a significant breakthrough in Natural Language Processing (NLP). Gordon Moore's Law increased computational capacity, leading to the creation of statistical model-based algorithms (Hutchins, 2005).

4.1 Attempts for Machine Translation

Back in 1994, Arbabi came up with a phoneme-based method of converting Arabic to English (Arbabi et al., 1994). Later on, between the years 2008 and 2010, statistical machine translation algorithms have been reported, those were not specific to any particular language. Various works have been reported for regional Indian languages. For example, Antony et al. (2010a) used an SVM kernel model that had been trained on over 40,000 names of Indian cities to solve the transliteration challenge from English to Kannada. It is based on the process of sequence labelling. The transliteration module employs an intermediary code that is intended to maintain the phonetic characteristics.

Antony et al. (2010b) and Kumari and Goyal (2012) compared their results to those produced by the Google Indic transliteration algorithm. Grapheme-to-phoneme (g2p) is the process of converting the spelling of a word into its pronunciation. Statistical g2p transliteration learning models are refined using specialized language pronunciation dictionaries, which are time-consuming and costly. Dong et al., developed a g2p transliteration model for low resource languages using phonological inventory data taken from Phoible (Dong et al., 2022), that is developed by (Norder et al., 2022). This data contained 37 phonological properties, including nasal, consonantal, sonorant, etc. Using high resource language terms with similar linguistic and phonological information, low resource language words are transformed to their pronunciation. To translate Hindi and Marathi into English, (Harish & Rangan, 2020), proposed a straight phonetic-based transliteration method without using a bilingual database.

Work reported by (Ekbal et al., 2007) greatly benefited Bengali-English transliteration, making a significant contribution to the development of translation systems for Indian languages to English. They have presented a modified combined source-channel model based on conventional and non-probabilistic expression. Linguistic expertise is required for transliterating human names from Bengali to English. Back-translation to the Kannada language is reported in Sowmya Lakshmi and Shambhavi (2019), where roman words are translated using Kannada script.

4.2 Attempts to Statistical Machine Translation

While MT is important and (Das et al., 2023) shows statistical approaches are necessary for SMTs and these methods are data-driven and uses parallel-aligned corpora. The chance of translation from the source language to the target language is determined using mathematical calculations, such as probability calculated using Bayes' theorem, as given in Eq. (1).

$$P(T_i|S_i) \propto P(T_i)_p(S_i|T_i) \tag{1}$$

where T_i and S_i represents the target and source language and $P(S_i|T_i)$ estimate the conditional likelihood of the intended language towards the source language. Any SMT method comprises three stages (a) Language Modelling (LM) are used for the Translation Model (TM), to calculates the probability of target language on given source language $P(T_i|S_i)$; (b) the decoder modelling (DM), which chooses the resource phrase with greatest likelihood among all potential sources (Kumawat & Chandra, 2014); (c) The most important and last stage of SMT is the DM.

The LM makes use of the n-gram model to determine the likelihood of a phrase. It assesses the likelihood of the translation and gives the final n words in the phrase the chance of a single word. The sentence may be divided into conditional probability products with the use of the chain rule., as shown in Eq. (2).

$$\begin{aligned} P(s) &= P(w_1, w_2, \cdots, w_n) \\ &= P(w_1)P(w_2 \mid w_1)\cdots P(w_n \mid w_1 w_2 \cdots w_{n-1}) \end{aligned} \tag{2}$$

where $P(s)$ is the likelihood that the phrase s, made up of the words $w_1, w_2, \ldots, w_n$ will occur in a k-gram model. It makes use of language pairs of bilingual paralleled corpus. It determines the chance of words or phrases in a sentence using a k-gram model, where k represents the length of the sentence. Finally, a DM is increasing the likelihood, it helps in deciding on the terms that have the best chance of being converted. i.e., $P(T_i)P(S_i|T_i)$.

The main, hm(y, x) indicates the feature operate while λm is the value of its weight. The grammar method, the reorganization model, both the word penalty and phrase penalty, overall reversible translational probabilities, or the bidirectional vocabulary translational probabil-ties are examples of common SMT characteristics. By using the minimal error rate training (MERT) approach, the feature weights may be adjusted (Och et al., 2004).

$$p(y|x) = \frac{\exp\left(\sum_{m=1}^{M} \lambda_m h_m(y,x)\right)}{\sum y'\left(\sum_{m=1}^{M} \lambda_m h_m(y',x)\right)} \tag{3}$$

$h_m(y,x)$ represents the characteristic function, while λm is the value of its weight. The linguistic model, rearrangement model, letter penalty, phrasing penalty, reversible translation likelihood, and reversible lexical translational probabilities are examples of common SMT features. The least probable error learning (MERT) approach can be used to adjust the feature weights (Och & Ney, 2004).

The SMT decoding chooses an appropriate target word or phrase translations for an unpublished source span from a bilingual phrase table in order to extend partial translation (referred to as translation proposition in SMT) $y<t=y_1,y_2,\ldots,y_t$.

4.3 Various Approaches for Enhancing the Language Processing Tasks

Various approaches reported for enhancing the performance of Indian low resource languages are categorised as (a) rule-based; (b) Statistical Machie Translation; (c) Neural Machine Translation. Table 2 summarises all the research works performed over low resource Indian languages.

Table 2. List of methods used for low resource Indian languages

Author	Rule Based	Statistic Based	Neural Based	Language	Methods
(Narayan et al., 2014)	-	-	✓	Hindi	Artificial Neural Network
(Todi et al., 2018)	-	-	✓	Kannada	RNN, LSTM, biLSTM
(Parikh, 2009)	-	-	✓	Hindi (ILMT corpus)	Multi-Neuro Tagger (Neural Network)
(Jamatia et al., 2015)	-	✓	-	Hindi, English (Codemixed)	Conditional Random, Fields, Sequential Minimal Optimization, Nave Bayes and , Random Forests
(BR & Kumar, 2012)	-	✓	-	Kannada	Hidden Markov Models Conditional Random Fields
(Antony & Soman, 2010)	-	✓	-	Kannada	Support Vector Machine
(Dhanalakshmi et al., 2009)	-	✓	-	Tamil	Support Vector Machine
(Selvam & Natarajan, 2009)	✓	✓	-	Tamil	Morphological Analysis, Statistical Projection and Injection Technique
(Ekbal et al., 2007)	-	✓	-	Bangla	Support Vector Machine
(Ekbal et al., 2007)	-	✓	-	Bangla	Conditional Random Field
(Dandapat et al., 2007)	✓	✓	-	Bangla	Hidden Markov Model, Maximum Entropy
(Shrivastava & Bhattacharyya, 2008)	-	✓	-	Hindi	Hidden Markov Models
(Pvs & Karthik, 2006)	-	✓	-	Hindi, Telugu, & Bengali	Conditional Random Field, Transformation based learning
(Dalal et al., 2006)	-	✓	-	Hindi	Maximum Entropy Markov Model
(Singh et al., 2006)	✓	-	-	Hindi	Decision Tree (CN2)

Rule-based Approach. To enhance the quality of language processing tasks rule-based methods like lexical rules, morphological analysis, and linguistic knowledge are used. Lexical rules must be precise and explicit in their judgments since they are responsible for managing language processing tasks. In literature three types of rule-based MT techniques were reported:

- Dictionary-based or direct-based, which uses multilingual dictionaries for translation and is easy to use. For instance, Goyal and Lehal (2011) developed a simple rule-based Hindi to Punjabi MT approach. Reddy and Hanumanthappa (2013) suggests the use of a dictionary-based English-Kannada and English-Telugu translation tool.
- The second type of translation focuses on the grammatical structures of the source and target languages and is called transfer-based translation.
- Lastly, there is interlingual translation, which produces target language from an intermediate representation called Interlingua, such as Universal Networking Language (UNL) (Kaur & Veer, 2016), with no language restriction. (Dave et al., 2001) used Interlingua to work on English to Hindi MT. (Poornima et al., 2011) recommends a rule-based phrase reduction strategy for the English to Tamil translation job.

Limitations of Rule-based Approach. Rule-based method for machine translation is limited in creating complex rules, resource-intensive, and time-consuming. Machine translation tasks rely on dictionaries and do not consider sentence structure beyond word morphology.

Statistical-based Approaches. It searches for statistical relationships in the data by using metrics like distance and likelihood. The characteristics of the data guides statistical models to create effective results. In translation, the probability distribution function is used to translate documents where, the likelihood probability $P(K|E)$ used to translating a sentence from English (E) to Kannada (K) is reflected by the score and demonstrates the possibility of translation an expression in the source language "E" into the target language "K".

Parallel corpora of languages are essential for accurate language processing. Statistical machine translation (SMT) systems have been developed for translating English to Kannada and Malayalam, addressing challenges like sentence restructuring, root and suffix separation, and morphological information (Unnikrishnan et al., 2010; Ramanathan et al., 2008).

Researchers have used statistical methods to build NER systems for regional languages like Hindi, Bengali, Kannada, and Tamil. The CRF approach, SVM statistical approach, and Hidden Markov Model (HMM) techniques were used to analyze Hindi and Bengali languages. A mixture of these methods was suggested for better outcomes in Bengali, resulting in better outcomes (Ekbal & Bandyopadhyay, 2009; 2010).

Performance and Limitations. The statistical approach, unlike rule-based methods, doesn't require extensive language knowledge, making it useful for limited resources and faster linguistic tasks. However, dictionaries are more accessible for managing verb phrase morphologies in highly inflected Indian languages (Ramanathan et al., 2008).

Neural Network-based Approaches. In recent times, many observations and approaches have been explored the Neural Network-based solutions for language processing tasks. While these techniques have shown great success in various language processing tasks, they may sometimes yield unsatisfactory results due to insufficient resources for specific activities that require processing of a particular regional language.

Learning models use artificial neural network topologies like Recurrent Neural Networks and LSTM. Neural Machine Translation (NMT) uses encoder-decoder systems to convert source phrases into fixed-length vectors. A study developed NMT for six Indian language pairings (Bahdanau et al., 2014). In the study of attempting first to developed a NMT for six Indian language pairings, including Telugu-Hindi, Konkani-Hindi, Gujarati-Hindi, Punjabi-Hindi, Tamil-Hindi, and Urdu-Hindi (Revanuru et al., 2017).

Attention-based NMT (Chorowski et al., 2015) takes a starting phrase, $x_1x_2x_3,\ldots,x_{T_x}$ and compresses it into a series of vectors. It then makes use of the resulting vector chain in order to generate the desired sentence, $y = y_1y_2,\ldots,y_{T_y}$

Attention-based natural language processing encodes the initial text during the encoding phase using a bidirectional RNN that comprises of an upward RNN and a backward RNN (Schuster & Paliwal, 1997). The forward looking RNN creates an array of forward subconscious states by reading the input text x in a forward direction. $\vec{h} = \left[\vec{h_1}, \vec{h_2}, \vec{h_3} \ldots\ldots \vec{h_{T_\infty}}\right]$ The reverse RNN creates a series of reverse states that are hidden by reading the beginning of text x backward. The inscription of a word at all the locations is formed by concatenating the two hidden states there, which results in the comments during the complete source phrase were $h = \left[h_1, h_2, \ldots, h_{T_\infty}\right]$ where,

$$h_j^T = \left[\overrightarrow{h_j^T};\ \overleftarrow{h_j^T}\right] \tag{4}$$

Following the result of the target sequence $y<t= y_1,y_2,\ldots,y_{t-1}$ the next word y_m is created with likelihood at the decoding step t.

$$p(y_t|y<t,x) = softmax(f(s_t,y_{t-1},c_t)) \tag{5}$$

If st is the concealed state of the processor at step *t* and *f*()is a non-stationary deactivation function:

$$s_t = f(s_{t-1}, y_{t-1}, c_t) \tag{6}$$

with $g()$ representing the non-stationary activation equation. Here, the signaling parameter for both the decoder and encoder is the gated repetitive unit (Cho et al., 2014). The situation vector that results or c_t, is calculated as a weighted average of the starting point sentence's descriptions:

$$c_t = \sum_{j=1}^{T_\infty} \alpha_t, j, h_j \tag{7}$$

The bi-directional LSTM neural architecture uses BLEU measure to access quality of MTs, outperforming Google Translate in Punjabi-Hindi translation. Radial Basis Function Neural Network and Generative Adversarial Network (GAN) ratio-based feature selection are used for sentiment analysis. Joshi et al. used an LSTM model for sub-word level compositions of Codemixed Hindi-English texts. Akhtar et al. proposed a hybrid deep learning approach using Convolution Neural Networks and SVM classifiers (Choudhary et al., 2018).

Performance and Limitations. Neural Machine Translation (NMT) is effective for sentiment analysis tasks in Indian languages, but interpreting words in low-resource languages can be challenging due to their agglutinative nature. Multitask learning and multilingual models are recommended (Bahdanau et al., 2014). During preprocessing, emoticons and punctuation are usually eliminated, but they are vital in analysing the sentiment or irony of a word or sentence in any language. For instance, the words "What!" and "What?" have distinct meanings, despite their widespread usage (Bhargava et al., 2019).

4.4 Comparative Analysis of the Present State-of-the-Art Language Processing Tasks

4.5 Improved language processing in low resource Indian languages requires high-quality dictionaries like WordNets and Corpora. Unexplored areas include code-mixed and opinion extraction. Neural network-based methods are not yet tested for many tasks across different Indian languages and datasets. Table 3 highlights a summary of various research papers or studies related to natural language processing (NLP) and machine learning tasks across different Indian languages and datasets.

Table 3. Comparative analysis of Indian state-of-the-art methods over low resource Indian languages

Authors	Languages	Dataset	Results (Accuracy)	Task	Methods Used
(Shalini et al., 2018)	Bengali-English (Code-Mixed) Telugu	SAIL-2017 (Code-mixed) 8500 reviews in (Telugu)	73.20% (Bengali-English) 51.30% (Telugu)	-	CNN
(Bhargava et al., 2019)	Hindi, Tamil, Bengali	SAIL-2015	77.63% (Hindi) 57.37% (Bengali) 71.56% (Tamil)	-	RNN, CNN with LSTM
(Choudhary et al., 2018)	Hindi, Telugu English, Spanish	English (Movie reviews), Spanish (Twitter), Hindi (Product review), Telugu (News Dataset)	80.50% (Hindi-English) 80.30% (Telugu- English) 81.5% (English-Spanish)		Bi-LSTM with RNN
(Akhtar et al., 2016)	Hindi	Own (Online product reviews, Online movie reviews) Hindi (SAIL-Twitter dataset)	62.52% (twitter) 65.96% (review) 44.88% (movie reviews)		CNN and SVM
(Joshi et al., 2016)	Hindi-English (Cross-Lingual)	Own (3879 Facebook comments, 7549 words)	69.70%		Sub word LSTM
(Ravi & Ravi, 2016)	Hindi-English (Cross-Lingual)	Own (300 news article, 276 Facebook comments)	86.01% (news) 84.88% (comments)	Sentiment Analysis	RBF and GAN
(Revanuru et al., 2017)	Telugu-Hindi, Konkani-Hindi, Gujarati-Hindi, Punjabi-Hindi, Tamil-Hindi, Urdu-Hindi	TDIL-DC and C-DAC	14.16%, 24.35%, 35.26% 45.97%, 7.56% 22.47% (BLEU)	Machine Translation	RNN with bi-LSTM
(Kumar et al., 2015)	Kannada	287 movie reviews	81.20% (Naïve Bayes) 89.70% (Baseline)		Semantic+ machine learning features
(Se et al., 2015)	Tamil, Hindi, Bengali	SAIL-2015	39.28% (Tamil) 55.67% (Hindi) 33.60% (Bengali)		Senti WordNet +Naïve Bayes
(Rohini et al., 2016)	Kannada	100 movie reviews	79% (Kannada) and 67% (English)	Sentiment Analysis	Decision tree Classifier
(Antony et al., 2010b)	English-Kannada	40,000 Indian place names	87.28%	Machine Translation	SVM
(Ekbal & Bandyopadhyay, 2010)	Bengali-English	6000 Indian person Names	89.80% (TUAR)		Modified joint-source channel

continues on following page

Table 3. Continued

Authors	Languages	Dataset	Results (Accuracy)	Task	Methods Used
(Paul et al., 2013)	Hindi	2500 words	89.08%	Lemmatization	Rule and Knowledge base model
(Prathibha & Padma, 2015)	Kannada	2720 words	85.00%		Linguistic Rule based method is used.
(Dave et al., 2001)	English-Hindi	180 sentences	95.00%	Machine Translation	Interlingua, UNL based method
(V. Goyal & G. S. Lehal, 2011)	Hindi-Punjabi	221 Documents	95.40%		Direct translation
(Poornima et al., 2011)	English-Tamil	200 sentences	57.50%		Rule-based approach
(Gupta & Lehal, 2011)	Punjabi	50 Punjabi news articles	86.25% (F1)	NER	Rule-based approach
(Balamurali et al., 2012)	Hindi-Marathi	Reviews (200 Hindi, 150 Marathi)	72.00% (Hindi) 84.00% (Marathi)	Sentiment Analysis	Linked WordNets of two languages
(Kumar et al., 2015)	Bengali-Hindi	Indian Tweets as part of SAIL-2015	46.25% (Hindi) 42.00% (Bengali)		Distributional thesaurus+ sentence level co-occurrences
(Unnikrishnan et al., 2010)	English-Kannada and Malayalam	1100 sentences of English-Kannada/ Malayalam	24.9% (Malayalam) 24.5% (Kannada) (BLEU)	Machine Translation	SMT with reordering & suffix Separation
(Ramanathan et al., 2008)	English-Hindi	5000 training 400 testing sentences	15.88 (BLEU-Score)		
(Ekbal & Bandyopadhyay, 2010)	Bengali- Hindi	IJCNLP-08 (1,22,467 tokens- Bengali & 5,02,974 tokens- Hindi)	78.29% (Hindi), 81.15% (Bengali) (F-Score)	Named Entity Recognition	CRF
(Ekbal & Bandyopadhyay, 2009)	Bengali	150k words	90.70% (F1)		CRF
(Vijayakrishna & Sobha, 2008)	Tamil	94k words (tourism)	80.44% (F1)		CRF
(Ekbal et al., 2007)	Bengali	150k words from Bengali Newspaper	91.80% (F1)		SVM
(Ekbal & Bandyopadhyay, 2010)	Bengali	34 million words from newspaper	83.79% (F1)		HMM
(Amarappa & Sathyanarayana, 2013)	Kannada	100k words, Mixture of EMILLE, Web, Books	85.40% (F1)		CRF

5. AVAILABLE INDIAN CORPUS FOR MACHINE TRANSLATION

Indian languages have diverse domains, allowing for the collection of parallel corpora for Indian Low Resourced Languages (LRLs). The EMILLE corpus, accessible through ELRA, contains 63 million words in six categories: consumer, education, health, housing, legal, and social documents, derived from informational leaflets and local authorities (Baker et al., 2002; Fillmore et al., 2002).

The EMILLE corpus has become a common data source for languages in this area. The English text in the parallel corpus has a total word count of 200,000 and is translated into Hindi, Bengali, Punjabi, Gujarati, and Urdu. By applying the sentence alignment technique provided by Moore (2002), we were able to sentence-align and recover over 8,000 sentences for all languages, partnering with English from its bilingual resources, which comprise over 13,000 sentences for all the accessible languages. Some of the uses-cases also reported with the Multi-Indic parallel corpus (Post et al., 2012). Table 4, listed all the available parallel corpus related to Indian LRLs, in which xx-yy in Type column represents the availability of multiple pairs.

Table 4. Opensource corpuses that are available for Indian low resource languages

Corpus Name	Pairs	Language	Type
IITB-en-hi (Kunchukuttan et al., 2017)	1.5M	2	en-hi
UPAL EnTam (Ramasamy et al., 2012)	170K	2	en-ta
WAT-ILMPC (Nakazawa et al., 2021)	800K	7	xx-en
ILCI (Jha, 2010)	550K	100 TB	xx-yy
OdiEnCrop(Nakazawa et al., 2021)	27K	2	En-or
Samaantar (Ramesh et al., 2022)	1.2M	6.7 GB	xx-yy
Backtranslated-Hindi	2.5M	2	en-hi
Backtranslated-Telugu	500k	2	en-te
CVIT Mann Ki Baat (Siripragada et al., 2020)	41K	10	xx-yy
PMIndia-Corpus (Haddow & Kirefu, 2020)	728K	13	xx-yy
CVIT-PIBv0.0 (Siripragada et al., 2020)	613K	11	xx-yy
CVIT-PIBv0.2	1.17M	11	xx-yy
CVIT-PIBv1.3	2.78M	11	xx-yy

Sometimes it is harden to depend on the datasets obtained from multiple sources as listed in Table 4 to create an Machine Translation system. (Haddow & Kirefu, 2020) used articles of Press Information Bureau (PIB)[9] as source material to enhance the

MT between Hindi and Telugu. The PIB is comparable to a newspaper that publishes in several languages, with the exception of strong one-to-one matches between publications and monotonous sentences that produce greater parallel sentences using automated sentence alignment methods. The following explains utilizing the same crawled content (Siripragada et al., 2020) and focuses on increasing alignment quality in an attempt to enhance corpus size and MNMT model performance.

6. AN OVERVIEW OF NEURAL MACHINE TRANSLATION

A promising approach for mapping words from source and target languages end to end is neural machine translation. It solves the shortcomings of conventional machine translation methods. Encoder and decoder are the two RNNs (Recurrent Neural Networks) that make up the NMT model. The decoder produces translated output text from the encoded vector, whereas the encoder network converts input into a fixed-length vector (Bahdanau et al., 2014). To get high performance, the architecture and the attention model can be integrated.

From the viewpoint of a probability, a target sentence t that can be maximises to it analogous for a given sentence's (Gheini & May, 2019). i.e., argmax $P(t|s)$. The encoder interprets source phrase s as an array of vectors, $s=(x_1,x_2,\ldots,x_n)$ and the output of a typical RNN architecture in the form vector v is calculated using the formula given in Eq. (3).

$$h_t = s(Wx_t + Wh_{t-1}) \tag{8}$$

The output of the hidden state Wh_{t-1} is added to the nonlinear mathematical function of input x_t multiplied by weight matrix W to produce the hidden state at time t, denoted by h_t. RNN generalizes feed-forward neural networks, which blend current input with stored previous input. Before making a judgment by RNN, the neural network reviews what transpired in the preceding nodes.

The researchers in NMT offered a number of architectures, some of which are mentioned in this study. NMT was proposed by (Bahdanau et al., 2014), to align and translate simultaneously. The aforementioned model has only been tested on languages with the same Subject Verb Object (SVO) order, which is problematic for machine translation, English and French.

Google created the GNMT (Google's Neural Machine Translation) architecture in 2017 to close the gap between machine translation and human translation. This proposed architecture composed of three modules, such as (a) vanishing gradient in RNN; (b) an encoder-decoder; and (c) attention network with 8 layers and LSTM (Long Short Term Memory Network) RNN units (Randhawa et al., 2013). In order to improve the performance, the attention network was added to the encoder-decoder model. This architecture promises to attain a 60% accuracy rate.

7. EVALUATION MATRICES

Evaluating machine translations is the most important part of any MT system. It can do manually using some language experts with gold standard data or automatically using available matrices by comparing machine translations with gold standards pairs. Multiple automated methods, such as the metric system for evaluation of translation are referred. Such as (a) METEOR (Joty et al., 2019); (b) the Bilingual Evaluation Understudy (BLEU) (Wołk & Marasek, 2015) (c) the Levenshtein method (Okuda et al., 1976) (d) the Rank-based Intuitive Bilingual Evaluation Score (RIBES) (Laskar et al., 2020) ; (e) the Word Error Rate (WER) (f) the National Institute of Standards and Technology (NIST) is also available for gauging the quality of MT output.

7.1 Bilingual Evaluation Understudy (BLEU)

The BLEU metric is the gold standard for assessing MT systems. This strategy, initially proposed in 2002 (Papineni et al., 2002) to evaluates the simulated interpretation to a selection of allusion translations. The MT assessment raises the rating when a large number of strings in the imagined translation match those in the authoritative interpretation. A score between 0 and 1 is given by the BLEU system for the text. However, it is most often shown as a percentage. The closer a translation is to 1, the closer it is to the standard translation. It uses word-by-word, and the order of words in both datasets and also performs the phrase matching. To determine a preliminary model's BLEU score, SacreBLEU is used.

7.2 Rank-Based Intuitive Bilingual Evaluation Score (RIBES)

It is computed by substituting rank correlation values for higher-order n-gram matches before performing the first round of unigram matching. The structure of words is the focus of this statistic. (Sellam et al., 2023) uses Kendall's tau coefficient (τ) based on word order to detect rank disparities between SMT and reference translators. The parameter is calibrated as stated below in Eq. (3) as normalized Kendall' s guarantees a positive value:

$$NKT(\tau) = \frac{\tau + 1}{2} \tag{9}$$

To adjust for the possibility of an overestimation of the correlation between the most relevant terms in SMT and reference translations, this coefficient may be used with the unigram-precision ($\rho 1_)$ and the brevity penalty BP, as shown in Eq. (4).

$$RIBES = NKT(\sigma_1^{\alpha}) \bullet (BP^{\beta}) \tag{10}$$

where α and β are parameters between 0 and 1.

7.3 Metric for Evaluation of Translation With Explicit Ordering (METEOR)

Meteor assigns a score to a translation based on the degree to which it matches a reference translation word for word (Banerjee & Lavie, 2005). In order to accurately reflect how humans, judge the quality of a translation. It is designed to provide ratings at the sentence area. Several metrics have shown the need of recall in conjunction with accuracy for a significant connection with human judgements, and this is something that METEOR makes use of and emphasizes. It aspires to solve the issue of inaccurate reference translated by using flexible word matching that takes into account synonyms and morphological variations. A perfect score of 1 indicates that all of the words from the machine-generated output can be found in the source material.

8. RECOMMENDATION FOR A MULTIFACED APPROACH

8.1 Government Support and Funding

The Technology Development for Indian Languages (TDIL) program, led by the Ministry of Electronics and Information Technology, aims to develop information processing tools for all 22 recognized languages, promote collaborative technology development, promote language technology proliferation, and offer solutions and standardization at all levels[10].

8.2 Academia and Industry Collaboration

National Language Translation Mission: Bhashini. The Hon'ble Finance Minister announced the National Language Translation Mission (NLTM), or "Bhashini," in the 2021 budget. The three-year mission aims to overcome language barriers and ensure digital inclusion in India, aiming to increase Indian language content and internet access.

Partnership with the tech industry and NGO. AI4Bharat, an open-source non-profit organization, aims to develop AI solutions for India's socio-economic and environmental issues, focusing on improving online experiences for vernacular language users, who face information shortages.

AI4Bharat, a Google India initiative, has partnered with Pratham Books, EkStep Foundation, and initiated a one-year AI residency program for B-Tech graduates. They are also in discussions with the government on the National Language Translation Mission.

9. INDIAN MACHINE TRANSLATION SYSTEMS

9.1 Indian Language Systems' Anusaaraka Systems (1995)

Rajeev Sangal initiated the Anusaaraka project by IIT Kanpur, but is right now being carried out at IIIT Hyderabad. The project's goal was to do machine translation (MT) between two Indian languages. The Technology Development Initiative for Indian Languages (TDIL), the nation's Ministry of Information Technology, the President of India, and Satyam Computing Corporation Private Limited are providing funding for the initiative. Hindi is the target language, while the source languages are {Telugu, Kannada, Bengali, Punjabi, and Marathi}. The system has been tested mostly for translating children's stories, but it is not domain-specific. The primary goal of the system's development was flawless "information preservation." The system's output only adhered to the grammar of the original language.

For instance, a Bengali to Hindi translation may take a piece of writing in Bengali and translate it into a Hindi outcome that is comprehensible for the person reading it, however it might not be perfectly correct in grammar. It is possible to find an individual Hindi phrase that perfectly captures the meaning of the originating Kannada language for 80% of the 30,000 initial phrases in the Anusaaraka dictionary (Bharati, et.al 2003).

9.2 Meta-Evaluation Studies

Assessment indicators had been thoroughly examined to determine their dependability. In their discussion of the necessity for meticulousness in examining assessment measures (Dixit, et.al 2023) point out a number of potential problems and oversights that might result in incorrect results.

9.3 Gathering Annotations from Humans

Research of metaevaluation mostly use human-annotated translates of other types of systems. Relative search engine results, or the ability to compare the attributes of multiple items together, are more easily provided by people over unchangeable scores, which is why WMT15–17 gathered Relative Rankings (Bojar et al., 2015, 2016a, 2017). Directed evaluation (DA) scores, which are quality evaluation scores overall results on an evaluation scale of 0-100, are quicker and simpler to compile owing to the fact that they need only an increasing percentage of ratings (Kocmi et al., 2021). In a subsequent study, Freitag et al. (2021b) used the power source Diverse Quality Metric (MQM) method to gather consumer feedback to stay translating computers. They got comments from qualified raters who had received MQM, which conditioning, as proposed by (Clark et al. 2021). In connection with this, human investigations are carried out by (Klubicka et al., 2018) for Croatian, while Fabbri et al. (2021) employed methodical techniques to gather and deliver multiple scores of tasks like summarizing.

9.4 Datasets on Move

In line with (Freitag et al. 2021b), one can gather MQM notes for five Indian languages such as Tamil (ta), Hindi (hi), Marathi (mr), Gujarati (gu), and Malayalam (ml). We use 200 words from the FLORES-101 datasets (Goyal et al., 2022) and get the translated results for each individual of the five Indian languages from 7 computerized translators (§3.1).

Modern models are employed to produce translation results in all five languages. These consist of translator outputs for English-XX from publicly available models with previous training such as NLLB (Costajussà et al., 2022), mBART (Liu et al., 2020), mT5 (Xue et al., 2021), IndicTrans (Ramesh et al., 2022), cvit (Philip et al., 2019), and mBART (Liu et al., 2020).

As it as results from Google Translation API4 and Microsoft Azure Cognitive Services API3. It should be noted that we regard all mBART outputs for Gujarati to be illegible and full of characters that are mixed from other languages. As a result, we reconsider the the funding on Gujarati to gather annotations on the references in place of these words. We note that these phrases contain mistakes as well as imperfect references, which is consistent with the findings of Clark et al. (2021). We discover that these mistakes are frequently less serious, however.

Figure 1. Frequency of the different sorts of errors and their severity in five Indian languages. The more serious the faults, the darker the shade. The types of mistakes are divided into two groups: accuracy (Acc.) and fluency (Flu.).

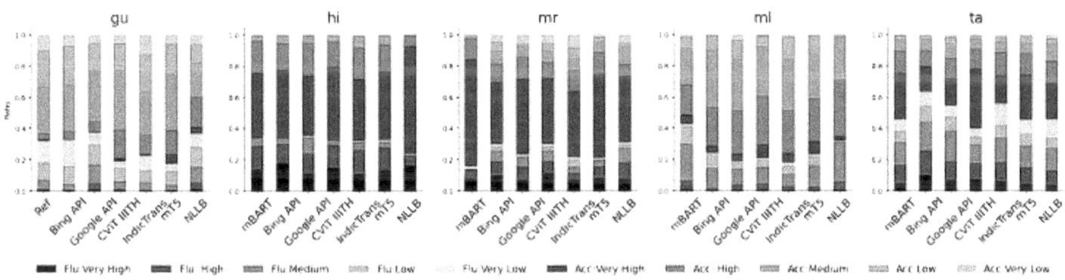

10. APPLICATION POINT OF RECENT MT

10.1 Emphasis on Solutions

Concentrating on solutions is essential in the dynamic field of machine translation in order to overcome obstacles and enhance the features of autonomous language translation platforms. This entails actively looking for solutions to issues as well as strategies to recognize and address them (Xiao et al., 2023).

10.2 Comparative Analysis

Hearing loss is expected to reach 700 million by 2050, affecting 430 million people globally. A third of those over 65 suffer from "presbycusis," which cannot be restored. Communication aids and AI-powered assistive devices are being developed to help. Sign language research focuses on synthesis, visualization, interpretation, and recognition (Joksimoski et al., 2022).

10.3 Practical Perspectives on Industry

With 27 research concentrating on clinical contexts, machine translation (MT) is being developed to get around language hurdles in health settings. Rule-based methods are not as accurate as statistical machine translation (SMT) systems. Enhancing multilingual communication and expanding access to health services are the goals of pilot projects (Dew et al., 2018).

10.4 E-Business and E-Commerce

Language difficulties in health settings are being addressed by machine translation (MT), with 27 research concentrating on clinical settings. In order to enhance multilingual communication and expand access to health services, statistical machine translation (SMT) systems are being created. E-commerce companies are also utilizing MT for product information, non-product websites, and marketing messages. Business procedures of e-commerce behemoths like Sportmaster and Alibaba have effectively used MT to facilitate timely and superior communication. Automation strategies are also being adopted by small-scale e-commerce suppliers in an effort to penetrate international markets[11].

11. CONCLUSION

This chapter has delved into the intricate landscape of Indian Low Resource Languages (LRLs) and their development within the context of natural language processing (NLP). We have explored the multifaceted aspects surrounding these languages, shedding light on their present state, significance in the modern world, and their potential to empower marginalized communities.

A deeper dive into the background of LRLs, both in India and globally, revealed the critical role they play in preserving cultural heritage and facilitating communication among diverse linguistic groups. The importance of LRLs extends beyond mere linguistic diversity; it touches upon social, economic, and educational aspects, making them vital assets in the modern world.

Furthermore, the chapter presented compelling case studies in NLP, showcasing various attempts at machine translation, statistical machine translation, preprocessing techniques, and approaches aimed at enhancing language processing tasks. These case studies offered insights into the state-of-the-art techniques being employed to tackle the challenges associated with LRLs.

The availability of Indian corpora for machine translation was discussed, underscoring the importance of quality linguistic resources in advancing NLP research and development. Traditional machine translation models were explored, providing a foundational understanding of the methods used in handling LRLs. Finally, the chapter offered recommendations for a multifaceted approach to address the challenges and opportunities presented by Indian LRLs. These recommendations included government support and funding, collaboration between academia and industry, and the rising awareness of the Government of India regarding the significance of LRLs.

REFERENCES

Akhtar, M. S., Kumar, A., Ekbal, A., & Bhattacharyya, P. (2016). A hybrid deep learning architecture for sentiment analysis. *Proceedings of COLING 2016, the 26th International Conference on Computational Linguistics: Technical Papers.*

Amarappa, S., & Sathyanarayana, S. (2013). Named entity recognition and classification in kannada language. *International Journal of Electronics and Computer Science Engineering*, *2*(1), 281–289.

Amarappa, S., & Sathyanarayana, S. (2015). Kannada named entity recognition and classification using conditional random fields. *2015 International Conference on Emerging Research in Electronics, Computer Science and Technology (ICERECT).* 10.1109/ERECT.2015.7499010

Ambati, V., Vogel, S., & Carbonell, J. G. (2011). Multi-strategy approaches to active learning for statistical machine translation. *Proceedings of Machine Translation Summit XIII: Papers.*

Ameta, J., Joshi, N., & Mathur, I. (2012). *A lightweight stemmer for Gujarati.* arXiv preprint arXiv:1210.5486.

Anand Kumar, M., Dhanalakshmi, V., Soman, K., & Rajendran, S. (2010). A sequence labeling approach to morphological analyzer for tamil language. *International Journal on Computer Science and Engineering*, *2*(06), 1944–1951.

Antony, P., Ajith, V., & Soman, K. (2010a). Kernel method for English to Kannada transliteration. *2010 International Conference on Recent Trends in Information, Telecommunication and Computing.*

Antony, P., Ajith, V., & Soman, K. (2010b). Statistical method for English to Kannada transliteration. *Information Processing and Management: International Conference on Recent Trends in Business Administration and Information Processing, BAIP 2010, Trivandrum, Kerala, India, March 26-27, 2010. Proceedings.* 10.1007/978-3-642-12214-9_57

Antony, P., & Soman, K. (2010). Kernel based part of speech tagger for kannada. *2010 International conference on machine learning and cybernetics.*

Arivazhagan, N., Bapna, A., Firat, O., Lepikhin, D., Johnson, M., Krikun, M., Chen, M. X., Cao, Y., Foster, G., & Cherry, C. (2019). Massively multilingual neural machine translation in the wild: Findings and challenges. *arXiv preprint arXiv:1907.05019.*

Baby, A., NL, N., Thomas, A. L., & Murthy, H. A. (2016). A unified parser for developing Indian language text to speech synthesizers. *Text, Speech, and Dialogue: 19th International Conference, TSD 2016, Brno, Czech Republic, September 12-16, 2016, Proceedings.*

Bahdanau, D., Cho, K., & Bengio, Y. (2014). Neural machine translation by jointly learning to align and translate. *arXiv preprint arXiv:1409.0473.*

Baker, P., Hardie, A., McEnery, T., Cunningham, H., & Gaizauskas, R. J. (2002). *67-Million Word Corpus of Indic Languages: Data Collection, Mark-up and Harmonisation*. LREC.

Bala Das, S., Panda, D., Mishra, T. K., & Patra, B. K. (2023). Statistical Machine Translation for Indic Languages. *arXiv e-prints*, arXiv: 2301.00539.

Balamurali, A., Joshi, A., & Bhattacharyya, P. (2012). Cross-lingual sentiment analysis for indian languages using linked wordnets. *Proceedings of COLING 2012: Posters, Banane, M., & Erraissi, A. (2022). A comprehensive study of Natural Language processing techniques Based on Big Data. 2022 International Conference on Decision Aid Sciences and Applications (DASA).*

Banerjee, S., & Lavie, A. (2005). METEOR: An automatic metric for MT evaluation with improved correlation with human judgments. *Proceedings of the acl workshop on intrinsic and extrinsic evaluation measures for machine translation and/or summarization.*

Banik, D., Ekbal, A., & Bhattacharyya, P. (2018). Machine learning based optimized pruning approach for decoding in statistical machine translation. *IEEE Access : Practical Innovations, Open Solutions*, *7*, 1736–1751. doi:10.1109/ACCESS.2018.2883738

Bharati, A., Chaitanya, V., Kulkarni, A. P., & Sangal, R. (2003). Anusaaraka: machine translation in Stages. *arXiv preprint cs/0306130.*

Bhargava, R., Arora, S., & Sharma, Y. (2019). Neural network-based architecture for sentiment analysis in Indian languages. *Journal of Intelligent Systems*, *28*(3), 361–375. doi:10.1515/jisys-2017-0398

BR, S., & Kumar, R. (2012). Kannada part-of-speech tagging with probabilistic classifiers. *International Journal of Computer Applications, 48*(17), 26-30.

Chakravarthi, A., & Raja, B. (2020). *Leveraging orthographic information to improve machine translation of under-resourced languages*. NUI Galway.

Cho, K., Van Merriënboer, B., Bahdanau, D., & Bengio, Y. (2014). On the properties of neural machine translation: Encoder-decoder approaches. *arXiv preprint arXiv:1409.1259*. doi:10.3115/v1/W14-4012

Chorowski, J. K., Bahdanau, D., Serdyuk, D., Cho, K., & Bengio, Y. (2015). Attention-based models for speech recognition. *Advances in Neural Information Processing Systems*, 28.

Choudhary, N., Singh, R., Bindlish, I., & Shrivastava, M. (2018). Emotions are universal: Learning sentiment based representations of resource-poor languages using siamese networks. *International Conference on Computational Linguistics and Intelligent Text Processing*.

Cui, J., Kingsbury, B., Ramabhadran, B., Sethy, A., Audhkhasi, K., Cui, X., Kislal, E., Mangu, L., Nussbaum-Thom, M., & Picheny, M. (2015). *Multilingual representations for low resource speech recognition and keyword search. In 2015 IEEE workshop on automatic speech recognition and understanding*. ASRU.

Dalal, A., Nagaraj, K., Sawant, U., & Shelke, S. (2006). Hindi part-of-speech tagging and chunking: A maximum entropy approach. *Proceeding of the NLPAI Machine Learning Competition*.

Dandapat, S., Sarkar, S., & Basu, A. (2007). Automatic part-of-speech tagging for Bengali: An approach for morphologically rich languages in a poor resource scenario. *Proceedings of the 45th Annual Meeting of the Association for Computational Linguistics Companion Volume Proceedings of the Demo and Poster Sessions*. 10.3115/1557769.1557833

Das, A., & Bandyopadhyay, S. (2010). Topic-based Bengali opinion summarization. *arXiv preprint arXiv:2301.00539*.

Dasgupta, S., & Ng, V. (2006). Unsupervised morphological parsing of Bengali. *Language Resources and Evaluation*, *40*(3-4), 311–330. doi:10.1007/s10579-007-9031-y

Datta, A., Ramabhadran, B., Emond, J., Kannan, A., & Roark, B. (2020). Language-agnostic multilingual modeling. *ICASSP 2020-2020 IEEE International Conference on Acoustics, Speech and Signal Processing (ICASSP)*. 10.1109/ICASSP40776.2020.9053443

Dave, S., Parikh, J., & Bhattacharyya, P. (2001). Interlingua-based English–Hindi machine translation and language divergence. *Machine Translation*, *16*(4), 251–304. doi:10.1023/A:1021902704523

Dew, K. N., Turner, A. M., Choi, Y. K., Bosold, A., & Kirchhoff, K. (2018). Development of machine translation technology for assisting health communication: A systematic review. *Journal of Biomedical Informatics*, *85*, 56–67. doi:10.1016/j.jbi.2018.07.018 PMID:30031857

Dhanalakshmi, V., Kumar, A., Shivapratap, G., Soman, K., & Rajendran, S. (2009). Tamil POS tagging using linear programming. *International Journal of Recent Trends in Engineering*, *1*(2), 166.

Diwan, A., Vaideeswaran, R., Shah, S., Singh, A., Raghavan, S., Khare, S., Unni, V., Vyas, S., Rajpuria, A., & Yarra, C. (2021). Multilingual and code-switching ASR challenges for low resource Indian languages. *arXiv preprint arXiv:2104.00235.*

Doddapaneni, S., Aralikatte, R., Ramesh, G., Goyal, S., Khapra, M. M., Kunchukuttan, A., & Kumar, P. (2023). Towards Leaving No Indic Language Behind: Building Monolingual Corpora, Benchmark and Models for Indic Languages. *Proceedings of the 61st Annual Meeting of the Association for Computational Linguistics (*Volume 1*: Long Papers).* 10.18653/v1/2023.acl-long.693

Dowling, M., Lynn, T., Graham, Y., & Judge, J. (2016). *English to Irish machine translation with automatic post-editing*. Academic Press.

Edunov, S., Ott, M., Auli, M., & Grangier, D. (2018). Understanding back-translation at scale. *arXiv preprint arXiv:1808.09381*. doi:10.18653/v1/D18-1045

Ekbal, A., & Bandyopadhyay, S. (2009). A conditional random field approach for named entity recognition in Bengali and Hindi. *Linguistic Issues in Language Technology*, *2*, 2. doi:10.33011/lilt.v2i.1203

Ekbal, A., & Bandyopadhyay, S. (2010). Named entity recognition using appropriate unlabeled data, post-processing and voting. *Informatica (Vilnius)*, *34*(1).

Ekbal, A., Haque, R., & Bandyopadhyay, S. (2007). Bengali part of speech tagging using conditional random field. *Proceedings of seventh international symposium on natural language processing (SNLP2007).*

Elkateb, S., Black, W. J., Vossen, P., Farwell, D., Rodríguez, H., Pease, A., Alkhalifa, M., & Fellbaum, C. (2006). Arabic WordNet and the challenges of Arabic. *Proceedings of the International Conference on the Challenge of Arabic for NLP/MT.*

Fillmore, C. J., Baker, C. F., & Sato, H. (2002). *The FrameNet Database and Software Tools*. LREC.

Gheini, M., & May, J. (2019). A universal parent model for low-resource neural machine translation transfer. *arXiv preprint arXiv:1909.06516.*

Goldsmith, J. (2001). Unsupervised learning of the morphology of a natural language. *Computational Linguistics*, *27*(2), 153–198. doi:10.1162/089120101750300490

Goyal, V., & Lehal, G. (2011). N-Grams Based Word Sense Disambiguation: A Case Study of Hindi to Punjabi Machine Translation System. *International Journal of Translation*, *23*(1), 99–113.

Goyal, V., & Lehal, G. S. (2011). Hindi to Punjabi machine translation system. International Conference on Information Systems for Indian Languages. *Journal of King Saud University. Computer and Information Sciences*, *33*(5), 497–507.

Gupta, V., & Lehal, G. S. (2011). Named entity recognition for Punjabi language text summarization. *International Journal of Computer Applications, 33*(3), 28-32.

Haddow, B., & Kirefu, F. (2020). PMIndia—A Collection of Parallel Corpora of Languages of India. *arXiv preprint arXiv:2001.09907.*

Harish, B., & Rangan, R. K. (2020). A comprehensive survey on Indian regional language processing. *SN Applied Sciences*, *2*(7), 1204. doi:10.1007/s42452-020-2983-x

Hedderich, M. A., Lange, L., Adel, H., Strötgen, J., & Klakow, D. (2020). A survey on recent approaches for natural language processing in low-resource scenarios. *arXiv preprint arXiv:2010.12309.*

Heitzman, J., & Worden, R. L. (1995). A country study. Academic Press.

Hutchins, J. (1997). Evaluation of machine translation and translation tools. *Iš: Survey of the State of the Art in Human Language Technology*, 418-419.

Hutchins, J. (2005). The first public demonstration of machine translation: the Georgetown-IBM system, 7th January 1954. *noviembre de.*

Hutchins, W. J. (1996). The state of machine translation in Europe. *Conference of the Association for Machine Translation in the Americas.*

Jha, G. N. (2010). *The TDIL Program and the Indian Langauge Corpora Intitiative (ILCI).* LREC.

Joksimoski, B., Zdravevski, E., Lameski, P., Pires, I. M., Melero, F. J., Martinez, T. P., Garcia, N. M., Mihajlov, M., Chorbev, I., & Trajkovik, V. (2022). Technological solutions for sign language recognition: A scoping review of research trends, challenges, and opportunities. *IEEE Access : Practical Innovations, Open Solutions, 10*, 40979–40998. doi:10.1109/ACCESS.2022.3161440

Joshi, A., Prabhu, A., Shrivastava, M., & Varma, V. (2016). Towards sub-word level compositions for sentiment analysis of hindi-english code mixed text. *Proceedings of COLING 2016, the 26th International Conference on Computational Linguistics: Technical Papers.*

Joty, S., Guzmán, F., Màrquez, L., & Nakov, P. (2019). DiscoTK: Using discourse structure for machine translation evaluation. *arXiv preprint arXiv:1911.12547.*

Kandimalla, A., Lohar, P., Maji, S. K., & Way, A. (2022). Improving English-to-Indian language neural machine translation systems. *Information (Basel), 13*(5), 245. doi:10.3390/info13050245

Kaur, B., & Veer, D. (2016). Translation challenges and universal networking language. *International Journal of Computer Applications, 133*(15), 36-40.

Khan, N. J., Anwar, W., & Durrani, N. (2017). Machine translation approaches and survey for Indian languages. *arXiv preprint arXiv:1701.04290.*

Koehn, P., & Knowles, R. (2017). Six challenges for neural machine translation. *arXiv preprint arXiv:1706.03872*. doi:10.18653/v1/W17-3204

Kugler, M., Ahmad, K., & Thurmair, G. (2013). *Translator's workbench: Tools and terminology for translation and text processing* (Vol. 1). Springer Science & Business Media.

Kumar, A., Kohail, S., Ekbal, A., & Biemann, C. (2015). IIT-TUDA: System for sentiment analysis in Indian languages using lexical acquisition. *Mining Intelligence and Knowledge Exploration: Third International Conference, MIKE 2015,* Hyderabad, India, December 9-11, 2015, *Proceedings*, 3.

Kumari, A., & Goyal, V. (2012). Font convertors for Indian languages—A survey. *Computer Science*, *1*(12).

Kumawat, S., & Chandra, N. (2014). Distance-based Reordering in English to Hindi Statistical Machine Translation. *International Journal of Computer Applications, 975*, 8887.

Kunchukuttan, A., Mehta, P., & Bhattacharyya, P. (2017). The iit bombay english-hindi parallel corpus. *arXiv preprint arXiv:1710.02855.*

Laskar, S. R., Khilji, A. F. U. R., Pakray, P., & Bandyopadhyay, S. (2020). Hindi-Marathi cross lingual model. *Proceedings of the Fifth Conference on Machine Translation.*

Magueresse, A., Carles, V., & Heetderks, E. (2020). Low-resource languages: A review of past work and future challenges. *arXiv preprint arXiv:2006.07264.*

Miao, Y., Blunsom, P., & Specia, L. (2021). A generative framework for simultaneous machine translation. *Proceedings of the 2021 Conference on Empirical Methods in Natural Language Processing*. 10.18653/v1/2021.emnlp-main.536

Moore, R. C. (2002). Fast and accurate sentence alignment of bilingual corpora. *Conference of the Association for Machine Translation in the Americas.*

Nakazawa, T., Nakayama, H., Ding, C., Dabre, R., Higashiyama, S., Mino, H., Goto, I., Pa, W. P., Kunchukuttan, A., & Parida, S. (2021). Overview of the 8th workshop on Asian translation. *Proceedings of the 8th Workshop on Asian Translation (WAT2021).*

Och, F. J., & Ney, H. (2004). The alignment template approach to statistical machine translation. *Computational Linguistics, 30*(4), 417–449. doi:10.1162/0891201042544884

Okuda, T., Tanaka, E., & Kasai, T. (1976). A method for the correction of garbled words based on the Levenshtein metric. *IEEE Transactions on Computers, 100*(2), 172–178. doi:10.1109/TC.1976.5009232

Pandey, A., Srivastava, B. M. L., & Gangashetty, S. V. (2017). Adapting monolingual resources for code-mixed hindi-english speech recognition. *2017 International Conference on Asian Language Processing (IALP).* 10.1109/IALP.2017.8300583

Pandey, A. K., & Siddiqui, T. J. (2008). An unsupervised Hindi stemmer with heuristic improvements. *Proceedings of the second workshop on Analytics for noisy unstructured text data.* 10.1145/1390749.1390765

Papineni, K., Roukos, S., Ward, T., & Zhu, W.-J. (2002). Bleu: a method for automatic evaluation of machine translation. *Proceedings of the 40th annual meeting of the Association for Computational Linguistics.*

Patel, P., Popat, K., & Bhattacharyya, P. (2010). Hybrid stemmer for Gujarati. *Proceedings of the 1st Workshop on South and Southeast Asian Natural Language Processing.*

Patra, B. G., Das, D., Das, A., & Prasath, R. (2015). Shared task on sentiment analysis in indian languages (sail) tweets-an overview. *Mining Intelligence and Knowledge Exploration: Third International Conference, MIKE 2015,* Hyderabad, India, December 9-11, 2015, *Proceedings,* 3.

Paul, S., Tandon, M., Joshi, N., & Mathur, I. (2013). Design of a rule based Hindi lemmatizer. *Proceedings of Third International Workshop on Artificial Intelligence, Soft Computing and Applications*. 10.5121/csit.2013.3408

Poornima, C., Dhanalakshmi, V., Anand, K., & Soman, K. (2011). Rule based sentence simplification for english to tamil machine translation system. *International Journal of Computer Applications, 25*(8), 38-42.

Post, M., Callison-Burch, C., & Osborne, M. (2012). Constructing parallel corpora for six indian languages via crowdsourcing. *Proceedings of the seventh workshop on statistical machine translation*.

Prahallad, K., Kumar, E. N., Keri, V., Rajendran, S., & Black, A. W. (2012). The IIIT-H Indic speech databases. *Thirteenth annual conference of the international speech communication association*. 10.21437/Interspeech.2012-659

Rajan, K., Ramalingam, V., Ganesan, M., Palanivel, S., & Palaniappan, B. (2009). Automatic classification of Tamil documents using vector space model and artificial neural network. *Expert Systems with Applications, 36*(8), 10914–10918. doi:10.1016/j.eswa.2009.02.010

Ramachandran, V. A., & Krishnamurthi, I. (2012). An iterative stemmer for Tamil language. *Intelligent Information and Database Systems: 4th Asian Conference, ACIIDS 2012, Kaohsiung, Taiwan, March 19-21, 2012, Proceedings*, 4.

Ramanathan, A., Hegde, J., Shah, R., Bhattacharyya, P., & Sasikumar, M. (2008). Simple syntactic and morphological processing can help English-Hindi statistical machine translation. *Proceedings of the Third International Joint Conference on Natural Language Processing: Volume-I*.

Ramanathan, A., & Rao, D. D. (2003). A lightweight stemmer for Hindi. *Proceedings of EACL*.

Ramani, B., Christina, S. L., Rachel, G. A., Solomi, V. S., Nandwana, M. K., Prakash, A., Aswin Shanmugam, S., & Raghava Krishnan, S. P. (n.d.). A Common Attribute based Unified HTS framework for Speech Synthesis in Indian Languages. *8th ISCA Speech Synthesis Workshop*.

Ramasamy, L., Bojar, O., & Žabokrtský, Z. (2012). Morphological processing for English-Tamil statistical machine translation. *Proceedings of the Workshop on Machine Translation and Parsing in Indian Languages*.

Ramesh, G., Doddapaneni, S., Bheemaraj, A., & Jobanputra, M. (2022). Samanantar: The Largest Publicly Available Parallel Corpora Collection for 11 Indic Languages. Transactions of the Association for Computational Linguistics, 10, 145-162. doi:10.1162/tacl_a_00452

Ranathunga, S., Lee, E.-S. A., Prifti Skenduli, M., Shekhar, R., Alam, M., & Kaur, R. (2023). Neural machine translation for low-resource languages: A survey. *ACM Computing Surveys*, *55*(11), 1–37. doi:10.1145/3567592

Randhawa, G., Ferreyra, M., Ahmed, R., Ezzat, O., & Pottie, K. (2013). Using machine translation in clinical practice. *Canadian Family Physician Medecin de Famille Canadien*, *59*(4), 382–383. PMID:23585608

Ranjan, P., & Basu, H. (2003). Part of speech tagging and local word grouping techniques for natural language parsing in Hindi. *Proceedings of the 1st International Conference on Natural Language Processing (ICON 2003).*

Ravi, K., & Ravi, V. (2016). Sentiment classification of Hinglish text. *2016 3rd International Conference on Recent Advances in Information Technology (RAIT).*

Revanuru, K., Turlapaty, K., & Rao, S. (2017). Neural machine translation of indian languages. *Proceedings of the 10th annual ACM India compute conference.* 10.1145/3140107.3140111

Rohini, V., Thomas, M., & Latha, C. (2016). Domain based sentiment analysis in regional Language-Kannada using machine learning algorithm. *2016 IEEE International Conference on Recent Trends in Electronics, Information & Communication Technology (RTEICT).* 10.1109/RTEICT.2016.7807872

Saharia, N., Sharma, U., & Kalita, J. (2012). Analysis and evaluation of stemming algorithms: a case study with Assamese. *Proceedings of the International Conference on Advances in Computing, Communications and Informatics.* 10.1145/2345396.2345533

Sai, A. B., Mohankumar, A. K., & Khapra, M. M. (2022). A survey of evaluation metrics used for NLG systems. *ACM Computing Surveys*, *55*(2), 1–39. doi:10.1145/3485766

Sailor, H. B., & Hain, T. (2020). Multilingual Speech Recognition Using Language-Specific Phoneme Recognition as Auxiliary Task for Indian Languages. *Interspeech*, 4756–4760. doi:10.21437/Interspeech.2020-2739

Sellam, T., Bapna, A., Camp, J., Mackinnon, D., Parikh, A. P., & Riesa, J. (2023). SQuId: Measuring speech naturalness in many languages. *ICASSP 2023-2023 IEEE International Conference on Acoustics, Speech and Signal Processing (ICASSP).*

Selvam, M., & Natarajan, A. (2009). Improvement of rule based morphological analysis and pos tagging in tamil language via projection and induction techniques. *International Journal of Computers, 3*(4), 357-367.

Shalini, K., Ravikurnar, A., Reddy, A., & Soman, K. (2018). Sentiment analysis of indian languages using convolutional neural networks. *2018 International Conference on Computer Communication and Informatics (ICCCI).*

Shrivastava, M., & Bhattacharyya, P. (2008). *Hindi POS tagger using naive stemming: harnessing morphological information without extensive linguistic knowledge.* International Conference on NLP (ICON08), Pune, India.

Siripragada, S., Philip, J., Namboodiri, V. P., & Jawahar, C. (2020). A multilingual parallel corpora collection effort for Indian languages. *arXiv preprint arXiv:2007.07691.*

Sowmya Lakshmi, B., & Shambhavi, B. (2019). Bidirectional Long Short-Term Memory for Automatic English to Kannada Back-Transliteration. *Emerging Research in Computing, Information, Communication and Applications: ERCICA 2018,* 1.

Sridhar, A., Ganesan, R. G., Kumar, P., & Khapra, M. (2020). Include: A large scale dataset for indian sign language recognition. *Proceedings of the 28th ACM international conference on multimedia.* 10.1145/3394171.3413528

Tan, Z., Wang, S., Yang, Z., Chen, G., Huang, X., Sun, M., & Liu, Y. (2020). Neural machine translation: A review of methods, resources, and tools. *AI Open*, *1*, 5–21. doi:10.1016/j.aiopen.2020.11.001

Todi, K. K., Mishra, P., & Sharma, D. M. (2018). Building a kannada pos tagger using machine learning and neural network models. *arXiv preprint arXiv:1808.03175.*

Tummalapalli, M., & Mamidi, R. (2018). Syllables for sentence classification in morphologically rich languages. *Proceedings of the 32nd Pacific Asia conference on language, information and computation.*

Unnikrishnan, P., Antony, P., & Soman, K. (2010). A novel approach for English to South Dravidian language statistical machine translation system. *International Journal on Computer Science and Engineering*, *2*(08), 2749–2759.

Vijayakrishna, R., & Sobha, L. (2008). Domain focused named entity recognizer for tamil using conditional random fields. *Proceedings of the IJCNLP-08 workshop on named entity recognition for South and South East Asian Languages.*

Wołk, K., & Marasek, K. (2015). Enhanced bilingual evaluation understudy. *arXiv preprint arXiv:1509.09088.*

Xiao, Y., Wu, L., Guo, J., Li, J., Zhang, M., Qin, T., & Liu, T.-y. (2023). A survey on non-autoregressive generation for neural machine translation and beyond. *IEEE Transactions on Pattern Analysis and Machine Intelligence*, 1–20. doi:10.1109/TPAMI.2023.3277122 PMID:37200120

Zhang, X., Su, J., Qin, Y., Liu, Y., Ji, R., & Wang, H. (2018). Asynchronous bidirectional decoding for neural machine translation. *Proceedings of the AAAI conference on artificial intelligence*. 10.1609/aaai.v32i1.11984

Zoph, B., Yuret, D., May, J., & Knight, K. (2016). Transfer learning for low-resource neural machine translation. *arXiv preprint arXiv:1604.02201*. doi:10.18653/v1/D16-1163

ENDNOTES

1 https://en.wikipedia.org/wiki/List_of_languages_by_number_of_native_speakers_in_India

2 https://censusindia.gov.in/census.website/data/census-tables

3 https://censusindia.gov.in/nada/index.php/catalog/22912

4 https://en.wikipedia.org/wiki/Languages_of_India

5 https://language-data-space.ec.europa.eu/related-initiatives/elrc_en

6 https://www.translateplus.com/blog/human-post-editing-for-accurate-generative-ai-translation/

7 https://www.washington.edu/doit/universal-design-process-principles-and-applications

8 https://www.logos.com/grow/translating-german-texts-with-logos-searching-for-definitions/

9 https://pib.gov.in/indexd.aspx

10 https://www.meity.gov.in/content/technology-development-indian-languages-tdil

11 https://summalinguae.com/e-commerce/machine-translation-software-for-e-commerce-businesses/

Chapter 5
Systematic Review of Morphological and Semantic Analysis in a Low Resource Language:
Tamil

P. Matan
College of Engineering Guindy, Anna University, Chennai, India

P. Velvizhy
College of Engineering Guindy, Anna University, Chennai, India

ABSTRACT

Natural language processing discusses the applications of computational technique analysis and synthesis of natural languages. Semantic and morphological analysis are the two basic percepts in the natural language processing domain. Semantic analysis is the process of analyzing the lexical, grammatical, and syntactical parts of the words. The study of words known as morphology focuses on the meaning and structure of words. In this chapter, the authors focus on various morphological analyzers developed for Tamil language. Developing a highly accurate and adaptable morphological analyser is a challenging task. Morphological analyser basically identifies the morphemes and parts of speech for tagging. The atomic version of a word that retains the original meaning is called a morpheme. Morphological analyzer type includes phrase level and word level analyzers. Universal networking language (UNL) is a declarative kind used to express the natural language text using a semantic network. The major applications of UNL are information retrieval system, machine translation system, and UNL-based search engine.

DOI: 10.4018/979-8-3693-0728-1.ch005

INTRODUCTION

Tamil is one of the oldest languages in history. Tamil Morphological study has been an interesting area in natural language understanding. Morphology is basically the process of analyzing the syntactic and semantic parts of the word. Morphological analysis can be done using Finite State Transducers, Finite State Machines, Tree Adjoining Grammars and Support Vector Machines. Semantic analysis primarily concentrates on word similarity. Semantics, which are employed in practical applications such as information retrieval/extraction, are used to measure word similarity. Semantic similarity is a most important measure in disciplines like Natural language processing, Artificial Intelligence, Sentiment Analysis and Information Retrieval techniques. Graph based semantic representations like Semantic networks, Dependency Graphs, Semantic relations and Universal Networking Language are the ways of semantic representation. The Universal Networking Language is a structured ontological graph-based intermediate representation of natural language. These structured representations of the data have a greater advantage in the Information Extraction/Retrieval during node search because of its lesser complexity. This book chapter focuses on the articles published in the Natural Language Processing area, which deals with the UNL, Morphological analysis and Semantic analysis. The paper organization is as follows: Section 2 reviews the ideology about Universal Networking Language. Section 3 discusses Morphological analysis and Section 4 elaborates on Semantic analysis, Section 5 provides conclusion and finally the References.

Review Methodology

Research articles have been collected from several sources like Springer, Elsevier, IEEE, ACM, arXiv. The articles were filtered based on the publication year starting from 2007 to 2022. Keywords like "Universal Networking Language", "Semantic Analysis", "Morphological Analysis", "Machine Translation", "Information Retrieval" were used to retrieve the relevant articles.

- The review sections are classified into three namely Universal Networking Language, Morphological Analysis and Semantic analysis.
- A comprehensive review of Universal Networking Language(UNL) is provided as a first attempt.
- The UNL Graph generation using Enconversion is discussed briefly.
- The models like Finite State Transducer, Support Vector Machines and Lexical Functional Grammar to develop a Morphological Analyser were discussed concisely.

- The Semantic analysis systems classified based on Word Embedding, Word Overlapping models were discussed.
- The challenges in the development of a Morphological Analyzer, Semantic Analysis and UNL are discussed.
- Finally, the future research directions on these domains are reviewed and concluded.

UNIVERSAL NETWORKING LANGUAGE: A SEMANTIC REPRESENTATION

The Universal Networking Language (UNL) is a formal language based on linguistics that is used to represent and connect diverse languages and knowledge systems. It tries to break down language barriers and facilitate cross-linguistic and cross-cultural communication and information exchange.

The UNL standardizes the representation of meaning and knowledge in a language-independent manner. It combines linguistic, logic, and computer science ideas to develop a universal representation of language that can be comprehended and processed by humans and machines alike.

The main components of UNL include a controlled vocabulary of concepts, a set of grammatical rules, and a notation system for representing linguistic structures. By mapping the meaning of words and sentences to a common underlying structure, UNL allows for the translation, transfer, and sharing of information across multiple languages. UNL has been used in a variety of domains, including machine translation, cross-lingual information retrieval, multilingual communication, and the creation of language technology. In an increasingly interconnected world, it is a great tool for encouraging linguistic diversity, facilitating global collaboration, and improving cross-cultural understanding.

Sitender and Bawa (2022) suggested a Universal Networking Language based Enconversion system using deep learning and context free grammar for Sanskrit language. By utilizing a Sanskrit stemmer with 23 prefixes and 774 suffixes with grammatical rules, the suggested approach improved POS tagging. Initially, a stemmer based tagging is used to remove morphological inflections. For POS tagging, the system employs Bidirectional Long Short-Term Memory (Bi-LSTM) and stacked LSTM. Further, a Cocke – Younger– Kasami (CYK) parser for parsing the input sentence was implemented. The parsed text is used to generate a node list, with each node containing a Sanskrit term tagged with an English counterpart. To resolve UNL relationships between nodes, a one-of-a-kind karaka analyzer is used. Eventually, after the ambiguities have been resolved, about 1500 rules are employed to construct the UNL expression for the input text in Sanskrit. The flaw of the proposed method is that it cannot be adopted for free order languages.

Sitender and Bawa (2021) designed a Universal Networking Language Enconverter system for Sanskrit language called SANSUNL. The proposed system consists of two databases, one for analysis and the other for the generation of UNL. In this work, Manual translation from English to Sanskrit is done initially. The sentence is then segmented into various tokens using a word splitter module. A blank space is used as a segmentation delimiter. The dependency parser is used to do parts of speech tagging and morphological analysis; this parser outputs labelled words. The node list contains tagged sanskrit words, equivalent English words as Universal Words (UW), and a Parts of Speech (POS) tag is used to eliminate the ambiguity of many entries for a single word in the dictionary. After finalizing the node list mapped with relations, UNL expression is generated. The system's shortcoming is that the procedure of manually translating English sentences into Sanskrit is taken from the Spanish language server.

Figure 1. Components of an UNL system

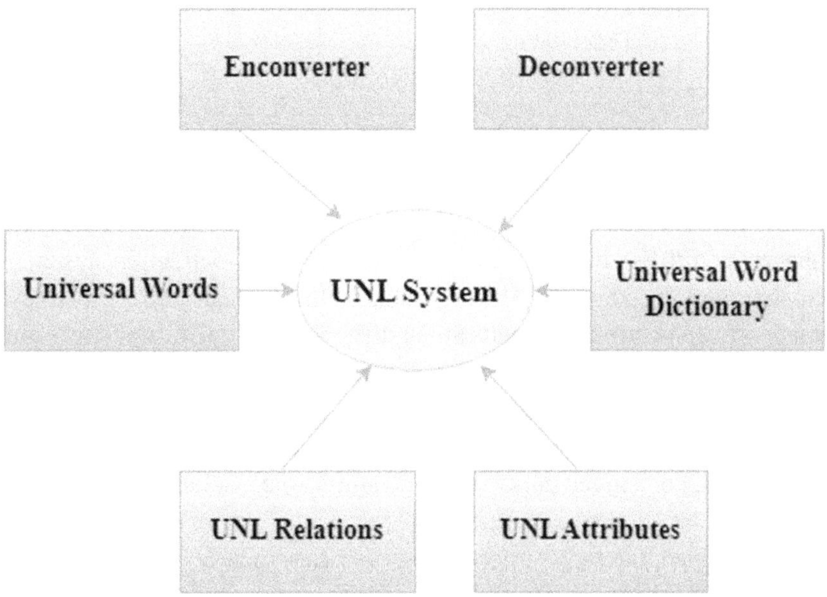

The components of an UNL system (shown in Figure 1) are:
Enconverter is used to transform Natural Language words into UNL expressions.
Deconverter is used to translate UNL expressions to Natural Phrases.

Universal Word Dictionary - A complete Knowledge Base (KB) of Universal Words

UNL Attributes - used to describe the subjectivity information

UNL Relations - used to connect the Universal Words

UNL Expressions are formed by labelling ideas, syntactic and semantic components with Universal Words.

Figure 2. A sample UNL expression

Let us consider an example sentence - "**Ganesh goes to Temple**".

The sentence is converted to an UNL Graph as shown in figure 3,

The UNL representation for the above sentence is as follows,
[UNL]
agt(go(icl > move).@present.@3S.@entry, Ganesh(iof >person))
obj(go(icl > move).@present.3S.@entry, Temple(icl >place)
[UNL]
Here,
agt - "Agent"
icl - "is a kind of" relation
iof - "is an instance of" relation
obj - "Thing in focus" are the abbreviations that are needed to be considered in the above UNL expression

Saha et al. (2019) have developed an Information extraction system using universal networking language. The suggested method's main goal is to extract target information from unstructured natural language input. Bengali sentences are used as an input for the UNL module. In this work, UNL relations are utilized to obtain the UNL expressions. These UNL expressions are nothing but the broken down sentences. The input sentences have been converted to UNL expressions using of binary relations. For a given input Sentence, among the available UNL expressions, the system decides to choose the respective relation(as shown in figure 3). Once the relation is obtained, the target information can be extracted.

Ali et al. (2021) based on the structure of UNL, suggested a machine translation system based on deep learning. The system converts a sentence of subject object verb (SOV) format to subject verb object (SVO) structure. The system employs two Recurrent Neural Networks (RNN). The first RNN uses encoding to generate a series of unique integers from the input phrase. Using a decoding approach, the second RNN generates the desired output from a series of numbers. The sentence is translated using both RNNs. The dataset used in the system is EMILLE corpus, Prothom-Alo corpus and Punjabi Monolingual Text Corpus ILCI –II.

Figure 3. A sample UNL graph

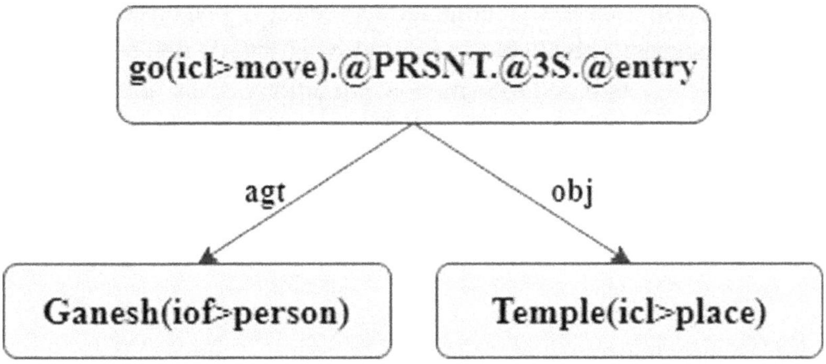

Sridhar et al. (2016) built an Machine translation system from English to Tamil based on Universal Networking Language. In this system, English sentences are enconverted to UNL using enconversion technique. Here, the UNL representation is modified in such a way to suit the translation process. It uses POS tagging with Standford POS tagger API. The Tamil terms in this work are manually inserted into the English Dictionary, which is a disadvantage. A Morphological Analyzer is built utilising the JAWS API. Tamil words must be generated for each English word in the UNL graph using a morphological generator. Finally, using a new sentence construction algorithm, Tamil words are rearranged into sentences. The system is evaluated with Bilingual Evaluation Understudy (BLEU). The system achieves a BLEU score of 0.581. Various Machine Translation approaches have been depicted in figure 4.

Figure 4. Machine translation approaches

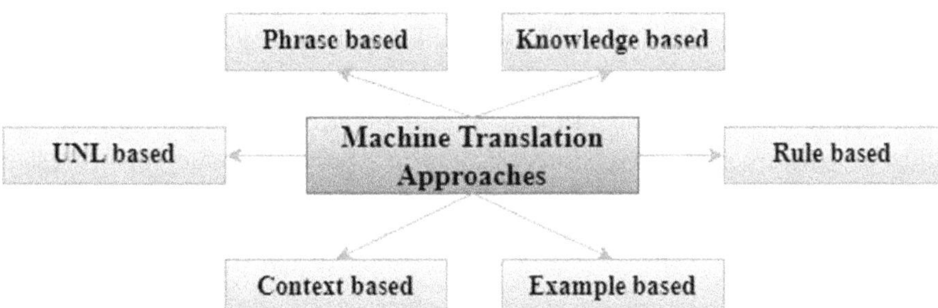

Subalalitha (2019) proposed an Information Extraction Framework for Kurunthogai. For Kurunthogai, a framework for information extraction (IE) based on templates is created. The framework extracts names of plants, foods, animals, objects, and waterbodies. There are extracted Noun Unigrams, Verb Unigrams, Adjective-Noun Bigrams, and Adverb-Verb Bigrams. N-grams are extracted with the help of a morphological analyzer. The proposed framework is able to extract information from bilingual text. A template has been designed on term based features and UNL-KB features. The UNL-KB is used when words don't match with term based features. Template based information extraction is used both in Kurunthogai as well as in English songs. The system is flexible such that it can be used for any literature texts, even in any kind of natural language applications. The framework achieved a precision score of 88.8%. The UNL graph generation process from Natural Language Data is shown in Figure 5.

Figure 5. UNL graph generation

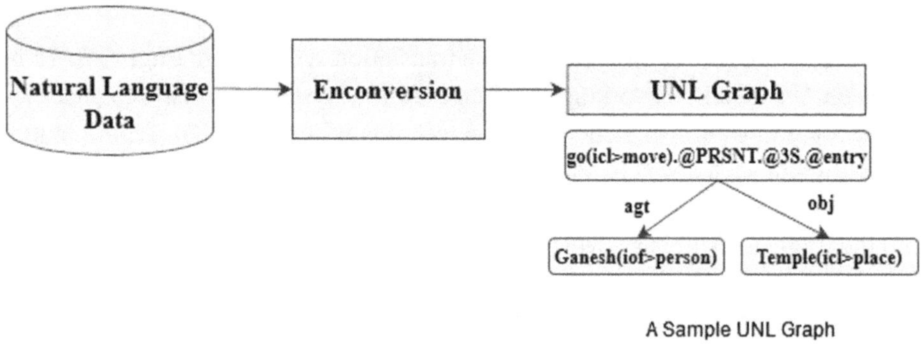

Despite being a promising strategy for linguistic interoperability, Universal Networking language (UNL) has some drawbacks. The substantial manual labour needed to create and maintain UNL materials represents one significant challenge. It takes a lot of time and resources to build UNL lexicons and semantic rules since they require a lot of human input. Additionally, because UNL primarily concentrates on generic language concepts, its capacity to handle highly particular domain knowledge or specialised terminology is constrained. Furthermore, the availability and precision of linguistic resources and semantic mappings—which might not always be complete or current—are crucial to UNL's success. It is necessary to conduct further research and development to improve UNL's ability to handle domain-specific information and to streamline the process of building UNL resources in order to address these inadequacies.

The UNL system's future developments have a great deal of promise to advance linguistic interoperability and ease communication across various linguistic communities. The incorporation of cutting-edge machine learning methods and NLP algorithms into UNL frameworks is a crucial component. By automating the process of developing and updating UNL materials, this can help make them more scalable and linguistically adaptive. The encoding and retrieval of information in UNL can also be improved by utilising semantic web technologies and knowledge graphs, enabling more precise, context-aware translations. The creation of UNL-based applications for cutting-edge technologies like virtual assistants, multilingual chatbots, and automatic language translation systems is another crucial direction. By pursuing these options, UNL may maintain its position as a potent force for advancing linguistic inclusion on a worldwide scale and dismantling language obstacles.

MORPHOLOGICAL ANALYSIS

A morphological analyser is a linguistic application or a software that analyses and deconstructs words into their constituent morphemes, which are the smallest meaningful units of a language. It aids in the comprehension of word structure and qualities by detecting prefixes, suffixes, roots, and other morphological features.

A morphological analyser can generate a morphological analysis of a given word by using rules and patterns specific to that language, providing information such as its lemma (base form), part of speech, tense, gender, number, and other pertinent grammatical aspects.

This tool is especially useful for natural language processing (NLP) tasks like text parsing, information retrieval, machine translation, and computational linguistics. It aids in a variety of language-related applications by improving language comprehension.

Sarveswaran et al. (2021) designed a Morphological Parser for Tamil Language called TamizhiMorph. The developed system is a morphological analyzer and generator (MAG) for the Tamil language that is open source and extensible. The Morphological analyser stores and retrieves the morphological and morpho-syntactic information. Machine translation of morphologically rich languages like Tamil can benefit from it. The TamizhiMorph works with the basic principle of Finite-State Transducer (FST). Morpheme labeling is done to mark the morphemes of a single morph together. This process is done to reduce the complexities in modelling. Finally, a Morphological guesser is implemented to analyse nouns, verbs, adverbs and adjectives. The system is integrated with Meta-Morph rules (Lexical Rules) and these rules are fed into a Foma Morphological analyser. Tamil textbook text and Tamil Universal Dependency treebank version 2.5 are used to assess the system.

Table 1. Tamil morphological analyzers

Name of the Morphological Analyzer	Methodology	Dataset
TamizhiMorph- Sarveswaran et al. (2021)	Finite State Transducer using Foma	Tamil Universal Depen- dency Tree Bank Version 2.5
Piripori- Suriyah et al. (2020)	Word level morphological rules	137144 Tamil words taken from internet
ThamizhiFST- Sarveswaran et al. (2018)	Support Vector Machine	Online Tamil Lexicon created by University of Madras

Suriyah et al. (2020) created a Morphological analyser for Tamil Language called Piripori. The Morphological Analyzer obtains the inflected/root/derived form from the input word. Piripori's concept is based on word-level morphological rules. When a root word is given as input, its parts of speech and translation are returned if the word itself is a root word. If the word is not a root word, rules are applied to the specific term in order to find the root word. During this process affixes are removed from the given input word to obtain the root word.

Sarveswaran et al. (2018) created ThamizhiFST, a Morphology Analyzer and Gener ator for Tamil Verbs. The System uses Finite State Transducer (FST) for developing the MAG (Morphological Analyzer and Generator). The FST is implemented with the help of FOMA Open Source software. The system employs 3250 Tamil verb set lemmas from 13 paradigms, as well as 260 conjugate forms. The morphosyntactic information is labelled with 27 different labels. The main advantage of TamizhiFST is its FST usage, the output can be easily adapted and changed according to the user's needs.

Premjith and Soman (2021) proposed a Deep Learning strategy for character-level morphological synthesis in Malayalam and Tamil. For morphological synthesis at the character level, the system employs Recurrent Neural Networks (RNN), Long Short Term Networks (LSTM), and Gated Recurrent Units (GRU). Using a process known as sequential labelling, input data is successively examined and morphologically synthesised data is created one character at a time. To extract patterns from the input data, RNN, LSTM, or GRU are employed. As an output, the Conditional Random Field (CRF) is employed to obtain the correlation among the predictions. An algorithm is constructed in such a way that root words satisfy the language's Sandhi Rules. However, the approach does not address the production of pronoun word forms.

Rajasekar and Geetha (2022) compared Machine Learning Methods for Tamil Morphological Analyzer. A paradigm based approach with the help of Finite State Machine (FSM) is used for Tamil Morphological Analyzer. A Tamil Morphological

Analyzer called TACOLA works on this principle. The methodology followed is to find the root word and with the help of Finite State Transducer (FST) morpheme affixes are found. Further Lemmatization guesser generates the output with affixes and word prefixes and generates the root word.

Table 2. Examples of morphological analysis

Word	Suffix	Suffix	Root Word
chedikkal(Plants)	kkal	plural	chedi
kanikkal(Fruits)	kkal	plural	kani
varudankkal(years)	nkkal	plural	varudam
maraththu(tree)	ththu	Oblique	maram
vasikka(to read)	kka	Non-finite verb form	vasi
avalai vita(than her)	ai-vita	Accusative postposition	aval
avalukkendru(for her)	ukkendru	Dative Postposition	aval
avalidamirundhu(from her)	Idam-irundhu	Locative Postposition	aval

Sheshasaayee and Deepa (2017) proposed an unsupervised approach ascertaining the Morphological Components of Tamil Language. Here, Preprocessing is done to remove stopwords and punctuations. P-similar technique is implemented to understand the morphological feature with the help of morpheme boundary of words. Further morph-suffix pairs are pruned, invalid morph-morph suffix pairs are removed. Finally, a paradigm model is designed for generation of morphs and suffixes.Various NLP Processes along with NLP when used as PaaS is listed out in figure 6.

Figure 6. NLP Systems and NLP as PaaS

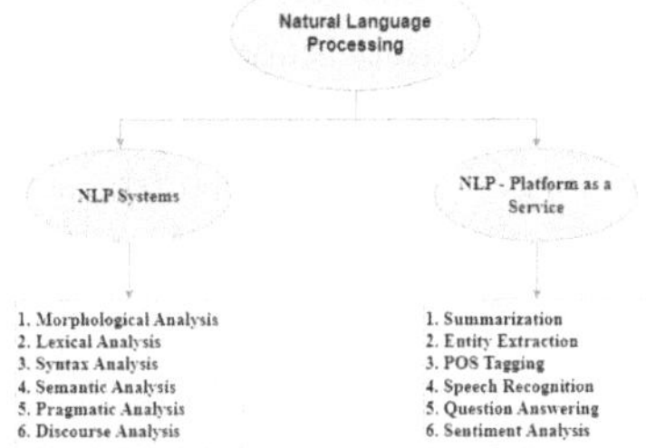

Menon et al. (2017) proposed employing Tree Adjoining Grammars for dependency resolution and semantic mining in the Tamil language. The syntax of Indian Languages is captured with Tree Adjoining Grammars (TAG). POS Tagging is done for the tree generated and the system is constructed with single anchor trees (a grammar tree lexicalized with a single lexicon). Further, TAG derived from the derived trees are constructed with the help of parser. TAG focusses on Machine Translation. This work focuses on grammar and parsing.

Ramalingam and Navaneethakrishnan (2021) developed a Tamil discourse literary text information retrieval system. The system is tested with two ancient literary works namely Thirukkural and Naladiyar. A Discourse parsing and indexing process is carried out in offline phase and query processing, ranking, searching is done in online phase. Since the Tamil literary text has a different style for word formulation, a word reformulation algorithm is proposed to support the morphological analyzer to find the discourse cues. The system tries to match the query words with synonyms of both Tamil and English Language. Semantic indices have been used for the mapping process. A mean average precision score of 89 percent was attained by the framework. Anita and Subalalitha (2019a) proposed a method for grouping Tamil literary works using discourse connectors. Discourse connectives are used to build K-clusters using the K-means clustering algorithm from Tamil literary text. A Morphological Analyzer tool developed by Anadhan in the year 2002 is used in this work. The Morphological analyzer receives Thirukkural as input. The discourse connectives are discovered, and clusters form. Cluster construction is achieved by combining semantically comparable couplets with discourse connectives. The system was assessed using a cluster purity metric, which yielded purity, rand index, precision, recall, and F-score of 0.79, 0.92, 0.79, 0.8, 0.79 respectively.

Srinivasan and Subalalitha (2019) suggested an Automatic Recognition of Named Entities in Tamil Documents. With the help of Regex, Date and Time, Named Entities are extracted as features. A Morphological analyzer is used to classify the Named Entity (NE) with the help of case markers. Also with the help of Morphological analyzer, the co-occurring entities are identified and context features are extracted. The above mentioned process is called feature extraction using context window. Thus, the features are extracted, using the methods namely Regular Expression, POS, and Context window. Naive Bayes algorithm is used for NE classification. The system achieved a F-score, Precision, Recall, F-measure of 83.54%, 89.52%, 84.51%, 86.94% respectively.

Mokanarangan et al. (2016) developed a Support vector machine-based Tamil morphological analyzer. The analyzer uses grammar rules and annotated corpus to determine the possible candidates for a given word. Support Vector Machine is used as a classifier for a given word in order to determine the most practical morphological deconstruction. Annotated Lexical Corpus and Grammar Rules are utilised to first tag each word for a given word using POS tagger. This process provides all possible candidates. Further, the SVM classifier is used for predicting Morphological Deconstruction. The accuracy of the system was 98.73%. The Higher Level Architecture of a sample Morphological Analyser is shown in figure 7.

Figure 7. A higher level architecture of morphological analysis

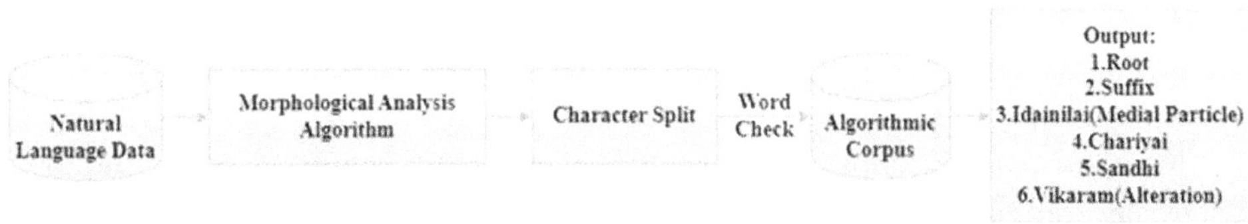

Even though they are useful tools for natural language processing, Tamil morphological analyzers have some drawbacks. The intricate word structures and rich morphology of the Tamil language provide a significant barrier. Accurately segmenting and analysing the morphemes is challenging due to the complex system of agglutination, in which numerous affixes are appended to the root word. A further degree of complication is added by the presence of homographs, which are words with the same spelling but different meanings. The precision and accuracy of the morphological analysis may be hampered by inaccurate disambiguation of such words. To improve the functionality and reliability of Tamil morphological analyzers, these issues demand additional research and development.

Tamil morphological analysis's future directions have tremendous potential for developing NLP and computer linguistics. One critical issue is the creation of more robust, all-encompassing morphological analyzers capable of handling the intricate morphological structures found in Tamil. This entails fine-tuning algorithms and rule-based systems to efficiently analyse affixation and other complicated word forms unique to the language. Furthermore, using machine learning techniques like neural networks and deep learning models can improve the accuracy and efficiency of Tamil morphological analysis. Incorporating semantic information and context awareness into morphological analysis can result in more accurate disambiguation and a better comprehension of word meanings. Tamil morphological analysis can help progress different language-related applications such as information retrieval, machine translation, and text parsing by studying these future directions.

SEMANTIC ANALYSIS

Semantic analysis is a natural language processing (NLP) procedure that focuses on comprehending and interpreting the meaning and interpretation of words, phrases, and sentences in a particular context. It goes beyond surface-level syntax and grammar analysis and digs into the deeper layers of language comprehension.

Semantic analysis seeks to elicit the intended meaning of a document by examining word relationships and contextual usage. It employs a number of approaches, including word sense disambiguation, entity recognition, semantic role labelling, and semantic parsing.

Semantic analysis helps computers to perceive the meaning of words and their interconnections by utilising computational techniques and linguistic expertise, hence easing tasks such as information extraction, question-answering systems, sentiment analysis, and machine translation. It assists in bridging the gap between human language and machine understanding, enhancing the accuracy and effectiveness of NLP applications.

Karuppaiah and Vincent (2021b) proposed using Indo-Wordnet and interlanguage semantic similarity to disambiguate word senses in Tamil. The process of determining a word's correct meaning is known as word sense disambiguation. Oxford Tamil Dictionary, Indo-WordNet, and English WordNet dictionary glosses make up the dataset used in the suggested method. The system eliminates all senses of a word except the meant one in its context, in order to improve the overall performance of the system. The system uses an unsupervised approach for disambiguating words in Tamil using two methods. The first technique determines the number of words that overlap between context-sensitive word glosses, while the second method determines the degree of similarity between context-sensitive word glosses and ambiguous terms. The second method is determined by the suggested system to be the most effective one.

Ajay et al. (2016) developed a word embedding approach for discovering semantic links between Tamil words. The system uses an unsupervised approach of feature extraction called word embedding to represent the natural language in terms of vectors. For word embedding, Gensim employs the Continuous Bag Of Words (CBOW) and skip gramme models. The model generates vectors for the words using neural network. A comparison of content-based word embedding versus context-based word embedding is performed. At last, the accuracy of semantic similarity models is calculated using a combination of feature vector size for the same word.

Figure 8. A higher level architecture of semantic similarity calculation

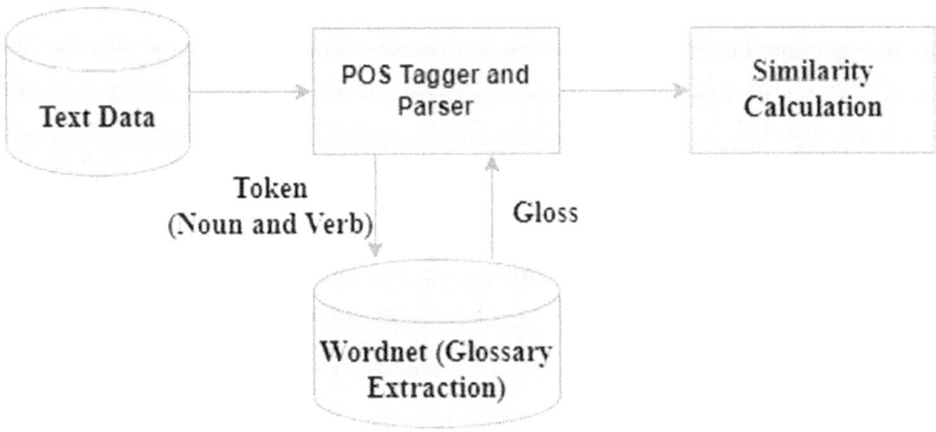

Table 3. Approaches of semantic analysis

Technique	Dataset	Methodology
Hybrid Approach - Deepa Karuppaiah and P M Durai Raj Vincent(2021)	Wordnet, Tamil Wikitionary, Oxford Tamil Dictionary	Word embedding
Word Sense Disambiguation in cross-lingual IR -Thenmozhi and Aravindan (2018)	WordNet	Word overlapping
Content Based Word Embedding-Ajay et. al. (2016)	Tamil newspaper- Political News Article	Word Embedding
Unsupervised Approach- Deepa Karuppaiah and P M Durai Raj Vincent(2021)	Indo-WordNet, Oxford Tamil Dictionary and English WordNet dictionary	Word Overlapping
Semantic Information Extraction-Lakshmana Pandian et. al. (2008)	Wordnet	Semantic Probability

Karuppaiah and Vincent (2021a) proposed a hybrid method for calculating the semantic similarity of Tamil words. Using data from datasets like Tamil IndoWordNet, Tamil Wiktionary, and Oxford Tamil Dictionary, a similarity finding technique is used. The Indo WordNet has more than 25000 synsets, each of which includes a noun and a verb as well as a gloss definition and examples. A link is created between words and the relations formed are of hypernyms and hyponyms forms. A group of words is described by Hypernyms, which is a broad term. Hyponym is a word which can group all the words of hypernym. Thus, the relations would help us to identify how the words are closely related (Semantic Similarity calculation as shown in figure 8). A sequence of steps are applied to obtain the similarity. As a first step, the Glosses are extracted from dictionary sources and then the input word senses are identified, further, the short gloss definition is identified. Then the supportive definitions are identified, extracted and filtered for choosing the right sense. Finally, the key terms are extracted and a similarity calculation is done using Jaccard similarity coefficient. The Miller Charles and Rubenstein Goodenough datasets, which are human-evaluated, are used to assess the approach.

Jagan et al. (2012) suggested a Semantic Parsing system for Tamil Sentences. A rule based approach is proposed for identifying the semantic sub graphs from Tamil Sentences. A Semantic graph based representation (a directed acyclic graphical representation) called the Universal Networking Language is implemented. To develop the semantic sub-graph, a classification is done with rule based morpho semantic features. Rule generation is done in two steps: Firstly during simple UNL graph construction and secondly after the graph construction. Basically a UNL graph is called a hypergraph, since it has several interlinked subgraphs. As a result, these subgraphs are utilised to define the boundaries of complicated semantic entities. The nested graph identification rules are defined. At last, evaluation is carried out using a rule-based technique.

Table 4. Available dataset for POS tagging

Reference	Target	No. of Tags
Sarveswaran et al. (2014)	New tagset	Highlevel = 7 and Low-level 10
Dhanalakshmi et al. (2009)	Amrita	32
BIS tagset - Pattabhi et el.(2007)	BIS	Highlevel = 11 and Lowlevel = 42
UD tagset - Nivre et al.(2016)	Universal Parts of Speech	17
Selvam et al. (2009)	POS+Morph	500

Pandian et al. (2008) proposed an extraction of semantic information from Tamil documents. Basically semantic extraction is the retrieval process of Entity – Relation, useful-concepts from a document. In the Training phase, Semi-automatic annotation for concepts, entities and relations is done for domain specific training documents. And then, the annotated documents are used to identify the clues, attributes for entity extraction and concept extraction. During the testing phase, the learned contexts are utilized to extract semantic information from unused documents from the testing phase. Finally, the information extracted is used to extract relations, entailments and facts from the given input documents.

Lakshmana Pandian and Geetha (2008) developed a morpheme-based language model for Tamil Part of Speech Tagging. The grammatical inflections are used to distinguish the noun and verb in parts of speech. The system uses a tagged corpus of 470910 words, with the help of morphological analyzer, tagging is done in a semi-automatic manner with 35 POS categories. This process separates the stem and other morphemes. Multilevel morphology is exploited to determine the POS category of the input word. Finally the language model is estimated using Bayes' Theorem.

Balaji et al. (2011) suggested a Morpho-Semantic feature for Rule-based Tamil Enconversion. The proposed System discusses the Tamil UNL enconversion. The enconversion process follows a morpho-semantic feature technique. The UNL relation is developed with the categories namely- Adjectival and Adverbial Suffixes, Connectives, Multiple Relations, Ambiguity resolution and Graph Construction. This work makes use of word based features rather than using structure based features. This is due to the Morphologically rich Tamil language. The result is a morphological information rather than syntactic structure. This is due to the enconversion process. Thenmozhi et al. (2018) proposed a deep learning method for translating verb phrases between Tamil and English and Hindi. Verb Phrase (VP) translation is adopted with the help of a neural machine translation model. For VP Translation, the system employs a Sequence to Sequence (Seq2Seq) deep neural network. Tagging is done for the input sentences. The tags used are sentence id and language information. The Seq2Seq maps the Source language VP to the target language VP. To predict the Tamil VP output for the given English sentences, a deep neural network model is used. The Model is evaluated using the VPT-IL@FIRE2018 dataset.

Jagan et al. (2019) proposed a Semi supervised learning approach of Semantic Relation. This article focuses on Semantic relation extraction bootstrapping for morphologically rich languages such as Tamil. Universal Networking Language (UNL) establishes a semantic similarity that exists between two parts in a sentence.To obtain word features, the system employs a rule-based approach. With the bootstrapping approach, all possible instances are captured to generate new patterns. With the help of UNL ontology, the approach is considered to be a general and domain independent one.

Subalalitha and Poovammal (2018) constructed a Thirukural automatic bilingual dictionary. The system makes use of an english and tamil explanatory text for Thirukural. The model is built with a three layered architecture using Thirukural and its explanation. Layer -1 has the Thirukkural written by Thiruvalluvar. In addition, layer 2 has the standard Tamil explanations. Finally, layer 3 consists of English explanations. A Naive Bayes Probabilistic model is implemented after Layer 2, to identify the most probable English word for a Tamil word. A Tamil - English word mapping is used to identify the maximum probability of a word occurring. Semantic relation can be used to find the word mapping with the feature set. The model achieves an efficiency score of 70 percent.

Table 5. POS tagger methodology

Reference	Methodology
Dhanalakshmi et al. (2009)	Support Vector Machine
Selvam et al. (2009)	Rule based, Projection and Injection technique
Mojanarangan et al. (2016)	Graph based neural approach
Avinesh et al. (2007)	BiLSTM and Conditional Random Fields
Thavareesan et al. (2020)	{BoW, TFIDF, fastText, GloVe, Word2Vec}+SVM and kNN
Qi P.et al. (2020)	BiLSTM
Nguyen et al. (2021)	Transformers

Rajasekar and Geetha (2021) developed a machine learning system in Tamil for information extraction from the gynaecological domain. A machine learning based classification model is implemented along with ontological representation, which is used to extract the required information. An ontological structure for the human body is created. Women Health issues for each part are identified and have been related in the ontological representation. Entity based relation extraction is used to retrieve information from ontological representation. The system acquired 75 percent accuracy for correctness in user queries.

Table 6. Available POS tagged datasets for Tamil

Reference	Tagset	Size
Dhanalakshmi et al. (2009)	Amrita	227,000
Computational Linguistic Research Group (CLRG), AU-KBC Research Cen- tre, MIT Campus of Anna University (2016)	BIS	515,283
UD Tamil Sarveswaran et al. (2020)	Universal Parts of Speech	2,625
UD Tamil Ramasamy and Zˇabokrtsky´ (2015)	Universal Parts of Speech	8,856

Roy et al. (2022) a deep ensemble framework to detect hate speech and abusive words in dravidian languages. Prediction of offensive language is done with CNN, BERT, MuRIL. To categorise offensive and non-offensive comments, a deep learning ensemble model is used. To detect hate speech and offensive language, the results of transforms and deep learning models are merged. F1 scores of 0.802 and 0.933 are achieved for Tamil and Malayalam languages respectively.

Jain et al. (2020) developed a Tamil to English neural machine translation. A model with two different architectures is used for Tamil to English Translation, based on the Encoder-Decoder concept. The system has three encoding layers and three decoding layers. The entire process is carried out in 3 parts namely - Encoder, Global Context Vector and Decoder. The transformer generates input with word embedding and positional encoding for the encoder step. Position 'j' must be predicted at the decoder stage, and it is entirely dependent on places before 'j'. The proposed model obtained a BLEU score of 7.5.

Premjith et al. (2019) designed a MTIL Parallel Corpus-based Neural Machine Translation System for English to Indian Language Translation. For four language pairs, namely English-Malayalam, English-Hindi, English-Tamil, and English-Punjabi, a Neural Machine Translation system is being developed. The suggested system's encoder is built with a Long Short Term Memory (LSTM) network and a Bi-Directional Recurrent Neural Network (Bi-RNN). The encoder uses the input sentence's fixed length vector. The decoder then guesses the output word based on the input embedding. The BLEU Score is utilised for automatic evaluation, whereas Adequacy, Fluency, and Overall Rating are used for manual review.

Sarveswaran and Dias (2021) Built a Part of Speech Tagger for Tamil Language. A neural POS tagger - TamizhiPOSt is developed. The development strategy employs the stanza deep learning framework, which is available off the shelf. Initially Tokenization is done, followed by Sentence Splitting and finally POS tagging is done. Stanza makes use of RNN and Bi-LSTM architecture. The main advantage of using Stanza is the flexibility of customizing the architecture and its hyperparameters. The number of layers, learning rate, activation function, lost functions can also be customized. The Bi-LSTM architecture is used for POS tagging, the POS tagging process also does the morphological analysis. The POS tagger achieved an accuracy of 93.27%. Various Tokenization processes have been listed out in figure 9

Anbukkarasi et al. (2022) proposed a Deep Learning-based Named Entity Recognition Method for the Tamil Language. With the aid of deep neural networks and transfer learning, a gated recurrent unit (GRU) model is created. The system consists of GRU, Bi-LSTM, LSTM, and RNN. The system classifies the newspaper data into Named Entity Tags. RNN helps to convert the independent activations to dependent ones by providing equal weights. LSTM is accomplished with the help of different gates called Activation function levels. The Bi-LSTM helps the formulation of Named Entity Recognition with the help of character level as well as word level formulation. The GRUs has been effective for smaller datasets, since GRUs are less operational than LSTM, and its advantage is that - its quicker training time. The system achieved an accuracy level of 99.62%.

Figure 9. Tokenization approaches

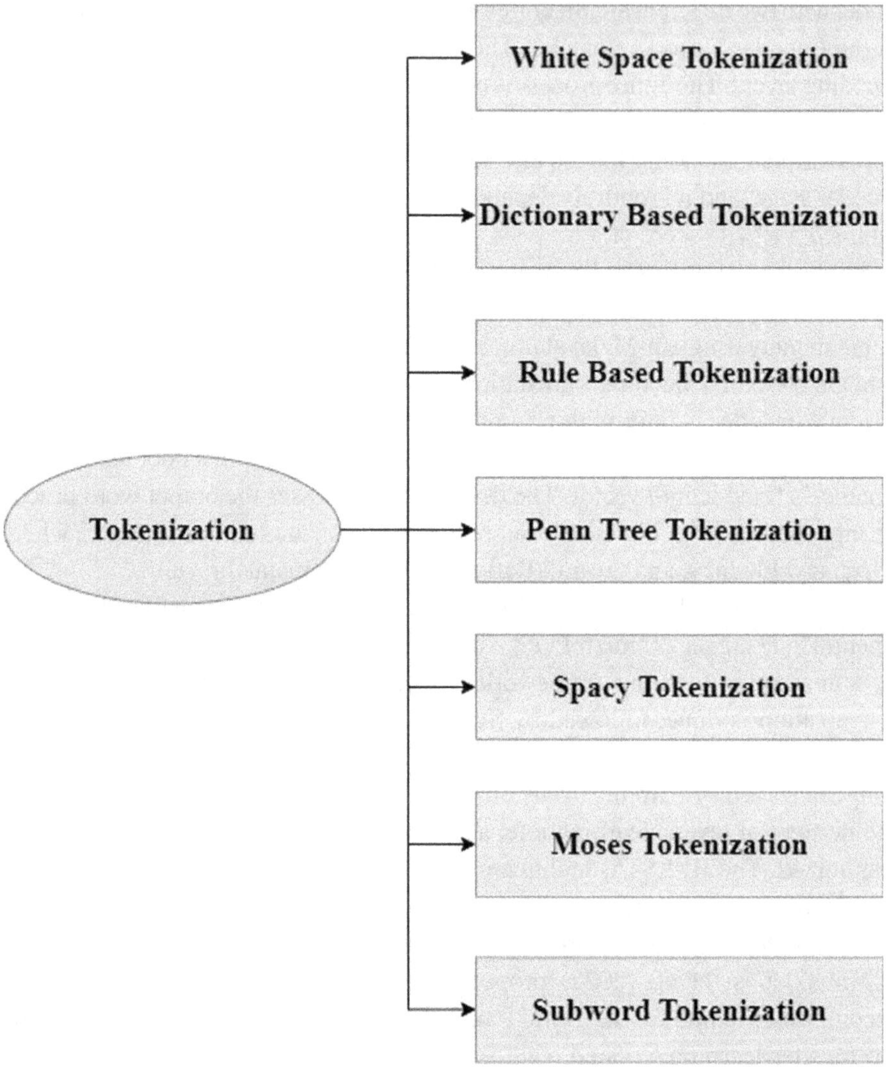

Thenmozhi and Aravindan (2018) developed a cross-lingual Tamil-English informa- tion retrieval system built on an ontology. The system uses the ontology to translate the source Tamil query into the intended English query. A Morphological analyser is implemented to remove suffixes and obtain the root word. A bilingual dictionary looks-up the English to Tamil word translation. Word sense disambiguation compares all the possible senses of the given query and returns the most matchable one called as the wordnet sense information. A Syntactic rearrangement is done for the language translated query. This rearrangement is done to provide better search results. Query Reformulation has to be done when the translated query provides ambiguous meaning. Query Reformulation can be done with the help of an ontology. The rewritten query is then turned into a Universal Resource Locator (URL), which is sent to the browser,which then obtains the necessary internet pages and displays the results.

Anita and Subalalitha (2019b) built a Discourse parser for Thirukkural. Information retrieval, question-answering systems, and text summarization are just a few examples of the Natural Language Processing applications that the system focuses on. It identifies relations in Thirukkural and discourse structure is developed with Thirukkural discourse parser. Input to the system is Tamil Thirukkural couplets. Discourse relation is identified by the Thirukkural Discourse parser, if it doesn't explicitly appear, then morphological analyzer is opted to identify the cue words. Cues are the words that uncover the buried information. If there exists two clauses, clause 1 can act as nucleus and clause 2 can act as satellite. The system derives Nucleus, Satellite and Discourse relations as output. It has achieved a precision of 84.26% and recall of 93.97%.

Harissh et al. (2018) proposed a text-based unsupervised domain ontology. The system operates in five stages: corpus collection, term extraction, taxonomic relationship extraction, non-taxonomic relationship extraction, and domain ontology construction. Iterative Focused Crawling is used to acquire corpora. Term Extraction is performed with Hyperlink Induced Topic Search (HITS) algorithm. Hearst and Morpho-Syntactic Patterns are used to extract taxonomic relationships. Association rule mining is used to find non-taxonomic relationships. Thus finally domain ontology is obtained as a result. Without the use of a manual annotated resource unsupervised HITS technique, domain ontologies are created. Ontology is built in such a way that it doesn't need any supervision from scratch. The system is designed in such a way that it can be extended with deep learning models to build domain ontology to make it useful and meaningful.

Sathiya and Geetha (2018) suggested an automatic ontology learning from multiple knowledge sources of text. Concept extraction, taxonomic relation extraction, and non-taxonomic relation extraction are the three stages of the automatic ontology construction process. With the help of contextual information, the Taxonomic Relation Extraction formulates two-level queries. Next, hyponyms and hypernyms are found using fitness scores, for which probase is used as input. This taxonomic relation gives concept hierarchy as output. Non-Taxonomic Relation (NTR) Extraction is carried out with dependency relation extraction - SVO triplet is extracted and the Non-Taxonomic Relation is discovered using COS(Co-occurrence Strength) measure helps to extract the relations.

Arul Deepa and Deisy (2012) developed an application of turing machine which is a rule based converter of Formal Tamil to Colloquial Tamil(FT2CT). The article is a kind of a Machine Translation technique which works on the basis of 7 important rules out of available 29 rules. These 29 rules are derived based on of morphology and phonology of Tamil language. The virtual turing machine is automated with the help of rules in such a way that, for any given formal tamil document, a word splitter module is used to split the words automatically and with the turing machine, the rules are applied automatically. This process is repeated for each word. Thus the document is generated with colloquial tamil based on the available 7 rules. The purpose of the system is to assist NRI Tamil learners in bridging the gap between formal and colloquial Tamil. The system has achieved a performance of 82%.

Balaji et al. (2016) developed an unsupervised learning method of semantic relations of morphologically rich language. Semantic relations are extracted with a minimal co-occurrence feature. The proposed system follows an morpho-semantic feature extraction. A tagged feature document corpus is given as input to the system. As a First Step, semantic sub-graphs are determined, which acts as a source node, further it can be developed with the help of the given POS tag and its morphological features. With the probabilistic learning model, possible connecting nodes are identified based on its probability, so that a semantic relation can be formed. When the probability reaches a limit and becomes unchanged, and at that stage, it could be decided that no more input instances are available for labeling the semantic relation. The system obtained an F-measure score of 0.5.

Despite being an essential part of interpreting natural language, Tamil semantic analysis has some restrictions. Getting the subtleties and intricate meaning of the Tamil language's complex and contextual meaning right is one of the biggest challenges. Like many other languages, Tamil exhibits polysemy, which allows a single word to have several meanings depending on the situation. Because of this ambiguity, it can be challenging to determine a sentence's intended meaning. Additionally, Tamil makes extensive use of idiomatic terms, metaphorical language, and cultural references, all of which can be difficult to grasp without a thorough knowledge of the language and its context. To address these issues, sophisticated algorithms and models must be created that can manage the complexity of Tamil semantic analysis and make use of contextual data for interpretations that are more precise and nuanced.

Tamil semantic analysis's future approaches have enormous potential for increasing natural language understanding and enabling more sophisticated communication in the Tamil language. One important area of research is to use advances in machine learning and artificial intelligence to increase the accuracy and depth of semantic analysis. This includes experimenting with deep learning models like neural networks and transformers to capture contextual nuances and disambiguation issues in Tamil. Furthermore, adding Tamil-specific knowledge graphs and ontologies might improve the encoding and retrieval of semantic information, allowing for more exact interpretations of meaning. Furthermore, combining cross-lingual and cross-modal semantic analysis can allow for effective translation and comprehension across languages and modalities. Tamil semantic analysis, by focusing on these future possibilities, can contribute to a wide range of applications, such as information retrieval, sentiment analysis, and intelligent virtual assistants, enabling improved language understanding and communication.

CONCLUSION

This book chapter examines the most well-known works in the field of Natural Language Processing. We have categorized the major areas of review into Universal Networking Language, Morphological Analysis, Semantic Analysis. It will create a new path for the researchers to develop new morphological analyzer systems, Semantic analysis models and UNL systems by knowing the gaps and pitfalls in those existing systems. Since, Tamil is evolving in terms of technological solution systems, it requires more and more researchers to look into the black box models of the systems that have been developed for the Tamil language. The novelty shown in this Book Chapter is to integrate UNL, Semantic and Morphological Analysis for an Information Retrieval System for Tamil Language. Thus, after the careful investigation of the research articles, these three areas deserve further study and will provide the researchers with more innovative ideas for the systems in future by overcoming the limitations and research gaps discussed in the Book Chapter

REFERENCES

Ajay, S., Srikanth, M., Kumar, M. A., & Soman, K. (2016). Word embedding models for finding semantic relationship between words in tamil language. *Indian Journal of Science and Technology*, *9*(45), 1–5. doi:10.17485/ijst/2016/v9i45/106478

Ali, M. N. Y., Rahman, M. L., Chaki, J., Dey, N., & Santosh, K. C. (2021). Machine translation using deep learning for universal networking language based on their structure. *International Journal of Machine Learning and Cybernetics*, *12*(8), 2365–2376. doi:10.1007/s13042-021-01317-5

Anbukkarasi, S., Varadhaganapathy, S., Jeevapriya, S., Kaaviyaa, A., Lawvanyapriya, T., & Monisha, S. (2022). *Named entity recognition for Tamil text using deep learning*. Institute of Electrical and Electronics Engineers Inc. doi:10.1109/ICCCI54379.2022.9740745

Anita, R., & Subalalitha, C. (2019a). An approach to cluster Tamil literatures using dis- course connectives. In *2019 IEEE 1st International Conference on Energy, Systems and Information Processing (ICESIP)* (pp. 1–4). IEEE.

Anita, R., & Subalalitha, C. (2019b). Building discourse parser for Thirukkural. *Proceedings of the 16th International Conference on Natural Language Processing*, 18–25.

Arul Deepa, K., & Deisy, C. (2012). A rule based converter of formal tamil to colloquial tamil (ft2ct). *11th International Tamil Internet Conference*.

Avinesh, P., & Karthik, G. (2007). Part-of-speech tagging and chunking using conditional random fields and transformation based learning. *Shallow Parsing for South Asian Languages*, *21*, 21–24.

Balaji, J., Geetha, T., Parthasarathi, R., & Karky, M. (2011). Morpho-semantic features for rule-based tamil enconversion. *International Journal of Computer Applications*, *26*(6), 11–18. doi:10.5120/3109-4269

Balaji, J., Ranjani, P., & Geetha, T. (2016). Unsupervised learning of semantic relations of a morphologically rich language. *International Journal of Information and Communication Technology*, *8*(4), 344–356.

Computational Linguistic Research Group (CLRG), AU-KBC Research Centre, MIT Campus of Anna University. (2016). *Aukbc-pos-corpus*. Available at www.au-kbc.org/nlp/corpusrelease.html

Dhanalakshmi, V., Kumar, A., Shivapratap, G., Soman, K., & Rajendran, S. (2009). Tamil pos tagging using linear programming. *International Journal of Recent Trends in Engineering*, *1*(2), 166.

Harissh, V. S., Vignesh, M., Kodaikkaavirinaadan, U., & Geetha, T. V. (2018). Unsupervised domain ontology learning from text. *Polibits*, *57*, 59–66. doi:10.17562/PB-57-6

Jagan, B., Geetha, T., & Parthasarathi, R. (2012). Semantic parsing of Tamil sentences. *Proceedings of the Workshop on Machine Translation and Parsing in Indian Languages*, 15–22.

Jagan, B., Parthasarathi, R., & Geetha, T. V. (2019). Bootstrapping of semantic relation ex- traction for a morphologically rich language: Semi-supervised learning of semantic relations. *International Journal on Semantic Web and Information Systems*, *15*, 119–149. doi:10.4018/IJSWIS.2019010106

Jain, M., Punia, R., & Hooda, I. (2020). Neural machine translation for Tamil to English. *Journal of Statistics and Management Systems*, *23*(7), 1251–1264. doi:10.1080/09720510.2020.1799582

Karuppaiah, D., & Vincent, P. D. R. (2021a). Hybrid approach for semantic similarity calculation between Tamil words. *International Journal of Innovative Computing and Applications*, *12*(1), 13–23. doi:10.1504/IJICA.2021.113609

Karuppaiah, D., & Vincent, P. D. R. (2021b). Word sense disambiguation in tamil using indo-wordnet and cross-language semantic similarity. *International Journal of Intelligent Enterprise*, *8*(1), 62–73. doi:10.1504/IJIE.2021.112320

Lakshmana Pandian, S., & Geetha, T. (2008). Morpheme based language model for tamil part-of-speech tagging. *Polibits*, *38*, 19–25. doi:10.17562/PB-38-2

Menon, V. K., Rajendran, S., Anandkumar, M., & Soman, K. (2017). Dependency resolution and semantic mining using tree adjoining grammars for tamil language. *arXiv preprint arXiv:1704.05611*.

Mokanarangan, T., Pranavan, T., Megala, U., Nilusija, N., Dias, G., Jayasena, S., & Ranathunga, S. (2016). Tamil morphological analyzer using support vector machines. *Natural Language Processing and Information Systems: 21st International Conference on Applications of Natural Language to Information Systems, NLDB 2016, Salford, UK, June 22-24, 2016 Proceedings*, *21*, 15–23.

Nivre, J., De Marneffe, M.-C., Ginter, F., Goldberg, Y., Hajic, J., & Manning, C. D. (2016). Universal dependencies v1: A multilingual treebank collection. *Proceedings of the Tenth International Conference on Language Resources and Evaluation (LREC'16)*, 1659–1666.

Pandian, S. L., Devakumar, J., & Geetha, T. (2008). Semantic information extraction from tamil documents. *International Journal of Metadata, Semantics and Ontologies*, *3*(3), 226–232. doi:10.1504/IJMSO.2008.023570

Pattabhi, R., Rao, T., Ram, R. V. S., Vijayakrishna, R., & Sobha, L. (2007). A text chunker and hybrid pos tagger for indian languages. *Proceedings of International Joint Conference on Artificial Intelligence Workshop on Shallow Parsing for South Asian Languages, IIIT Hyderabad, Hyderabad, India*.

Premjith, B., Kumar, M. A., & Soman, K. P. (2019). Neural machine translation system for english to indian language translation using mtil parallel corpus. *Journal of Intelligent Systems*, *28*(3), 387–398. doi:10.1515/jisys-2019-2510

Premjith, B., & Soman, K. P. (2021). Deep learning approach for the morphological synthesis in malayalam and tamil at the character level. *ACM Transactions on Asian and Low-Resource Language Information Processing*, 20.

Qi, P., Zhang, Y., Zhang, Y., Bolton, J., & Manning, C. D. (2020). Stanza: A python natural language processing toolkit for many human languages. *arXiv preprint arXiv:2003.07082*. doi:10.18653/v1/2020.acl-demos.14

Rajasekar, M., & Geetha, A. (2021). Machine learning algorithm for information extraction from gynaecological domain in tamil. *J. Math. Comput. Sci.*, *11*(6), 7140–7153.

Rajasekar, M., & Geetha, A. (2022). Comparison of machine learning methods for tamil morphological analyzer. In *Intelligent Sustainable Systems Proceedings of ICISS, 2021*, 385–399.

Ramalingam, A., & Navaneethakrishnan, S. C. (2021). A discourse-based information retrieval for tamil literary texts. *Journal of Information and Communication Technology*, *20*, 353–389. doi:10.32890/jict2021.20.3.4

Ramasamy, L., & Zˇabokrtsky´, Z. (2015). *Ud tamil ttb*. Available at https://universaldependencies.org/treebanks/tattb/index.html

Roy, P. K., Bhawal, S., & Subalalitha, C. N. (2022). Hate speech and offensive language detection in dravidian languages using deep ensemble framework. *Computer Speech & Language*, *75*, 75. doi:10.1016/j.csl.2022.101386

Saha, A. K., Mridha, M. F., Rafiq, J. I., & Das, J. K. (2019). *Information extraction from natural language using universal networking language* (Vol. 924). Springer Verlag. doi:10.1007/978-981-13-6861-5_24

Sarveswaran, K. P., Krishnamurthy, K., & Balasubramani. (2020). *Ud tamil-mwtt*. Available at https://universaldependencies.org/treebanks/ta$_m$wtt/index.html

Sarveswaran, K., & Dias, G. (2021). *Building a part of speech tagger for the tamil language*. Institute of Electrical and Electronics Engineers Inc. doi:10.1109/IALP54817.2021.9675195

Sarveswaran, K., Dias, G., & Butt, M. (2018). Thamizhifst: A morphological analyser and generator for tamil verbs. *2018 3rd International Conference on Information Technology Research (ICITR)*, 1–6. 10.1109/ICITR.2018.8736139

Sarveswaran, K., Dias, G., & Butt, M. (2021). Thamizhi morph: A morphological parser for the tamil language. *Machine Translation*, *35*(1), 37–70. doi:10.1007/s10590-021-09261-5

Sarveswaran, K., & Mahesan, S. (2014). Hierarchical tagset for rulebased processing of tamil language. *International Journal of Multidisciplinary Studies*, *1*(2), 67–74. doi:10.4038/ijms.v1i2.53

Sathiya, B., & Geetha, T. V. (2018). Automatic ontology learning from multiple knowledge sources of text. *International Journal of Intelligent Information Technologies*, *14*(2), 1–21. doi:10.4018/IJIIT.2018040101

Selvam, M. and Natarajan, A. (2009). Improvement of rule based morphological analysis and pos tagging in Tamil language via projection and induction techniques. *International Journal of Computers*, *3*(4), 357–367.

Sheshasaayee, A., & Deepa, V. R. A. (2017). *Ascertaining the morphological components of tamil language using unsupervised approach*. Institute of Electrical and Electronics Engineers Inc.

Sitender, & Bawa, S. (2021). Sansunl: A Sanskrit to unl enconverter system. *Journal of the Institution of Electronics and Telecommunication Engineers*, *67*(1), 117–128. doi:10.1080/03772063.2018.1528187

Sitender & Bawa, S. (2022). Sanskrit to universal networking language enconverter system based on deep learning and context-free grammar. Springer Science and Business Media Deutschland GmbH.

Sridhar, R., Sethuraman, P., & Krishnakumar, K. (2016). English to tamil machine trans- lation system using universal networking language. *Sadhana - Academy Proceedings in Engineering Sciences*, *41*, 607–620.

Srinivasan, R., & Subalalitha, C. (2019). Automated named entity recognition from tamil documents. *2019 IEEE 1st international conference on energy, systems and information processing (ICESIP)*, 1–5. 10.1109/ICESIP46348.2019.8938383

Subalalitha, C. (2019). Information extraction framework for kurunthogai. *Sadhana*, *44*(7), 156. doi:10.1007/s12046-019-1140-y

Subalalitha, C. N., & Poovammal, E. (2018). Automatic bilingual dictionary construction for tirukural. *Applied Artificial Intelligence*, *32*(6), 558–567. doi:10.1080/08839514.2018.1481590

Suriyah, M., Anandan, A., Narasimhan, A., & Karky, M. (2020). Piripori: morphological analyser for tamil. In *Proceedings of International Conference on Artificial Intelligence, Smart Grid and Smart City Applications: AISGSC 2019* (pp. 801–809). Springer. 10.1007/978-3-030-24051-6_75

Thavareesan, S., & Mahesan, S. (2020). Word embedding-based part of speech tagging in tamil texts. In *2020 IEEE 15th International conference on industrial and information systems (ICIIS)* (pp. 478–482). IEEE. 10.1109/ICIIS51140.2020.9342640

Thenmozhi, D., & Aravindan, C. (2018). Ontology-based tamil-english cross-lingual information retrieval system. *Sadhana*, 43.

Thenmozhi, D., Kumar, B. S., & Aravindan, C. (2018). Deep learning approach to English- Tamil and Hindi-Tamil verb phrase translations. In *FIRE* (pp. 323–331). Working Notes.

Van NguyenM.LaiV. D.VeysehA. P. B.NguyenT. H. (2021).Trankit: A light-weight transformer-based toolkit for multilingual natural language processing. *arXivpreprint arXiv:2101.03289*. doi:10.18653/v1/2021.eacl-demos.10

Chapter 6
Machine Learning Approach for Kashmiri Word Sense Disambiguation

Aadil Ahmad Lawaye
https://orcid.org/0000-0003-4072-2043
Baba Ghulam Shah Badshah University, India

Tawseef Ahmad Mir
https://orcid.org/0000-0001-9723-8995
Alliance University, India

Mahmood Hussain Mir
https://orcid.org/0000-0002-8497-9126
Alliance University, India

Ghayas Ahmed
https://orcid.org/0000-0002-1400-1528
Baba Ghulam Shah Badshah University, India

ABSTRACT

Studying the senses of words in a given data is crucial for analysing and understanding natural languages. The meaning of an ambiguous word varies based on the context of usage and identifying its correct meaning in the given situation is a famous problem known as word sense disambiguation (WSD) in natural language processing (NLP). In this chapter, the authors discuss the important WSD research works carried out in the context of different languages using different techniques. They also explore a supervised approach based on the hidden Markov model (HMM) to address the WSD problem in the Kashmiri language, which lacks research in the NLP domain. The performance of the proposed approach is also examined in detail along with future improvement directions. The average results produced by the proposed system are accuracy=72.29%, precision=0.70, recall= 0.70, and F1-measure=0.70.

DOI: 10.4018/979-8-3693-0728-1.ch006

INTRODUCTION

Natural Language Processing (NLP), an important branch of Artificial Intelligence (AI), enables machines to understand and generate natural languages like humans (Chowdhary and Chowdhary 2020; Eisenstein 2019; Fanni et al. 2023). To interpret or generate the natural language, it is necessary to identify the desired meaning of words in the given data. However, many words in every natural language are ambiguous and may give different meanings based on the context of usage. Interpreting the meaning of a given natural language text becomes complex due to these ambiguous words. For example, look at the following two sentences using the ambiguous word "passage":

This **passage** *is difficult for me to understand.* *(1)*

Don't bother he will change with the **passage** *of time.* *(2)*

In sentence (1) it gives the sense of "*a section in a book*" whereas in sentence (2) it means "*the act of passing from one state or place to the next*". Similarly, consider the four sentences in Kashmiri below:

ہیوٗر تخس،رطأخ ن۔ دوٗہوٚی ونپاَ وزیزان *(3)*

Nazeezo apnove yahoodeyen khater sakht ravaye (Transliteration)

سأ یلأز نَپات تخس *(4)*

Sakht tapen zeal aes (Transliteration)

ترٗورض تخس زنٛہ نَسنٛوپ ِھچ ساتیس *(5)*

Sita's che poonsen hanz sakht zaruret (Transliteration)

ہنرَک دَر ناوی یڑأگ ہکاڈ ہنےٚھچ ہت زنٛمَ نَتلاح لِکشُم تخ *(5)*

Sakht mushkil halaten manz te che ne daek gaed yewaan raed karne (Transliteration)

The four Kashmiri sentences 3,4,5 and 6 above use the word تخس in four different contexts. In sentence 3 it translates to "*strict*", in sentence 4 it translates to "*severe*", in sentence 5 it translates to "*substantially*" and in sentence 6 it translates to "*hard*".

The process of making the correct sense prediction of ambiguous words in the given natural language data is given the name Word Sense Disambiguation (WSD). WSD has a direct influence on different NLP applications like machine translation, question answering, text classification, sentiment analysis, information extraction and retrieval, etc. It is considered a difficult problem as ambiguity may arise at different levels. Homonymy exists when we have words with ditto spellings and sounds but exhibit unalike senses. For example, the "*ugly woman*" or "*flexible container used for carrying personal items*" senses of the word **bag**. On the other hand, polysemy exists when the different senses of a word are connected. For example, the word "mouse" may refer to an "animal" or "peripheral connected to a computer" and these senses are related due to resemblance in shape. The overall WSD process has two steps. In the first step list of possible senses of the underlying word is collected from a sense inventory and in the second step the feasible sense to the word is assigned.

The research on WSD started many decades ago and is still considered an interesting problem in NLP. The main challenges that fuel its complexity are the lack of unified sense representations, different sense granularities in different sense inventories, non-availability of computational resources required and many others. Research on WSD is carried out using three different methodological approaches; supervised WSD approaches, unsupervised WSD approaches and semi-supervised approaches. In the supervised approach, the WSD model is trained on a manually crafted or automatically generated sense-tagged corpus (Gujjar et al. 2023; Janz and Piasecki, 2019; Wang and Wang 2019). In the unsupervised approach, the WSD model captures the similarity between the words existing in different instances and uses this similarity to perform disambiguation (Jha et al. 2023; Zhang et al. 2021). In the semi-supervised approach, the WSD model is trained on a limited sense-tagged corpus and a large untagged corpus is used to increase the training data in order to enhance the system performance (Chen et al. 2016). Even though ample research efforts have already been made to solve this problem this is still not completely solved. Also, the researchers have focused on limited languages like English, Spanish, French, etc. with few efforts on other languages. When the research on said topic is analyzed in the context of Indian languages, especially Kashmiri language there is a huge void present. This chapter is a step towards narrowing this research gap in the context of Kashmiri language. In this chapter, we put forward a WSD approach for the Kashmiri language implementing supervised machine learning methodology. We assessed the performance of the proposed system on a set of ambiguous Kashmiri words and reported the results produced in terms of precision, recall, F1 score and accuracy.

This chapter is further distributed into different sections. The chapter discusses different real-world applications of WSD in the next section. Different WSD approaches along with the important research works conducted previously are then discussed. Important challenges concerning WSD in Indian languages are then presented. Then a brief introduction to the Kashmiri language is given along with its linguistic features and the different research works related to NLP. The chapter then discusses the methodology adopted to handle WSD in the Kashmiri language. Finally, the summary of the chapter is provided.

WSD Real-World Application Scenarios

Machine Translation (MT)

It refers to translating given text from one language to another. If the given natural language data is not deciphered correctly the output of this application may be incorrect. For example, while translating sentence 1 from English to Urdu if the word "***passage***" is interpreted as "*the act of passing from one state or place to the next*" instead of "*a section in a book*" the result translation will be wrong. This highlights the significance of WSD in machine translation.

Information Retrieval (IR)

This is another important NLP application that deals with finding out the intended information from the given data. To achieve better results in the IR process it is necessary to identify the correct sense of the words in the search query. Without properly deciphering the words the search engine may retrieve the documents containing the words in the search query but with different senses. For example, if the user searches for information regarding the "apple", the search engine may produce documents containing the word "apple" with the sense "fruit" or documents containing the word "apple" with the sense "technology company". However, with the proper handling of the WSD more relevant documents with the intended meaning may be retrieved.

Text Classification

Text classification is an NLP application that predicts the category to which a document belongs. In this WSD also plays an important role. For example, in a scenario where news articles about the word "*bank*" are to be classified into different categories like "technology", "finance", "river conservation", and "technology". A document containing the sentence "This year the bank reported a huge profit in sales". If the WSD is not handled properly the classifier may incorrectly decipher the word "bank" in this sentence as "financial institution instead of a term related to technology and hence categorize the document into "finance category" instead of "technology". This shows the role of WSD in text classification.

Question Answering

The objective of question-answering systems is to provide the answers to the user queries. Here the WSD also needs proper attention as the system may give irrelevant answers to the user queries. Question-answering systems use the WSD techniques to interpret the intended meaning of the query words and then produce the relevant answers. For example, the user fires the query: "What are the most visited banks?". Here the word "bank" is ambiguous and without deciphering the query words correctly the question-answering system may produce answers about financial institutions instead of river banks.

Sentiment Analysis

Sentiment analysis an important NLP task determines the sentiment of the given text. This task is also highly influenced by the way WSD is handled. If the WSD technique is not used properly the text may get tagged with the false sentiment. For example, consider a scenario where the user sentiments (positive, neutral or negative) regarding product review are to be classified. The model classifies the reviews of customers for a smartphone and the user review is: "The mobile speed is nice, but the bank is not good." If the word "bank" is misinterpreted in this review the sentiment regarding the smartphone may be classified as negative due to the words "not good" following it. But if the word "bank" is interpreted correctly then the sentiment regarding the speed of the mobile may be tagged as positive and that of the bank with negative sentiment.

Related Work

Research works dealing WSD problem have used machine learning techniques. As the study is related to the WSD for Kashmiri language which is a South Asian language and lacks research on this topic we studied the already existing work in other languages. Papers surveyed to take this research work include those employing different machine-learning approaches in different languages.

Supervised WSD:

Kokane et al (2023) used a supervised machine-learning technique for WSD. The experiments are carried out using two neural networks on two standard datasets;

OMSTI (Taghipour and NG, 2015) and SemCor (Miller et al. 2003) and a newly generated dataset Adaptive-Lex. To train the proposed model utilized Adaptive-Lex along with WordNet (Miller 1995) to generate word embeddings for polysemous words. Leveraging adaptive word embeddings for WSD enhanced the performance of the proposed system.

Mir et al. (2023) proposed a supervised WSD model for the Kashmiri language. In this research work experiments are carried out using three basic machine learning algorithms namely; decision trees, SVM and k-NN. The experiments are carried out on 60 ambiguous Kashmiri words and it is observed that SVM based classifier performs better than other algorithms used.

Yadav et al. (2021) proposed a supervised approach implemented using the Tsetlin Machine to find the appropriate sense of an ambiguous word in the given text. in this system word senses are distinguished using conjunctive clauses. Contextual features extracted from the given text are used to obtain these clauses. The results obtained from experimentation indicate that the senses dredged out by the proposed model can comprehended easily by assessing the converged model of the Tsetlin Machine.

Pal et al. (2019) used a novel supervised approach to tackle WSD in Bengali. The authors first evaluated four basic supervised algorithms; decision tree, Naïve Bayes, SVM and artificial neural networks on the 13 most commonly used Bangali ambiguous words. The baseline methodology is then extended in two directions; in the first modification bootstrapping is applied and in the other modification lemmatization is applied to the baseline strategy. When these two extensions were subjected to evaluation it was observed both these extensions enhanced the performance of the baseline methodology. The dataset for this research work is fetched from Bengali Corpus (Pan and Saha 2019) and Bengali WordNet (Das and Bandyopadhyay, 2010).

Raganato et al. (2017) utilized the sequence learning models to solve the WSD problem. The authors thoroughly investigated different end-to-end neural architectures customized for the WSD task and tested these models on different standard WSD datasets. the results showed that the sequence learning models implanted using LSTMs are better for the all-words WSD task. (Vial et al. 2019) also used the same strategy with modifications to carry out the WSD task. Here the authors used an ensemble of transformers instead of the LSTM decoder and the contextual embeddings from BERT (Devlin et al. 2018) are used as inputs to the all-words WSD model.

Walia et al. (2017) used the Naïve Bayes algorithm to solve WSD in the Gurmukhi language. The proposed model is implemented on a Gurmukhi dataset obtained from "Evaluations and Language Resources Distribution Agency, Paris, France" which is sense-tagged for 100 ambiguous words. Experiments are carried out using different window sizes to analyze its role in the disambiguation and it is observed that when window size is increased the performance gets elevated.

Melamud et al. (2016) presented a neural model that uses bidirectional LSTM to learn context embeddings from a large corpus. Then the model is tested for carrying out different NLP tasks. When the model was tested for the WSD task in a supervised manner it produced results near to or higher than the existing prominent systems.

Chun-Xiang et al. (2015) used the Hidden Markov Model (HMM) to tackle WSD for Chinese. Senses are obtained from Chinese Tongyici Cilin and the results produced showed improvements. (Zhou et al. 2014) came up with a unified solution for resolving ambiguity using different algorithms. Initially, HMM is used and then the Maximum Entropy Markov Model (McCallum et al. 2000), Conditional Random Fields (Lafferty et al. 2001) and tree-structured Conditional Random Fields algorithm are employed. The authors employed beam search, and appropriate training sets to reduce the time complexity of the proposed technique and the results produced were better than many previous studies.

Unsupervised WSD:

Jha et al. (2023) employed graph-based unsupervised WSD approach in the context of Hindi language. The weighted graph is created where the various senses of the ambiguous word are represented by nodes and the edges of the graph give the relations between them. Edges are assigned weights according to the semantic similarity extracted from Hindi WordNet and the most appropriate sense to the ambiguous term is then decided by a random walk algorithm.

Meng (2022) proposed a graph and knowledge base WSD approach to enrich the existing WSD approaches with the required information. Contextual information is obtained with the help of dependency parsing and a disambiguation graph is constructed using the sentences available in the knowledge base that give the proper distinction of the various senses of the ambiguous words. The disambiguation is then carried out using both the contextual graph and the disambiguation graph.

Rahman and Borah (2022) proposed a novel unsupervised approach for the WSD task. In this work, both WordNet and Wikipedia are considered to predict the correct sense of the ambiguous term. The model first identifies all senses that an ambiguous word can have from the WordNet and then computes its collocation score with other words in the context. The collocation score computes the possibility with which the two words co-exist in Wikipedia. The maximum collocation score gives the correct sense of the ambiguous word in the concerned context.

Han and Shirai (2021) used an unsupervised technique for WSD. In this research work features in the form of word embeddings and collocations are leveraged to implement the model. Both these features are aggregated in the final WSD system and the results reported by the model on SensEval-3 Lexical Sample WSD Task showed a 4.7% increment in the precision than the baseline.

Gogoi et al. (2021) proposed an unsupervised technique for Assamese WSD. In this research work, the Cuckoo algorithm is used for implementation purposes. the dataset is extracted from the Assamese corpus (Sarma et al. 2012). The results produced by the proposed model (precision= 87.5%, recall=84% and F1-score=85.71%) are better when compared with the results produced by the research work presented in (Gogoi et al. 2020).

Hou et al. (2020) proposed an unsupervised technique to handle WSD in Chinese. Authors exploited the masked language model task of large pre-trained language models. In addition to this, a novel WSD dataset based on HowNet (Dong and Dong, 2003) is also created. The model reported better results than the other baseline models used.

Abed et al. (2016) proposed an unsupervised approach based on a genetic algorithm to counter WSD. To get better semantic similarity results the genetic algorithm is improved by leveraging local search techniques. The model first assigns all possible senses to the words extracted from WordNet and then the improved genetic algorithm finds out the appropriate senses based on the relatedness and semantic similarity measures. The results produced by the proposed model are better than the previously proposed solutions when evaluated on the same dataset extracted from SemCor.

Semi-Supervised WSD:

Barba et al. (2020) proposed a semi-supervised technique to WSD in a multilanguage setting. The model uses a label propagation scheme that takes benefits from multilingual information available in the knowledgebase and contextual word embeddings and projects senses from resource-rich language to resource-poor language. The proposed model showed that the automatically generated datasets are of better quality than other datasets and the model produced better results than the other counterparts.

Sausa et al. (2020) proposed a semi-supervised WSD technique. The input to the proposed model is given in the form of word embeddings prepared with the help of the Word2Vec (Church 2017) model, FastText (Bojanowski et al. 2016) and BERT models concatenated with part-of-speech (PoS) tags. SSL algorithms are used for carrying out WSD and it is observed that these models perform as par with supervised approaches and can predict the senses of words that are out-of-vocabulary as well in contrast to supervised approaches. From the results, it is observed that Word2Vec using skip-gram variant is better for performing WSD whereas BERT gives the best embeddings.

Yuan et al. (2016) used the LSTM algorithm to carry out WSD in a semi-supervised manner. The main reason for using the semi-supervised classifier was to capture the syntactic as well as sequential mappings from the data in a better way.

The semi-supervised model produced state-of-art results when a graph is prepared from the sense-tagged instances augmented with large untagged data obtained from online resources and sense labels are impregnated in this.

WSD Challenges Specific to Indian Languages

From the literature review section, it is apparent that the research work on the WSD topic is smoothly going on. But when the same topic is discussed in the context of Indian languages specifically in Kashmiri there is a lack of such efforts. The major challenges in WSD specific to Indian languages are discussed here:

- Indian languages exhibit huge inflectional complexity which makes the morphological analysis of these languages difficult.
- Indian languages lack the resources required for the efficient handling of the WSD problem. In the case of foreign languages large datasets, preprocessing tools and efficient WSD models are reachable whereas Indian languages lack such resources. when we talk of the Kashmiri language there is no publicly reachable WSD dataset.
- Spelling variation is a common problem in Indian languages and the same word has different spellings which adds the WSD complexity.
- Semantic variations in the Indian languages are also found in Indian languages.
- Some sentences are smaller in length giving less contextual information to predict the correct sense of an ambiguous word whereas some sentences are very large containing huge vague information concerning WSD.
- Research efforts for WSD in Indian languages are restricted to a few languages like Hindi, Gurmukhi, Bengali and Assamese but there is a huge scarcity of such work for the Kashmiri language.
- Furthermore, the research on the WSD problem in the context of Indian languages is still stuck on traditional methods and the utilization of the latest techniques like deep learning approaches, Large Language Models (LLMs), and hybrid approaches is still missing.
- The datasets that are available for the WSD task for some Indian languages are smaller in size in comparison to foreign languages and these limited-size datasets have been used for the WSD research efforts.

Kashmiri Language, Its Linguistic Features, and NLP

Kashmiri is a language used in day-to-day communication by around 6.8 million people mostly residing in the Kashmir Valley of Jammu and Kashmir, a region in northern India. Kashmiri is a member of the Dardic branch of the Indo-Aryan languages and has similarities with other languages in the region such as Punjabi, Dogri, and Pahari (Kachru 2016). The language has a rich cultural heritage and is known for its unique phonology, grammar, and vocabulary. With time it has been influenced by different languages like Arabic, English, Urdu, Persian, and Sanskrit (Kak 2005). Kashmiri is known for its complex grammar, including a system of noun declensions and a variety of verb tenses and moods.

Despite having millions of users' research work in the field of NLP for the Kashmiri language is flimsy. To make progress in research in NLP there is a requirement for different linguistic tools. Due to the impetus in research in different NLP applications over the last many years development of such resources took place for different languages. But as far as the Kashmiri language is concerned it is still on the back foot which finally barres the research in this language on different NLP applications. There are several problems that we found during the course of this research work. Like many other Indian languages, Kashmiri has a rich linguistic structure with different scripts. There are different writing systems used in Kashmiri that pose challenges for NLP. Sharada script and Perso-Arabic script are commonly used scripts for writing Kashmiri and Perso-Arabic is treated as official script. The dataset collected for this research is in the Perso-Arabic script. There is no standardization in the Kashmiri writing system, and different writers use different scripts, which makes it challenging to develop NLP models that can handle different scripts, dialects, and writing styles (Koul 1996). Other issues that are present in the Kashmiri writing system include redundancy of symbols, repetition of words, variations in spellings of the same word, and compound words. The presence of diacritic marks in the Kashmiri language like Arabic adds fuel to the complexity of its processing. There are a number of diacritic marks like (ً, ٔ, ٖٚ, etc.) available in the Perso-Arabic script and the presence of these has a great impact on the meanings of the words in some cases. For example, رود and رۄد only differ in the diacritic mark (ٔ) but these words have totally different meanings. رود gives the sense of '*run*' whereas the word رۄد gives the sense of '*eradicate*'.

Kashmiri language also differs from other Indian languages from many perspectives. It has verb-second (V2) word order much like German with a lot of inflection (Wali & Koul, 1997). In contrast to remaining Indo-Aryan languages Kashmiri adheres to Subject-Verb-Object (SVO) word order. Keeping the verb position aside, word order in Kashmiri is considered flexible (Koul & Wali, 2004). This means that the same sentence can be expressed in multiple ways, depending on the context and emphasis, posing a challenge to interpreting a sentence. Words in Kashmiri are highly inflected, meaning that they can be modified to indicate different grammatical functions or relationships within a sentence (Wani 2017). Another challenge is that the agglutinative nature of Kashmiri can lead to long, complex words that can be difficult to analyze and disambiguate. Kashmiri has a complex system of noun declensions, with different forms for singular and plural, masculine and feminine, and direct and oblique cases. There are also different declensions for animate and inanimate nouns (Wali & Koul, 1997). Kashmiri verbs have a variety of tenses and moods, including present, past, future, imperative, and subjunctive. Verbs are conjugated differently depending on the person, number, and gender of the subject (Verbeke 2018). Kashmiri has a rich system of pronouns, with different forms for different levels of formality and politeness. The same pronoun can refer to different entities based on the context. For each personal pronoun, there are many Kashmiri equivalents. In the case of nominative, the ratio of pronouns between English and Kashmiri is 6:15 (Wani 2021). Kashmiri is a language that has a gender system and the gender of a noun can affect the form of adjectives, pronouns, and verbs that refer to that noun. This can make it difficult to accurately disambiguate the meaning of a word or phrase in context, especially if the gender of the noun is not explicitly stated. The gender system in Kashmiri is not binary, meaning that there are more than two gender categories. For example, Kashmiri has a separate gender category for non-human animals, which is different from the gender categories for male and female humans.

All the linguistic features discussed above make processing Kashmiri data a complex task. In the realm of NLP, research in the Kashmiri language is in the primitive phase. As from the literature review section, it may be visible that the Kashmiri language lacks research in WSD and the utilization of the latest techniques to handle the WSD problem. The only research paper we find handling the WSD problem in Kashmiri using (Mir et. al 2023) as discussed in the literature review section. The lack of research on this research problem is due to the non-availability of required datasets and the other resources required. Also due to the complex nature of the Kashmiri language halts the research on the said topic. However, some research efforts have been made for problems other than WSD. Furthermore due to the linguistic complexities discussed above utilizing of machine learning approaches for processing the Kashmiri language is more difficult. This has also impacted the research exploration of machine learning approaches for Kashmiri language. Here we will present some remarkable research efforts made so far in the NLP domain with respect to the Kashmiri language. In (Lone et al. 2022a) survey of resources available for NLP research in the Kashmiri language is presented. (Kak et al. 2017) discussed various issues, and problems faced in the development of Kashmiri Wordnet. A tag set comprising of 26 tags is proposed for Kashmiri part-of-speech (PoS) tagging in (Kak et al. 2009). Research work to develop a PoS tagger for the Kashmiri language utilizing a hybrid technique and CRF-based technique are presented in (Lawaye & Purkayastha, 2013) and (Lawaye & Purkayastha, 2014) respectively. In (Malik & Bansal, 2015) Named Entity Recognition (NER) system for Kashmiri is discussed. In (Lone et al. 2022b) various issues related to machine translation are discussed with Kashmiri as a case study.

METHODOLOGY

In this section, we will discuss the step-wise methodology adopted to carry out WSD. The proposed WSD model is shown in Figure 1 below.

Figure 1. Proposed methodology for Kashmiri WSD

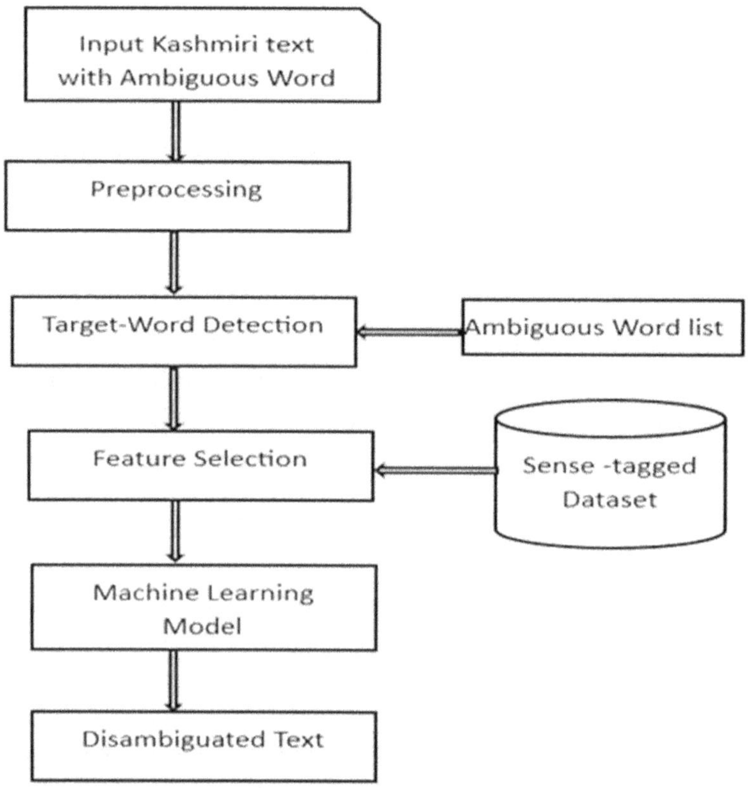

Data Collection

Kashmiri a language mainly spoken by the people of Kashmiri and is morphologically very rich but it does not have data available like other languages like English, Hindi, Urdu, etc. A variety of resources that were considered to fetch raw data for this research work include Kashmiri WordNet (Kak et al. 2017), PoS tagged dataset (Lawaye and Purkayastha, 2014), Trilingual Sense Dictionary (Banday et al. 2009) and Internet.

Preprocessing

To convert the raw corpus collected into the normalized form we proceed with a few preprocessing tasks.

Tokenization: The first preprocessing step employed is tokenization which dissolves the data into fundamental units called tokens. To carry out tokenization we used a method named 'word-tokenize' present in NLTK (Natural Language Processing Toolkit) Python library.

Data Cleaning: In the next step of preprocessing all the unwanted characters like punctuation marks present in the dataset are removed. Some unwanted characters that we found in our dataset include quotation marks ("", '', ' '), colon (:), brackets ([],()), semicolon (؛), inverse comma (،), hyphen (-), repeated symbols (----), other symbols like (*,/,<,>,\,|, @, #, $, %). All these unwanted symbols that do not have a role in future processing are ousted from the dataset. Also, the uneven number of blank lines and extra spaces are eradicated.

Another important issue that we need to look into while data cleaning is variations in spelling. Due to the lack of writing standardization for the Kashmiri language the data we collected contains the same words with different spellings which complicates the data processing. Also like the Arabic language diacritic marks are used in the Kashmiri language that needs to be handled. For example, the word written in Kashmiri WordNet as نظر (nazar) is written as نَظر in Trilingual E-Dictionary. If the same word is spelled differently at different places, we have used the spellings for the word as is present in Kashmiri WordNet and replaced all the word occurrences with the same spellings.

Target-Word Detection

Once the input text is preprocessed, finding out the presence of ambiguous words in it is the next step. Kashmiri WordNet is a repository of Kashmir words that gives the different concepts words give in different situations. We fetched the list of available ambiguous words available in it. This ambiguous-word list is used to check the presence of ambiguous words in the given input. If an ambiguous word is available in the input text, it becomes our target word for which the correct sense is to be predicted by the WSD model.

Sense-Tagged Dataset

Out of the preprocessed dataset, sixty ambiguous Kashmiri words having the highest frequency were selected. Instances for these ambiguous words were retrieved and then sense-tagging was performed using the sense definitions from Kashmiri

WordNet. The sense-tagged dataset with 9570 instances obtained is used to develop the WSD model.

Feature Selection

In the next phase, we extract the features from the data that are used to achieve the desired objective of WSD. As we employ a machine learning approach to perform WSD, a machine learning model requires input in the form of features to learn the WSD task and to predict the correct sense of an ambiguous word in the given input. In this research work, local lexical features of the target word are considered as clues to resolve ambiguity. These features are present on both sides of the target word and for this study, we considered the ambiguous word, the words that are present in two positions before and after the target word. These lexical features giving a 5-gram window are then transformed into vector form and given to the WSD model to learn the WSD task.

Machine Learning Model

The next step is to employ a machine learning model to carry out the WSD task in Kashmiri. In this research work, the Hidden Markov Model (HMM) algorithm is used to build the WSD model. HMM is fed the features prepared in the previous step and infers the correct sense of an ambiguous word in the given input. For each sense, there is a corresponding state in HMM. Transition probabilities are then defined between these states that represent how feasible is it to go from one state to another state from the given list of states. We computed the transition and emission probabilities of different senses of target words available in the sense-tagged dataset. To test the performance of the WSD model created we subjected it to unseen data containing the ambiguous word. It uses the Viterbi algorithm to find the most probable sequence of states (word senses) that best explains the observations in the sentence. This is actually the appropriate sense for the target word in the given text.

Observation and Interpretation

In the last step, we analyzed the reliability of the system. The reliability of the system is assessed using 10-fold cross-validation technique. The results are then presented using different metrics i.e., accuracy, precision, recall and F1-measure. These evaluation metrics help to get clear insights into the predictions made by the system. The sense predicted by the developed model may be the desired one or may be wrong, hence the outputs are divided into four classes.

True-Positive (TN): The scenario where the system properly identifies the intended meaning of an ambiguous word when presented with text containing that ambiguous term.

True-Negative (TN): The scenario where the ambiguous word is not tagged and the model also does not predict its sense.

False-Positive (FP): The scenario where the model incorrectly tags sense to the ambiguous word in a given input.

False-Negative (FN): The scenario where the model estimates that a given sense is not suitable to the ambiguous word when it is actually.

Based on the above four types of outputs produced by the system accuracy, precision, recall and F1-score may be defined as follows:

Accuracy(A): Taking all the sense predictions into consideration accuracy computes the share of right sense predictions (including positive and negative ones) made by the system.

Precision(P): Precision metric estimates the proficiency of the WSD model to make right positive predictions. It gives the count of true positive predictions out of the total positive predictions made by the model.

Recall(R): Recall metric estimates the proficiency of the WSD model to accurately determine positive instances out of the total actual positive instances.

F1-measure: F1-measure considers both false positives as well as false negatives and is obtained by calculating the harmonic mean of precision and recall.

Mathematical equations to obtain accuracy, precision, recall and F-measure are given below:

$$\text{Accuracy}(A) = (TN+TP) / (TN+TP+FN+FP) \quad (1)$$

$$\text{Precision}(P) = TP / (TP+FP) \quad (2)$$

$$\text{Recall}(R) = TP / (TP+FN) \quad (3)$$

$$F1 - \text{Measure} = (2 \times P \times R) / (P+R) \quad (4)$$

Out of the 60 ambiguous words, the results of 20 ambiguous words obtained during the test phase are presented in Table 1 below. The Table shows the ambiguous word, precision, recall and F1-measure and accuracy reported by the system during the testing phase.

From Table 1 above it is observed that the proposed WSD model shows good results for every word tested. We also analyzed the impact of the level of ambiguity on the accuracy of the model. Figure 2 shows the sense distribution of the 20 words shown in Table 1.

Table 1. Results reported for 20 ambiguous words

S. No.	Ambiguous Word	Accuracy (%)	Precision	Recall	F1-Score
1	آب (Aab)	82.41	0.82	0.78	0.80
2	دٔوھت (thud)	75.83	0.73	0.71	0.72
3	زیٔت (taiz)	72.66	0.70	0.69	0.69
4	رود (door)	69.56	0.68	0.68	0.68
5	ھتار (rath)	71.75	0.70	0.68	0.69
6	دٔور (roed)	80.20	0.78	0.77	0.77
7	تخس (sakhet)	73.31	0.70	0.71	0.70
8	فاص (saaf)	68.64	0.65	0.66	0.65
9	مأک (kaem)	70.26	0.68	0.68	0.68
10	لاک (call)	73.22	0.70	0.71	0.70
11	رٔوک (koer)	71.76	0.69	0.70	0.69
12	نٔگال (lagun)	69.78	0.68	0.68	0.68
13	لام (mall)	69.88	0.68	0.68	0.68
14	لٔوم (moel)	70.17	0.69	0.70	0.69
15	ھتٔو (weth)	69.35	0.68	0.69	0.68
16	ؤن (nuve)	70.54	0.68	0.69	0.68
17	رٔشأک (kashur)	71.61	0.70	0.70	0.70
18	مارآ (aram)	70.74	0.68	0.67	0.67
19	ھتٔب (buth)	72.52	0.71	0.72	0.71
20	دٔوىس (seud)	71.65	0.69	0.69	0.69

Figure 2. Distribution of words based on the number of senses used in the annotation process

From Figure 2 it is shown out of twenty selected ambiguous words five words have two senses, three words have three senses, seven words have four senses, two words have five senses, and one word has six, seven and eight senses each. Figure 3 then shows the impact of the number of senses on the accuracy of the WSD model.

Figure 3. Accuracy based on the number of senses used in annotation

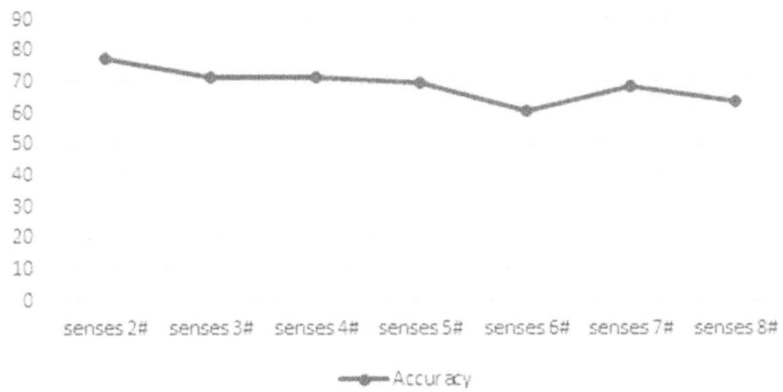

Figure 3 illustrates that more ambiguous words show less accuracy than words that are less ambiguous i.e., the more senses a word has more complex is to predict its right senses in a given situation. There seems one exception to this conclusion i.e., for the word that has six different senses but this is not true. The word ژگال (*lagun*) is the only word that has six different senses used in the dataset used for the test. It shows lower accuracy than words having seven and eight different senses not because it contradicts the above reaches conclusion but has a smaller number of instances (98) available in the dataset i.e., only 16.33 per sense on average whereas the word فاصل with seven different senses has 202 instances (28.85 per sense) in the dataset and the word زیت having eight different senses has 177 instances (22.12) in the dataset. From this, it is proved that the greater the size of the dataset used for training the WSD model better its accuracy.

CONCLUSION

This chapter focuses on the WSD problem for the Kashmiri language. The problem is countered in this chapter with a supervised technique based on the HMM algorithm. The WSD model is trained on a sense-tagged dataset which contains instances of

60 ambiguous Kashmiri words. The model is then tested on 20 ambiguous words and results are reported in terms of accuracy, precision, recall and F1-measure. Evaluation is carried out using the 10-fold cross-validation technique. The overall performance of the WSD model to decipher the exact interpretation of ambiguous words in different situations seems satisfactory. While completing this study we faced different challenges like collection of the dataset, inconsistency in data, preparation of training sets, etc. Kashmiri being a resource-poor language in terms of computational linguistics work on the NLP domain is in the preliminary phase. This study is an important step towards advancing the research in Kashmiri language in the NLP domain and opens the doors for exploring other NLP problems in Kashmiri language.

The WSD model proposed in this model can be improved in the future in many ways. Firstly, the model has been tested on only 20 ambiguous words and in the future more ambiguous words may be tested by supplying training and test sets for other ambiguous words. Secondly, we have used only one machine learning algorithm i.e., HMM to develop the WSD model and in the future other algorithms from different categories like supervised, unsupervised, and Knowledge-based algorithms may be experimented. This will give us more insights into using different techniques for analyzing the WSD problem in Kashmiri. We have explored only the Lexical-Sample variant of the WSD task in this research and in the future All-Words variant of the WSD task may also be explored.

REFERENCES

Abed, S. A., Tiun, S., & Omar, N. (2016). Word sense disambiguation in evolutionary manner. *Connection Science*, *28*(3), 226–241. doi:10.1080/09540091.2016.1141874

Banday, T. A., Panzoo, O., Lone, F. A., Nazir, S., Malik, K. A., Rasoool, S., & ... . (2009). Developing A Trilingual (English-Hindi-Kashmiri) E-Dictionary: Issues And Solutions. *Interdisciplinary Journal of Linguistics.*, *2*(1), 295–304.

Barba, E., Procopio, L., Campolungo, N., Pasini, T., & Navigli, R. (2020). Mulan: Multilingual label propagation for word sense disambiguation. In *Proceedings of the Twenty-Ninth International Joint Conference on Artificial Intelligence* (pp. 3837-3844). 10.24963/ijcai.2020/531

Bojanowski, P., Grave, E., Joulin, A., & Mikolov, T. (2017). Enriching word vectors with subword information. *Transactions of the Association for Computational Linguistics*, *5*, 135–146. doi:10.1162/tacl_a_00051

Chen, J., Zhong, L., & Cai, C. (2016). Using exponential kernel for semi-supervised word sense disambiguation. *Journal of Computational and Theoretical Nanoscience*, *13*(10), 6929–6934. doi:10.1166/jctn.2016.5649

Chowdhary, K., & Chowdhary, K. R. (2020). Natural language processing. *Fundamentals of Artificial Intelligence*, 603-649.

Chun-Xiang, Z., Yan-Chen, S., Xue-Yao, G., & Zhi-Mao, L. (2015). Chinese Word Sense Disambiguation Based on Hidden Markov Model. *International Journal of Database Theory and Application*, *8*(6), 263–270. doi:10.14257/ijdta.2015.8.6.24

Church, K. W. (2017). Word2Vec. *Natural Language Engineering*, *23*(1), 155–162. doi:10.1017/S1351324916000334

Das, D., & Bandyopadhyay, S. (2010). Developing bengali wordnet affect for analyzing emotion. In *International Conference on the Computer Processing of Oriental Languages* (pp. 35-40). Academic Press.

Devlin, J., Chang, M. W., Lee, K., & Toutanova, K. (2018). *Bert: Pre-training of deep bidirectional transformers for language understanding.* arXiv preprint arXiv:1810.04805.

Dong, Z., & Dong, Q. (2003, October). HowNet-a hybrid language and knowledge resource. *International conference on natural language processing and knowledge engineering Proceedings*, *2003*, 820–824.

Eisenstein, J. (2019). *Introduction to natural language processing*. MIT Press.

Fanni, S. C., Febi, M., Aghakhanyan, G., & Neri, E. (2023). Natural language processing. In *Introduction to Artificial Intelligence* (pp. 87–99). Springer International Publishing. doi:10.1007/978-3-031-25928-9_5

Gogoi, A., Baruah, N., & Sarma, S. K. (2020, December). Assamese word sense disambiguation using genetic algorithm. In *Proceedings of the 17th International Conference on Natural Language Processing (ICON)* (pp. 303-307). Academic Press.

Gujjar, V., Mago, N., Kumari, R., Patel, S., Chintalapudi, N., & Battineni, G. (2023). A Literature Survey on Word Sense Disambiguation for the Hindi Language. *Information (Basel)*, *14*(9), 495. doi:10.3390/info14090495

Han, S., & Shirai, K. (2021, February). Unsupervised Word Sense Disambiguation based on Word Embedding and Collocation. ICAART, (2), 1218-1225. doi:10.5220/0010380112181225

Hou, B., Qi, F., Zang, Y., Zhang, X., Liu, Z., & Sun, M. (2020, December). Try to substitute: An unsupervised chinese word sense disambiguation method based on hownet. In *Proceedings of the 28th International Conference on Computational Linguistics* (pp. 1752-1757). 10.18653/v1/2020.coling-main.155

Janz, A., & Piasecki, M. (2019). A weakly supervised word sense disambiguation for Polish using rich lexical resources. *Poznán Studies in Contemporary Linguistics*, *55*(2), 339–365. doi:10.1515/psicl-2019-0013

Jha, P., Agarwal, S., Abbas, A., & Siddiqui, T. J. (2023). A Novel Unsupervised Graph-Based Algorithm for Hindi Word Sense Disambiguation. *SN Computer Science*, *4*(5), 675. doi:10.1007/s42979-023-02116-1

Kachru, B. B. (2016). Kashmiri and other Dardic Languages'. *Current Trends in Linguistics*, *5*, 284–306.

Kak, A. A. (2005). Globalization of English and its Reflection on Kashmiri. *South Asian Language Review*, *15*(1), 37–50.

Kak, A. A., Ahmad, F., Mehdi, N., Farooq, M., & Hakim, M. (2017). Challenges, Problems, and Issues Faced in Language-Specific Synset Creation and Linkage in the Kashmiri WordNet. *The WordNet in Indian Languages*, 209-220.

Kak, A. A., Mehdi, N., & Lawaye, A. (2009). What should be and What should not be? Developing a POS tagset for Kashmiri. *Interdisciplinary Journal of Linguistics*, *2*, 185–196.

Kokane, C., Babar, S., & Mahalle, P. (2023, March). An Adaptive Algorithm for Polysemous Words in Natural Language Processing. In *Proceedings of Third International Conference on Advances in Computer Engineering and Communication Systems: ICACECS 2022* (pp. 163-172). Singapore: Springer Nature Singapore. 10.1007/978-981-19-9228-5_15

Koul, O. N. (1996). On the standardisation of Kashmiri Script. *Standardisation and Modernisation Dynamics of Language Planning*.

Lafferty, J., McCallum, A., & Pereira, F. C. (2001). *Conditional random fields: Probabilistic models for segmenting and labeling sequence data*. Academic Press.

Lawaye, A. A., & Purkayastha, B. S. (2013). Towards Developing a Hierarchical Part of Speech Tagger for Kashmiri: Hybrid Approach. In *Proceedings of the 2nd National Conference on Advancement in the Era of Multidisciplinary Systems* (pp. 187-192). Academic Press.

Lawaye, A. A., & Purkayastha, B. S. (2014). Kashmir part of speech tagger using CRF. *Computer Science*, *3*(3), 3.

Lone, N. A., Giri, K. J., & Bashir, R. (2022a). Natural Language Processing Resources for the Kashmiri Language. *Indian Journal of Science and Technology*, *15*(43), 2275–2281. doi:10.17485/IJST/v15i43.1964

Lone, N. A., Giri, K. J., & Bashir, R. (2022b). Machine intelligence for language translation from Kashmiri to English. *Journal of Information & Knowledge Management*, 2250074.

Malik, A. B., & Bansal, K. (2015). Named Entity Recognition for Kashmiri Language using Noun Identification and NER Identification Algorithm. *International Journal on Computer Science and Engineering*, *3*(9), 193–197.

McCallum, A., Freitag, D., & Pereira, F. C. (2000, June). Maximum entropy Markov models for information extraction and segmentation. In Icml (Vol. 17, No. 2000, pp. 591-598). Academic Press.

Melamud, O., Goldberger, J., & Dagan, I. (2016, August). context2vec: Learning generic context embedding with bidirectional lstm. In *Proceedings of the 20th SIGNLL conference on computational natural language learning* (pp. 51-61). 10.18653/v1/K16-1006

Meng, F. (2022). Word Sense Disambiguation Based on Graph and Knowledge Base. In *4th EAI International Conference on Robotic Sensor Networks* (pp. 31-41). Springer International Publishing. 10.1007/978-3-030-70451-3_3

Miller, G. A. (1995). WordNet: A lexical database for English. *Communications of the ACM*, *38*(11), 39–41. doi:10.1145/219717.219748

Miller, G. A., Leacock, C., Tengi, R., & Bunker, R. T. (1993). A semantic concordance. *Human Language Technology: Proceedings of a Workshop Held at Plainsboro, New Jersey, March 21-24, 1993.*

Mir, T. A., Lawaye, A. A., Rana, P., & Ahmed, G. (2023). Building Kashmiri Sense Annotated Corpus and its Usage in Supervised Word Sense Disambiguation. *Indian Journal of Science and Technology*, *16*(13), 1021–1029. doi:10.17485/IJST/v16i13.2396

Molina, A., Pla, F., & Segarra, E. (2002, November). A hidden markov model approach to word sense disambiguation. In *Ibero-American Conference on Artificial Intelligence* (pp. 655-663). Springer Berlin Heidelberg. 10.1007/3-540-36131-6_67

Pal, A. R., Saha, D., Dash, N. S., Naskar, S. K., & Pal, A. (2019). A novel approach to word sense disambiguation in Bengali language using supervised methodology. *Sadhana*, *44*(8), 1–12. doi:10.1007/s12046-019-1165-2

Pan, S., & Saha, D. (2019). An automatic identification of function words in TDIL tagged Bengali corpus. *International Journal on Computer Science and Engineering*, *7*(1), 20–27.

Rabiner, L. R. (1989). A tutorial on hidden Markov models and selected applications in speech recognition. *Proceedings of the IEEE*, *77*(2), 257–286. doi:10.1109/5.18626

Raganato, A., Bovi, C. D., & Navigli, R. (2017, September). Neural sequence learning models for word sense disambiguation. In *Proceedings of the 2017 conference on empirical methods in natural language processing* (pp. 1156-1167). 10.18653/v1/D17-1120

Rahman, N., & Borah, B. (2022). An unsupervised method for word sense disambiguation. *Journal of King Saud University. Computer and Information Sciences*, *34*(9), 6643–6651. doi:10.1016/j.jksuci.2021.07.022

Sarma, S. K., Bharali, H., Gogoi, A., Deka, R., & Barman, A. (2012, December). A structured approach for building Assamese corpus: insights, applications and challenges. In *Proceedings of the 10th workshop on Asian language resources* (pp. 21-28). Academic Press.

Sousa, S., Milios, E., & Berton, L. (2020, July). Word sense disambiguation: an evaluation study of semi-supervised approaches with word embeddings. In *2020 International Joint Conference on Neural Networks (IJCNN)* (pp. 1-8). IEEE. 10.1109/IJCNN48605.2020.9207225

Taghipour, K., & Ng, H. T. (2015, July). One million sense-tagged instances for word sense disambiguation and induction. In *Proceedings of the nineteenth conference on computational natural language learning* (pp. 338-344). 10.18653/v1/K15-1037

Verbeke, S. (2018). Some linguistic features of the Old Kashmiri language of the Bāṇāsurakathā. *Acta Orientalia Academiae Scientiarum Hungaricae*, *71*(3), 351–367. doi:10.1556/062.2018.71.3.7

Vial, L., Lecouteux, B., & Schwab, D. (2019). *Sense vocabulary compression through the semantic knowledge of wordnet for neural word sense disambiguation*. arXiv preprint arXiv:1905.05677.

Wali, K., & Koul, O. N. (1997). *Kashmiri: A cognitive-descriptive grammar*. Psychology Press.

Walia, H., Rana, A., & Kansal, V. (2017, September). A Naïve Bayes Approach for working on Gurmukhi Word Sense Disambiguation. In *2017 6th International Conference on Reliability, Infocom Technologies and Optimization (Trends and Future Directions) (ICRITO)* (pp. 432-435). IEEE. 10.1109/ICRITO.2017.8342465

Wang, M., & Wang, Y. (2021, August). Word sense disambiguation: Towards interactive context exploitation from both word and sense perspectives. In *Proceedings of the 59th Annual Meeting of the Association for Computational Linguistics and the 11th International Joint Conference on Natural Language Processing* (Volume 1*: Long Papers)* (pp. 5218-5229). 10.18653/v1/2021.acl-long.406

Wani, S. H. (2014). Divergence patterns in kashmiri-english machine translation: A view from translation of tenses. *Interdisciplinary Journal of Linguistics*, 6.

Wani, S. H. (2021). Kashmiri to English machine translation: A study in translation divergence issues of personal and possessive pronouns. *Indian J Multiling Res Dev*, *2*(1), 1–9. doi:10.34256/ijmrd2111

Yadav, R. K., Jiao, L., Granmo, O. C., & Goodwin, M. (2021, February). Interpretability in Word Sense Disambiguation using Tsetlin Machine. ICAART, (2), 402-409. doi:10.5220/0010382104020409

Yuan, D., Richardson, J., Doherty, R., Evans, C., & Altendorf, E. (2016). *Semi-supervised word sense disambiguation with neural models.* arXiv preprint arXiv:1603.07012.

Zhang, C. X., Liu, R., Gao, X. Y., & Yu, B. (2021). Graph convolutional network for word sense disambiguation. *Discrete Dynamics in Nature and Society*, *2021*, 1–12. doi:10.1155/2021/2822126

KEY TERMS AND DEFINITIONS

Ambiguity: Ambiguity is a concept in NLP that refers to describing circumstances where a lexical term phrase or a sentence might have distinct interpretations. The ambiguity may arise at different levels like lexical level, syntactic level, pragmatic level or semantic level.

Context-Window: Context-Window lists the words that are present in the surrounding of a particular word within a specified range.

Cross-Validation: Cross-validation is a valuable technique that gives a reliable estimate of the performance of the machine learning model. It is helpful in spotting the overfitting issues as well as deciding the relevant parameters and best model for the task at hand.

Machine Learning: Machine learning is a part of Artificial Intelligence concerned with the development of models that let computers learn and make judgments without the requirement of being programmed explicitly. The machine learning models are designed with the aim of elevating their performance through experience or exposure to data.

Natural Language Processing: Natural Language Processing is a derivative of Artificial Intelligence that unfolds the rules to facilitate the interaction between humans and machines. Understanding, generating and interpreting the natural languages by machines just like humans do is the aim objective that NLP fulfills.

Sense-Inventory: Lexical resource that contains the structured set of senses for words. WordNet is considered de facto standard sense inventory for English and has been developed for other languages also.

Word Sense Disambiguation: The task of deciding the most relevant sense of a dubious term that has numerous potential meanings or senses is called word sense disambiguation. This relevant sense of the term is decided by the surrounding words.

Chapter 7
Implementation and Analysis of Shallow Parsing Techniques in Khasi Language

Eusebius Lawai Lyngdoh
North-Eastern Hill University, India

Aiom Minnette Mitri
North-Eastern Hill University, India

Goutam Saha
North-Eastern Hill University, India

Arnab Kumar Maji
https://orcid.org/0000-0002-3320-9965
North-Eastern Hill University, India

ABSTRACT

In the realm of natural language processing (NLP), after part-of-speech (POS) tagging, the subsequent crucial step is shallow parsing. In this endeavour, the authors have undertaken the development of a shallow parser for the Khasi language. The work explores an array of techniques from both traditional machine learning (ML) and modern deep learning (DL) methodologies. They have employed a variety of ML algorithms, including decision trees, logistic regression, support vector machines, random forest, and multinomial naive bayes. Additionally, they have harnessed the power of DL with models such as the vanilla recurrent neural network, long short-term memory network, gated recurrent units, and bidirectional LSTM, all geared towards achieving the shallow parsing objective. The crux of the effort lies in the meticulous comparative analysis of these techniques. The chapter delves into a comprehensive discussion of their individual performances.

DOI: 10.4018/979-8-3693-0728-1.ch007

INTRODUCTION

The primary speakers of the Khasi language are the Khasi tribes in India's Meghalaya region. The Austro-Asian language family, which includes the South-east Asian language Mon Khmer, has a branch called the Khasian branch, which includes the Khasi language (Thabah et al., 2022). Numerous Indian languages have had computational linguistics research done on them, but Khasi has had notably less of it. Thus, the goal of this work is to close this gap by investigating the Khasi language from the standpoint of natural language processing (NLP) and language computation. Parsing is a fundamental NLP phase that involves breaking down phrases into their constituent components and analyzing each one's grammatical structure. Chunking, also known as shallow parsing is a compressed kind of parsing that focuses on identifying specific phrase types without delving deeply into complex syntactic relationships or grammatical accuracy. Shallow parsing may extract structured data from text and perform a surface-level analysis, which makes it suitable for tasks like text summarization and information extraction despite its limitations. This study seeks to contribute to the field of interlanguage communication and linguistic computation by doing research and building NLP tools specifically customized to the Khasi language. The difficulties encountered in successfully tagging Khasi words and performing parsing tasks highlight the significance of more study and the acquisition of more tagged Khasi data in order to achieve higher accuracy and performance of NLP systems for this language.

LITERATURE REVIEW

Osborne (2000) provides a novel method for approaching shallow parsing by viewing it as a POS tagging problem. The method described in the article produces a shallow parsing procedure that is more accurate and efficient by using POS tags to denote chunk boundaries. Experimental findings reveal the potency of this strategy and highlight its potential as a different and computationally effective method for shallow parsing problems. The study advances the topic of shallow parsing and provides insightful information on the connection between POS tagging and shallow parsing.

Sha & Pereira (2003) focuses on the use of CRF model for shallow parsing tasks. In addition to their success in parsing, CRF models are discussed for their ability to capture dependencies between neighbouring word labels. In order to illustrate the promise of CRFs for precise and effective shallow parsing, the paper presents experimental findings that prove that CRF-based models have higher performance when compared to other techniques.

The use of shallow NLP techniques for extracting noun phrases is covered in the paper Subhashini & Kumar (2010). The study investigates various approaches to recognise and extract noun phrases from text, including statistical and rule-based approaches. The evaluation of these methods' accuracy in accurately capturing noun phrases is presented in the paper, demonstrating the potential uses of shallow NLP for noun phrase extraction tasks.

Asopa et al. (2016), outlines the creation and assessment of a rule-based chunker. With a focus on nouns, adverbs, verbs, and adjectives, the chunker has been developed utilising hand generated linguistic rules for various phrases and conjuncts. For annotations, the Indian Languages Chunk Tagset is employed. 500 Hindi sentences have been entered into the chunker and then subject to an HMM tagger evaluation. Precision, recall, and F-measure values of 79.68, 69.36, and 74.16 were attained by the system. Although the rule-based technique proves to be less effective, it is recommended that the system's effectiveness can be increased by producing more chunk rules.

Warjri et al. (2018) present the various POS in Khasi's grammatical structure and 54 tags from the POS tag set have also been published by them. Their work provides a foundation and acts as a background for future computational processing of Khasi language in machine learning (Warjri et al., 2018).

M. J. Tham (2018a) investigates the problems and difficulties of creating an annotated corpus and HMM POS tagger for Khasi. It is found that creating language technology tools for a language with limited resources like Khasi is difficult. However, expanding the annotated corpus to allow for further analysis and combining HMM tagger with the features inherent in the language provides good performance as reported in the literature pertaining to HMM POS taggers.

In the paper "Khasi Shallow Parser" by M. J. Tham (2018b), a shallow parser for the Austro-Asiatic language Khasi is developed, with an emphasis on recognising noun and verb phrase pairs. Khasi noun and verb phrases are created manually and recorded in a corpus of tagged words. The parser, which is developed using a Hidden Markov Model (HMM), produces encouraging results and is an important first step when knowledge of other phrases or potential lexical/syntactic errors is limited.

The paper "NLP tools for Khasi, a low resource language" by M. Tham (2020), describes the creation of NLP tools for the low-resource language Khasi. It has shallow parsers and POS taggers, which enable it to function on par with other Indian languages. The creation of a Khasi corpus, creation of the Khasi tagset, and use of hybrid methods and Hidden Markov Models (HMM) for POS tagging and shallow parsing accuracy are highlighted in the paper.

The usage of a Bidirectional Gated Recurrent Unit (BiGRU) for shallow parsing problems is examined in the study "Bidirectional Gated Recurrent Unit for Shallow Parsing" by M. J. Tham (2020). In order to increase parsing accuracy, the study examines how well BiGRU captures contextual information from both past and future words. The BiGRU based strategy performs better in experiments than other approaches, indicating its potential as a useful tool for shallow parsing problems.

Warjri et al. (2021) discuss Part Of Speech (POS) tagging in the Khasi language and train a conditional random fields (CRF) model with a Khasi POS corpus and achieve accuracy higher in comparison to other state-of-the-art techniques. They find that few words have been tagged incorrectly which may be because of the issue of ambiguity, where the same word may have different tags, and the problem where words are unknown or have not been encountered (Warjri et al., 2021).

DATASET AND PRE-PROCESSING

The corpus that has been utilised in this work for training and testing is the publicly available POS tagged corpus from the BIS tagset for Khasi M. J. Tham (2018a). The corpus consists of 4386 sentences. After processing of the rules, which are elaborated in the Methodology section that follows, on the BIS tagset for Khasi M. J. Tham (2018b), the total count of the Noun Phrases is 12395 and the total count of Verb Phrases is 17474. The total count of tokens outside phrases is 46713. Using the machine learning models from Scikit learn (Pedregosa et al., 2011), as a pre-processing step, for each word in the input sentence, we extract features such as token, lowercase version of the token, previous token, POS tag and previous token's POS tag and we employ a python dictionary for storing them which is as shown in Figure 1. A special case is when the token happens to be that of the sentence's first word where the 'prev token' and 'prev pos tag' will then, not be present.

The example above shows that the word "Slem" is the current token to be parsed, its lower case is "slem", the preceding token is "Katno", the POS tag is "RB" and the preceding token's POS tag is "RB".

We implement the RNN models using the keras Chollet et al. (2015) open source library. The training data is prepared such that the length of the input data sequence should be fixed. We fix the input sequence length to the length of the longest sentence. Sentences which are shorter are padded with zeros at the beginning for both the training and testing data. Each input word and each output tag is given a distinct integer, which is how each individual integer in the input and output data is indexed. Word embedding has been used, which enables efficient sequence handling, and the vector size is 100 for each input token (Pennington et al., 2014).

Figure 1. Feature of a token "slem"

```
{ 'token' : 'slem' ,
'lower_cased_token' : 'slem' ,
'prev_token' : 'Katno' ,
'pos_tag' : 'RB' ,
'prev_pos_token' : 'RB' }
```

METHODOLOGY

Ramshaw & Marcus (1995), propose a method for parsing using BIO tagging technique where BIO is the abbreviation for Beginning, Inside, Outside. BIO tagging can only be applied to a corpus where POS tagging has been done. A description of BIO tags is as follows, B-XX: labels a word that begins a chunk of type XX, I-XX: labels a word contained within a block of type XX. O: labels a word that is not part of any chunk.

Here "XX", is simply a placeholder for the exact chunk label that is utilized. It helps in distinguishing distinct types of chunks within a sequence.

We have utilized the publicly available Khasi POS tagged corpus M. J. Tham (2022), that uses the BIS tagset, to further tag the annotated corpus with noun and verb chunks for this work. The task of BIO tagging has been done manually on a corpus size of 4386 Khasi sentences. The shallow parser is then trained on this annotated corpus.

Rules for Shallow Parsing in Khasi Language

Grammatical and syntactic rules of the language have been extracted from renowned Khasi grammar publications. We have used 15 of those rules for our work and have focused only on noun phrases and verb phrases. We elaborate the rules for labelling chunks of nouns and verbs as follows:

- A noun phrase's basic building block, according to Jyrwa (1989), is a pronominal marker (PM), which functions as a number/gender marker, a noun word, and then a subject enclitic (SE). Jyrwa's description of this structure emphasizes the crucial elements that constitute a fundamental noun phrase in the subject context. (M. J. Tham, 2018b).
- Adjectives can take on a variety of roles in Khasi sentences, and they are only counted as part of a noun chunk if they come right before or right after the noun they modify (M. J. Tham, 2018b).
- A Khasi noun chunk may contain demonstratives, cardinal numbers, quantifiers, pronominal markers, distributive particles, and adjectives as pre-modifiers. However, a pronominal marker is occasionally dropped in Khasi. These include verb followed noun clauses, locative expressions, and vocative sentences. In these cases, a noun chunk is only the noun word itself, without the pronominal marker (M. J. Tham, 2018b).
- In Khasi, it is usual for two or more nouns to be used together, with the combined meaning deriving from the total of the separate terms. These noun collocations are categorised as belonging to the same noun chunk since they can function as pre or post modifiers within a noun phrase. When they follow a noun, verbs that have been designated as nouns also contribute to these collocations and become a component of the noun phrase (M. J. Tham, 2018b).
- When a noun is followed by a verb, the verb joins the noun phrase that includes the preceding noun. Except in cases of stylistic writing when repetition occurs without the necessity for punctuation, it is generally suggested to use a comma (,) to separate a noun from the verb that follows it. In such circumstances, the verb is joined to the noun that comes before rather than the word that is repeated (M. J. Tham, 2018b).
- Imitative words are created in the Khasi language by joining a string of words whose pronunciations are phonetically related to each other, such as ancestor and successor. The aesthetic aspects of certain words, such as their sound patterns or rhythmic effect, are chosen more often than their semantic meaning (M. J. Tham, 2018b).
- A term that is imitative may be made up of an ancestor and a successor, each having a unique pronominal marker. The ancestor and successor are treated as discrete noun chunks in these instances, denoting different grammatical units inside the phrase. But, occasionally, the pronominal marker only appears before the ancestor and not the successor. In these situations, the entire phrase

is taken into account as a single noun chunk, highlighting how closely related the ancestor and successor are and how their meanings are unified (M. J. Tham, 2018b).

- The word "bad" can be used as a substitute for the English word "and" in Khasi and can also be a part of a noun phrase. The exact context will determine whether or not it belongs to the noun chunk. The conjunction "bad" may be left out of the noun chunk if the pronominal marker comes before the second word, designating a separate noun chunk. This demonstrates that the allowed pre-modifiers for Khasi noun chunks are restricted to the particular elements described before and do not overlap with the conjunction (M. J. Tham, 2018b).
- A possessive marker in Khasi is represented by the word "la". It is classified as a noun chunk member because it can appear as the initial component of a noun phrase when the noun phrase is the subject of a preposition or a verb. As a result, "la" can be used to denote a possessive connection within the noun chunk, denoting ownership or possession (M. J. Tham, 2018b).
- In Khasi, a basic verb phrase can indeed consist of just the main verb or include preceding auxiliaries. For example, the verb "bam" means "eat" and can function as a standalone verb phrase. However, it can also be accompanied by the auxiliary "la" to form the verb phrase "la bam," which conveys the meaning of "have eaten." The inclusion of auxiliaries in the verb phrase provides additional information about tense, aspect, or other grammatical features (M. J. Tham, 2018b).
- There are times when a major verb is absent from a Khasi sentence and just an auxiliary verb is present. In these situations, only the auxiliary verb is present in the verb chunk. In other words, the auxiliary verb serves as a stand-alone component in the verb phrase (M. J. Tham, 2018b).
- Two consecutive verbs are treated as two different verb chunks in Khasi when they appear in a phrase. This implies that each verb is viewed as a distinct part of the verb phrase. For instance, the words "sdang" and "hap" are regarded as different verb chunks in the phrase "sdang hap," which means "starts falling." The second word "hap" denotes the action of falling, whereas the first verb "sdang" denotes the action of starting (M. J. Tham, 2018b).
- A separate verb chunk is considered to be the infinitive phrase in Khasi, which consists of the infinitive "ban" (to) up to the main verb. This means that the entire phrase, including any auxiliary verbs that may appear between "ban" and the main verb, is regarded as a single unit in the verb phrase (M. J. Tham, 2018b).
- The inclusion or absence of the conjunction "bad" as a component of a verb chunk in Khasi follows a similar pattern to the formation of noun chunks.

Similar to how noun chunks include the conjunction "bad" when it is connected to both the ancestor and the successor, verb chunks also include the conjunction when it is connected to both the preceding and the following verb (M. J. Tham, 2018b).

- Tokens in the corpus that do not belong to the verb chunks, noun chunks, or other designated chunks are identified by the "O" tag. These tokens are outside of the specified chunks and do not have any particular labelling or grouping attached to them, according to this tag. When chunking or labelling operations are being performed, the "O" tag is frequently used to designate tokens that do not fall into any preset categories or patterns (M. J. Tham, 2018b).

In our chunk tagset, we have designated the noun phrase as NP and verb phrase as VP as in Table 1. Rules that generate noun phrases are shown in Table 2 while those that generate verb phrases are as shown in Table 3 respectively.

Table 1. Description of Indian language chunk tagset

Sl. No.	Chunk	Description
1.	NP	Noun Phrase
2.	VP	Verb Phrase

Table 2. Rules for noun phrase

S. No.	Chunk
1.	NP ->JJ N NN
2.	NP ->JJ N NNP
3.	NP ->JJ N NST
4.	NP ->PR PRP M N NN JJ
5.	NP ->PR PRP M N NNP JJ
6.	NP ->PR PRP M N NNP JJ

In Table 2 the Common Noun is represent by N NN tag, N NNP tag for Proper Noun, N NST tag for Nloc Noun, JJ tag for Adjective and PR PRP M tag is for Pronominal Personal Pronoun. While In Table 3, the V VM tag is for the Main Verb, V VAUX tag is for Auxiliary Verb and V VAUX VINF tag is for Infinitive Auxiliary Verb.

Table 3. Rules for verb phrase

Sl. No.	Chunk
1.	VP ->V VAUX V VM
2.	VP ->V VM
3.	VP ->V VAUX VINF

We demonstrate the steps to create the chunk dataset to train the different models as a block diagram in Figure 2.

Figure 2. The steps involved in the development of chunk dataset

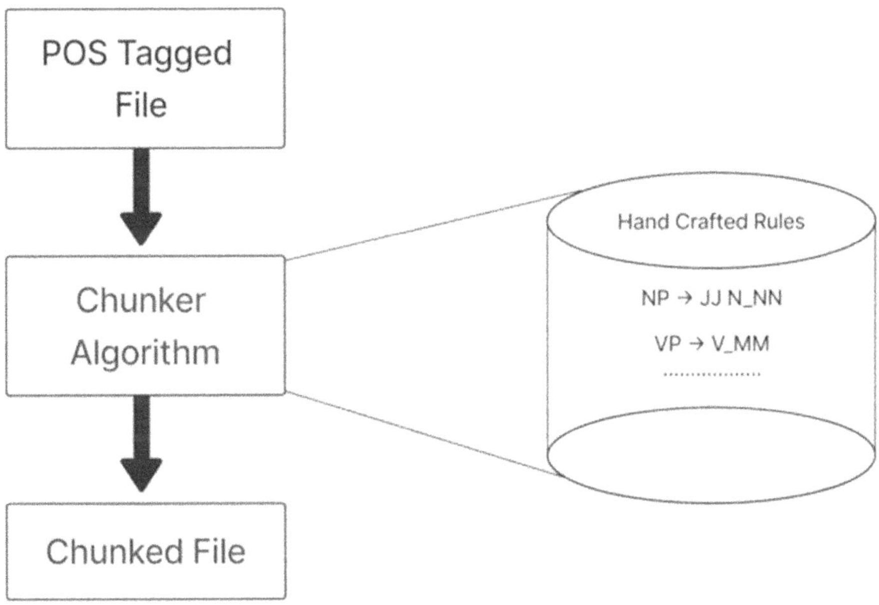

Background of the Models Employed

For our experiment, we train the corpus on different models, namely, Hidden Markov Model (HMM), Conditional Random Fields (CRF), Naives Bayes, Logistic regression, Support Vector Machine (SVM), Decision Tree, Random Forest, Vanilla RNN, Long short-term memory (LSTM), Gated Recurrent Units (GRUs) and Bidirectional LSTM(BiLSTM). A detailed description of each of the models employed is given as follows.

Hidden Markov Model (HMM)

A statistical model called the HMM is used to create tag sequences. It determines the most probable tag sequences. The transition probability is calculated as a result. The likelihood of a transition between two tags, such as a forward tag and a backward tag is represented by the transition probability. The sequence is used as an input, and the transition probability is typically estimated based on the previous and subsequent tags (Kanakaraddi & Nandyal, 2018).

Conditional Random Fields (CRFs)

A CRF is a sequence modelling technique used to locate objects or textual patterns, such as POS tags. Additionally to believing that features are interdependent, future observations are also taken into account while learning a pattern. In terms of performance, it is considered the best method for entity recognition. We employ features that are modelled from the data to feed into the CRF since these models consider the prior data. These feature functions describe specific aspects of the sequence that the data point represents, such as the tag order B-NP-> I-NP.

Naive Bayes

The Multinomial Naive Bayes algorithm (MultinomialNB) is a Bayesian learning approach popular in Natural Language Processing. The Bayes theorem is employed by the programs to determine the tag of a text, such as an email or a news story. It computes the probability of each tag for a given sample and out- puts the tag with the greatest likelihood (Bulusu & Sucharita, 2019). Using the grid search to find the best combination of hyper parameters and K-Fold cross validation from Scikit-learn (Pedregosa et al., 2011), we find that for Multinomial Naive Bayes the best value for the regularization hyper parameter, alpha, is 0.1.

Logistic Regression

Among the best-known algorithms for machine learning, categorized as supervised learning, is logistic regression. It predicts the category of the dependent variable using a collection of independent variables (Pedregosa et al., 2011). Logistic regression predicts a dependent categorical variable's output. It provides probability numbers between 0 and 1 since the result must be discrete or categorical. The dependent variable in multinomial logistic regression may be any one of three or more potential unordered kinds, such as "O," "NP," or "VP". For our work the best value for the hyper parameter, inverse regularization strength, C, is 1.The smaller the values of C the higher the regularization.

Support Vector Machine (SVM)

The SVM algorithm seeks to identify the most effective decision boundary or line that can categorize n-dimensional space into classes, enabling quick classification of following data points. The phrase "hyper plane" refers to the ideal decision boundary. SVM chooses the extreme points and vectors to form the hyper plane. The Support Vector Machine technique gets its name from the vectors used to represent these extreme cases (Support Vector Machine, n.d.). SVMs have been claimed to perform better at text classification, despite long training time (Morwal et al., 2012). In this work, it is found that the best value of the hyper parameter, C is 1 with a linear kernel.

Decision Tree

Both classification and regression problems are handled using a decision tree, a non-parametric supervised learning technique. Its hierarchical tree structure consists of leaf nodes, internal nodes, branches, and a root node (Decision tree, n.d.). We set the following hyper parameter values,

criterion (a hyper parameter that determines a split's quality) = log loss,
max features (number of features for the best split) = log2 and,
min samples split (minimal number of samples necessary to separate an internal node) = 3.

Random Forest

The Random Forest classifier uses numerous decision trees to different subsets of the input dataset and aggregates the results to enhance the estimated accuracy of the dataset. It takes shorter training time than other algorithms (Random Forest, n.d.). Even with a big dataset, it runs efficiently and predicts the outcome with excellent accuracy. At tree leaves, an RF classifier assigns class probabilities. It examines every tree and adds the leaf distributions before classifying. By choosing random node tests and employing various data subsets for each tree, randomness is added. The data and predictors will determine how many trees are required. It is simple to use and has few parameters (Boateng et al., 2020). Decision trees (DTs), which are a component of RF, use conditions to classify input for each tree. Due to its adaptability to numerous data kinds and applications, RF is widely utilized and very adaptable (Boateng et al., 2020). For our work we set the following hyper parameter values,

criterion (a hyper parameter that determines a split's quality) = log loss,
max features (number of features for the best split) = log2 and,
min samples split (minimal number of samples necessary to separate an internal node) = 3.

Recurrent Neural Network

Recurrent neural networks (RNN) are a kind of neural network in which the results of earlier phases are used as input in the current phase. RNN has many variants, which include Vanilla RNN, Long short-term memory (LSTM), Gated recurrent units (GRUs) and Bidirectional LSTM (BiLSTM).

Traditional deep neural networks often assume that inputs and outputs are independent, while recurrent neural networks create outputs by taking into ac- count data from earlier parts in the sequence. Recurrent neural networks use the context of prior inputs to form their outputs in contrast to ordinary neural networks, which regard each input as a discrete, unconnected input. Although unidirectional recurrent neural networks might be helpful in predicting the out- come of a given sequence, they are unable to take into account future events in their predictions. (Long short-term memory (LSTM), n.d.). Because it contains feedback connections, LSTM can analyze the entire sequence of data. This has uses in speech recognition, automated translation, etc. The vanishing gradient issue associated with a conventional recurrent neural network is what the GRU (Gated Recurrent Unit) seeks to address. Due to their similar designs and occasionally identically excellent results, GRU and LSTM can both be seen as variations of one another (Gated recurrent unit, n.d.).

The main difference between the LSTM and BiLSTM designs is the bidirectional processing of the BiLSTM. Both architectures share comparable parts and methods. The BiLSTM is better equipped to detect complex connections in sequential data because of its bidirectional approach's ability to take information into account from both sides. In both architectures, the fundamental concepts of gates, activation functions, and peephole connections hold true, demonstrating their efficiency in information management and prediction (Kawakami, 2008). Bidirectional LSTMs process the data in both ways inside two hidden layers before pushing the results toward a single output layer. This ability empowers bidirectional LSTMs to catch and use long-range setting data from both the past and future bearings while handling successive information (Bidirectional LSTMs, n.d.).

Figure 3. LSTM model

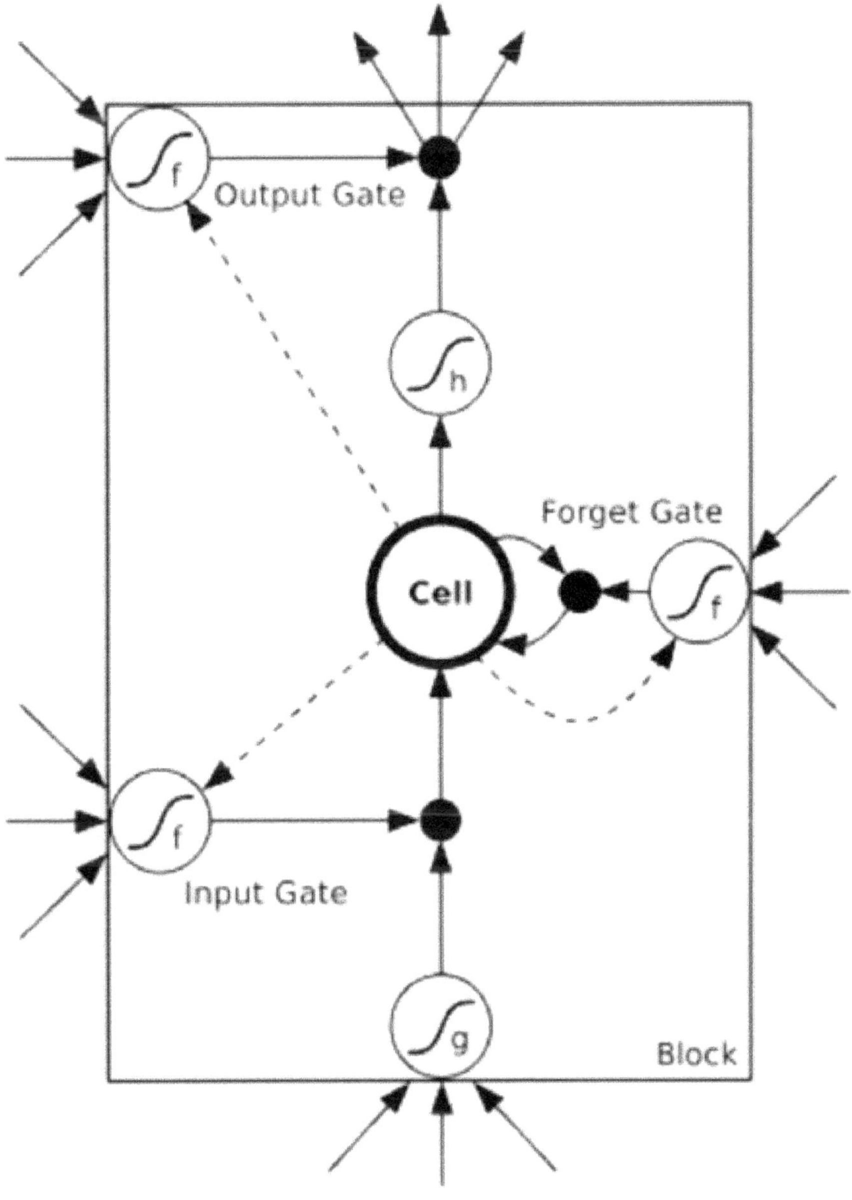

Figure 4. BiLSTM model (Bidirectional LSTMs, n.d.)

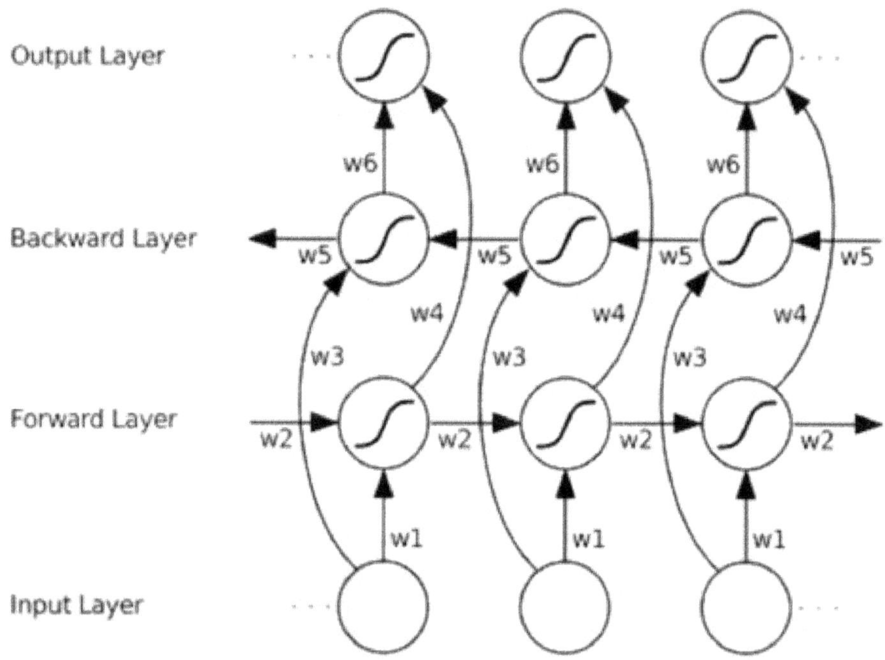

EXPERIMENTAL RESULTS AND ANALYSIS

We experiment with HMM and CRF and various Scikit-learn machine learning models which include Decision Tree, Logistic regression, SVM, Random forest and Multinomial Naive Bayes (MultinomialNB) classifier on Tham's Khasi corpus (M. J. Tham, 2022). We split the corpus into two parts - 80% for training and the 20% for validation.

A comparison of the outcomes from various models is shown in Table 4.

From the Table 4 it is seen that the HMM model achieves an accuracy of 96.79%, whereas the CRF model achieves an accuracy of 95.64%. Taggers that utilize ML models achieve accuracy ranging from 85% - 95% with Decision tree reporting 94.49%, Logistic Regression, 93.35%, SVM 85.72%, Random Forest, 92.76% and Multinomial NB reporting 88.7% accuracies. Decision tree achieves the highest accuracy among these ML models. Various RNN models have also been implemented, including Vanilla RNN, Long short-term memory (LSTM), Gated recurrent units (GRUs) and Bidirectional LSTM (BiLSTM) on M. J. Tham (2022) Khasi corpus. For the train-validation data split, we utilise the same proportion as before.

Table 4. Performance of HMM, CRF, machine learning, and deep learning models on M. J. Tham (2022) Khasi corpus

S No.	Model	Precision	Recall	F1 - Score	Accuracy (%)
1.	HMM	0.97	0.97	0.98	96.79
2.	CRF	0.93	0.94	0.93	95.64
3.	Decision Tree	0.93	0.91	0.92	94.49
4.	Logistic Regression	0.96	0.93	0.91	93.35
5.	SVM	0.32	0.75	0.67	85.72
6.	Random Forest	0.95	0.86	0.91	92.76
7.	Multinomial NB	0.89	0.91	0.89	92.10
8.	VNN	0.79	0.86	0.83	85.68
9.	LSTM	0.99	0.99	0.99	99.67
10.	GRU	0.99	0.99	0.99	99.69
11	Bi LSTM	0.99	0.99	0.99	99.67

A Comparative Analysis With Existing System

In this section, we make a comparative analysis with the existing work on Shallow Parsing in Khasi Language found in the literature that has been developed by M. J. Tham (2018b), developed a Shallow parser using HMM (M. J. Tham, 2018b).

Table 5. Comparison with M. J. Tham (2018b) HMM

	Precision (%)	Recall (%)	F1 Score
M. J. Tham (2018b) HMM	94.39	96.65	95.51
HMM	97.75	97.75	98.00
CRF	93.0	94.0	93.75
Decision Tree	93.5	91.25	92.5
Logistic Regression	96.0	93.0	90.5
SVM	83.0	75.25	75.25
Random Forest	95.75	86.75	91.0

Figure 5. Comparison with M. J. Tham (2018b) HMM

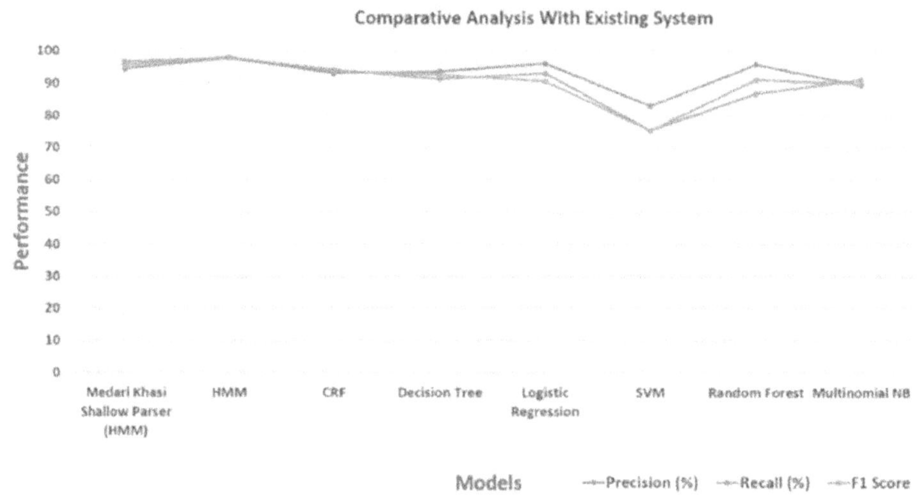

The HMM model used in our work gives higher values compared to same model used in M. J. Tham (2018b). The reason is because M. J. Tham (2018b) takes only the POS tag as input data whereas in our work the input data consists of the word and its associated POS tag. The use of this word-tag pair for input data, as proposed by Osborne (2000), shows that it gives better results than using only the POS tag or just the word.

M. J. Tham (2020) develop a shallow parser using Bidirectional gated recurrent unit. Here the author uses only POS tags as input data where the output data consist of a concatenation of POS tags as well as the chunk tag. A comparison of the results reported by M. J. Tham (2020) with our results is depicted in Table 6.

Table 6. Comparison with M. J. Tham (2020) BiGRU model

Models	Precision (%)	Recall (%)	F1 Score
M. J. Tham (2020) Bi- GRU 256 neurons	98.79	99.03	98.91
VNN	80.75	86.75	83.75
LSTM	99.75	99.75	99.75
GRU	99.75	99.75	99.75
BiLSTM	99.75	99.75	99.5

Our Recurrent Neural Network (RNN) models employ 64 neurons, in contrast to the utilization of 256 neurons by M. J. Tham (2020). Our experimentation with various neuron counts indicates that the number of neurons has no discernible impact on model performance. Consequently, the optimal count of 64 neurons has been adopted, resulting in parameter reduction. The diminished efficacy of the VNN model relative to others can be attributed to the vanishing gradient problem and constrained memory span. Our work exhibits better performance in precision, recall, and F1 score compared to Tham's BiGRU model. A noteworthy inclusion in our approach is the incorporation of word embeddings, which facilitate accurate data feature capture. Additionally, our model demonstrates proficiency in identifying instances of new words not already present in the vocabulary.

CONCLUSION

In this work we have investigated the significance of parsing, specifically focusing on shallow parsing or chunking, as an effective technique for analyzing grammatical structures within sentences. Diverse machine learning (ML) models, including Decision Tree, Logistic Regression, Support Vector Machines (SVM), Random Forest, and Multinomial Naive Bayes (MultinomialNB), have been assessed in this investigation. Notably, the Decision Tree model stands out with the highest accuracy of 94.49%.

Furthermore, recurrent neural network (RNN) models, namely Vanilla RNN (VNN), Long Short-Term Memory (LSTM), Gated Recurrent Units (GRUs), and Bidirectional LSTM (BiLSTM), have also been incorporated. The RNN models consistently outperform others, exhibiting accuracy rates ranging from 85% to 99%. The individual performance metrics for these RNN models are as follows: VNN achieves an accuracy of 85.68%, LSTM attains 99.67%, GRU achieves 99.69%, and BiLSTM demonstrates 99.67% accuracy.

Through comparative analysis against existing models in the literature for Khasi, as discussed in the preceding sections, our models emerge with heightened performance levels. They exhibit the capacity to proficiently perform parsing and analysis of the Khasi language with a notably enhanced degree of accuracy.

REFERENCES

Asopa, S., Asopa, P., Mathur, I., & Joshi, N. (2016). Rule based chunker for hindi. In *2016 2nd international conference on contemporary computing and informatics (ic3i)* (pp. 442–445). 10.1109/IC3I.2016.7918005

Bidirectional LSTMS. (n.d.). https://intellipaat.com/blog/what-is-lstm/

Boateng, E. Y., Otoo, J., & Abaye, D. A. (2020). Basic tenets of classifica- tion algorithms k-nearest-neighbor, support vector machine, random forest and neural network: A review. *Journal of Data Analysis and Information Processing*, *8*(4), 341–357. doi:10.4236/jdaip.2020.84020

Bulusu, A., & Sucharita, V. (2019). Research on machine learning techniques for pos tagging in nlp. *International Journal of Recent Technology and Engineering, 8*(1S4).

Chollet, F., (2015). *Keras.* GitHub. Retrieved from https://github.com/ fchollet/keras

Decision tree. (n.d.). https://www.ibm.com/in-en/topics/decision-trees#:~:text=A\%20 decision\%20tree\%20is\%20a,internal\%20nodes\%20and\%20leaf\%20nodes

Gated Recurrent Unit. (n.d.). https://towardsdatascience.com/understanding-gru-networks-2ef37df6c9be

Jyrwa, M. B. (1989). *A descriptive study of the noun phrase in Khasi. Academic Press.*

Kanakaraddi, S. G., & Nandyal, S. S. (2018). Survey on parts of speech tagger techniques. In 2018 International Conference on Current Trends Towards Converging Technologies (ICCTCT).

Kawakami, K. (2008). *Supervised sequence labelling with recurrent neural networks* [Unpublished doctoral dissertation]. Technical University of Munich.

Long Short-Term Memory (LSTM). (n.d.). https://www.ibm.com/cloud/learn/ recurrent-neural-networks#toc-variant-rn-2xvhbyi.

Morwal, S., Jahan, N., & Chopra, D. (2012). *Named entity recognition using hidden markov model (hmm). International Journal on Natural Language Computing* (Vol. 1). IJNLC.

Osborne, M. (2000). Shallow parsing as part-of-speech tagging. *Fourth Conference on Computational Natural Language Learning and the Second Learning Language in Logic Workshop.* 10.3115/1117601.1117636

Pedregosa, F., Varoquaux, G., Gramfort, A., Michel, V., Thirion, B., & Grisel, O. (2011). Scikit-learn: Machine learning in python. *Journal of Machine Learning Research, 12*, 2825–2830.

Pennington, J., Socher, R., & Manning, C. (2014, October). GloVe: Global vectors for word representation. In *Proceedings of the 2014 conference on empirical methods in natural language processing (EMNLP)* (pp. 1532–1543). Association for Computational Linguistics. doi:10.3115/v1/D14-1162

Ramshaw, L., & Marcus, M. (1995). Text chunking using transformation- based learning. In *Third workshop on very large corpora.* Retrieved from https://aclanthology.org/W95-0107

Random forest. (n.d.). https://www.ibm.com/cloud/learn/random-forest

Sha, F., & Pereira, F. (2003). *Shallow parsing with conditional random fields.* Academic Press.

Subhashini, R., & Kumar, V. J. S. (2010). Shallow nlp techniques for noun phrase extraction. In Trendz in information sciences & computing (tisc2010) (pp. 73–77). doi:10.1109/TISC.2010.5714612

Support vector machine. (n.d.). https://www.analyticsvidhya.com/blog/ 2017/09/understaing-support-vector-machine-example-code/

Thabah, N. D. J., Mitri, A. M., Saha, G., Maji, A. K., & Purkayastha, B. S. (2022). A deep connection to khasi language through pre-trained embedding. *Innovations in Systems and Software Engineering*, 1–15. doi:10.1007/s11334-022-00497-9

Tham, M. (2020). Nlp tools for khasi, a low resource language. In *Proceedings of the 17th international conference on natural language processing (icon): System demonstrations* (pp. 26–27). Academic Press.

Tham, M. J. (2018a). Challenges and issues in developing an annotated corpus and hmm pos tagger for khasi. *The 15th international conference on natural language processing.*

Tham, M. J. (2018b). Khasi shallow parser. In *Proceedings of the 15th interna- tional conference on natural language processing (icon 2018). patiala, punjab, india* (pp. 43–49). Academic Press.

Tham, M. J. (2020). Bidirectional gated recurrent unit for shallow parsing. *Indian Journal of Computer Science and Engineering*, *11*(5), 517 521. doi:10.21817/indjcse/2020/v11i5/201105167

Tham, M. J. (2022). *Tham khasi annotated corpus.* https://catalog.elra.info/en- us/repository/browse/ELRA-W0321/

Warjri, S., Pakray, P., Lyngdoh, S., & Kumar Maji, A. (2018). Khasi language as dominant part-of-speech (pos) ascendant in nlp. *International Journal of Computational Intelligence & IoT*, *1*(1).

Warjri, S., Pakray, P., Lyngdoh, S. A., & Maji, A. K. (2021). Part-of-speech (pos) tagging using conditional random field (crf) model for khasi corpora. *International Journal of Speech Technology*, *24*(4), 853–864. doi:10.1007/s10772-021-09860-w

Chapter 8
Named Entity Recognition (NER) in Low Resource Languages of Ho

Satya Ranjan Dash
https://orcid.org/0000-0002-7902-1183
KIIT University, India

Bikram Biruli
KISS University, India

Yasobanta Das
KISS University, India

Prosper Abel Mgimwa
Real Hope Secondary School, Mafinga, Tanzania

Muhammed Abdur Rahmaan Kamaldeen
KIIT University, India

Aloka Fernando
University of Moratuwa, Sri Lanka

ABSTRACT

The Ho tribe is an indigenous community that primarily inhabits the Indian states of Odisha, Jharkhand, West Bengal, Assam, and Chhattisgarh. The Ho language, which belongs to the Austroasiatic language of Munda family, is their primary means of communication. Warang Chiti is the script for writing Ho language. Creating user-friendly tools, applications, and resources that support Ho language users in various aspects, such as typing, spell-checking, dictionary lookup, text conversion between UNICODE and 8-bit encodings, speech-to-text, and text-to-speech translation, this

DOI: 10.4018/979-8-3693-0728-1.ch008

chapter discusses data augmentation techniques, transfer learning methods, domain adaptation strategies, and the importance of resource creation. It also emphasizes the need for collaborative efforts and community-driven initiatives to advance NER research in low resource language settings.

1. INTRODUCTION

The HO tribe is an indigenous community that primarily inhabits the Indian states of Odisha, Jharkhand, West Bengal, Assam and Chhattisgarh. Their population is 5 million. The Ho language, which belongs to the Austroasiatic language of Munda family, is their primary means of communication (Kumar & Kumar, 2019). Warang Chiti is the script for writing Ho language. Pandit Lako Bodra created Warang Chiti Script in 1954. Jharkhand tribes are primarily found in the eastern and western parts of Singhbhum Ranchi, Dumka, Hazaribagh, Palamu, and Giridih. According to the 2011 census, the total ST population in the state is 8,645,042, with rural areas having 7,868,130 and urban areas having 776,892. Scheduled tribes accounted for 26.3% of the population in 2001.

The Ho community is a notable Munda tribe in India, predominantly centred in the Chotanagpur Plateau area. They have a rich cultural legacy, including traditional traditions, festivals, and ceremonies. They are noted for their art, music, and dancing, showing their affinity for nature and agrarian methods. Social cohesiveness is a fundamental part of their communal life. Historically, the Ho people have been involved in agriculture, farming crops like rice, millet, and pulses, and manufacturing handicrafts like jewellery and textiles.

However, due to the lack of documentation and language resources, the Ho language is currently facing the threat of extinction. Therefore, there is a growing interest in applying NLP and NER techniques to the Ho language to preserve and document this endangered language. This paper presents a survey of existing work in this area, along with future research directions. Named Entity Recognition (NER) in low resource languages presents unique challenges due to limited annotated data and linguistic resources. This research article investigates the specific difficulties associated with NER in low resource languages and explores various approaches and solutions to address these challenges. The article discusses data augmentation techniques, transfer learning methods, domain adaptation strategies, and the importance of resource creation (Das & Mandal, 2020). It also emphasizes the need for collaborative efforts and community-driven initiatives to advance NER research in low resource language settings. There are several different tribes represented in Odisha's population, with the Kolha, Ho, and Munda tribes having the largest populations. Odisha is also home to a number of additional indigenous cultures in addition to these tribes. There is a sizable community of the Kolha tribe in the state, which is renowned for its distinctive cultural legacy. The Ho tribe, with its own language and customs, is also well-represented (Mohanty, 2008). The Munda tribe, known for their extensive cultural traditions, also makes up a portion of Odisha's tribal population. Other indigenous tribes, each with a unique character, also live in Odisha besides the Kolha, Ho, and Munda tribes. The Santal, Oraon, Kondh, Gond, Juang, and several more tribes are among them (Das, 2015). Each tribe has its own unique language, culture, and traditions, which add to the state's rich cultural diversity. These tribes are spread out throughout various areas of Odisha in terms of population. While certain tribes are mostly found in a few districts, others are dispersed among several districts. Odisha is a key centre of indigenous communities in India as a result of the variety of its tribal inhabitants, which adds to the state's cultural richness and legacy (Behera, 2017).

The foundation of human culture and identity is language, which embodies millennia of knowledge, tradition, and history (Panda, 2018). Unfortunately, many indigenous languages are slowly dying out in the face of globalisation and dominant languages, putting the priceless information they contain in peril (Das, 2021). One such endangered language is Ho, a tribal tongue spoken mostly by the Ho tribe in the Indian state of Jharkhand and nearby areas (Tribal Research Institute).

The Ho language is a valuable storehouse of indigenous knowledge since it has a distinctive linguistic structure and a vibrant oral tradition (Tribal Language Development Authority). However, the preservation and recording of the Ho language have encountered significant difficulties as a result of numerous socioeconomic issues and constrained technical resources.

1.1. Named Entity Recognition (NER)

The Named Entity Recognition (NER) is a subtask of natural language processing (NLP) that includes detecting and categorising entities inside a text into present categories such as individuals, organizations, places, dates, numerical values, and other particular sorts of entities. The fundamental purpose of NER is to extract structured information from unstructured text material. The Named Entity Recognition (NER) (Jain, 2019) job (Konkol et al., 2015; Marrero et al., 2013; Rao et al., 2015) is a challenging automated sequence labelling problem that entails identifying names and categorising them into groups. Identification entails indicating the existence of Named Entities (NEs), which were once restricted to proper nouns but are now inclusive of other noun types and associated tags inside a particular text corpus, as we address in this thesis. Classification is the process of putting recognised NEs into distinct categories. Some examples of these NE categories include: Person name, such as first name, middle name, and last name; Location name, such as village, town, city, state, region, and continent; Organisation name, such as government agency, private sector, and company names; and Miscellaneous names, such as date, time, distance, quantity, and percent, respectively.

When identified entities are seen to be more significant than the acts they carry out, NER is advised. According to Friburger et al. (Friburger et al., 2002), entities make up around 10% of news items in both English and French. In numerous exciting Natural Language Processing (NLP) application areas, such as Question Answering (Wang et al., 2017), Machine Translation (Babych & Hartley, 2003), Text Summarization (Gupta & Lehal, 2011), Information Retrieval (Chen et al., 1998), Word Sense Disambiguation (Moro et al., 2014), Coreference Resolution (Dimitrov et al., 2005), Semantic Search (Han & Zhao, 2010), social media (Jung, 2012), Information Linking (Derczynski et al., 2015), and others, NE recognition has been successfully applied over the years.

1.2. Significance of NER

Information Extraction: NER plays a critical role in extracting important information from enormous amounts of text data. By detecting and categorising named items, NER aids in translating unstructured text into structured data that can be conveniently studied.

Enhanced Search and Retrieval: NER increases search engines' performance by letting users to obtain more relevant and detailed information. For example, a search query for "Apple" may be adjusted to differentiate between the technological business and the fruit.

Knowledge Graph Construction: NER is crucial in generating knowledge graphs, which reflect interactions between items. By detecting entities and their relationships in a text, NER contributes to constructing a structured knowledge base.

Text summarising: In the context of text summarising, NER helps identify essential entities and events, enabling the development of short and useful summaries. This is especially important for rapidly comprehending the major aspects of a paper.

Question Answering Systems: NER is crucial for question-answering systems. It helps identify the entities relevant to a user's query, helping the extraction of accurate and contextually suitable replies from a corpus of text.

Event Extraction: Identifying entities in a text enables for the extraction of events and their participants. NER is a vital component of event extraction systems, contributing in the knowledge of who did what, where, and when.

Entity attaching and Disambiguation: NER aids in attaching named entities to knowledge bases and disambiguating between entities with similar names. This verifies that the proper entity is connected with the recognised name.

Information Retrieval for Business Intelligence: In business intelligence and analytics, NER aids in extracting insights from unstructured text data, such as news articles, social media, and customer evaluations. This might be important for identifying market trends, rival actions, and client attitudes.

Legal and Regulatory Compliance: NER is used in legal and regulatory areas to detect and categorize organisations referenced in documents. This is critical for compliance, contract analysis, and due diligence activities.

Customization for Domain-Specific Applications: NER systems may be adjusted for domain-specific applications, making them suitable to numerous industries such as healthcare, banking, and legal services.

NER has a significant influence on society and makes it possible to track trends (Xian-Yi et al., 2010) in the textual media that are regularly created by a variety of organisations as well as by people. The Twitter-based systems can presently use NER in a variety of languages. (Baksa et al., 2016; Lopez et al., 2017).

The purpose of this thesis is to systematically investigate various attributes and various named entity recognition strategies in Hindi. In order to achieve this, we examine the NER systems for several Indian languages and for foreign languages in depth before examining the NER system for Hindi.

1.3. Named Entity Recognition (NER) In Various Languages

On a variety of corpora, NER systems are successfully created for the resource-rich English language (Leaman & Lu, 2016; Shaalan & Raza, 2008). Examples include the following: EMLMED—medical emails; WRISCI—written scientific texts; SPOREL—spoken religious texts; SPOMISC—spoken miscellaneous texts; NCBI—disease corpus; CDR—chemical disease connection; and provide performance assessment metric—F-measure of 82%–95%. NER systems are created for languages other than English as well.

By labelling each outgoing connection with NEs of the target article, Nothman et al. (Nothman et al., 2013) demonstrate a method to automatically produce NE annotation in five languages, including English, German, Spanish, Dutch, and Russian from Wikipedia. This method achieves Fmeasure of 94.9% on coarse NEs and 89.9% on fine-grained NEs, respectively. For the purpose of classifying the articles, they make use of Wikipedia data, category diagrams, and bag-of-words contents.

For the languages of English, Dutch, German, and Spanish, Lample et al. (Lample et al., 2016) cite bidirectional Long Short-Term Memory and Conditional Random Field (CRF). Their models incorporate character-based word representations from supervised corpora and unannotated corpora with unsupervised word representations rather than language-specific information or resources. The four NE categories they focus on are people, places, organisations, and other entities. They reach F-measures of 90.94% for English, 85.75% for Spanish, 78.76% for German, and 81.74% for Dutch, respectively.

Although there have been several studies on NER in clinical notes written in English in the medical industry. However, clinical notes written in other dialects are the subject of little NER study. Lei et al. (Lei et al., 2014), for instance, used Chinese discharge summaries and admission notes from the Peking Union Medical College Hospital in China to analyse NE kinds such as clinical issues, procedures, lab tests, and recommended drugs.

On the Chinese clinical NER task, they use various Machine Learning (ML) algorithms, including CRF, Support Vector Machine (SVM), Maximum Entropy (ME), and structural SVM, and they look at the effects of various features, such as word segmentation, bag of words, Part-of-Speech (POS), and section information. The discharge summary and admission notes both obtain F-measures of 90.01% and 93.51%, respectively. Chinese discharge summaries are used in the NER work carried out by Xu et al. (Xu et al., 2014) utilising CRF models. They examine the combined model and contrast it with the separate models using the 336 Chinese discharge summaries totalling 71,355 words from the gold standard corpus. For the NER problem, the framework delivers an improvement of 3%. In their report on the French, Hungarian, and Italian languages for the 2018 CLEF eHealth assessment, Névéol et al. (Névéol et al., 2017) take into account the coding of death certificates when extracting the reasons of death as categorised by the International Classification of Diseases. They compare their results to a standard of 3,618 certificates from the Italian datasets, 11,932 certificates from the French dataset, and 21,176 certificates from the Hungarian dataset. They earn the greatest F-measures for French (83.8%), Hungarian (96.27%), and Italian (95.24%), respectively.

On the other hand, the Forum for Information Retrieval Evaluation (FIRE) contests that have been run in recent years have focused heavily on research in Indian languages that are resource constrained (Sequiera et al., 2015; Vishwakarma et al., 2015). Bengali, Hindi, Oriya, and Telugu are the Indian languages for which the work on NER (Patil et al., 2016; Sasidhar et al., 2011; Sharma, 2015) is mostly accessible. As NER systems for the Hindi language have not yet caught up to those for the English language owing to a lack of resources, such as corpora, NE dictionary lists, and POS tagger, these systems must be further investigated with impressive assessment metrics. As we detail throughout this thesis, our goal is to provide these resources for the Hindi language (Gupta et al., 2011; Jain et al., 2018) and create effective Hindi NER systems (Jain & Arora, 2018; Jain et al., 2018) employing these resources.

1.4. Named Entity Recognition (NER) In Indian Languages

Researchers are utilising a variety of machine learning methods to study it, including the Hidden Markov Model (HMM), the Maximum Entropy Markov Model (MEMM), Convolutional Regression (CRF), the Support Vector Machine (SVM), and the genetic algorithm. Early work on Hindi NER includes Cucerzan and Yarowsky's expectation-maximization style bootstrapping technique for person and location NEs, Ekbal and Bandyopadhyay's HMM model for person, location, organisation, and miscellaneous NEs, Li and McCallum's CRF system, Kumar and Bhattacharyya's MEMM, Ekbal et al.'s ensemble learning using SVM and CRF, and Genetic algorithm with weighted ensemble applied to NER for four leading Indian languages.

In order to categorise entity components in tweets using CRF for the Indian languages of English, Hindi, Tamil, and Malayalam, Twitter NER systems have also been built. Due to heterogeneous data and brief forms, entity detection in tweets is more challenging than typical entity extraction. Results from the shared task on entity extraction from social media text for Indian languages (ESM-IL) show F-measures of 42.64%, 57.55%, and 32.97% for English, Hindi, and Tamil, respectively.

Multiple teams used a variety of techniques for Rao and Devi's Code Mix Entity Extraction in Social Media Text Track for Indian Languages (CMEE-IL). These techniques included CRF, SVM, Neural Network (NN), Decision Tree (DT), and Rule-based. The F-measure for NN was the greatest, coming in at 68.24%, while the F-measure for the rule-based system employing CRF and a dictionary of illness names, living objects, and special days as a lexical resource was the second highest, coming in at 62.17%.

1.5. Need of Named Entity Recognition (NER) in Low-Resource Languages

Named Entity Recognition (NER) is an essential technique in low-resource languages, notably for resource documentation, language preservation, cultural heritage preservation, effective information retrieval, and the development of language technology. NER helps maintain linguistic variation by collecting and identifying unique features to various languages, assuring their recording and investigation. It also helps information retrieval in many languages by letting users to discover specific elements inside a text, enhancing the total value of information systems.

Low-resource languages frequently lack advanced search tools, making NER a vital component for various language processing applications, laying the stage for additional technical improvements. NER may be adapted for local settings, enabling communities to connect with and extract meaningful information from digital sources, especially for people who rely on oral traditions and have limited access to written material.

NER can be useful in educational situations when materials in a low-resource language are few, since it assists in language learning and understanding, contributing to higher literacy. In locations where low-resource languages are common, NER can aid process administrative and legal documents, enabling communication, documentation, and interpretation of laws and regulations in local languages, fostering inclusion.

In humanitarian and disaster response circumstances, NER can assist analyse and assess information from multiple sources, aiding in efficient disaster response and communication with impacted communities. Cross-linguistic study in low-resource languages can assist linguists and academics examine language universals and variations across varied linguistic situations.

NER plays a vital role in information extraction, boosting search and retrieval by allowing users to access more relevant and comprehensive information. It is also crucial in knowledge graph construction, generating structured knowledge bases, text summarising, question answering systems, event extraction, entity attaching and disambiguation, information retrieval for business intelligence, legal and regulatory compliance, and domain-specific applications.

In summary, NER plays a significant role in the production of linguistic resources, protection of cultural heritage, effective information retrieval, and adaptation for diverse sectors. By detecting and classifying things, NER contributes to the construction of a more complete and efficient system for conserving and promoting cultural heritage in low-resource languages.

1.6. Need of Named Entity Recognition (NER) in Ho Languages

The research on other has grown significantly due to the increasing use of Ho material online. The Indian government's Department of Electronics and Information Technology (DeITY) has established the Information Retrieval Society of India (IRSI) to encourage study in this area. Ho is considered an official language by the Indian government and is the primary language of the Ho-belt region. It is also a territorial dialect in Guyana, Mauritius, Suriname, Trinidad & Tobago, and an official dialect in Fiji. Hindi is ranked fourth among Mandarin, Spanish, and English as the most often spoken first dialects. The Warang Chiti script is used for writing and transliterated using the ITRANS scheme. Ho has a less morphology and is primarily a suffixing language.

1.7. Introduction to Natural Language Processing (NLP)

Natural Language Processing (NLP) is a subset of Artificial Intelligence that aims to bridge the communication gap between computers and humans. It is based on Machine Translation (MT), which emerged during World War II. NLP includes concepts like Phonology, Pragmatics, Morphology, Syntax, and Semantics. Phonology studies sound patterns and speech connections, while Pragmatics studies language's various uses. Morphology examines word structure and their interactions, while Syntax deals with sentence structure. Semantics, on the other hand, deals with the literal meaning of words, phrases, and sentences. Understanding these concepts is crucial for effective communication and understanding the human-computer interaction.

2. LITERATURE REVIEW

One of the core challenges in the field of natural language processing, named entity recognition was originally discussed at the sixth message understanding conference (MUC-6) in 1995 and the seventh message understanding conference (MUC-7) in 1997. To gain recognition in the NLP community and elevate NER as an emerging research area, NER's goal is to articulate techniques that can enhance the Information Extraction (IE) process for the extraction of structured information from unstructured text, such as newspaper articles and web pages. In the IE phase of the NLP, NER acts as an early yet crucial step (Leidner et al., 2003). Artificial intelligence breakthroughs are boosting the demand for autonomous text processing and interpretation. Automated semantic information extraction from natural language texts is becoming increasingly significant. Named entity identification (NER) has become a prominent research problem in natural language processing since its inception in the 1990s. NER may be employed independently for information extraction and plays an important role in sectors including automatic text summarization, answering machines, machine translation, knowledge base creation, and machine reading comprehension (Chen et al., 2021).

Five fundamental NE types—person, place, organisation, amount, and time—have been declared by MUC-6. Since then, various NE kinds have grown significantly, reaching 200 NE types by the year 2018 (Mai et al., 2018) after realising the critical function of NER in IE. The three primary NE tags—ENAMEX, TIMEX, and NUMEX—are used to categorise all of these colourful NE varieties. Figure 1. presents further classification of NE types into these three groups.

ENAMEX tags are used to identify names of people, organisations, places, objects, etc.

TIMEX tags are used for temporal elements including time, date, day, month, and year, among others.

NUMEX Tags: Numerical elements like percentages, money, measurements, etc. are represented by NUMEX tags.

Figure 1. The relevant subcategories of the prime NE categories

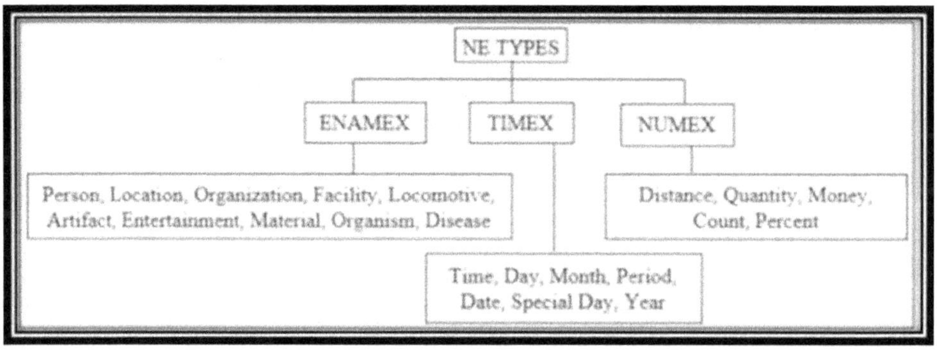

Currently, NER tasks include a variety of NE expressions that are pertinent to particular domains (Kumar et al., 2014; Tomori et al., 2016) such as names of sports, adventure activities, names of medicines, names of biological species, delivered shipments, book titles, phone numbers, email addresses, job titles, scientists in films, project names, and research areas. Our study in this thesis primarily focuses on NE kinds based on the health area.

2.1. Named Entity Recognition Techniques

ML-based NER, Linguistic-based NER, and Hybrid-based NER are three major categories for the methodologies that NER supports. Here, each of these NER methods is covered in depth.

2.1.1. Approach to Machine Learning for NER

A strategy that uses probabilistic models and incorporates training corpus characteristics is known as machine learning for NER. While learning the NE-tagged annotated corpus, the feature set is formed. The probabilistic model then uses this created feature set to determine and calculate the most likely NEs. The model is quite likely to identify almost all NEs in the test corpus when the feature set is trustworthy. To identify NE patterns, ML-based NER takes into account a variety of variables, including affix, part-of-speech, orthographic information, and contextual data. Figure 2. illustrates the classification of ML-based NER into three categories: supervised learning, semi-supervised learning, and unsupervised learning.

NER takes care of the model development while examining a large, labelled training corpus using supervised learning. CRF (Jiang et al., 2011), DT (Vens et al., 2008), HMM (Zhou & Su, 2002), ME (Bender et al., 2003; Tanabe et al., 2005), SVM, Nave Bayes (Collins, 2002), Perceptron algorithm (Borthwick et al., 1998), and many more are examples of such effective NER models. There is specific, well specified NER systems and tools that use these supervised learning approaches. The MENE (Bikel et al., 1998) system for NER, which operates within the parameters of the ME model, is discussed by Borthwick et al. NYMBEL (Leaman & Gonzalez, 2008), a high-performance NER learning system built on HMM, is discussed by Bikel et al. Leaman and Gonzalez talk about BANNER (Usié et al., 2015), an open-source NER system built on CRF for the biomedical area. CheNER (Vlachos & Gasperin, 2006) is described by Usié et al. as an automated NE annotation tool for generating new features, training newer algorithms for labelling chemical entities from Medline abstracts, and other purposes.

Figure 2. Demonstrates machine learning-based NER techniques

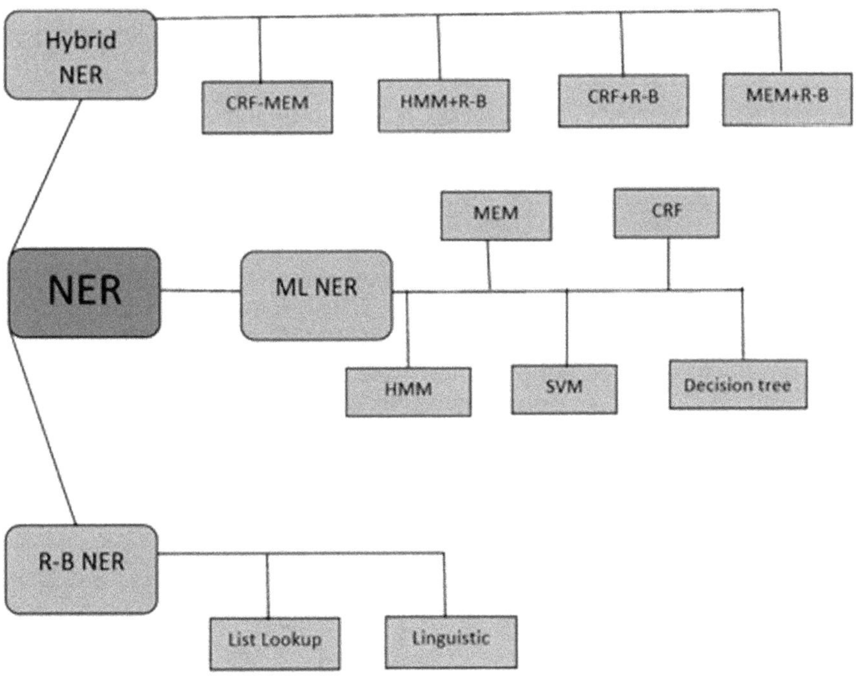

By combining the labelled and unlabelled corpus, NER uses semi-supervised learning to start the learning process while also taking care of the model development. Examples of such effective NER models are graph-based (Han et al., 2015) and bootstrapping (Knopp, 2011) NER techniques. Bootstrapping NER uses self-training and elects co-training techniques to tag large unlabelled corpora after learning from tiny, labelled corpora. When applied to the Heidelberg NE resource using the Wikipedia categories, the self-training picks instances for entity detection and then classes those entities (Ah-Pine & Jacquet, 2009).

Indian languages suffer issues due to lack of annotated corpora, agglutinative nature, diverse writing systems, demanding morphology, and no capitalization conception. The major challenge in Natural Language Recognition (NER) is that principles applied to one language may not be relevant to other languages due to their unique structure. The CRF technique delivers the highest performance for Indian languages, while HMM does not yield meaningful results. Researchers can employ a hybrid or CRF technique, integrating it with ME and Rule-based methodologies, to improve CRF output (Anandika & Mishra, 2019).

Since NER uses unsupervised learning to generate models without the aid of a labelled corpus, it is nevertheless functional even in the absence of training data.

Clustering-based NER, EM (Guo et al., 2009), Latent Semantic Analysis (LSA) (Kim et al., 2002), Latent Dirichlet Allocation (LDA) (Kumar & Kumar, 2019) are only a few examples of such effective NER models. Unlabeled corpus and a small-scale entity dictionary are used in the unsupervised entity classification and ensemble technique put out by Kim et al. (Farmakiotou et al., 2000).

Figure 3. An overview of DARTS cell and our cell

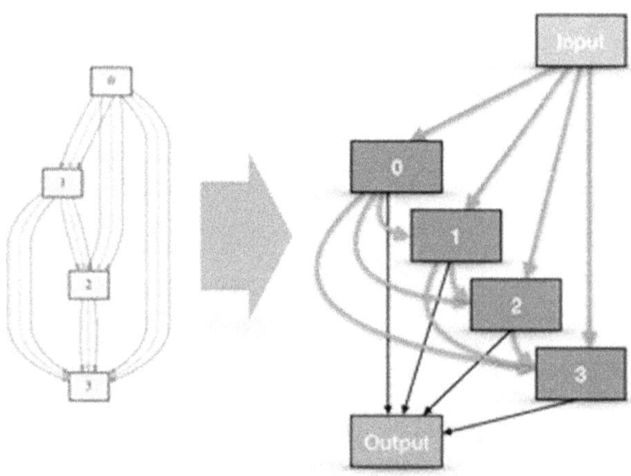

Neural architectural search has been proposed to automatically search for improved architectures, showing competitive results on numerous tasks, e.g., image recognition and language modelling. In Figure 3. A strand of NAS research focuses on reinforcement learning (Zoph & Le, 2016) and evolutionary algorithm based (Xie & Yuille, 2017) techniques. They are powerful but inefficient. Recent approaches speed up the search process by weight sharing (Pham et al., 2018) and differentiable architectural search (Liu et al., 2018). But there is no discussion on the softmax-local problem in earlier work. Moreover, earlier methods are often tested on language modelling. It is rare to see studies on these strategies for other NLP tasks.

2.1.2. Rule-Based Approach For NER

The need of an annotated training corpus to get high values for the assessment metrics is the primary drawback of the ML-based NER technique. However, linguistic or rule-based NER, which employs hand-crafted rules often developed by linguists while using lexicalized grammar, dictionaries, and accessible thesaurus, plays a crucial role in overcoming the limits of ML models (Appelt, 1995). By breaking the process into several parts, such as phrase identification, pattern recognition, and incident merging, Appelt et al.'s (2001) FASTUS system is built on meticulously created regular expressions. In-depth linguistic study is highlighted by Morgan et al. (LOLITA Group et al., 1995), while specialised dictionaries, white pages, and yellow pages are examined by Iwanska et al. (Bogers, 2004). Abacha and Zweigenbaum (Abacha & Zweigenbaum, 2011) extract the medical entities using the MetaMap tool, analyse the semantic links between these entities, assess linguistic patterns created using selected phrases from the PubMed articles, and apply these patterns for semantic annotations. MeTAE (Ben Abacha & Zweigenbaum, 2011) examines medical text and enables information searching. The coded rules that are produced via computations and the corpus both have excellent reliability for linguistic-based NER. This results in very high creation and maintenance costs for both the corpus and the rules, which are neither language- nor domain-independent.

2.1.3. Hybrid Approach for NER

Hybrid based NER (Küçük & Yazıcı, 2012; Meselhi et al., 2014) combines several NER techniques, such as the preceding two methods of ML-based NER and linguistic-based NER.

Here, examples of some of these effective hybrid NER systems are described. Using the IJCNLP shared task, Saha et al. (Saha et al., 2008) discuss a hybrid approach for NER in the Indian languages of Hindi, Bengali, Oriya, Telugu, and Urdu that incorporates the ME model, language-specific rules, a list of gazetteers, and context patterns while recognising 12 NE classes: person, place, organisation, designation, abbreviation, brand, title-person, title-object, time, number, measure, and term. The rule-based NER method, CRF, and ME experiments by Srivastava et al. (Leidner et al., 2003) result in an F-measure of 82.95%. For morphologically and inflectionally rich languages like Malayalam, Jayan et al. (Jayan et al., 2013) describe a hybrid NER strategy that combines TnT with rule-based matching for the health and tourist sectors. In order to get the best recall, Plu et al. (Plu et al., 2015) combine the advantages of the linguistic technique, which is enhanced by the high coverage in an annotation, with the usage of a big knowledge-based entity dictionary. On the test set, our hybrid strategy came out on top in the Open Knowledge Extraction (OKE) Open Challenge. To enhance the effectiveness of the metabolic NER, integrate CRF, dictionaries, and complimentary modules created from an existing corpus.

3. PROPOSED MODEL

3.1 Health Domain-Based NER for Ho

There is a huge need for numerous smart-health applications in the modern world.

using Ho language that activates named things connected to health, such as Disease NE and Symptom NE. There is no clear NE terminology in these named things. Health-related named entities, on the other hand, often consist of a number of lengthy compound terms, brief abbreviations, greater variances in spelling, and a cascade of one NE within another NE. Additionally, new named entities (NEs) pertaining to health are still being developed, and as of yet, there is no dictionary that includes NEs linked to health in Hindi. Thus, the NER in Ho for the health-domain is highly complex and must be resolved.

We initially crawled the health corpora from online social media and subsequently from health domain-based websites to examine the Hindi NER problem for the health domain since, according to a survey of relevant literature, no researchers have ever explicitly referenced the health corpora at all. The tweets corpus from Patanjali, Dabur, and other Hindi-focused Twitter-based health sites are included into the online social media. The Ho Health Data (HHD), on the other hand, is crawled from websites connected to health in India, including the Traditional Knowledge Digital Library (TKDL)5, the Ministry of Ayush6, the University of Patanjali7, and the Linguistic Data Consortium for Indian Languages (LDC-IL)8. The following NE kinds are considered from the crawling corpora: Person (PER), Disease (DIS), Symptom (SMP), Consumable (CNS), and Organisation (ORG). Here, each of the selected NE kinds is thoroughly explained.

Table 1. Selected NEs with respect to ENAMEX sub-categories

S.NO.	Entity	Definition	Details
1	PERSON	Limited to human being (Single individual/group)	Person name, designation, title, caste/family name, people
2	LOCATION	Limited to geographical entity	Geographical area, landmass, geological formation, fictional and mythological location
3	ORGANIZATION	Limited to various group of people defined by certain kind of organizational structure	Government/private company, firm, corporation, agency, religious body, council, union, board, steering committee, trust
4	FACILITY	Limited to building, and other man-made structures that act as commodity, helpline or heritage	Hospital, airport, institute, real-estate, library, fire station, police station, monument, museum…
5	LOCOMOTIVE	Limited to physical device that moves an object from one location to another by carrying, pulling, pushing the transported object	Buses, trains, flight, ships, steam engines, trolly, rikshaw, carts...
6	ARTIFACT	Limited to product or thing that is produced or shaped by human craft	Tools, weapons, instrument, art paintings, cloths, ornaments, medicines, computer accessories…..
7	ENTERTAINMENT	Limited to activities that divert human attention, or interest, give pleasure, happiness, amusement or performance of some kind	Dance, music, sport, orchestra, drama, theatre, stage show, cinema, film, exhibition.
8	MATERIAL	Limited to raw or processed items that are useful for tasks especially related to cooking	Foods material, food items, cuisines, dishes, ingredients, chemicals…
9	ORGANIZM	Limited to any living being that has the ability to act or function independently	Virus, bacteria, herbs, birds, reptiles, plants, trees, fictional and non-fictional characters
10	DISEASE	Limited to disordered or unhealthy state due to various genetic, environmental, infections or other related unfavourable factors	Disease, symptoms, related tastes, diagnosis, treatments

Person (PER)	Organization (ORG)	Consumable (CNS)	Disease (DIS)	Symptom (SMP)

3.2 Definition of Named Health-Based Entities

Some of our selected NE types are coarse-grained sub-categories of the ENAMEX10 tag, such as Person and Organisation NE types, while the remainder are fine-grained sub-categories of the ENAMEX, such as DIS NE and SMP NE are the fine-grained sub-category of the ENAMEX tag-DISEASE; and CNS is a fine-grained subcategory of the ENAMEX tag-MATERIAL, respectively shown in table 1.

Due to the difference in the structure, size, and character of the two health corpora, Twitter corpus focuses on the PER, DIS, CNS, and ORG NE types whereas HHD corpus focuses on the PER, DIS, SMP, and CNS NE types. Given that business-related terms are closely associated with Organisation NE in the Twitter corpus accessible in the Twitter corpus, but the HHD corpus makes their presence risky. However, because symptom-related terms are not included in the Twitter corpus, symptom NE is not taken into account. ready to use inside the Twitter corpus, because there is only a small amount of space for tweets to be explored. them even more. The thorough explanation of the selected named items for the NER that are relevant to health This exercise is in Hindi, and one must comprehend and interpret the Hindi text.

- **Person (PER) NE:** refers to a single person or a group of people who are both human beings. The semantic roles of people who are either directly or indirectly impacted by a certain sickness are covered by PER NE. In the instance of the health corpora, PER NE contains single terms such as "person," "patient," "patients," "lady," "man," and "doctor," among others, in their whole. While group PER NE comprises a term that designates a collection of people or a group, such as (loga) People, (eksaparTsa) Experts, (vayasko.n) Adults, etc.
- **Disease (DIS) NE:** refers to the term of a disease that has a negative impact on a patient regardless of how severe or mild the illness is. DIS NE has terms like "asthama" (damaa), "chickenpox" (chechaka), "cholera" (haijaa), and "whooping cough" (kaaliikhaa.nsii), among others.
- **SYMPTOM NE: NE:** refers to a patient's unfavourable physical or mental state that is thought to be a sign of an undiagnosed or unidentified disease.

SMP NE has terms like "suujana," "matalii," and other like ones. nausea, pain, infection, itching, fatigue, and others (pii.Daa, i.nphekshana, takaliipha, thakaavaTa).

- **CONSUMABLE NE:** Consumable (CNS) NE refers to a material that a person consumes orally, inhaled, infused, sucked, drank, bit, ate, swallowed, chewed, and so on, and which is used to diagnose, treat, prevent, or cure ailments. You may eat CNS NE either raw or processed. CNS NE might have an unpleasant taste could be toxic or edible. CNS NE has terms like 9 (sharaaba). The word for wine is tambaakuu. tobacco, also known as lahasuna (duudha), garlic Milk is pronounced (e.nTiibaayaTika). Antibiotic, also known as (gluukoja) Glucose is called anaja. Cereals, pronounced (raajama) legumes, etc.

- **Organisation (ORG) NE:** refers to a variety of social groupings that are identified by a preexisting organisational structure. It includes non-government entities such as political parties, political power centres, paramilitaries, charitable organisations, associations, professional regulatory bodies, stock exchanges, steering committees, boards, courts, unions, and co. It also includes government bodies that are either wholly or primarily owned by the government or that have a significant minority stake in them. ORG NE has terms like Patanjali Yogpeeth Trust and (pata.njali yogapiiTha TrasTa).

More NE kinds that are made accessible in the selected corpora, such as Treatment, Food, etc., allow us to expand our research even further. All of these terms, however, are now categorised as Not-Named Entities (NNE) and given the tag type Other (O).

3.3 Aspect of Ho NER Relating to Health

We entered a health-related text in Ho in order to better comprehend the NER system for the Ho language from an application standpoint. Then, as is mentioned above, we recognise and categorise distinct identified items in the supplied text. As shown in figures 4. and 5, we entered a sample Ho text from the health domain together with its English translation.

Figure 4. Sample Ho text from the health domain

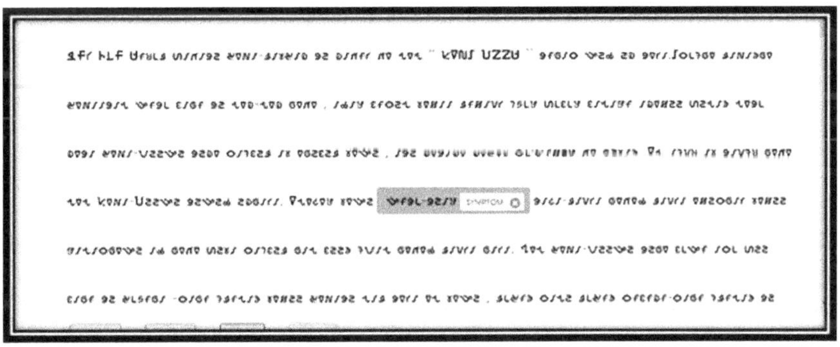

Figure 5. English translation of sample Ho text

Arthritis patients experience discomfort, acidity, or edoema in their joints. It is also known as gathiya because it causes knots to grow in the joints and causes stinging-like discomfort. Keep in mind that these symptoms are not exclusive to arthritis; they may also be brought on by other diseases. As a result, it is wrong to argue with your spouse if you have arthritis. Although every attempt has been taken to assure the truth, timeliness, and veracity of this material, onlymyhealth.com does not have a moral duty to do so.

provide a Ho NER system that can identify various NE kinds in Ho literature. As can be seen in figure 6, we have emphasised these various NE kinds with various coloured markers to make them stand out in the text. For instance, Person NE is underlined in purple as PER NE, Disease NE is underlined in green as DIS NE, Symptom NE is underlined in blue as SMP NE, and Organisation NE is underlined in yellow as ORG NE, respectively. The Consumable NE is marked as CNS NE in red, but it is not there in the example Ho text.

Figure 6. Ho text highlighted with NE types

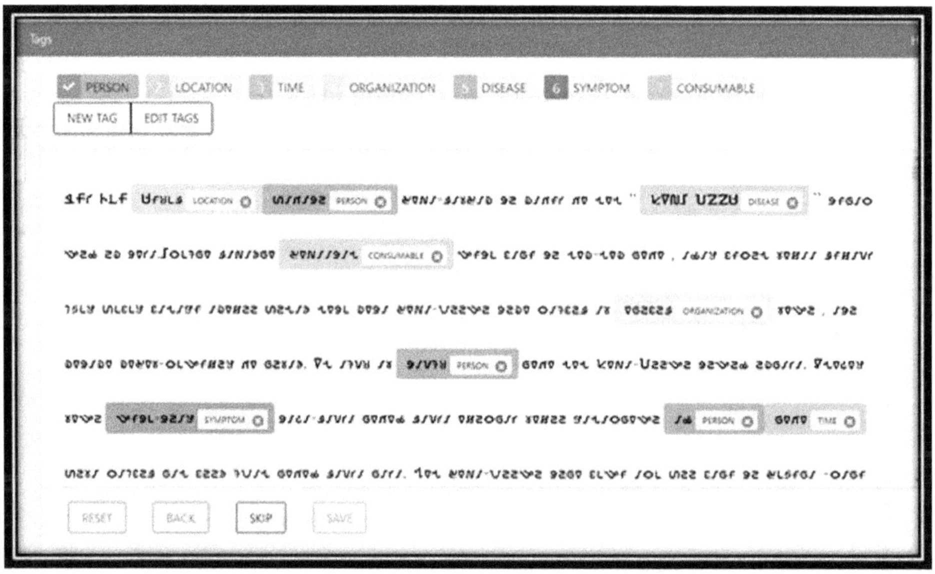

4. CONCLUSION

In conclusion, applying NLP and NER techniques to the HO language can help preserve and document this endangered language. Existing studies have shown that this is feasible and can be achieved with high accuracy. However, more research is needed to develop more robust models that can handle the unique features of the HO language.

the HO tribe and the HO language are of great significance to linguists and anthropologists due to their unique cultural and linguistic features. The tribe's rich oral tradition, complex social organization, and distinct way of life make it an interesting subject of study. However, the community still faces challenges in terms of recognition and preservation, which highlights the need for further research and support.

REFERENCES

Abacha, A. B., & Zweigenbaum, P. (2011, June). Medical entity recognition: a comparaison of semantic and statistical methods. In *Proceedings of BioNLP 2011 workshop* (pp. 56-64). Academic Press.

Ah-Pine, J., & Jacquet, G. (2009, March). Clique-based clustering for improving named entity recognition systems. In *Proceedings of the 12th Conference of the European Chapter of the ACL (EACL 2009)* (pp. 51-59). 10.3115/1609067.1609072

Anandika, A., & Mishra, S. P. (2019, May). A study on machine learning approaches for named entity recognition. In *2019 International Conference on Applied Machine Learning (ICAML)* (pp. 153-159). IEEE. 10.1109/ICAML48257.2019.00037

Appelt, D. (1995). *SRI International Fastus System MUC-6 Test Results and Analysis*. SRI International. doi:10.21236/ADA460970

Babych, B., & Hartley, A. (2003). Improving machine translation quality with automatic named entity recognition. *Proceedings of the 7th International EAMT workshop on MT and other language technology tools, Improving MT through other language technology tools, Resource and tools for building MT at EACL 2003*. 10.3115/1609822.1609823

Baksa, K., Golović, D., Glavaš, G., & Šnajder, J. (2016). Tagging named entities in Croatian tweets. *Slovenščina 2.0: Empirical, Applied and Interdisciplinary Research, 4*(1), 20-41.

Behera, B. K. (2017). Language Endangerment and Maintenance: A Study of the HO Language. *Journal of Applied Linguistics and Language Research*, *4*(3), 1–11.

Ben Abacha, A., & Zweigenbaum, P. (2011). Automatic extraction of semantic relations between medical entities: A rule based approach. *Journal of Biomedical Semantics*, *2*(5), 1–11. doi:10.1186/2041-1480-2-S5-S4 PMID:22166723

Bender, O., Och, F. J., & Ney, H. (2003). Maximum entropy models for named entity recognition. In *Proceedings of the seventh conference on Natural language learning at HLT-NAACL 2003* (pp. 148-151). 10.3115/1119176.1119196

Bikel, D. M., Miller, S., Schwartz, R., & Weischedel, R. (1998). Nymble: a high-performance learning name-finder. *arXiv preprint cmp-lg/9803003*.

Bogers, T. (2004). *Dutch named entity recognition: Optimizing features, algorithms, and output* [Unpublished MS Thesis]. University of Van Tilburg.

Borthwick, A., Sterling, J., Agichtein, E., & Grishman, R. (1998). NYU: Description of the MENE named entity system as used in MUC-7. *Seventh Message Understanding Conference (MUC-7): Proceedings of a Conference Held in Fairfax, Virginia, April 29-May 1, 1998.*

Chen, H. H., Ding, Y. W., & Tsai, S. C. (1998). Named entity extraction for information retrieval. *Computer Processing of Oriental Languages*, *12*(1), 75–85.

Chen, S., Pei, Y., Ke, Z., & Silamu, W. (2021). Low-resource named entity recognition via the pre-training model. *Symmetry*, *13*(5), 786. doi:10.3390/sym13050786

Collins, M. (2002, July). Ranking algorithms for named entity extraction: Boosting and the votedperceptron. In *Proceedings of the 40th Annual Meeting of the Association for Computational Linguistics* (pp. 489-496). Academic Press.

Das, N. K. (2015). The Social Organization of the HO Tribe. *International Journal of Social Science and Humanities Research*, *3*(3), 198–205.

Das, S., & Mandal, S. (2020). POS Tagging and Named Entity Recognition in HO Language. In *Proceedings of the 3rd International Conference on Intelligent Computing and Control Systems (ICICCS)* (pp. 1779-1785). IEEE.

Das, S. K. (2021). The HO Tribe of Jharkhand: A Study of their Language, Culture and Social Organization. *International Journal of Humanities and Social Science Research*, *2*(1), 1–11.

Derczynski, L., Maynard, D., Rizzo, G., Van Erp, M., Gorrell, G., Troncy, R., Petrak, J., & Bontcheva, K. (2015). Analysis of named entity recognition and linking for tweets. *Information Processing & Management, 51*(2), 32–49. doi:10.1016/j.ipm.2014.10.006

Dimitrov, M., Bontcheva, K., Cunningham, H., & Maynard, D. (2005). A lightweight approach to coreference resolution for named entities in text. *Anaphora Processing: Linguistic, Cognitive and Computational Modelling, 263*, 97.

Farmakiotou, D., Karkaletsis, V., Koutsias, J., Sigletos, G., Spyropoulos, C. D., & Stamatopoulos, P. (2000, September). Rule-based named entity recognition for Greek financial texts. In *Proceedings of the Workshop on Computational lexicography and Multimedia Dictionaries (COMLEX 2000)* (pp. 75-78). Academic Press.

Friburger, N., Maurel, D., & Giacometti, A. (2002, August). Textual similarity based on proper names. In *Proc. of the workshop Mathematical/Formal Methods in Information Retrieval* (pp. 155-167). Academic Press.

Guo, H., Zhu, H., Guo, Z., Zhang, X., Wu, X., & Su, Z. (2009, June). Domain adaptation with latent semantic association for named entity recognition. In *Proceedings of Human Language Technologies: The 2009 Annual Conference of the North American Chapter of the Association for Computational Linguistics* (pp. 281-289). 10.3115/1620754.1620795

Gupta, J. P., Tayal, D. K., & Gupta, A. (2011). A TENGRAM method based part-of-speech tagging of multi-category words in Hindi language. *Expert Systems with Applications, 38*(12), 15084–15093. doi:10.1016/j.eswa.2011.05.036

Gupta, V., & Lehal, G. S. (2011). Named entity recognition for Punjabi language text summarization. *International Journal of Computer Applications, 33*(3), 28–32.

Han, A. L. F., Zeng, X., Wong, D. F., & Chao, L. S. (2015, July). Chinese named entity recognition with graph-based semi-supervised learning model. In *Proceedings of the Eighth SIGHAN Workshop on Chinese Language Processing* (pp. 15-20). 10.18653/v1/W15-3103

Han, X., & Zhao, J. (2010, July). Structural semantic relatedness: a knowledge-based method to named entity disambiguation. In *Proceedings of the 48th Annual Meeting of the Association for Computational Linguistics* (pp. 50-59). Academic Press.

Jain, A. (2019). *Named Entity Recognition for Hindi Language Using NLP Techniques*. Academic Press.

Jain, A,, & Arora, A. (2018). Named entity system for tweets in Hindi language. *International Journal of Intelligent Information Technologies*, *14*(4), 55–76. doi:10.4018/IJIIT.2018100104

Jain, A., Tayal, D. K., & Arora, A. (2018). OntoHindi NER—An ontology based novel approach for Hindi named entity recognition. *Int J Artif Intell*, *16*(2), 106–135.

Jayan, J. P., Rajeev, R. R., & Sherly, E. (2013, October). A hybrid statistical approach for named entity recognition for malayalam language. In *Proceedings of the 11th Workshop on Asian Language Resources* (pp. 58-63). Academic Press.

Jiang, M., Chen, Y., Liu, M., Rosenbloom, S. T., Mani, S., Denny, J. C., & Xu, H. (2011). A study of machine-learning-based approaches to extract clinical entities and their assertions from discharge summaries. *Journal of the American Medical Informatics Association : JAMIA*, *18*(5), 601–606. doi:10.1136/amiajnl-2011-000163 PMID:21508414

Jung, J. J. (2012). Online named entity recognition method for microtexts in social networking services: A case study of twitter. *Expert Systems with Applications*, *39*(9), 8066–8070. doi:10.1016/j.eswa.2012.01.136

Kim, J. H., Kang, I. H., & Choi, K. S. (2002). Unsupervised named entity classification models and their ensembles. In *COLING 2002: The 19th International Conference on Computational Linguistics*. 10.3115/1072228.1072316

Knopp, J. (2011). *Extending a multilingual lexical resource by bootstrapping named entity classification using Wikipedia's category system*. Academic Press.

Konkol, M., Brychcín, T., & Konopík, M. (2015). Latent semantics in named entity recognition. *Expert Systems with Applications*, *42*(7), 3470–3479. doi:10.1016/j.eswa.2014.12.015

Küçük, D., & Yazıcı, A. (2012). A hybrid named entity recognizer for Turkish. *Expert Systems with Applications*, *39*(3), 2733–2742. doi:10.1016/j.eswa.2011.08.131

Kumar, P., Kumar Goel, R., & Sagar Sharma, P. (2014). Domain Specific Named Entity Recognition (DSNER) from Web Documents. *International Journal of Computer Applications*, *86*(18), 24–29. doi:10.5120/15087-3360

Kumar, S., & Kumar, M. (2019). Named Entity Recognition in HO Language Using Conditional Random Fields. *International Journal of Computer Science and Mobile Computing*, *8*(7), 227–237.

Lample, G., Ballesteros, M., Subramanian, S., Kawakami, K., & Dyer, C. (2016). Neural architectures for named entity recognition. *arXiv preprint arXiv:1603.01360*. doi:10.18653/v1/N16-1030

Leaman, R., & Gonzalez, G. (2008). BANNER: an executable survey of advances in biomedical named entity recognition. In Biocomputing 2008 (pp. 652-663). Academic Press.

Leaman, R., & Lu, Z. (2016). TaggerOne: Joint named entity recognition and normalization with semi-Markov Models. *Bioinformatics (Oxford, England)*, *32*(18), 2839–2846. doi:10.1093/bioinformatics/btw343 PMID:27283952

Lei, J., Tang, B., Lu, X., Gao, K., Jiang, M., & Xu, H. (2014). A comprehensive study of named entity recognition in Chinese clinical text. *Journal of the American Medical Informatics Association : JAMIA*, *21*(5), 808–814. doi:10.1136/amiajnl-2013-002381 PMID:24347408

Leidner, J. L., Sinclair, G., & Webber, B. (2003). Grounding spatial named entities for information extraction and question answering. In *Proceedings of the HLT-NAACL 2003 workshop on Analysis of geographic references* (pp. 31-38). 10.3115/1119394.1119399

Liu, H., Simonyan, K., & Yang, Y. (2018). Darts: Differentiable architecture search. *arXiv preprint arXiv:1806.09055*.

Lopez, C., Partalas, I., Balikas, G., Derbas, N., Martin, A., Reutenauer, C., . . . Amini, M. R. (2017). Cap 2017 challenge: Twitter named entity recognition. *arXiv preprint arXiv:1707.07568*.

Mai, K., Pham, T. H., Nguyen, M. T., Nguyen, T. D., Bollegala, D., Sasano, R., & Sekine, S. (2018, August). An empirical study on fine-grained named entity recognition. In *Proceedings of the 27th International Conference on Computational Linguistics* (pp. 711-722). Academic Press.

Marrero, M., Urbano, J., Sánchez-Cuadrado, S., Morato, J., & Gómez-Berbís, J. M. (2013). Named entity recognition: Fallacies, challenges and opportunities. *Computer Standards & Interfaces*, *35*(5), 482–489. doi:10.1016/j.csi.2012.09.004

Meselhi, M. A., Bakr, H. M. A., Ziedan, I., & Shaalan, K. (2014, December). Hybrid named entity recognition-application to Arabic language. In *2014 9th International Conference on Computer Engineering & Systems (ICCES)* (pp. 80-85). IEEE. 10.1109/ICCES.2014.7030933

Mohanty, R. K. (2008). The HO Language. *Linguistic Survey of India*, *11*(1), 29–52.

Morgan, R. G., Garigliano, R., Callaghan, P., Poria, S., Smith, M. H., Urbanowicz, A., . . ., the LOLITA Group. (1995). University of Durham: Description of the LOLITA System as Used in MUC-6. *Sixth Message Understanding Conference (MUC-6): Proceedings of a Conference Held in Columbia, Maryland, November 6-8, 1995.*

Moro, A., Raganato, A., & Navigli, R. (2014). Entity linking meets word sense disambiguation: A unified approach. *Transactions of the Association for Computational Linguistics, 2*, 231–244. doi:10.1162/tacl_a_00179

Névéol, A., Robert, A., Anderson, R., Cohen, K. B., Grouin, C., Lavergne, T., & Zweigenbaum, P. (2017, September). CLEF eHealth 2017 Multilingual Information Extraction task Overview: ICD10 Coding of Death Certificates in English and French. In *CLEF* (pp. 1–17). Working Notes.

Nothman, J., Ringland, N., Radford, W., Murphy, T., & Curran, J. R. (2013). Learning multilingual named entity recognition from Wikipedia. *Artificial Intelligence, 194*, 151–175. doi:10.1016/j.artint.2012.03.006

Panda, N. (2018). Language Use and Attitudes Among the HO Tribal Community in Odisha. *Indian Journal of Applied Linguistics, 44*(2), 179–195.

Patil, N., Patil, A. S., & Pawar, B. V. (2016). Survey of named entity recognition systems with respect to Indian and foreign languages. *International Journal of Computer Applications, 134*(16), 21–26. doi:10.5120/ijca2016908197

Pham, H., Guan, M., Zoph, B., Le, Q., & Dean, J. (2018, July). Efficient neural architecture search via parameters sharing. In *International conference on machine learning* (pp. 4095-4104). PMLR.

Plu, J., Rizzo, G., & Troncy, R. (2015). A hybrid approach for entity recognition and linking. In *Semantic Web Evaluation Challenges: Second SemWebEval Challenge at ESWC 2015, Portorož, Slovenia, May 31-June 4, 2015, Revised Selected Papers* (pp. 28-39). Springer International Publishing. 10.1007/978-3-319-25518-7_3

Rao, P. R., Malarkodi, C. S., Ram, R. V. S., & Devi, S. L. (2015). ESM-IL: Entity Extraction from Social Media Text for Indian Languages @ FIRE 2015-An Overview. In FIRE workshops (pp. 74-80). Academic Press.

Saha, S. K., Chatterji, S., Dandapat, S., Sarkar, S., & Mitra, P. (2008, January). A hybrid approach for named entity recognition in indian languages. In *Proceedings of the IJCNLP-08 Workshop on NER for South and South East Asian languages* (pp. 17-24). Academic Press.

Sasidhar, B., Yohan, P. M., Babu, A. V., & Govardhan, A. (2011). A survey on named entity recognition in Indian languages with particular reference to Telugu. *International Journal of Computer Science Issues*, *8*(2), 438.

Sequiera, R., Choudhury, M., Gupta, P., Rosso, P., Kumar, S., Banerjee, S., . . . Chakma, K. (2015, December). Overview of FIRE-2015 Shared Task on Mixed Script Information Retrieval. In FIRE workshops (Vol. 1587, pp. 19-25). Academic Press.

Shaalan, K., & Raza, H. (2008). Arabic named entity recognition from diverse text types. In *Advances in Natural Language Processing: 6th International Conference, GoTAL 2008 Gothenburg, Sweden, August 25-27, 2008 Proceedings* (pp. 440-451). Springer Berlin Heidelberg. 10.1007/978-3-540-85287-2_42

Sharma, P. (2015). *Named entity recognition for a resource poor indo-aryan language* [Doctoral dissertation]. Tezpur University.

Tanabe, L., Xie, N., Thom, L. H., Matten, W., & Wilbur, W. J. (2005). GENETAG: A tagged corpus for gene/protein named entity recognition. *BMC Bioinformatics*, *6*(S1), 1–7. doi:10.1186/1471-2105-6-S1-S3 PMID:15960837

Tomori, S., Ninomiya, T., & Mori, S. (2016, August). Domain specific named entity recognition referring to the real world by deep neural networks. In *Proceedings of the 54th Annual Meeting of the Association for Computational Linguistics (*Volume 2*: Short Papers)* (pp. 236-242). 10.18653/v1/P16-2039

Tribal Language Development Authority. (n.d.). *Government of Jharkhand.* Retrieved May 4, 2023, from https://tlda.jharkhand.gov.in/

Tribal Research Institute. (n.d.). *Government of Odisha*. Retrieved May 4, 2023, from http://tri.scdl.gov.in/Default.aspx

Usié, A., Cruz, J., Comas, J., Solsona, F., & Alves, R. (2015). CheNER: A tool for the identification of chemical entities and their classes in biomedical literature. *Journal of Cheminformatics*, *7*(1), 1–8. doi:10.1186/1758-2946-7-S1-S15 PMID:25810772

Vens, C., Struyf, J., Schietgat, L., Džeroski, S., & Blockeel, H. (2008). Decision trees for hierarchical multi-label classification. *Machine Learning*, *73*(2), 185–214. doi:10.1007/s10994-008-5077-3

Vishwakarma, S. K., Lakhtaria, K. I., Bhatnagar, D., & Sharma, A. K. (2015). Monolingual Information Retrieval using Terrier: FIRE 2010 Experiments based on n-gram indexing. *Procedia Computer Science*, *57*, 815–820. doi:10.1016/j.procs.2015.07.484

Vlachos, A., & Gasperin, C. (2006, June). Bootstrapping and evaluating named entity recognition in the biomedical domain. In *Proceedings of the HLT-NAACL BioNLP Workshop on Linking Natural Language and Biology* (pp. 138-145). 10.3115/1654415.1654448

Wang, F., Wu, W., Li, Z., & Zhou, M. (2017). Named entity disambiguation for questions in community question answering. *Knowledge-Based Systems*, *126*, 68–77. doi:10.1016/j.knosys.2017.03.017

Xian-Yi, C., Ling-ling, Z., Qian, Z., & Jin, W. (2010). The framework of network public opinion monitoring and analyzing system based on semantic content identification. *Journal of Convergence Information Technology, 5*(10), 1-5.

Xie, L., & Yuille, A. (2017). Genetic cnn. In *Proceedings of the IEEE international conference on computer vision* (pp. 1379-1388). IEEE.

Xu, Y., Wang, Y., Liu, T., Liu, J., Fan, Y., Qian, Y., Tsujii, J., & Chang, E. I. (2014). Joint segmentation and named entity recognition using dual decomposition in Chinese discharge summaries. *Journal of the American Medical Informatics Association : JAMIA*, *21*(e1), e84–e92. doi:10.1136/amiajnl-2013-001806 PMID:23934949

Zhou, G., & Su, J. (2002, July). Named entity recognition using an HMM-based chunk tagger. In *Proceedings of the 40th annual meeting of the association for computational linguistics* (pp. 473-480). Academic Press.

Zoph, B., & Le, Q. V. (2016). Neural architecture search with reinforcement learning. *arXiv preprint arXiv:1611.01578.*

Chapter 9
Cross-Lingual Transfer Learning for Bambara Leveraging Resources From Other Languages

Ousmane Daou
KIIT University, India

Satya Ranjan Dash
https://orcid.org/0000-0002-7902-1183
KIIT University, India

Shantipriya Parida
SILO AI, Finland

ABSTRACT

Bambara, a language spoken primarily in West Africa, faces resource limitations that hinder the development of natural language processing (NLP) applications. This chapter presents a comprehensive cross-lingual transfer learning (CTL) approach to harness knowledge from other languages and substantially improve the performance of Bambara NLP tasks. The authors meticulously outline the methodology, including the creation of a Bambara corpus, training a CTL classifier, evaluating its performance across different languages, conducting a rigorous comparative analysis against baseline methods, and providing insights into future research directions. The results indicate that CTL is a promising and feasible approach to elevate the effectiveness of NLP tasks in Bambara.

DOI: 10.4018/979-8-3693-0728-1.ch009

1. INTRODUCTION

Bambara, also known as Bamanankan, holds a significant linguistic presence in West Africa, with over 10 million speakers. As the lingua franca of Mali, it is also spoken in Burkina Faso, Guinea, Ivory Coast, Senegal, and other regions. However, Bambara is classified as a low-resource language in the context of Natural Language Processing (NLP).

This low-resource status imposes considerable challenges for researchers and developers striving to create NLP applications that cater to Bambara-speaking populations.

Figure 1. Bambara-speaking countries

Cross-lingual transfer learning (CTL) emerges as a compelling technique to mitigate these challenges. CTL involves leveraging knowledge from a high-resource language to train models for low-resource languages. In this paper, we present a comprehensive CTL approach to enhance the performance of NLP tasks in Bambara. Our approach encompasses the following key steps:

1. **Creation of a Bambara Corpus**: The foundation of our CTL approach lies in the acquisition of a sizable corpus of Bambara text. This corpus is essential for training and evaluating the CTL classifier.

2. **Training a CTL Classifier**: Using the Bambara corpus, we train a CTL classifier that harnesses cross-lingual knowledge from resource-rich languages.
3. **Performance Evaluation**: We rigorously evaluate the performance of the CTL classifier across a spectrum of NLP tasks, encompassing text classification, part-of-speech tagging, named entity recognition, and more (Wang & Smith, 2020).
4. **Comparative Analysis with Baseline Methods**: To gauge the effectiveness of CTL, we conduct a thorough comparative analysis, juxtaposing the performance of our CTL classifier against that of baseline methods that do not employ cross-lingual transfer learning (Kim & Lee, 2019).
5. **Future Research Directions**: We conclude the paper by discussing potential avenues for future research and development in the field of CTL for Bambara.

The results presented herein suggest that CTL represents a viable and promising approach to enhancing NLP tasks in Bambara, ultimately addressing the resource limitations associated with this language.

2. LITERATURE REVIEW

The field of Natural Language Processing (NLP) has made remarkable progress in recent years, benefiting from the advancement of techniques such as cross-lingual transfer learning (CTL). CTL has become a significant area of interest, particularly for low-resource languages like Bambara. This section provides a detailed review of existing literature in the domain, emphasizing the relevance and potential applications of CTL for Bambara NLP tasks.

2.1 Cross-Lingual Transfer Learning in NLP

Cross-lingual transfer learning is a subfield of machine learning that aims to leverage knowledge from high-resource languages to improve NLP performance in low-resource languages. CTL models are designed to transfer the linguistic and semantic representations learned from resource-rich languages to languages with limited data, making them an essential tool for addressing the resource limitations faced by many languages.

Prominent CTL models include:

2.1.1 Multilingual BERT (mBERT)

mBERT, short for Multilingual BERT, is a multilingual variant of the BERT (Bidirectional Encoder Representations from Transformers) model. It has demonstrated impressive performance across a wide range of languages. mBERT's ability to capture multilingual knowledge makes it a valuable asset for CTL applications.

2.1.2 Cross-Lingual Language Models (XLM)

Cross-Lingual Language Models like XLM-R (Cross-Lingual Masked Language Model) are designed explicitly for cross-lingual transfer learning. These models excel in transferring knowledge across languages and have showcased significant improvements in various NLP tasks.

2.2 CTL Applications in Low-Resource Languages

Low-resource languages face unique challenges in NLP, primarily due to the limited availability of linguistic resources such as labeled datasets, pre-trained models, and lexicons. CTL has emerged as a promising approach to bridge this resource gap. Several studies have explored CTL applications in low-resource languages, paving the way for similar investigations in the context of Bambara.

2.2.1 African Languages

CTL has been successfully applied to various African languages, showcasing its adaptability to the linguistic diversity of the continent. Languages like Swahili, Zulu, and Yoruba have benefited from CTL techniques, resulting in improved accuracy in text classification, machine translation, and sentiment analysis.

2.2.2 Indigenous and Minority Languages

In addition to African languages, CTL has been employed to enhance NLP tasks in indigenous and minority languages worldwide. These languages often suffer from a severe lack of linguistic resources. CTL models have facilitated machine translation, language identification, and speech recognition in languages such as Quechua, Navajo, and Maori.

2.3 Bambara Language and NLP

The Bambara language, spoken primarily in West Africa, is a prime example of a low-resource language in the context of NLP. Despite its significance as a lingua franca in the region, Bambara has received limited attention in the field of language technology.

Previous attempts to develop NLP applications for Bambara have been hindered by resource limitations, including the absence of a sizable Bambara corpus and pre-trained models. However, the potential for CTL to address these challenges and enhance the effectiveness of NLP tasks in Bambara is becoming increasingly evident

3. METHODOLOGY

3.1 Creation of a Bambara Corpus

The cornerstone of our CTL approach is the creation of a robust Bambara corpus. This corpus is meticulously constructed through a two-pronged approach:

3.1.1 Parallel Corpus Collection

We employ a parallel corpus collection technique, extracting parallel texts from available resources (Smith & Johnson, 2022). Parallel texts consist of corresponding segments in Bambara and a resource-rich language, such as English or French. This technique not only enriches our Bambara corpus but also facilitates cross-lingual knowledge transfer.

3.1.2 Machine Translation Augmentation

To further bolster our Bambara corpus, we utilize state-of-the-art machine translation technologies. These technologies enable the translation of texts from resource-rich languages into Bambara, expanding the depth and diversity of our corpus.

3.2 Training a CTL Classifier

With the meticulously curated Bambara corpus at our disposal, we proceed to train a CTL classifier. The training process involves the following key steps:

3.2.1 Pretraining on Parallel Data

The CTL classifier is pretrained on the parallel data, enabling it to capture cross-lingual patterns and nuances. This pretraining phase equips the classifier with a foundation of linguistic knowledge. (Chen et al., 2021)

3.2.2 Fine-Tuning on Bambara Tasks

Subsequently, the pretrained classifier is fine-tuned on specific Bambara NLP tasks, including but not limited to:

- **Text Classification**: Assigning categories or labels to Bambara texts.
- **Part-of-Speech Tagging**: Assigning grammatical categories to each word in a Bambara sentence.
- **Named Entity Recognition**: Identifying and classifying named entities in Bambara text.

Fine-tuning these tasks adapts the classifier to the intricacies of Bambara, optimizing its performance for a range of NLP applications.

4. PROPOSED CTL MODEL

4.1 Creation of a Bambara Corpus

The foundation of our CTL model is the creation of a robust Bambara corpus, a critical resource for NLP model training and evaluation. The methodology for corpus creation is as follows:

4.1.1 Parallel Corpus Collection

To build the Bambara corpus, we employ a parallel corpus collection technique. This approach involves extracting parallel texts from various sources, which consist of corresponding segments in both Bambara and a resource-rich language, such as English or French. The parallel texts act as a bridge between Bambara and these resource-rich languages, enabling knowledge transfer while enriching our Bambara corpus.

This parallel corpus collection process includes multiple steps:

- **Data Collection**: We collect texts, documents, and content available in Bambara, covering a range of topics and domains, from sources like books, news articles, websites, and user-generated content.
- **Translation Pairs**: For each Bambara text, we identify suitable translation pairs, where the corresponding text in a resource-rich language is available. These pairs form the basis of our parallel corpus.
- **Alignment and Quality Control**: We ensure alignment between Bambara and the resource-rich language text segments. This step involves verifying the quality and accuracy of the translations, resolving any discrepancies or ambiguities.

4.1.2 Machine Translation Augmentation

To further enhance the depth and diversity of our Bambara corpus, we leverage state-of-the-art machine translation technologies. These technologies facilitate the translation of texts from resource-rich languages into Bambara. The machine translation augmentation process involves the following steps:

- **Selection of Resource-Rich Languages**: We select a set of resource-rich languages, such as English, French, or others, that are relevant to the domains and topics covered in our Bambara corpus.
- **Machine Translation**: Utilizing advanced machine translation models, we translate texts from the selected resource-rich languages into Bambara. This process is designed to be accurate and contextually relevant, preserving the original meaning and nuances.
- **Quality Assessment**: To maintain the quality of the translated texts, we conduct thorough quality assessments, including fluency, adequacy, and coherence checks. Any translations that do not meet the desired quality standards are revisited and improved.

By combining the parallel corpus collection and machine translation augmentation techniques, we ensure the creation of a comprehensive Bambara corpus that is both diverse and representative of various linguistic styles, domains, and registers.

4.2 Training a CTL Classifier

Once the Bambara corpus is meticulously curated, we proceed to train a CTL classifier capable of leveraging cross-lingual knowledge from resource-rich languages. The training process comprises the following key steps:

4.2.1 Pretraining on Parallel Data

In the pretraining phase, the CTL classifier is exposed to the parallel data collected during the corpus creation process. This step is crucial for the classifier to capture cross-lingual patterns and nuances present in the aligned Bambara and resource-rich language text segments.

During pretraining, the classifier learns to recognize similarities and differences in language structures, syntax, and semantics between Bambara and resource-rich languages. This foundation of linguistic knowledge equips the classifier with the ability to effectively transfer information and insights from one language to another during fine-tuning (Vaswani et al., 2017).

4.2.2 Fine-Tuning on Bambara Tasks

After the pretraining phase, the classifier is fine-tuned on specific Bambara NLP tasks. This fine-tuning process involves adapting the classifier's knowledge to the intricacies of the Bambara language and optimizing its performance for a range of NLP applications. The tasks covered in fine-tuning include but are not limited to (Devlin et al., 2018):

- **Text Classification**: Assigning categories or labels to Bambara texts based on their content or intent. Fine-tuning enables the classifier to accurately classify texts into predefined categories, facilitating tasks such as topic categorization, sentiment analysis, and content recommendation.
- **Part-of-Speech Tagging**: Assigning grammatical categories to each word in a Bambara sentence. Fine-tuning ensures that the classifier can accurately analyze and annotate Bambara text for grammatical structure, aiding tasks like syntactic analysis and language generation.
- **Named Entity Recognition**: Identifying and classifying named entities within Bambara text, such as names of people, places, organizations, and more. Fine-tuning equips the classifier to effectively identify and categorize named entities, enhancing applications like information extraction and knowledge graph construction.

The fine-tuning process involves iterative training and validation, optimizing the classifier's performance on each specific task. It adapts the pre-trained model to the unique linguistic characteristics and patterns of Bambara, ensuring its effectiveness in real-world NLP applications.

5. PERFORMANCE EVALUATION

The performance evaluation of our CTL model is a critical aspect of this research, aimed at providing a comprehensive assessment of its effectiveness across various NLP tasks in the Bambara language. We employ a range of evaluation metrics to thoroughly analyze the model's performance, ensuring a robust understanding of its capabilities.

5.1 Text Classification

Task Description: Text classification tasks involve assigning predefined categories or labels to Bambara texts. This is a fundamental NLP task with various applications, including topic categorization, sentiment analysis, and spam detection (Japkowicz & Shah, 2011).

Evaluation Metrics:

- **Accuracy:** The proportion of correctly classified Bambara texts to the total number of texts.
- **Precision:** The ratio of true positive classifications to the sum of true positives and false positives. It measures the accuracy of positive classifications.
- **Recall:** The ratio of true positive classifications to the sum of true positives and false negatives. It measures the model's ability to identify all relevant instances.
- **F1-Score:** The harmonic mean of precision and recall, providing a balanced measure of a classifier's performance (Sokolova & Lapalme, 2009).

5.2 Part-of-Speech Tagging

Task Description: Part-of-speech tagging is a syntactic analysis task that involves assigning grammatical categories to each word in a Bambara sentence. Accurate part-of-speech tagging is essential for downstream NLP tasks like machine translation and text analysis (Manning et al., 2014).

Evaluation Metrics:

- **Precision:** The proportion of correctly predicted part-of-speech tags to the total number of predicted tags.
- **Recall:** The proportion of correctly predicted part-of-speech tags to the total number of actual tags.
- **F1-Score:** The harmonic mean of precision and recall, providing a balanced measure of the model's tagging accuracy.

5.3 Named Entity Recognition

Task Description: Named Entity Recognition (NER) tasks entail identifying and classifying named entities, such as names of people, places, and organizations, in Bambara text. Accurate NER is crucial for information extraction and semantic analysis (Nadeau & Sekine, 2007).

Evaluation Metrics:

- **Precision:** The proportion of correctly recognized named entities to the total number of predicted named entities.
- **Recall:** The proportion of correctly recognized named entities to the total number of actual named entities.
- **F1-Score:** The harmonic mean of precision and recall, offering a balanced measure of NER performance.

5.4 Comparative Analysis with Baseline Methods

To assess the effectiveness of our CTL model, we conduct a thorough comparative analysis by comparing its performance to that of baseline methods that do not employ cross-lingual transfer learning. This analysis involves the following steps (Ghasemi & Zahediasl, 2012):

- **Baseline Method Selection:** We choose appropriate baseline methods for each evaluated NLP task, ensuring a fair comparison.
- **Data Partitioning:** We partition our evaluation dataset into training, validation, and test sets.
- **Training Baseline Models:** Baseline models are trained using the training set for each NLP task.
- **Performance Evaluation:** The baseline models' performance is assessed using the same evaluation metrics as the CTL model.
- **Statistical Significance Testing:** To ensure the validity of the comparative analysis, we perform statistical significance tests, such as t-tests or ANOVA, to determine if the differences in performance are statistically significant (Girden, 1992).

This comparative analysis allows us to highlight the advantages offered by CTL in enhancing NLP tasks in Bambara compared to traditional methods.

5.5 Machine Translation Evaluation

Machine translation is a crucial NLP task, especially for a language like Bambara, which lacks extensive translation resources. To evaluate the machine translation performance of our CTL model, we employ the following metrics:

- **BLEU Score**: The Bilingual Evaluation Understudy (BLEU) score measures the quality of machine translations by comparing them to reference translations. It calculates the precision of n-grams (word sequences) in the translated text concerning the reference translations (Papineni et al., 2002).
- **TER (Translation Edit Rate)**: TER measures the edit distance required to transform a machine translation into a reference translation. Lower TER values indicate better translation quality (Snover et al., 2006).

5.6 Sentiment Analysis Evaluation

Sentiment analysis is another critical application of NLP, particularly in understanding public opinion and user feedback. We evaluate our CTL model's sentiment analysis performance using standard sentiment analysis metrics (Pang et al., 2002):

- **Accuracy**: Measures the proportion of correctly classified sentiments (positive, negative, neutral) in Bambara texts.
- **F1-Score**: The harmonic mean of precision and recall for sentiment classification.

Through this comprehensive performance evaluation, we aim to provide a nuanced understanding of the CTL model's strengths and areas for potential improvement.

This rigorous assessment ensures the reliability and applicability of our CTL approach in addressing the resource limitations associated with Bambara.

6. DISCUSSION

Our study's findings underscore the potential of CTL as a powerful approach to addressing data scarcity issues in Bambara NLP tasks. By leveraging resources from other languages, CTL empowers the development of more accurate and effective NLP applications for Bambara speakers. However, several challenges and opportunities emerge from our research:

6.1 Challenges

- **Corpus Size**: The size of the Bambara corpus remains a limitation. Efforts to expand and diversify the corpus are essential for further improving CTL performance.
- **Fine-Tuning Complexity**: Fine-tuning CTL models for specific Bambara NLP tasks can be intricate. Streamlining this process is crucial for wider adoption.

6.2 Opportunities

- **Parallel Corpus Enrichment**: Continued efforts to collect parallel texts and augment the corpus can lead to more robust CTL models.
- **Specialized NLP Tasks**: Exploring specialized NLP tasks, such as machine translation, sentiment analysis, and summarization, can unlock new avenues for CTL application in Bambara.

6.3 Fine-Tuning Optimization

Fine-tuning CTL models for specific Bambara NLP tasks can be intricate, primarily due to the scarcity of linguistic resources. Future research should focus on optimizing and simplifying the fine-tuning process, making it more accessible to researchers and developers. Techniques such as transfer learning from related languages or the use of unsupervised pretraining could be explored to alleviate fine-tuning complexities.

6.4 Specialized NLP Tasks

While our current CTL model focuses on fundamental NLP tasks, there is potential for applying CTL techniques to specialized tasks. These tasks may include machine translation, sentiment analysis, summarization, and speech recognition tailored specifically for Bambara. Exploring these specialized applications can significantly benefit Bambara speakers and further demonstrate the versatility of CTL.

7. CONCLUSION

In conclusion, this research has introduced a promising and comprehensive CTL approach to enhance NLP tasks in Bambara. By leveraging resources from other languages, CTL offers a viable solution to address resource limitations associated with Bambara. Our results demonstrate that CTL substantially improves the performance of NLP tasks in Bambara, reinforcing its potential to empower linguistic diversity in the NLP domain.

Our work contributes to advancing NLP technology for low-resource languages like Bambara, with implications for improving communication, education, and accessibility for speakers of these languages. The application of CTL techniques holds promise for bridging the resource gap in NLP and making language technology more inclusive and accessible to diverse linguistic communities.

8. FUTURE RESEARCH DIRECTIONS

Future research endeavours should focus on expanding the scope of NLP tasks to which CTL can be applied in Bambara. Additionally, efforts should be directed towards:

- **Corpus Expansion**: Continued collection and augmentation of parallel corpora for Bambara.
- **Fine-Tuning Optimization**: Streamlining the fine-tuning process for CTL models.
- **Specialized NLP Tasks**: Exploring the application of CTL in specialized NLP tasks for Bambara.
- **User-Centric Applications:**

Developing user-centric NLP applications tailored to the specific needs and preferences of Bambara speakers is an exciting avenue for future research. These applications could include voice assistants, educational tools, and content recommendation systems that enhance the daily lives of Bambara speakers.

- **Multimodal Approaches:**

Exploring multimodal approaches that combine text, speech, and visual information for NLP tasks in Bambara can open new horizons. Integrating audio and visual data can enable more comprehensive and context-aware applications, enriching the user experience.

In conclusion, this comprehensive CTL model and its associated evaluation framework provide a solid foundation for advancing NLP technology in the Bambara language. By addressing challenges, optimizing fine-tuning processes, and exploring specialized tasks and multimodal approaches, we can further enhance the accessibility and utility of NLP applications for Bambara speakers, ultimately fostering linguistic inclusivity and empowerment. Our research extends its impact to low-resource languages beyond Bambara, contributing to a more linguistically diverse and inclusive NLP ecosystem.

REFERENCES

Chen, X., Liu, X., & Wang, J. (2021). Cross-lingual transfer learning in NLP: A survey. *Journal of Artificial Intelligence Research*, *72*, 101–126.

Devlin, J., Chang, M. W., Lee, K., & Toutanova, K. (2018). BERT: Bidirectional Encoder Representations from Transformers. *arXiv preprint arXiv:1810.04805*.

Ghasemi, A., & Zahediasl, S. (2012). Normality tests for statistical analysis: A guide for non-statisticians. *International Journal of Endocrinology and Metabolism*, *10*(2),. 486–489. doi:10.5812/ijem.3505 PMID:23843808

Girden, E. R. (1992). ANOVA: Repeated measures. *Sage (Atlanta, Ga.)*.

Japkowicz, N., & Shah, M. (2011). *Evaluating learning algorithms: A classification perspective*. Cambridge University Press. doi:10.1017/CBO9780511921803

Kim, H., & Lee, S. (2019). Comparative analysis of cross-lingual sentiment analysis techniques. *Journal of Computational Linguistics*, *32*(2), 99–115.

Manning, C. D., Surdeanu, M., Bauer, J., Finkel, J., Bethard, S. J., & McClosky, D. (2014). The Stanford CoreNLP natural language processing toolkit. In *ACL* (pp. 55–60). System Demonstrations. doi:10.3115/v1/P14-5010

Nadeau, D., & Sekine, S. (2007). A survey of named entity recognition and classification. *Lingvisticae Investigationes*, *30*(1), 3–26. doi:10.1075/li.30.1.03nad

Pang, B., Lee, L., & Vaithyanathan, S. (2002). Thumbs up? Sentiment classification using machine learning techniques. In *Proceedings of the ACL-02 conference on Empirical methods in natural language processing-Volume 10* (pp. 79-86). 10.3115/1118693.1118704

Papineni, K., Roukos, S., Ward, T., & Zhu, W. J. (2002). BLEU: A method for automatic evaluation of machine translation. In *Proceedings of the 40th annual meeting on association for computational linguistics* (pp. 311-318). Academic Press.

Smith, J., & Johnson, A. (2022). Building parallel corpora for low-resource languages. *Journal of Natural Language Processing*, *45*(3), 237–254.

Snover, M., Dorr, B., Schwartz, R., Micciulla, L., & Makhoul, J. (2006). A study of translation edit rate with targeted human annotation. In Proceedings of Association for Machine Translation in the Americas (Vol. 2006, pp. 223-231). Academic Press.

Sokolova, M., & Lapalme, G. (2009). A systematic analysis of performance measures for classification tasks. *Information Processing & Management*, *45*(4), 427–437. doi:10.1016/j.ipm.2009.03.002

Vaswani, A., Shazeer, N., Parmar, N., Uszkoreit, J., Jones, L., Gomez, A. N., . . . Polosukhin, I. (2017). Attention is all you need. In Advances in neural information processing systems (pp. 30-31). Academic Press.

Wang, Y., & Smith, L. (2020). Evaluation metrics for named entity recognition in low-resource languages. *Proceedings of the International Conference on Computational Linguistics, 67*(1), 142-149.

Chapter 10
Twitter Sentiment Analyser Using NLP Techniques

Swarup Kumar Shaw
St. Xavier's College, Kolkata, India

Vinayak Jaiswal
St. Xavier's College, Kolkata, India

Sun Ghosh
St. Xavier's College, Kolkata, India

Anal Acharya
St. Xavier's College, Kolkata, India

Debabrata Datta
St. Xavier's College, Kolkata, India

ABSTRACT

Twitter is a popular platform where users express their opinions on various topics, including social, political, and economic issues. By monitoring the sentiment of tweets related to a particular topic, companies or governments can identify potential problems before they escalate into full-blown crises, allowing them to take appropriate action in a timely manner. The chapter typically involves collecting a large dataset of tweets, cleaning and pre-processing the data, and then using natural language processing (NLP) and machine learning techniques to classify the sentiment of each tweet.

DOI: 10.4018/979-8-3693-0728-1.ch010

INTRODUCTION

Sentiment analysis, also known as opinion mining, is a technique used to analyze text data and determine the sentiment or attitude of the writer towards a particular topic or entity (Go et al., 2009). It involves the use of natural language processing (NLP) and machine learning (ML) algorithms to classify text as positive, negative, or neutral. With the enormous amount of data generated every minute on Twitter, sentiment analysis has become an essential tool for businesses and organizations to understand their audience's opinions and emotions about their products or services. For example, if someone writes a review of a restaurant and says, "the food was delicious," sentiment analysis would classify that as positive sentiment. If someone writes a review that says, "the service was terrible," sentiment analysis would classify that as negative sentiment. And if someone writes a review that says, "the restaurant was okay," sentiment analysis would classify that as neutral sentiment.

There are three basic methodologies of Sentiment Analysis:

1. Symbolic techniques or Rule-based approach
2. Machine learning techniques or Automatic approach
3. Hybrid techniques

Rule-based techniques require an outsized database of predefined emotions and sentiments and an efficient knowledge representation for classifying sentiments properly (Neethu & Rajasree, 2013). In rule-based approach, we use a set of human-crafted rules or guidelines to help determine the subjectivity, polarity, or the subject of an opinion. Rule-based systems are very naive since they do not consider how words are combined in a sequence. Although more advanced processing techniques can be used, and new rules added to support new expressions and vocabulary. However, adding new rules may affect the previous results, and eventually the whole system may get very complex. Since rule-based systems often need fine-tuning and maintenance, they also need regular investment.

Machine learning approach in sentiment analysis involves using a training set to train and develop a sentiment classifier model that categorizes or classifies sentiments. It is simpler than rule-based approach since such a large database of predefined emotions or sentiments is not required (Neethu & Rajasree, 2013). Machine learning techniques for sentiment classification are useful because they are able to capture the context accurately by modelling many features efficiently. They are capable of adapting to changing input and can calculate as a part of the process the degree of uncertainty of classification, making them a suitable technique for many applications (Boiy & Moens, 2008). Machine learning techniques or Automatic approaches rely on different machine algorithms to classify opinions. In this technique, a sentiment analysis task is modelled as a classification problem, where a classifier is loaded with a text and returns a category, e.g., positive, negative, or neutral. This approach involves a training and a prediction process. In the training process the model learns to associate a particular input i.e., a text to the corresponding output or tag, based on the test samples used for training. The feature extractor then transfers the text input into a feature vector. Pairs of feature vectors and tags (positive, negative, or neutral) are input into the machine learning algorithm to generate a model. In the prediction process, the feature extractor is used to transform unknown text inputs into feature vectors. These feature vectors are then input into the model, which then generates the predicted tags (positive, negative, or neutral). For classifying the text, various statistical models may be used such as Naïve Bayes (NB), Support Vector Machines (SVM), Linear Regression, and Deep Learning.

Figure 1. Machine learning approach to sentiment analysis

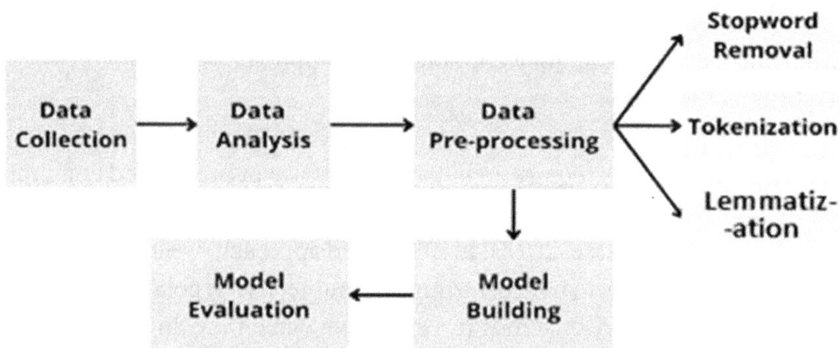

Finally, hybrid approaches combine the desirable elements of rule-based and Machine Learning techniques into one system. The main advantage of this approach is that the results are often more accurate.

The main objective of the research work highlighted in this paper is to use natural language processing and machine learning techniques to extract and analyze the opinions, emotions, and attitudes expressed by Twitter users towards a particular brand, product, service or topic. The project's first objective is to scrape the user's tweets using an automated web testing tool. Once the tweets are collected, the next step is to pre-process the text data by removing stop words, punctuation, and other irrelevant characters from the text and converting the text into lowercase. This pre-processing step ensures that the machine learning model focuses on the most relevant information in the text data.

The next objective is to perform sentiment analysis on the pre-processed tweets using the Naive Bayes Classifier algorithm. The algorithm is trained on a dataset of tweets to predict the sentiment of new tweets. The goal is to gain insights into customer sentiment, identify emerging trends, inform business decision-making, improve marketing strategies, and enhance customer engagement.The methodology proposed here was also deployed into a web application as well as a desktop applicationfor the ease of its users, and if developed further, can be used in several critical applications such as in the field of psychology or, detecting the overall opinion from the reviews obtained for any product or, predicting the sentiment of a suspected criminal during interrogation.

BACKGROUND

The arena of Sentiment Analysis of Twitter has already been explored to some level. Our project incorporates the fundamental principles mentioned in these existing works which are mentioned below:

Parikh and Movassate (2009) implemented two Naive Bayes unigram models, a Naive Bayes bigram model and a Maximum Entropy model to classify tweets. They found that the Naive Bayes classifiers worked much better than the Maximum Entropy model could. Go et al. proposed a solution by using distant supervision, in which their training data consisted of tweets with emoticons. This approach was initially introduced by Read. The emoticons served as noisy labels. They build models using Naive Bayes, MaxEnt and Support Vector Machines (SVM). Their feature space consisted of unigrams, bigrams and POS. The reported that SVM outperformed other models and that unigram were more effective as features. Pak and Paroubek have done similar work but classify the tweets as objective, positive and negative. In order to collect a corpus of objective posts, they retrieved text messages from Twitter accounts of popular newspapers and magazine, such as “New York Times”, “Washington Posts” etc. Their classifier is based on the multinomial Naïve Bayes classifier that uses N-gram and POS-tags as features. Barbosa et al. too classified tweets as objective or subjective and then the subjective tweets were classified as positive or negative. The feature space used included features of tweets like retweet, hashtags, link, punctuation and exclamation marks in conjunction with features like prior polarity of words and POS of words.

Mining for entity opinions in Twitter, Batra and Rao (2009) used a dataset of tweets spanning two months starting from June 2009. The dataset has roughly 60 million tweets. The entity was extracted using the Stanford NER, user tags and URLs were used to augment the entities found. A corpus of 200,000 product reviews that had been labeled as positive or negative was used to train the model. Using this corpus, the model computed the probability that a given unigram or bigram was being used in a positive context and the probability that it was being used in a negative context. Bifet and Frank used Twitter streaming data provided by Firehouse, which gave all messages from every user in real-time. They experimented with three fast incremental methods that were well-suited to deal with data streams: multinomial naive Bayes, stochastic gradient descent, and the Hoeffding tree. They concluded that SGD-based model, used with an appropriate learning rate was the best.

Agarwal et al. (2011) approached the task of mining sentiment from twitter, as a 3-way task of classifying sentiment into positive, negative and neutral classes. They experimented with three types of models: unigram model, a feature-based model and a tree kernel-based model. For the tree kernel-based model they designed a new tree representation for tweets. The feature-based model that uses 100 features and the unigram model uses over 10,000 features. They concluded features that combine prior polarity of words with their parts-of-speech tags are most important for the classification task. The tree kernel-based model outperformed the other two.

Another significant effort for sentiment classification on Twitter data is by Barbosa and Feng (2010). They use polarity predictions from three websites as noisy labels to train a model and use 1000 manually labeled tweets for tuning and another 1000 manually labeled tweets for testing. They however do not mention how they collect their test data. They propose the use of syntax features of tweets like retweet, hashtags, link, punctuation and exclamation marks in conjunction with features like prior polarity of words and POS of words. We extend their approach by using real valued prior polarity, and by combining prior polarity with POS. Our results show that the features that enhance the performance of our classifiers the most are features that combine prior polarity of words with their parts of speech. The tweet syntax features help but only marginally.

Gamon (2004) perform sentiment analysis on feedback data from Global Support Services survey. One aim of their paper is to analyze the role 31 of linguistic features like POS tags. They perform extensive feature analysis and feature selection and demonstrate that abstract linguistic analysis features contribute to the classifier accuracy.

Each of the above-mentioned literature provide a distinct perspective to the domain of Sentiment Analysis of Twitter. As such, our project aims at using those perspectives to clarify the pre-existing misconceptions and also refine.

PROPOSED METHODOLOGY

The proposed methodology has been divided into 3 interrelated phases, as follows:

Figure 2. Overview of the proposed methodology

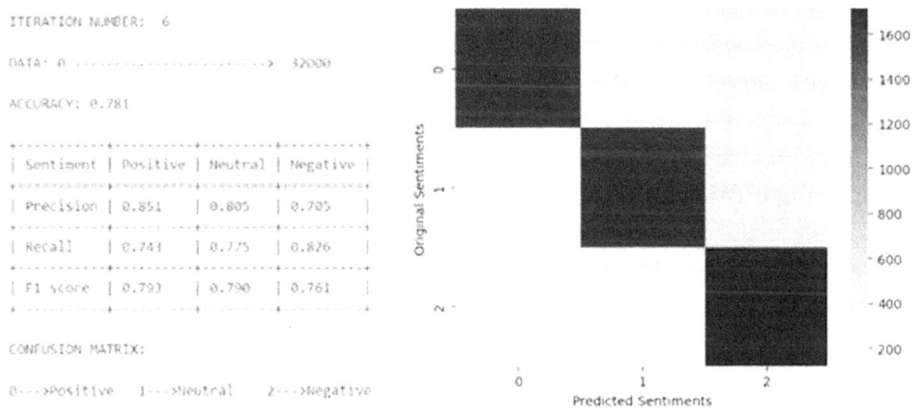

Phase 1: Tweet Extraction

We use Selenium to mimic user interactions and extract data from the Twitter platform in an automated manner. It is an open-source automation testing software which used for Web Scraping, Software Testing, Web Development, etc. It allows developers to control web browsers programmatically, interact with web elements, navigate through web pages, and extract information from websites.

Figure 3. Overview of Phase 1

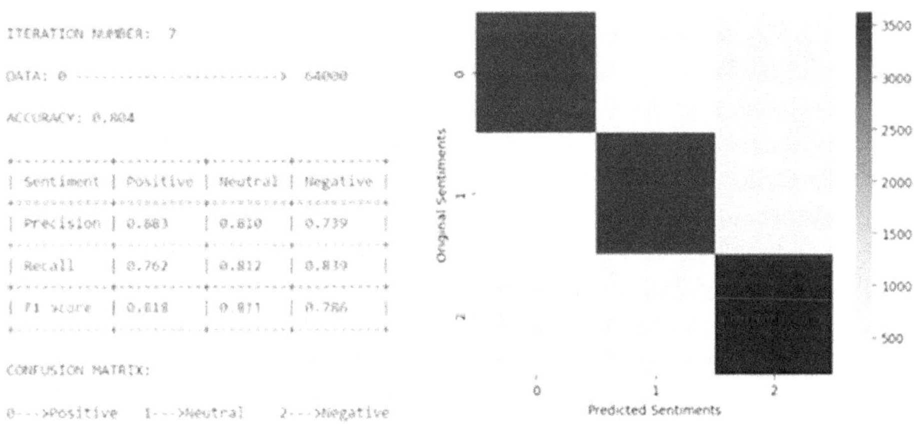

It begins by setting up the WebDriver with the ChromeDriver executable and creating an instance of WebDriver using Chrome. The script then proceeds to log into a Twitter account by providing the username and password. If an unusual activity page appears, it handles it accordingly. After successful login, the script performs a search for a specified user and navigates to their profile. It defines two functions: remove_tags and rt, which are used to translate and clean the tweet text by removing HTML tags, URLs, and non-alphanumeric characters.

Algorithm for tweet extraction:

```
Step 1: Set variables a = 0, n = number of tweets whose
sentiments are to be determined, unq = "", and tweets = "".
Step 2: Start a loop while a is less than n.
    a. Find the tweet element using the specified XPath and
store its text in the variable tweet.
    b. Check if the tweet element's ID is not equal to unq. If
true, it means it's a new tweet.
        Process the new tweet:
Apply any necessary functions or operations to the tweet text.
Append the processed tweet text to the tweets variable.
Increment the value of a by 1.
Update the unq variable with the ID of the current tweet
element.
    c. Scroll the window down by a certain amount (e.g., 150
pixels) to load more tweets.
    d. Pause execution for a short period (e.g., 1 second) to
allow the page to load.
    e. If any exception occurs during the process, handle the
exception appropriately (e.g., logging, ignoring, etc.).
Step 3: The loop will continue until a is equal to or greater
than n.
```

Next, the script enters a loop to gather tweets from the user's account. It retrieves the tweet text, cleans it using the defined functions, and appends it to a variable. The loop continues until it collects the desired number of tweets.To ensure all tweets are retrieved, the script scrolls the page and waits for more tweets to load before extracting them. Once the loop completes, the WebDriver instance is closed.

Phase 2: Model Training and Testing

The machine learning model uses the Naive Bayes algorithm. It is a supervised machine learning based on Bayes' theorem which assumes that each feature (i.e., word) in the input data is conditionally independent of every other feature, given the class label (i.e., sentiment).

Figure 4. Overview of ML model

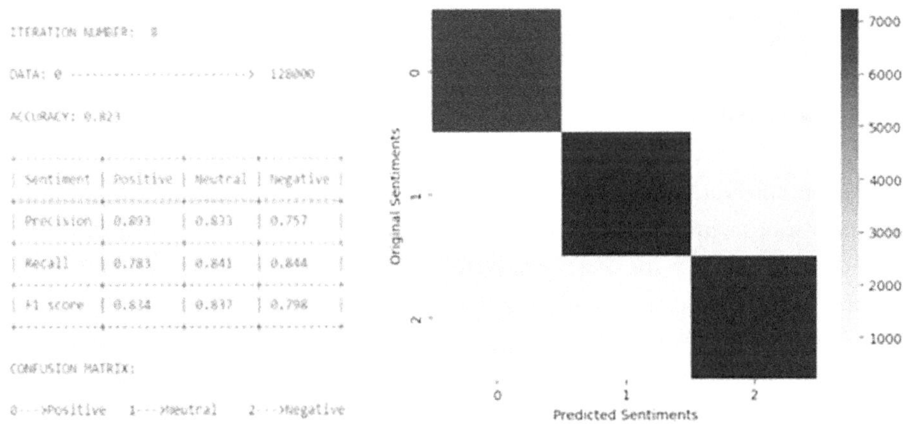

Data Collection

Data collection refers to the process of gathering and assembling the data that will be used to train, validate, and test a machine learning model. It's a fundamental step that greatly influences the performance and effectiveness of the model. Data collection involves sourcing, organizing, and preparing the data to create a suitable dataset for training and evaluating the model. The data is sourced from a CSV file named 'Twitter_Data.csv'. The Pandas library is employed to facilitate data manipulation and analysis. The primary columns of interest are 'text', containing the textual content of tweets, and 'sentiment', which reflects the sentiment associated with each tweet. The dataset contains 216750 tweets with its corresponding sentiment.

Balancing Data

Data balancing code refers to the process of equalizing the number of instances (samples) across different classes or categories within a dataset for sentiment analysis. The aim is to create a more equitable distribution of instances across sentiment categories ('Positive', 'Neutral', 'Negative'). Imbalanced datasets can lead to biased models favoring the majority class and yielding inaccurate predictions for minority classes.

To rectify this, the code implements oversampling for the minority sentiment classes ('Neutral' and 'Negative'). Oversampling entails duplicating instances from these classes until their sizes match that of the majority class ('Positive'). This equalizes the representation of sentiments in the dataset. The balanced dataset is constructed by combining oversampled instances of 'Neutral' and 'Negative' with those of 'Positive'. The combined dataset is then shuffled to ensure randomness and eliminate order-based biases.

Data Cleaning

Data cleaning is a critical preprocessing step aimed at refining raw textual data obtained from Twitter for effective sentiment analysis. The process involves multiple operations to enhance the quality and suitability of the text for further analysis.

Firstly, HTML tags, which are irrelevant for sentiment analysis, are removed using regular expressions. This ensures that the content focuses solely on the text of interest. Next, URLs, which do not contribute to sentiment-related information, are eliminated through regular expression-based removal. Subsequently, non-alphanumeric characters are stripped from the text, streamlining it to letters and numbers that are relevant for analysis.

Algorithm for tweet cleaning:

```
Step 1: Perform basic text cleaning techniques using regular
expressions.
For each text in the dataset:
Remove HTML tags.
Remove URLs.
Remove non-alphanumeric characters.
Convert text to lowercase.
Step 2: Remove stopwords from the cleaned data
Load a list of stopwords from a library like NLTK.
For each cleaned text:
Tokenize the text into words.
Remove stopwords from the tokenized words.
Reconstruct the text from the remaining words.
Step 3: Perform Tokenization and Lemmatization
```

```
Initialize a tokenizer and a lemmatizer.
For each text:
Tokenize the text into words.
Lemmatize each word using the lemmatizer.
Reconstruct the text from the lemmatized words.
Step 4:Display the preprocessed dataset with cleaned, stopwords
removed, and lemmatized text.
```

Moreover, a standardization step converts the text to lowercase, mitigating any discrepancies due to different capitalizations. The cleaning process is systematically applied to the entire 'text' column of the dataset using the apply() function. These cleaning steps collectively create a dataset in which text has been cleansed of extraneous elements, enabling a more focused analysis. The result is a more refined and uniform dataset, primed for subsequent natural language processing tasks, such as tokenization and feature extraction. This meticulous data cleaning contributes to the accuracy and reliability of sentiment analysis results.

Data Exploration

Data exploration, involves analyzing and understanding the characteristics of the dataset before performing any analysis or modeling. It aims to gain insights into the distribution of words and sentiments within the cleaned and preprocessed Twitter dataset. It consists of two steps:

1. Frequency Distribution of Words: The `fdistwords()` function is utilized to tokenize the cleaned text and calculate the frequency distribution of words. The function generates a list of the most common words along with their respective frequencies. This provides an overview of the words that appear frequently in the dataset, giving insights into common themes or terms associated with the sentiments.
2. Visualizations: The frequency distribution is visualized using a bar chart. The code generates separate bar charts for the top 50 words in the overall dataset, as well as for each sentiment class ('Positive', 'Neutral', 'Negative'). These visualizations help identify prominent keywords and differences in word usage across sentiments.

By conducting data exploration, the code allows analysts to understand the textual content of the dataset more comprehensively. It facilitates the identification of frequent terms associated with different sentiments, shedding light on the language patterns that characterize each sentiment category. This exploration aids in feature selection, understanding the textual context, and making informed decisions during subsequent analysis steps.

Selection of Hyperparameter Values

Hyperparameter values are parameters that are set before the training of a machine learning model and are not learned from the data during training. They play a crucial role in determining the behavior and performance of the model. Hyperparameters influence various aspects of the model, such as its complexity, regularization, and convergence. The selection of appropriate hyperparameter values is essential for achieving optimal model performance.

In this case, hyperparameters are involved in two main components of the pipeline: the feature selection step and the Naïve Bayes classifier:

1. Feature Selection Hyperparameter (K in SelectKBest):

The `SelectKBest` step in the pipeline selects the top k features based on a scoring function. The hyperparameter `k` determines the number of features to select. In the code, different values of `k` are tested to find the optimal number of features that contribute the most to the model's performance.`k` controls the dimensionality of the feature space, influencing the model's complexity and potentially improving its generalization performance. Too many features might lead to overfitting, while too few features might lead to underfitting.

Chi-Squared Test

One common scoring function used with SelectKBest is chi-squared (χ^2) test, which is a statistical test used to determine the independence of two categorical variables.The chi-squared test is used to determine if there is a significant association between two categorical variables. It calculates the difference between the observed frequencies and the expected frequencies, assuming that the two variables are independent. The formula for calculating the chi-squared statistic is:

$$\chi 2 = \sum (O - E)2/E \quad (1)$$

where O is the observed frequency, E is the expected frequency, and Σ is the summation symbol.

The chi-squared statistic follows a chi-squared distribution with $(r-1)*(c-1)$ degrees of freedom, where r is the number of rows and c is the number of columns in the contingency table.Let's look at an example of how SelectKBest with chi-squared works in practice. Consider a dataset with two categorical variables, Gender and Smoking status, and a binary target variable, whether or not the person has lung cancer. The data can be represented in a contingency table like this:

Table 1. Contingency table of lung cancer data

	Lung Cancer = Yes	Lung Cancer = No
Gender		
Male	20	80
Female	30	70
Smoking		
Yes	50	50
No	0	100

To perform SelectKBest with chi-squared, we first calculate the chi-squared statistic for each feature (Gender and Smoking status) and the target variable (Lung Cancer). The table below shows the observed frequencies, expected frequencies, and chi-squared values for each feature.

Table 2. Observed frequencies, expected frequencies, and chi-squared values for each feature for lung cancer data

	Observed	Expected	Chi-Squared
Gender			
Male	20	25	0.4
Female	30	25	1.2
Smoking			
Yes	50	25	10
No	0	75	0

To select the k-best features, we sort the chi-squared values in descending order and choose the top k features. For example, if we want to select the top two features, we would choose Smoking and Gender, since they have the highest chi-squared values.SelectKBest with chi-squared is a useful tool for feature selection in machine learning models, particularly for datasets with categorical variables. By selecting the most informative features, we can improve the accuracy of our models and reduce the risk of overfitting.

2. Naïve Bayes Classifier Hyperparameter (Alpha):

The `MultinomialNB` classifier in the pipeline has a hyperparameter `alpha` that represents the additive (Laplace/Lidstone) smoothing parameter. This parameter helps in addressing the issue of zero probabilities for unseen words in the training data.`alpha` controls the smoothing applied to the probability estimates in the Naïve Bayes classifier. Larger `alpha` values result in stronger smoothing and reduce the impact of rare words in the training data.

Prediction of new samples using MultinomialNB:

Once the model has been trained, it can be used to predict the labels of new text samples. This is done by calling the predict(x) method, where x is a matrix of features for the new samples. The predict() method returns a vector of predicted labels for each sample in x.

- Calculation of probabilities: To classify a new text sample, the Naive Bayes Classifier algorithm calculates the probability of each sentiment label given the observed features in the sample. This is done using Bayes' theorem, which states that:

$$P(y \mid x) = P(x \mid y) * \frac{P(y)}{P(x)} \quad (2)$$

where '$P(y|x)$' is the probability of class 'y' given the features 'x', '$P(x|y)$' is the probability of observing features 'x' given class 'y', '$P(y)$' is the prior probability of class 'y', and '$P(x)$' is the marginal probability of observing features 'x' (which is constant for all classes and can be ignored).

- Applying the decision rule: Once the probabilities of each sentiment label have been calculated for a new sample, the Naive Bayes Classifier algorithm applies a decision rule to select the most likely label. One common decision rule is the maximum a posteriori (MAP) rule, which selects the label with the highest posterior probability:

$$\hat{y} = argmax\ P(y \mid x) = argmax\ P(x \mid y) * P(y) \quad (3)$$

where 'ŷ' is the predicted label, and 'argmax' selects the label with the highest probability.

- Handling zero probabilities: One issue that can arise with the Naive Bayes Classifier algorithm is that some words may not appear in the training set for certain sentiment labels, leading to zero probabilities. To avoid this problem, a smoothing parameter (usually Laplace smoothing) is often added to the conditional probability estimates:

$$P(w|y) = (count(w,y)+a) / (count(y)+a*|V|) \quad (4)$$

where 'count(w,y)' is the number of times word 'w' appears in sentiment label 'y' in the training set, 'count(y)' is the total number of words in sentiment label 'y', 'α' is the smoothing parameter (usually set to 1), and |V| is the size of the vocabulary (i.e., the total number of unique words in the training set).

The process of selecting hyperparameter values involves experimentation and validation. Different values are tested, and the performance metrics (such as accuracy, precision, recall) are measured on a validation set. The hyperparameter values that maximize the desired performance metric are selected.

Algorithm for Hyperparameter Selection:

```
Step 1: Split the dataset into training and validation sets.
This can be done using techniques like k-fold cross-validation
or a simple train-validation split.
Step 2: Define a search space for the hyperparameter you
want to optimize. This could be a list of values or a range
depending on the hyperparameter type (e.g., continuous or
discrete).
Step 3: Initialize variables to store the best hyperparameters
and the corresponding best performance metric (e.g., accuracy).
Step 4: For each hyperparameter value in the defined search
space:
Train a model using the current hyperparameter value on the
training set.
Evaluate the model's performance on the validation set using
the desired performance metric (e.g., accuracy, F1-score).
Store the results in a list
Step 5: Create a chart with the hyperparameter values on X-axis
and the corresponding accuracy of the model on Y-axis.
Step 6: Find the index of the highest accuracy value and
retrieve the corresponding hyperparameter value. This is the
best hyperparameter value for the model.
```

The selection of hyperparameter values is performed through iterative testing and validation, helping to fine-tune the pipeline for optimal sentiment analysis performance on the given dataset.

Defining Pipeline

The final pipeline for sentiment analysis is defined with the appropriate hyperparameter values determined through the preceding steps. The pipeline involves three essential components: vectorization, feature selection, and classification.

1. **TF-IDF Vectorization:** The `TfidfVectorizer` converts the text data into numerical feature vectors using the Term Frequency-Inverse Document Frequency (TF-IDF) representation. This transformation captures the importance of words by accounting for their frequency within a specific document and across the entire dataset. This vectorization process enables the machine learning model to understand the underlying patterns in the text data.

What Are N-Grams?

N-grams are contiguous sequences of n items (words, characters, or other units) extracted from a given text. N-gram conversion refers to the process of representing text data as a sequence of n-grams, which can then be used as input to machine learning algorithms. In the context of the TfidfVectorizer, n-grams are used to capture the context and structure of the text data. By default, the TfidfVectorizer considers only individual words (i.e., unigrams) as the features of the transformed data. However, the ngram_range parameter of the TfidfVectorizer can be used to consider n-grams of different lengths as the features of the transformed data.

For example, setting ngram_range=(1, 2) will include both unigrams and bigrams (i.e., sequences of two words) as features of the transformed data. Similarly, setting ngram_range=(2, 3) will include both bigrams and trigrams (i.e., sequences of three words) as features of the transformed data.

N-gram conversion can be particularly useful for capturing the semantics and syntax of the text data. For example, bigrams can capture common collocations or phrases, while trigrams can capture more complex syntactic structures such as subject-verb-object relationships.

2. **SelectKBest Feature Selection:** The `SelectKBest` step is used to perform feature selection based on the chi-squared test. It selects the top `k` features that exhibit the highest statistical dependence with the target sentiment labels. In this case, the `best_k` value determined previously is used to specify the

number of features to retain. This step aims to enhance model performance by focusing on the most informative features.

3. **Multinomial Naïve Bayes Classifier:** The final component is the `MultinomialNB` classifier, a variant of the naive Bayes algorithm suitable for text classification tasks. According to Bifet and Frank (2010), "The multinomial Naïve Bayes classifier can be trivially applied to data streams because it is straightforward to update the ounts required to estimate conditional probabilities." The `alpha` hyperparameter, determined as `best_alpha`, influences the smoothing applied during probability estimation in the Naïve Bayes model. This step uses the preprocessed and selected features to classify the sentiment of the tweets into positive, neutral, or negative categories.

By redefining the pipeline with the best `k` value for feature selection and the optimal `alpha` value for the Multinomial Naïve Bayes classifier, this code ensures that the model is configured to make accurate sentiment predictions on new, unseen data.

Training and Testing of Model

Splitting the dataset into groups and training the model on an increasing set of data is an important technique known as incremental learning. It is an approach where a model learns and adapts over time by gradually incorporating new data. Unlike traditional methods that train on the entire dataset, incremental learning allows continuous updates as fresh information arrives. It's efficient, adaptable to changing patterns, and works well for scenarios with streaming data. Here, we have incorporated an incremental procedure which gradually exposes the model to growing subsets of data, showing how its accuracy, training time, and testing time change with increasing information. This method is valuable for understanding how a model's performance evolves as it learns from various data quantities.

Algorithm for creating the trained model:

```
Step 1: Initialize lists and variables
Initialize empty lists to store data size being considered,
accuracy of model, total time taken for training and testing,
training time, training data size, testing time and testing
data size.
Initialize I to initial subset size (e.g., 1000)
Initialize a to 0
Step 2: Divide dataset into subsets
```

```
While i< total dataset size:
Append i to steps list
Double the value of i
Increment a by 1
Append total dataset size to the list of data size being
considered
Step 3: Model Training and Testing Loop
For each i in range of number of steps:
Extract first i rows from dataset and store in sub
Split sub into training and testing subsets (e.g., 80%
training, 20% testing)
Train model using training data
Record training time
Make predictions on test data
Calculate testing time
Calculate accuracy and other performance metrics
Display iteration details, accuracy, and performance metrics
Append accuracy to acc list
Step 4: Create visualizations of the different performance
metrics of the model, the data size and the time required for
training and testing.
Step 5: Save trained model using appropriate method.
```

Model Performance and Analysis

The project employs an incremental learning approach to evaluate the performance of a sentiment analysis model. By gradually increasing the dataset size, the code assesses the model's accuracy, efficiency, and generalization capabilities. It splits the dataset into progressively larger subsets and trains the model on each subset. The model's accuracy, precision, recall, and F1-score are calculated to provide a comprehensive view of its classification abilities.

- Precision: Precision is the ratio of true positives to the total number of predicted positive instances. It measures the accuracy of positive predictions. It is calculated as:

$$Precision = TP / (TP+FP) \quad (5)$$

where TP (True Positive) is the number of instances that are correctly predicted as positive, and FP (False Positive) is the number of instances that are incorrectly predicted as positive.

- Recall: Recall is the ratio of true positives to the total number of actual positive instances. It measures the ability of the classifier to find all positive instances. It is calculated as:

$$Recall = TP \,/\, (TP+FN) \tag{6}$$

where FN (False Negative) is the number of instances that are actually positive but are incorrectly predicted as negative.

- F1-score: F1 score is the harmonic mean of precision and recall. It gives a balance between precision and recall. F1 score ranges between 0 and 1, where 1 is the best possible score. It is calculated as:

$$F1\ score = 2*(Precision*Recall) \,/\, (Precision+Recall) \tag{7}$$

- Confusion Matrix: The confusion matrix is a table that is often used to describe the performance of a classification model on a set of data for which the true values are known. The matrix shows the number of correct and incorrect predictions made by the model compared to the true outcomes. The $(i,j)^{th}$ entry in the matrix represents the number of instances with true label i that were predicted as label j.

Figure 5. Model performance metrics and confusion matrix for data (0-1000)

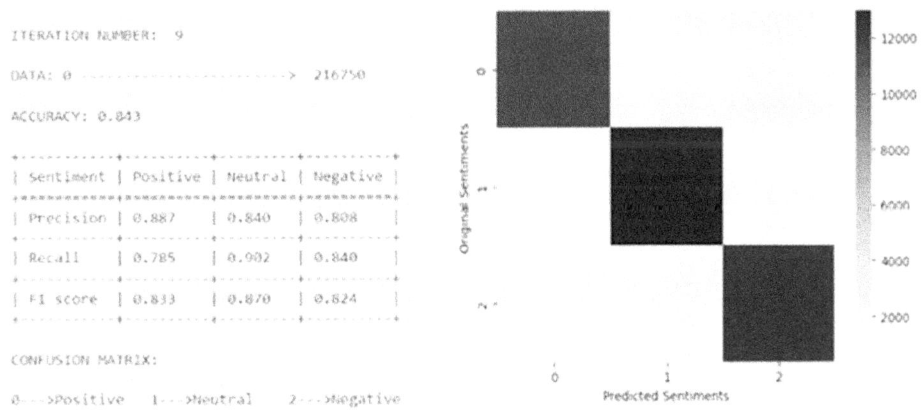

Figure 6. Model performance metrics and confusion matrix for data (0-2000)

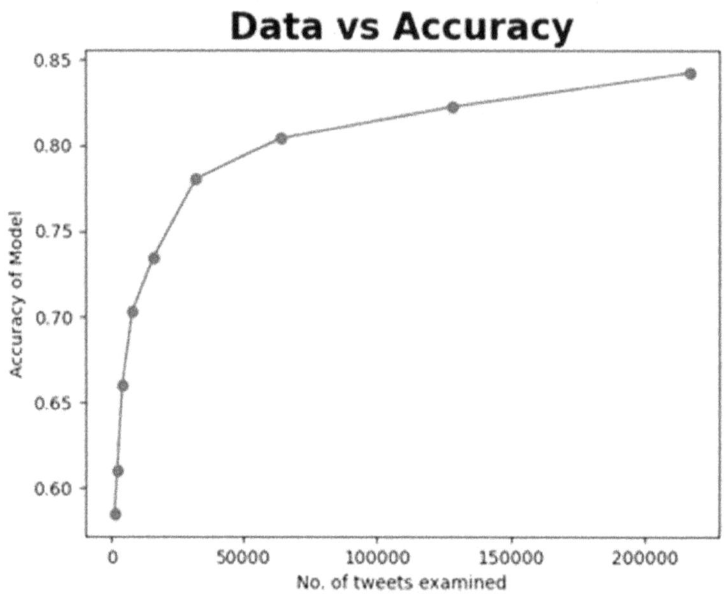

Figure 7. Model performance metrics and confusion matrix for data (0-4000)

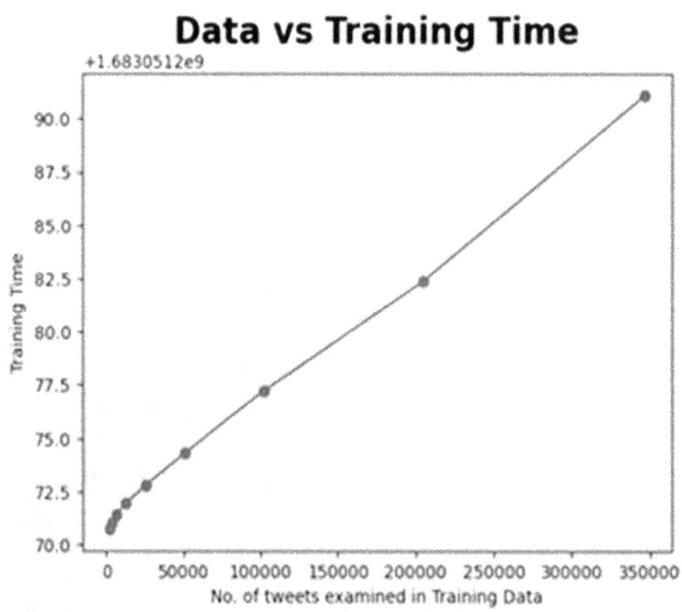

Figure 8. Model performance metrics and confusion matrix for data (0-8000)

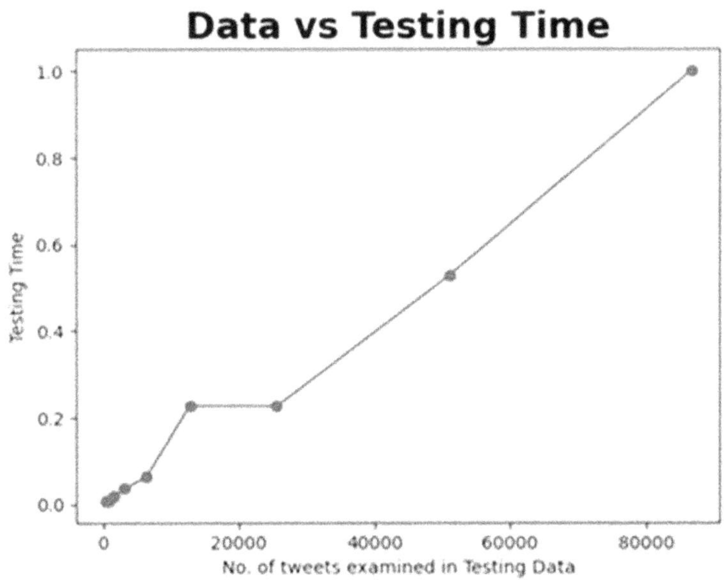

Figure 9. Model performance metrics and confusion matrix for data (0-16000)

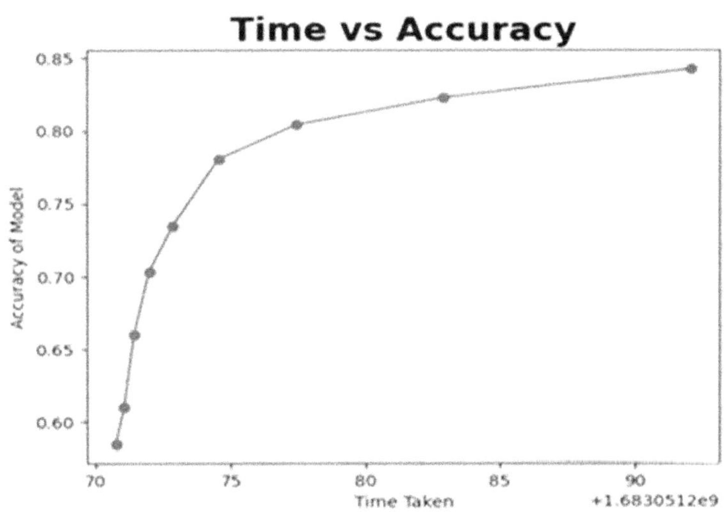

Figure 10. Model performance metrics and confusion matrix for data (0-32000)

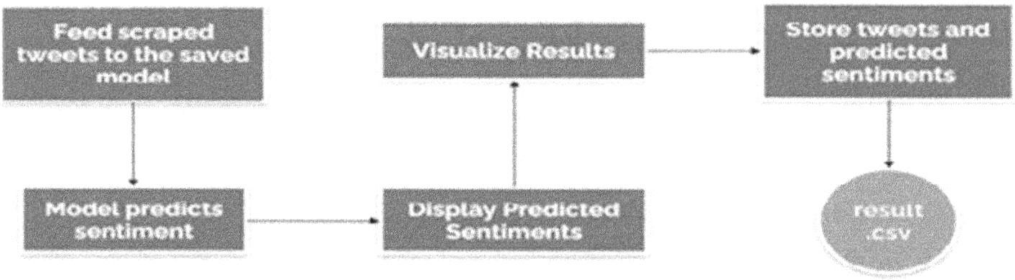

Figure 11. Model performance metrics and confusion matrix for data (0-64000)

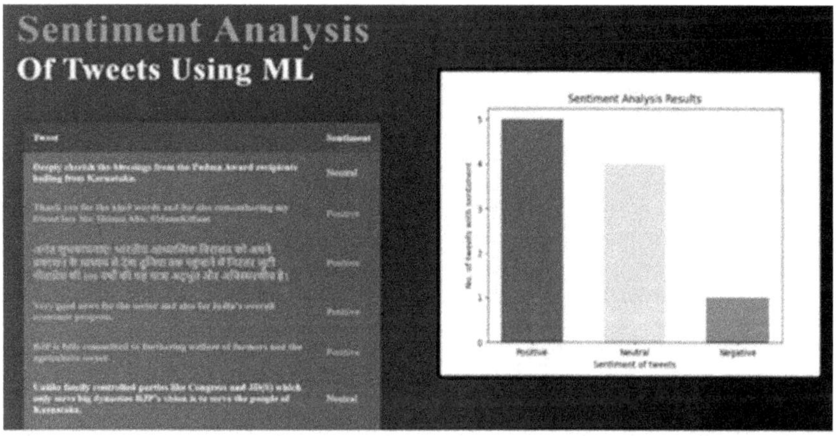

Figure 12. Model performance metrics and confusion matrix for data (0-128000)

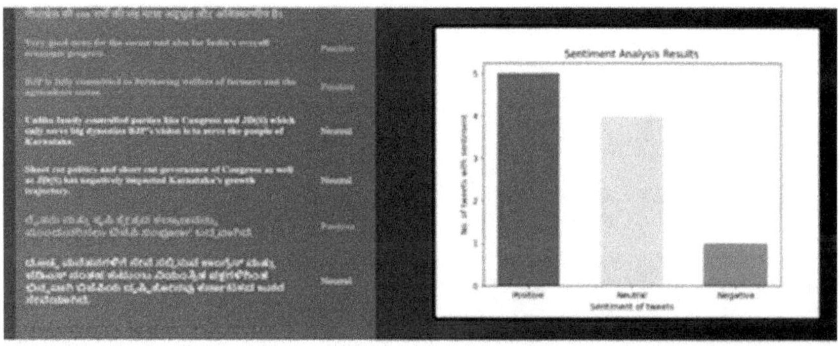

Figure 13. Model performance metrics and confusion matrix for data (0-216750)

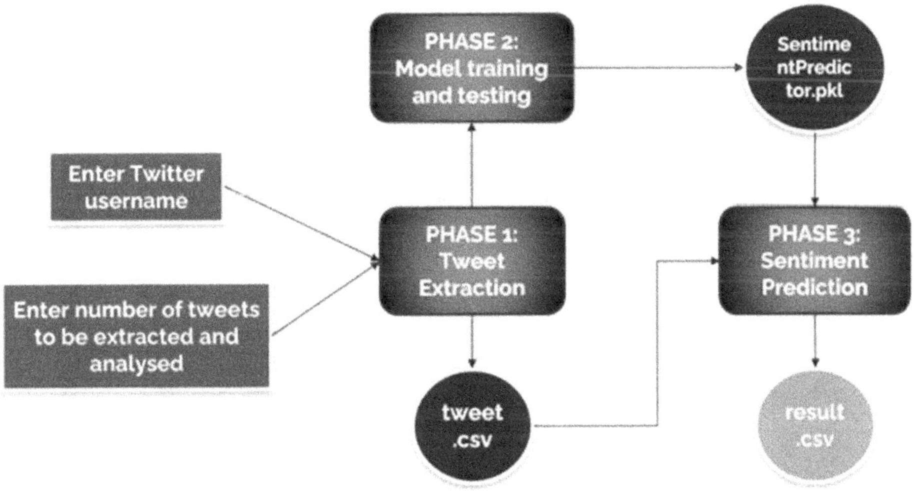

The accuracy of the model is **0.843**, which means that it correctly predicts the sentiment of 84.3% of the tweets in the dataset. Based on the precision, recall, and F1 scores, we can see that the model performs best on the positive sentiment category, with a precision of 0.887, recall of 0.785, and F1 score of 0.833. It performs slightly worse on the neutral sentiment category, with a precision of 0.840, recall of 0.902, and F1 score of 0.870. It performs worst on the negative sentiment category, with a precision of 0.808, recall of 0.840, and F1 score of 0.824.

Visualizations of accuracy trends, training and testing times, and accuracy over time are generated, aiding in intuitive interpretation. The code's strengths lie in its incremental learning strategy, allowing the model to learn from diverse data volumes, and in its inclusion of key performance metrics. By tracking training and testing times, the code gauges the model's efficiency.

This visualization helps us to optimize the training process by identifying any bottlenecks in the training time. For example, if the training time increases rapidly beyond a certain number of tweets examined, you may need to optimize the algorithm or the hardware used for training.

This helps us to determine if there is a point where adding more data significantly increases the testing time. It can be used to optimize the testing process.

This visualization is useful in analyzing the relationship between the time taken and the accuracy of the model. It helps us assess the trade-off between the time taken and the accuracy of the model. If the accuracy increases rapidly in the initial stages but slows down as the time taken increases, we may need to decide if the marginal increase in accuracy is worth the additional time required to train or test the model.

Figure 14. Graph for data v/s accuracy

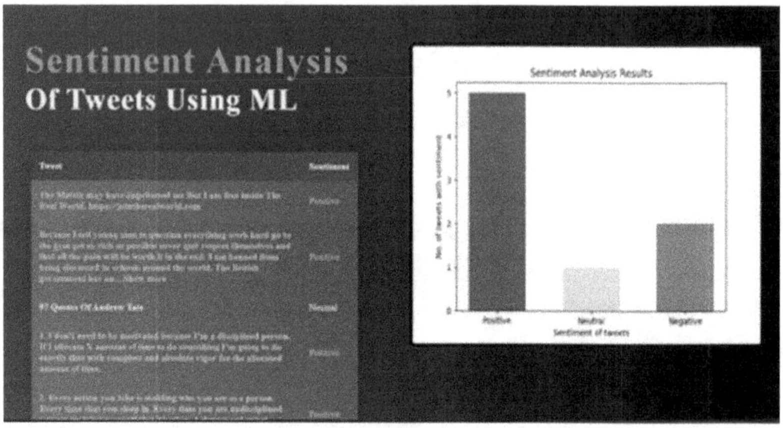

Figure 15. Graph for data v/s training time

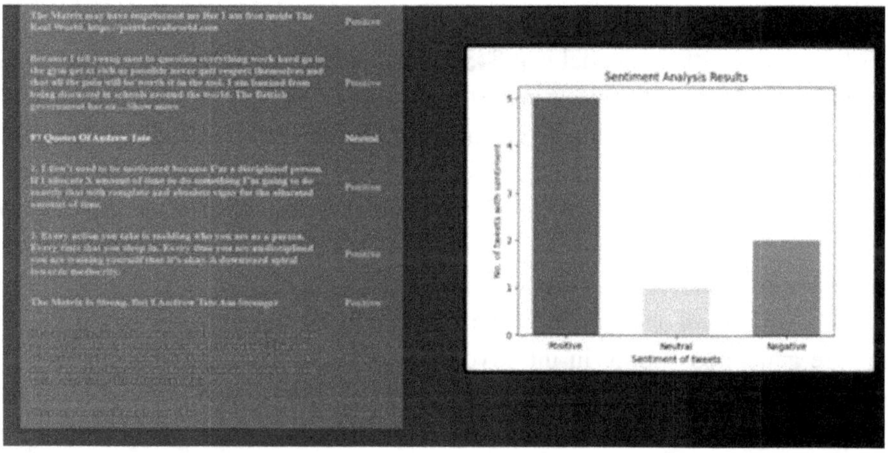

Figure 16. Graph for data v/s testing time

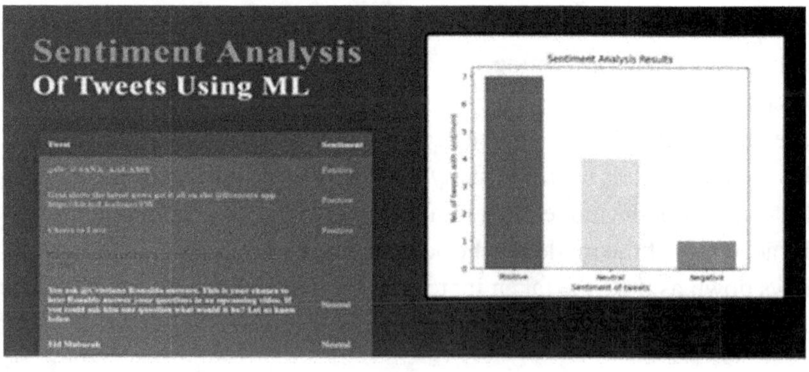

Figure 17. Graph for time v/s accuracy

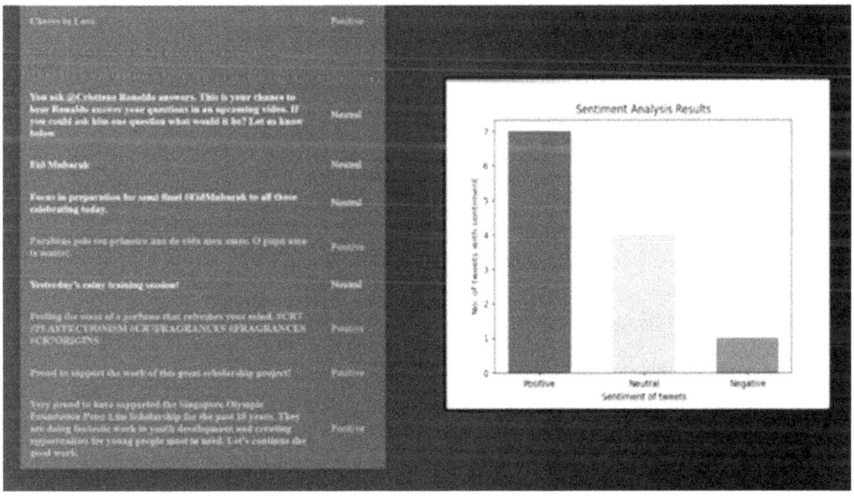

Phase 3: Sentiment Prediction

We apply the trained pipeline to the collected cleaned and translated tweets. The model processes the input and predicts sentiment category for the tweet. The sentiment categories can be positive, negative, or neutral. These results are displayed as tweets and its predicted sentiment and is visualised with the help of a bar graph which is drawn using matplotlib. The bar graph indicates the number of positive, negative and neutral tweets. We then store these tweets and their sentiments in a csv file.

Figure 18. Overview of sentiment prediction process

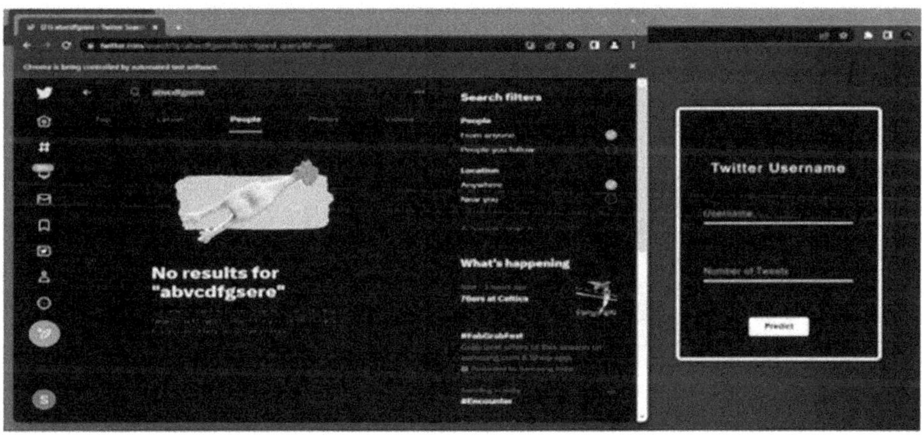

RESULTS

The proposed algorithm has been tested over several Usernames and have generated satisfactory results. Out of these, a few of the examples have been incorporated within this section.

Web App Results:

Example 1: Username used @narendramodi, Number of tweets 10

Figure 19. Web app result for username @narendramodi and number of tweets 10

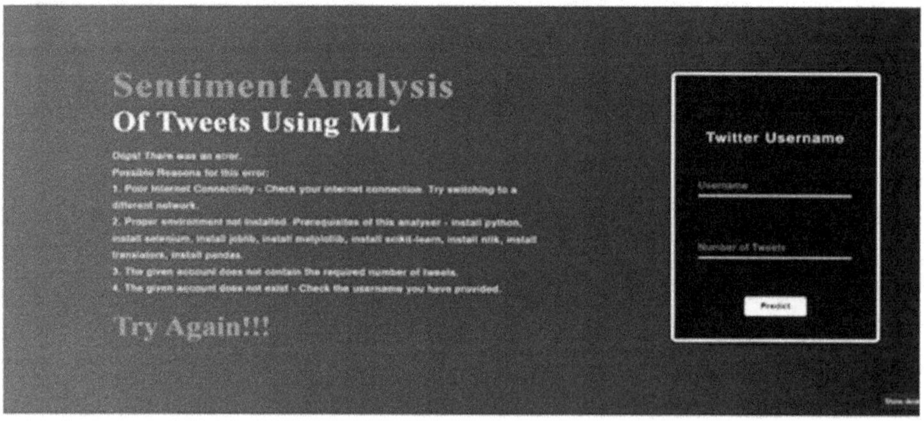

Figure 20. Web app result for username @narendramodi and number of tweets 10

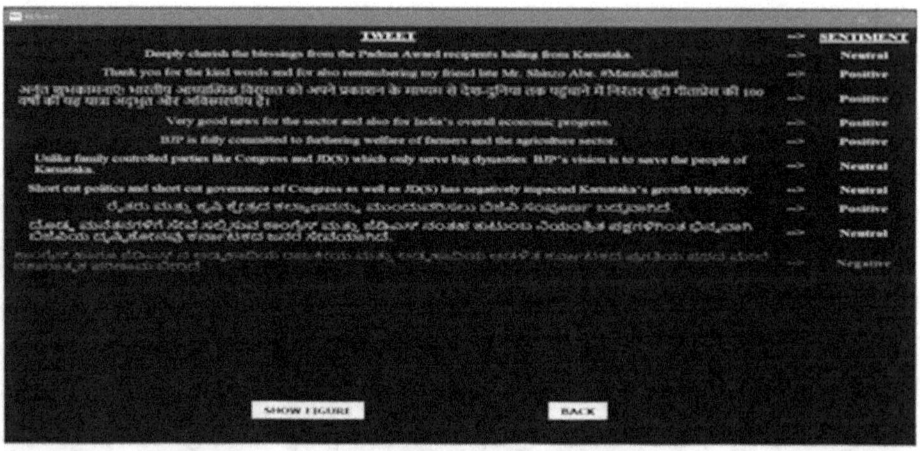

Example 2: Username used @Cobratate, Number of tweets 8

Figure 21. Web app result for username @cobratate and number of tweets 8

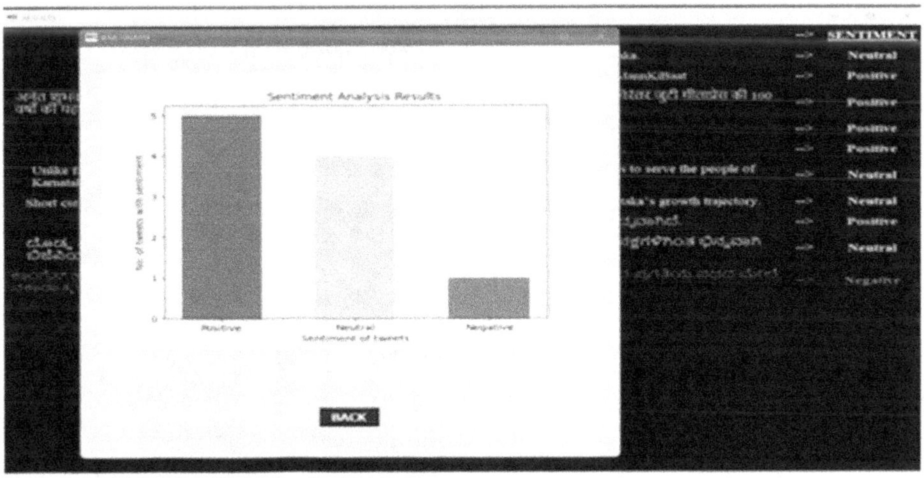

Figure 22. Web app result for username @cobratate and number of tweets 8

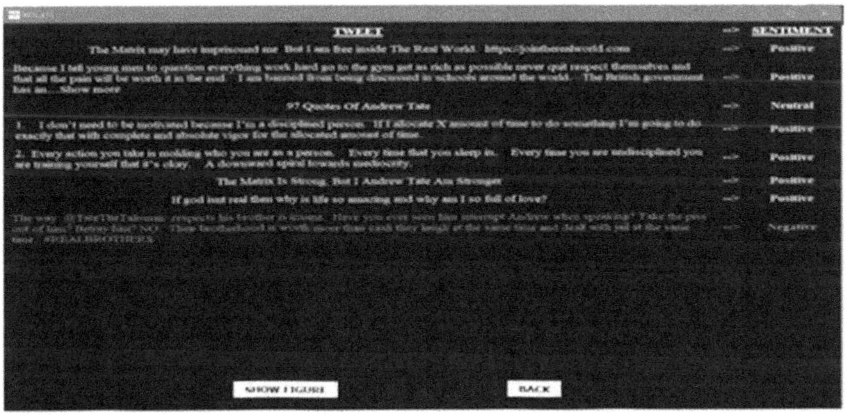

Example 3: Username used @Cristiano, Number of tweets 12

Figure 23. Web app result for username @cristiano and number of tweets 12

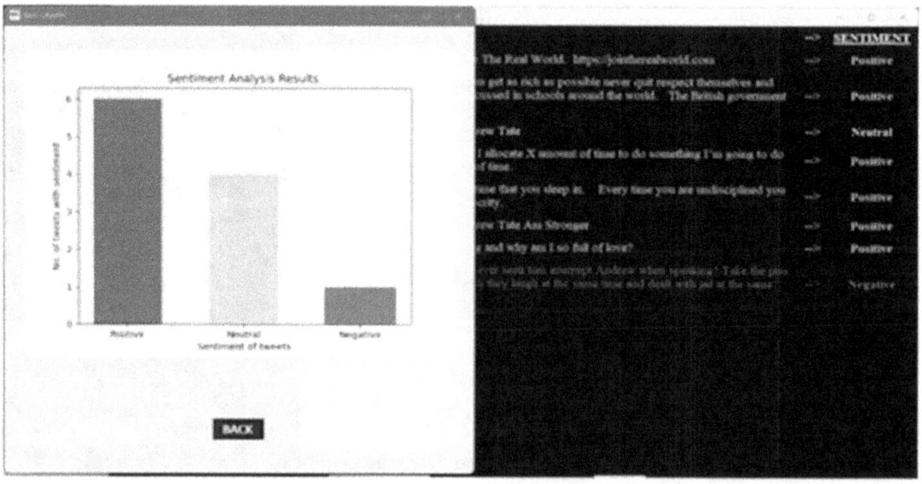

Figure 24. Web app result for username @cristiano and number of tweets 12

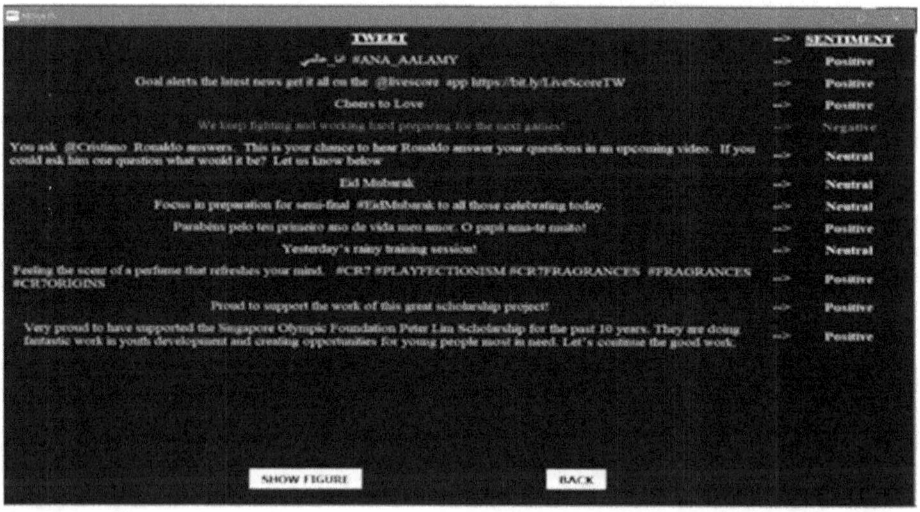

Example 4: Username used @abvcdfgsere (username that does not exist), Number of tweets 5

Figure 25. Web app result for username @abvcdfgsere and number of tweets 5

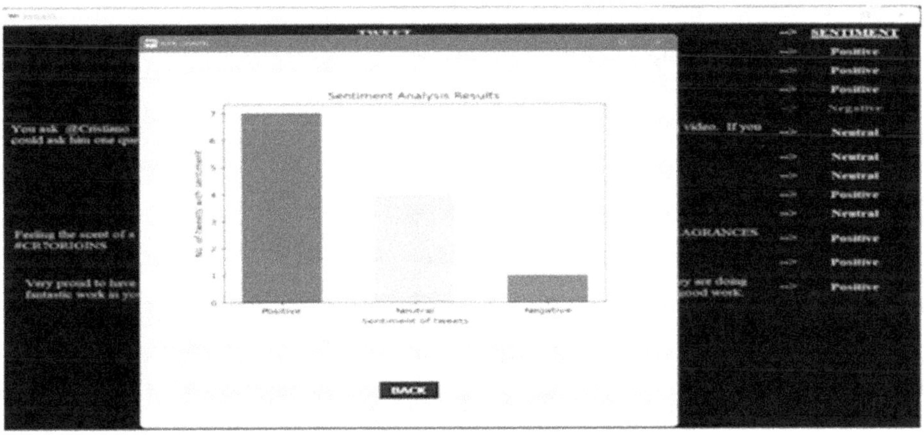

Figure 26. Web app result for username @abvcdfgsere and number of tweets 5

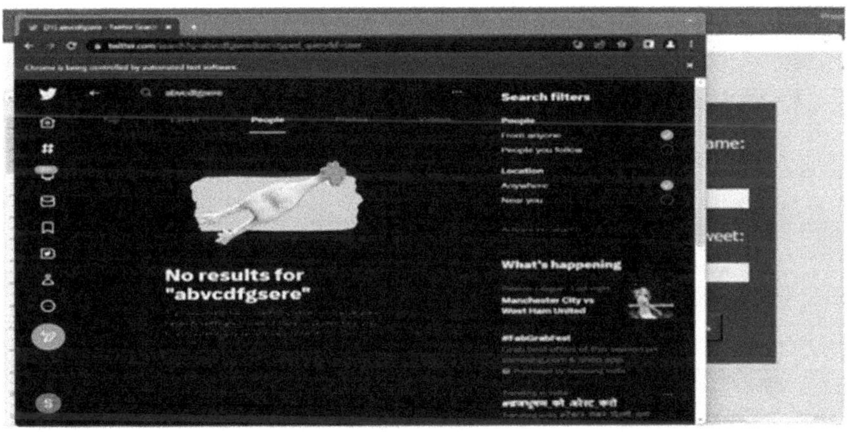

Desktop App Results:

Example 1: Username used @narendramodi, Number of tweets 10

Figure 27. Desktop app result for username @narendramodi and number of tweets 10

Figure 28. Bar graph of sentiment analysis for username @narendramodi and number of tweets 10

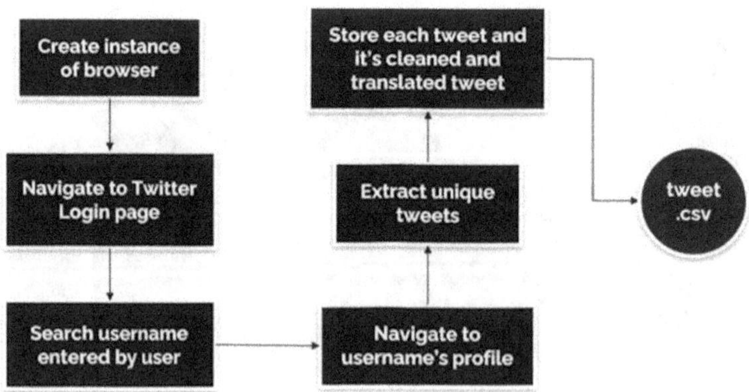

Example 2: Username used @Cobratate, Number of tweets 8

Figure 29. Desktop app result for username @corbratate and number of tweets 8

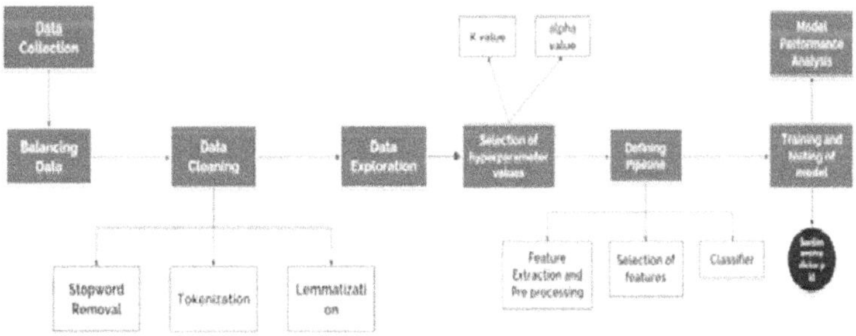

Figure 30. Bar graph of sentiment analysis for username @cobratate and number of tweets 8

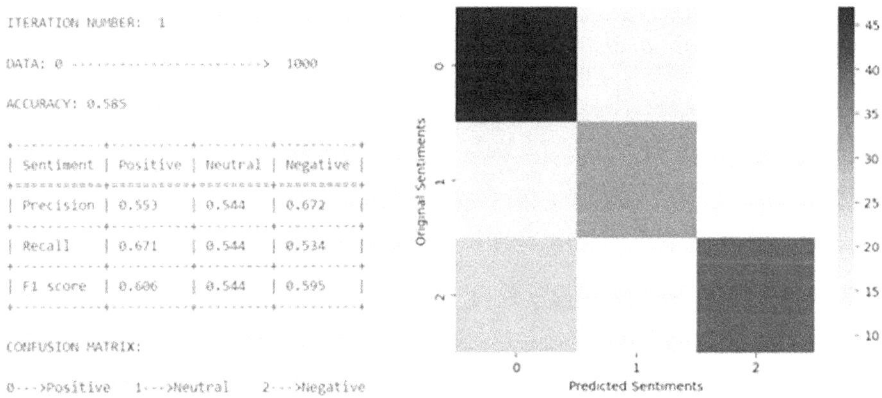

Example 3: Username used @Cristiano. Number of tweets 12

Figure 31. Desktop app result for username @cristiano and number of tweets 12

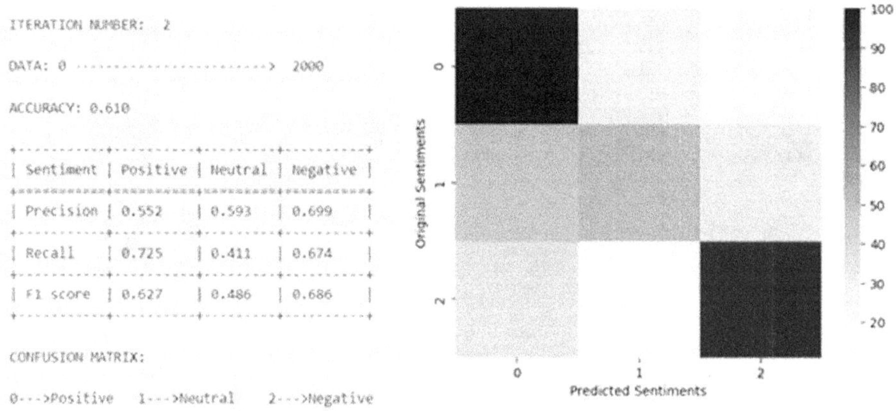

Figure 32. Bar graph of sentiment analysis for username @cristiano and number of tweets 12

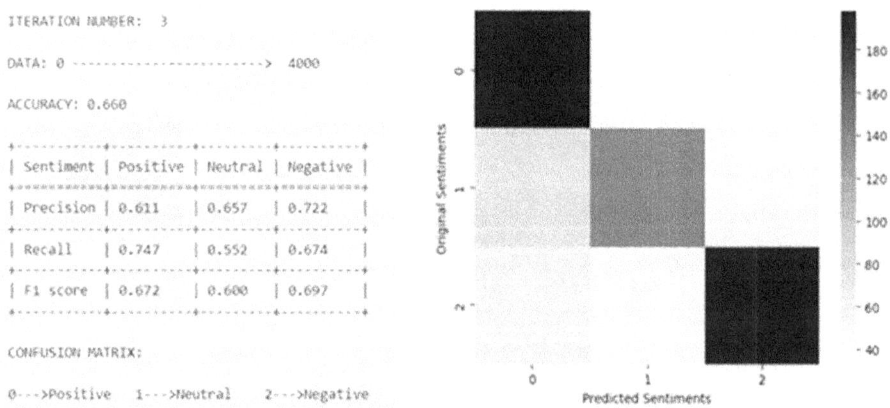

Example 4: Username used @abvcdfgsere (username that does not exist), Number of tweets 5

Figure 33. Username @abvcdfgsere not found

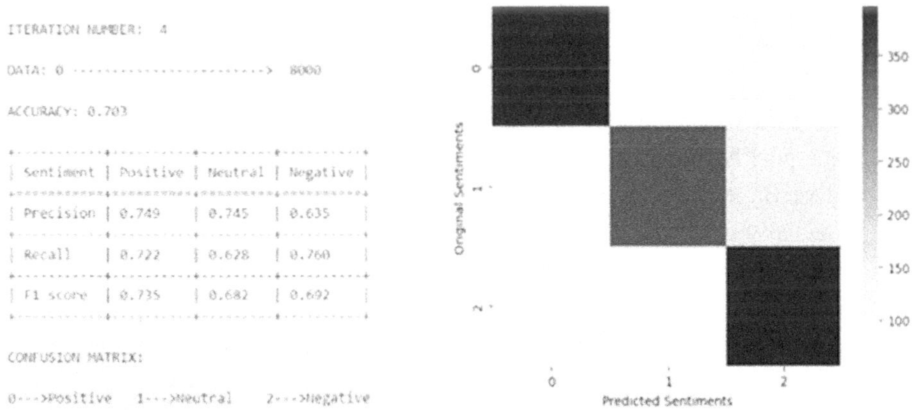

Figure 34. Web app result for username @abvcdfgsere and number of tweets 5

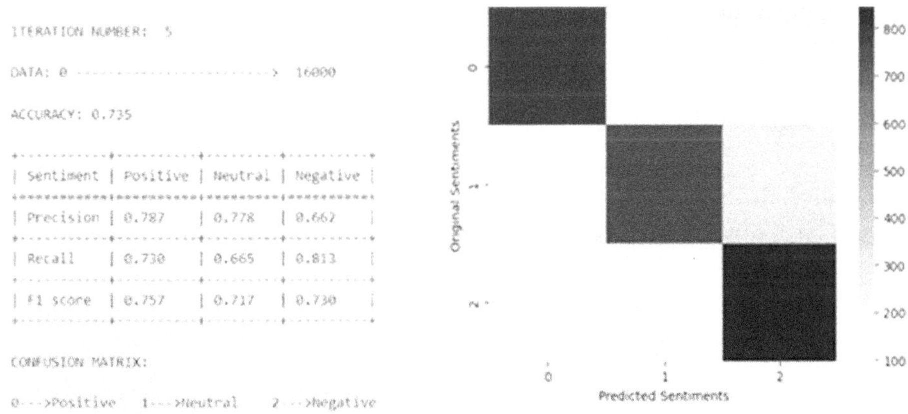

CONCLUSION

In conclusion, the above code implements a sentiment analysis model for Twitter data using the Naive Bayes algorithm. The model extracts tweets from a user's account using Selenium and Google Cloud Translate API to translate them into English. It then applies a pre-trained Naive Bayes model to predict the sentiment of the tweets as positive, negative, or neutral. Finally, the results are displayed on a web page along with a bar chart showing the number of positive, negative, and neutral tweets. The user can enter a username, and the code extracts the tweets of that user and performs the sentiment analysis. The implementation can be improved further by using other algorithms, adding more pre-processing steps, and incorporating more features to increase the accuracy of the model.

Advantages of the implemented method:

- Naive Bayes is a simple and fast algorithm that can process large amounts of data quickly. This makes it ideal for processing large volumes of tweets.
- Naive Bayes has been shown to perform well in sentiment analysis tasks, especially when the data is pre-processed properly. It can accurately classify tweets into positive, negative, or neutral sentiment categories.
- Naive Bayes requires only a small amount of training data to achieve high accuracy. This means that it can be trained quickly and used to analyse tweets in real-time.
- Naive Bayes is a language-independent algorithm, which means that it can be used to analyse tweets in any language. This makes it a versatile tool for sentiment analysis.
- Naive Bayes is easy to implement and requires minimal tuning of hyperparameters. This makes it accessible to researchers and developers who may not have a deep understanding of machine learning algorithms.

Limitations of the implemented method:

- Naive Bayes assumes that the features (words) in a tweet are independent of each other, which is not always true in natural language. This can lead to inaccurate predictions.
- Naive Bayes cannot easily detect sarcasm and irony in tweets, which can lead to misinterpretations of sentiment.
- The accuracy of Naive Bayes depends on the quality and quantity of training data. If the training data does not contain certain words or phrases, Naive Bayes will not be able to recognize them in new tweets.
- Naive Bayes treats all words as positive or negative, which can lead to incorrect sentiment analysis when negation is used in a tweet.
- Naive Bayes can be sensitive to irrelevant features (words) in a tweet, which can lead to overfitting and inaccurate predictions.

FUTURE SCOPE

The future scope of sentiment analysis of tweets using NB is bright as it has several potential applications in various fields such as marketing, politics, and customer service. Some of the possible future developments in this area include:

- One of the main challenges in sentiment analysis is the accuracy of the classification. Researchers are continuously working to improve the accuracy of the NB model by using advanced algorithms and techniques.
- Real-time analysis of tweets using NB can be used to monitor the sentiment of the public on various issues such as political events, product launches, and social causes.
- Sentiment analysis of tweets using NB can be used to monitor the sentiment of customers on social media platforms such as Twitter and Facebook. This can help companies to respond quickly to customer complaints and feedback.

REFERENCES

Agarwal, A., Xie, B., Vovsha, I., Rambow, O., & Passonneau, R. (2011). Sentiment analysis of Twitter data. *Proceedings of the Workshop on Languages in Social Media.*

Barbosa, L., & Feng, J. (2010). *Robust Sentiment Detection on Twitter from Biased and Noisy Data.* AT&T Labs - Research.

Batra, S., & Rao, D. (2009). *Entity Based Sentiment Analysis on Twitter.* Department of Computer Science, Stanford University.

Bifet, A., & Frank, E. (2010). Sentiment knowledge discovery in Twitter streaming data. *Proceedings of the Fourth International Workshop on Knowledge Discovery from Sensor Data.*

Gamon, M. (2004). *Sentiment classification on customer feedback data: noisy data, large feature vectors, and the role of linguistic analysis.* Microsoft Research.

Go, A., Bhayani, R., & Huang, L. (2009). Twitter sentiment classification using distant supervision. CS224N Project Report, 1(12).

Pak, A., & Paroubek, P. (2010). Twitter as a corpus for sentiment analysis and opinion mining. *Proceedings of the Seventh International Conference on Language Resources and Evaluation (LREC'10).*

Parikh, R., & Movassate, M. (2009). Sentiment Analysis of User-Generated Twitter Updates using Various Classification Techniques. Academic Press.

Chapter 11
Transformer-Based Memes Generation Using Text and Image

Dhirendra Kumar Sharma
https://orcid.org/0000-0002-8003-9671
University of Petroleum and Energy Studies, India

Rishab Jain
University of Petroleum and Energy Studies, India

Anshika Saini
University of Petroleum and Energy Studies, India

ABSTRACT

Memes are gaining popularity day by day to convey humor, news, social commentary, etc., but they can spread hatred and offence in the society. In this chapter, the authors create an automatic meme generator that generates relevant memes. In this chapter, Memebotics tool takes input as image or text and uses multiple pre-trained models of GPT to make memes more creative and quicker. Memebotics uses sentiment analysis to verify that created memes are relevant and do not hurt the sentiment of any society. The authors use VADAR, SVM techniques to identify the best model for sentiment analysis. They tested the model with different versions of EleutherAI GPT-Neo to find the model that can work on low configuration and saves time and money. As a result, they have created a model that generates memes that are relevant to all culture, language, and religion.

DOI: 10.4018/979-8-3693-0728-1.ch011

INTRODUCTION

Memes, as is well known, have exploded in popularity as a means of online expression and communication. People utilize it to express themselves humorously, emotionally, socially and politically, and so on. Making your own meme from the ground up, though, calls for some imagination and creative chops and can take a while. One solution to this problem is a meme generator called "memebot" that uses a deep learning model to create interactive memes. Misanthropes are able to propagate offensive content in our society through the ease of creating memes. Too many people use this to propagate racist, sexist, or otherwise harmful memes that target specific religious or cultural groups.

In the paper (Rohan Kashyap, 2022), "memeBot" model, developed, which uses deep learning to automatically generate memes. To create memes, their suggested model, memeBot, employs a mix of CNNs and RNNs. As we've seen, this tool has the potential to be exploited to make cruel memes, which can hurt the feelings of any society.

We discovered that Generative Pre-trained Transformers (GPT) is a popular approach for developing various generative tools, which helps with this problem. To prevent the production of hostile content, we have utilized the scope of GPT in our suggested model to produce suitable memes (Rohan Kashyap, 2022).

Using either a picture or a textual query as input, the "Memebotics" model may produce aesthetically pleasing and contextually appropriate memes. Every culture and religion should be able to find something meaningful in memes. By automating the process of producing memes, these models make meme culture more accessible and facilitate the sharing of ideas and emotions through them. The developers of Memebotics are working on an easy-to-use platform that will facilitate the online dissemination of sentiment, humor, and social criticism.

The study is structured as follows: in section 2, we covered relevant work, which includes information on recently published works. We have emphasized the central topic of our research in section 3, which deals with problem statements. We have detailed the components of the system and our technique in Section 4, where we described the proposed task. In section 5, "Results and Discussion," we covered our experimental findings. In addition, we have covered our final outcome in the part devoted to conclusions. Our work has been concluded and future plans for it have been mentioned in section 6.

RELATED WORK

The paper (Beskow, 2020) using the 2018 US midterm elections as a case study for detecting and classifying internet memes using multi-modal deep learning. The authors compare uni-modal approaches using a model they call Meme-Hunter, which classifies images as memes or non-memes. They found and analyzed meme families shared on Twitter during the election using picture similarity, meme-specific optical character recognition, and face detection; this technology might be used to research the usage of memes in political campaigns. This sheds light on the ways in which memes can reinforce preexisting biases within a society. In the paper (Aadhavan Sadasivam, 2020) introduces a method for autonomously creating memes using deep learning. Using a mix of CNNs and RNNs, the proposed model, memeBot, can output memes. The input image is processed by CNN to extract visual information, while the text captions are generated by RNN. Possible applications of the research's method to autonomous meme generation include online communication, social media marketing, and other similar fields.

In SemEval-2022 Task 5 (Mayukh Sharma, 2022), to find misogynist memes, this study examines and contrasts several deep learning systems. The authors examined a few well-known designs. The networks in question were DenseNet-201, ResNet-50, Inception-v3, and VGG-16. On top of that, they suggested MemXNet, a cutting-edge method that fuses convolutional and graph neural networks for enhanced performance. The results demonstrate that MemXNet achieved better performance than the other models, illustrating the difficulty of detecting misogynous memes. Ensemble approaches could potentially boost performance, according to the study, which also urges further investigation into the subject. In the paper (Pimpalkar, 2022) authors proposed a machine learning-based approach to extracting sentiment from image-based memes. The authors test their approach on a dataset of 5,000 memes collected from social media platforms such as Twitter and Instagram. They assert that their method achieves a higher accuracy of 87.5% in sentiment categorization compared to other state-of-the-art methods. This allows us to identify which machine learning-based approach yields a more accurate sentiment identification of memes, which is useful for the analysis of image-based memes and for sentiment analysis. In the paper (Qu, 2023) author uses OpenAI's CLIP model for multimodal contrastive learning to examine the development of racist memes on 4chan's /pol/ board. The authors examine the origins and dissemination of racist memes using a dataset consisting of 12.5 million image-text pairs collected from 4chan's /pol/ board from June 2016 to July 2017. It proves how well their system detects and groups similar illogical memes. In our proposed project, we describe images for the purpose of making memes using OpenAI's CLIP model.

In the article (Gonsalves, 2021) incorporates AI-Memer models into the process of meme development (Gonsalves, 2022). Their technique consists of three steps: locating backdrop photos, creating captions, and last, typing the captions onto the photographs. The author details their process for finding related images using the semantic search in the OpenImages and Wikimedia Commons datasets. Ai models developed by Eleuther, GPT-3 Da Vinci or GPT-Neo, are thereafter used to provide captions for the selected photos. The article provides examples of automatically generated captions and compares the results of GPT-3 and GPT-Neo. The author concludes by discussing typesetting and presenting examples of memes created with AI-Memer. Instead of annotations, we relied on picture descriptions. Because the description helps with understanding the picture more than the annotations.

PROBLEM STATEMENT

Memes are a popular way for people to express themselves on social media and share photos and videos from their lives. Making memes, though, may be a huge pain for a lot of individuals because not everyone is as creative or has the same design abilities. Creators and social media influencers have long followed the practice of making memes that attack a particular religion, language, or culture. We are all aware that religious matters are among the most delicate. We must refrain from mocking anyone's religious or cultural views lest we offend their sensibilities. However, there are many who persist in spreading hate speech and memes that insult religious and cultural practices. There will be more objectionable content and a negative influence on society if these memes succeed in inciting hatred and polarizing a big portion of the people. Tools like memeBot and AI-memers are already available for the purpose of automatically creating memes. As illustrated in Figure 1, the "AI Memers" program (Gonsalves 2022) uses user-supplied text to search OpenImage and Wikipedia.

After choosing a picture and adding any necessary annotations, it was run through the CLIP text encoder and CLIP image encoder to embed text and determine the best image and caption to use as a meme. Unfortunately, vile memes can be made using these techniques. Using both visual and written means, they are able to incite social animosity. (Gonsalves, 2022).

"Memebotics" uses a mix of text and image sentiment analysis to generate relevant memes. Caption creation, which is based on an image description model, receives the generated meaningful text description of the image, which makes memes funnier.

Figure 1. Flow diagram of AI-Memers

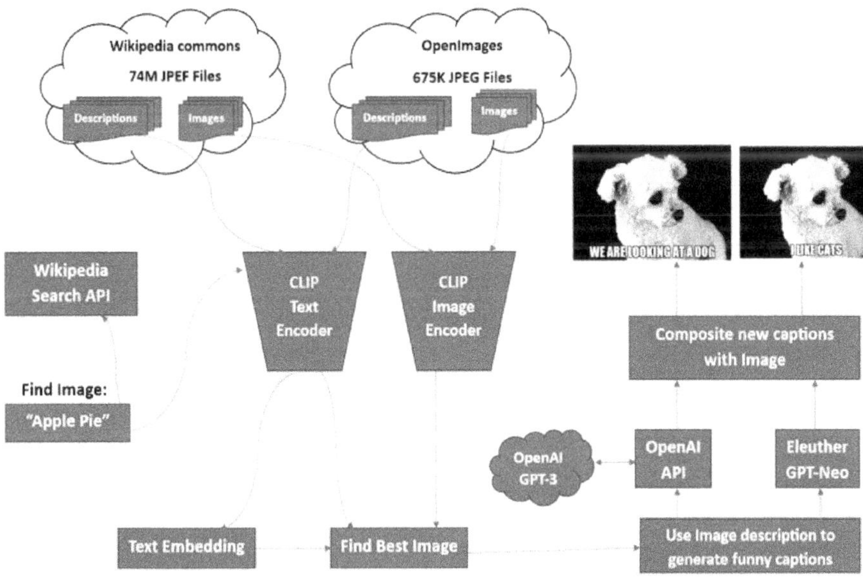

PROPOSED WORK

An improved version of AI-Memers, Memebotics is our proposed tool (Gonsalves, 2022). As input, our suggested model is capable of handling both text and images. In this case, we have tried out various GPT-Neo versions to discover the optimal model that requires little in the way of processing resources. Additionally, Memebotics use sentiment analysis to evade offensive and irrelevant memes.

System Model

Model components have been described below:

- **User Query** – our model accepts the input as image or text.
- **Image search and Selection** – here the images are searched for the text prompt using the datasets of different APIs. Then, the user can select any image according to their interest.
- **API**- APIs of Wikipedia and OpenImages are used to search the images (Gonsalves, 2022).
- **Image description** – A pre-trained model "clip_prefix_caption", is used to generate image description. The model can be fine-tune on different datasets for generating relevant descriptions.

Figure 2. Proposed model flow chart

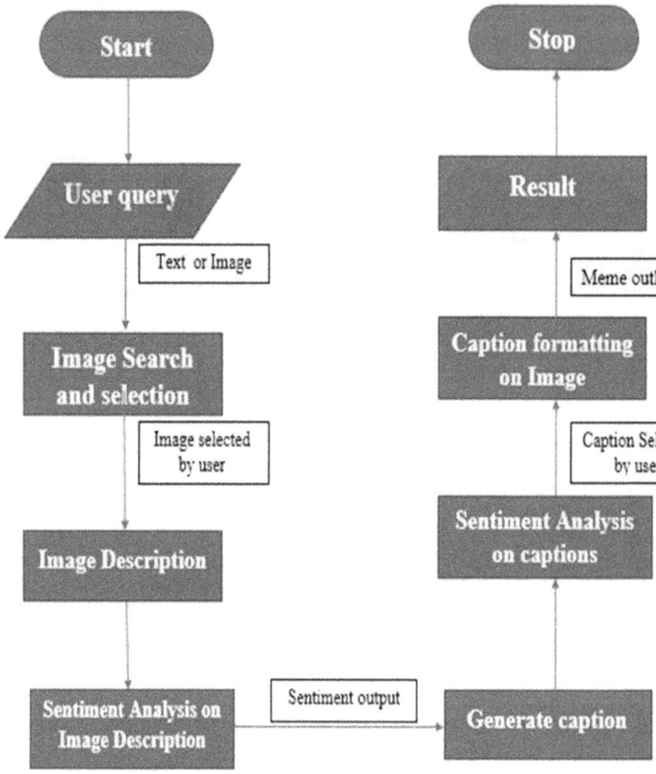

- **Clip_prefix_caption** – This CLIP model can generate semantic encodings for each image without additional information because it has previously been trained on a very large number of images (Mokady, n.d.).
- **GPT** – It stands for Generative Pre-trained Transformers. These models used deep learning techniques to generate natural language content. Our model uses the GPT2 and GPT3 based model to generate image and text.
- **Caption Generation** – A pre-trained model "GPT Neo" which is a replica of GPT3, is used for generating captions (Rohan Kashyap, 2022).
- **Sentiment Analysis** – Our proposed model used the sentiment analysis technique for finding the relevant image and captions (Hutto, 2014).
- **Caption formatting**- PIL library is used to format the generated captions over the image.

In this, VADER (Amit Pimpalkar, 2020) is used to find the polarity score of the unlabeled datasets. The labeled datasets are passed through the SVM model (Keswani, 2020) after creating the features vectors using Word2Vec model (Rohan Kashyap, 2022) for finding positive and negative (Pimpalkar, 2022) sentences.

Methodology

The complete working of "Memebotics" is explained below. This diagram tells us about how different functions are called and used in proposed model (Hutto, 2014). To generate a pertinent meme for our proposed project, we used sentiment analysis (Qu, 2023) on both text and images. If the user has already provided an image, it will automatically generate a text description of it. It searches images for the text prompt given by the user instead of an image query if the input query is in text form. In order to find the relevant image, our model searches the Wikipedia and OpenImages APIs (Gonsalves, 2022). In this case, a pre-trained model (Clip_prefix_caption; Mokady, n.d.)) has been used to construct an image description. After that, it checks for relevant images by doing sentiment analysis on the image description. To create meme captions, the caption generation model is now exclusively fed positive image descriptions (Pimpalkar, 2022). Our methodology returns the top 10 most relevant captions for users to choose from. The user's chosen caption and image are now part of the model. We detail our planned effort in the area below.

RESULT AND DISCUSSION

A simple text prompt consisting of an image and pertinent text was all it took for the "AI-Memers" tools to generate memes. Memes made with it have the potential to offend people of all faiths, languages, and cultures, leading to an increase in bigotry. "Memebotics" application allows users to input both text and images to generate memes; this allows us to generate memes that are not only topical but also creative, humorous, and original. Memebotics uses sentiment analysis to identify offensive and irrelevant memes and then makes new ones. Additionally, this will have a positive impact on society by raising awareness.

We compare the output of AI-Memers and Memebotics.

To create memes, we put both models through their paces using the identical input, "pet dog," and then choose a picture of a dog from the outputs provided.

From all the output images shown (in Figure 4) by the model following the image search command, the user chose the one up there. To get captions from this picture, we feed it to the model.

Figure 3. Flow diagram of proposed work

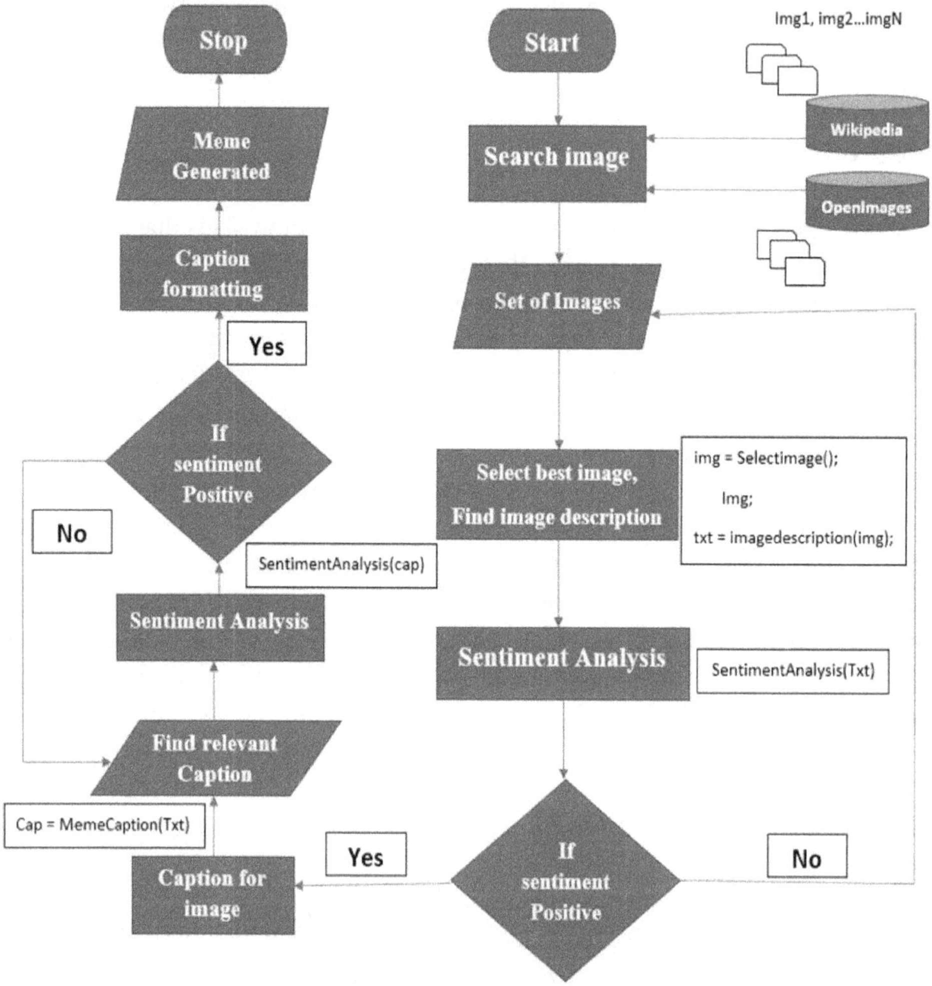

The result of the caption generating models of the two models are shown in the two photos up top, figure 5 and figure 6. The results produced by Memebotics, as shown in Figure 5, outperform those of AI-Memers, as shown in Figure 6.

In Memebotics work, models trained and optimized several models, however we encounter numerous challenges while trying to choose the optimal dataset.

Figure 4. Image selected by user

Figure 5. Output generated by Memebotics

```
Captions:
 1: A FUNNY PICTURE OF A DOG
 2: HE'S A KITTEN..
 3: WE'RE A GROUP OF DOGS THAT LOVE CATS
 4: A DOG WITH GREAT PAWS
 5: WE'RE DOGS. WE'RE NOT CATS
 6: THE SMELL THAT IS COMING FROM A MOUTHFUL OF WATER
 7: A CUTE WHITE DOG WHO LOOKS MAD
 8: HE LOOKS SAD
 9: I DON'T LIKE MONDAYS
10: A DOG WITH SHORT LEGS
```

Figure 6. Output generated by AI-Memers

```
Captions:
 1: I'M A DOG
 2: I HATE MONDAYS
 3: THIS IS WHAT HAPPENS WHEN YOU LET YOUR DOG DRINK OUT OF THE TOILET
 4: I LIKE PUPPIES
 5: I LOVE MY DOG
 6: A DOG HAS A MOUTH OF ITS OWN
 7: I'M A DOG
 8: I'M A DOG
 9: MY CAT IS PRETTY
10: THIS IS A PICTURE OF A DOG
```

Sentiment Analysis

We train our sentiment analysis model on a dataset with 56,000 entries to ensure that memes do not inadvertently offend anyone. In order to assess the dataset's quality and obtain these results, we trained a support vector machine model using varying batch sizes of the same dataset.

Figure 7. Simulations results

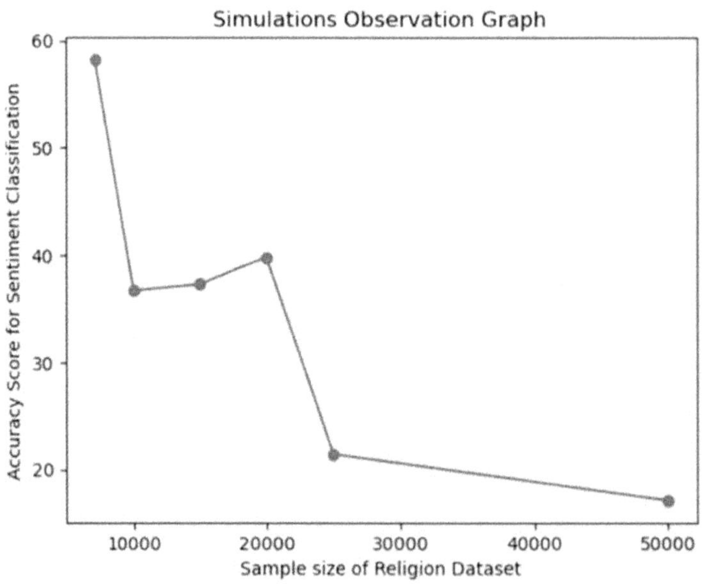

Table 1. Simulations observation

Sample Size of Religion Dataset	Accuracy Score for Sentiment Classification
7000	58.25%
10000	36.7%
15000	37.27%
20000	39.82%
25000	21.46%
50000	17.15%

Model simulations with varying sample sizes of religion datasets exhibit changes in accuracy score. On one side, we can see the dataset sample sizes, and on the other, we can see the corresponding simulations' accuracy scores for sentiment classification. Because the dataset has a lot of positive labels, the model gets biased when testing, but it also gets neutral and negative sentences, as seen in the graph, which causes the accuracy score to drop gradually between the first two simulations. The model's performance improves between 10,000 and 20,000 rows of data, as it is trained with negative and neutral sentences in this range. However, after 20,000 rows, the graph starts to decline again, indicating that the model's performance is poor due to the dataset's bias. This is because the model is incorrectly classifying some sentences as positive, leading to a gradual drop in accuracy. Therefore, we are utilizing VADAR to determine the emotion rather than an SVM model.

Caption Generation

For this reason, we have experimented with various "EleutherAI GPT Neo" models to identify the most efficient, least resource-intensive, and least expensive one.

Table 2. Evaluation of different models of caption generation on personal computers

S.no	Name	Parameter	Pile (Tokens)	No. of Steps	Experiment Remarks
1.	GPT-Neo 2.7B	2.7B	420B	400,000	High computation required
2.	GPT-Neo 1.3B	1.3B	380B	362,000	High computation required
3.	GPT-Neo 125M	125M	300B	572,300	Works on low computation

- **Parameters**- In order to run the model, this is the amount of neurons utilized.
- **Pile**- Here we can see how many datasets or tokens were utilized by these models.
- **Number of steps**- The total number of iterations used to train the models is this.

Based on our analysis of all the models, we have determined that "GPT-Neo 125M" is the best fit for content creators' typical system configurations. Their systems will be protected because it uses less processing power when employed.

Figure 8. Output generated by Memebotics

CONCLUSION AND FUTURE WORK

This work introduces a strategy for automatic meme production that has demonstrated encouraging outcomes in producing high-quality, entertaining, and coherent memes. Social media marketing, entertainment, education, and content moderation are just a few of the many possible uses for these models, which might completely alter the way memes are made and shared.

Everyone, regardless of their culture, religion, language, etc., can benefit from the memes generated by the "Memebotics" application. We keep an eye out for inappropriate and offensive content in the generated memes, and we try to improve their quality by selecting the most effective captions to draw in viewers with humor or useful information.

Looking ahead, we plan to This study presents a method for automated meme generation that has shown promising results in creating amusing, well-structured memes. Among the several potential applications for these models that might fundamentally change the meme creation and sharing process are social media marketing, entertainment, education, and content moderation.to create memes that can be meaningfully shared across all faiths and cultures. To that end, we are compiling a database of information about the gods and sacred symbols used by various faiths. Our model will be trained using cultural views related to religion. We are striving to make memes that honor different faiths and cultural practices.

REFERENCES

Aadhavan SadasivamK. G. (2020, April 30). *memeBot: Towards Automatic Image Meme Generation*. https://arxiv.org/abs/2004.14571

Amit Pimpalkar, J. R. (2020)). Influence of Pre-processing Strategies on the Performance of ML Classifiers Exploiting TF-IDF and BOW Features. *Advances in Distributed Computing and Artificial Intelligence Journal*, 49-68.

David, M., & Beskow, S. K. (2020). The evolution of political memes: Detecting and characterizing internet memes with multi-modal deep learning. *Information Processing & Management*, 1–13.

Gonsalves, R. A. (2021, June 3). *towardsdatascience*. Retrieved from TowardsDataScience: https://towardsdatascience.com/ai-memer-using-machine-learning-to-create-funny-memes-12fc1fe543e4

Gonsalves, R. A. (2022, September 18). *AI-Memer: Using Machine Learning to Create Funny Memes*. Retrieved from AI-Memer: https://colab.research.google.com/github/robgon-art/ai-memer/blob/main/AI_Memer.ipynb

Hutto, C. &. (2014). VADER: A Parsimonious Rule-Based Model for Sentiment Analysis of Social Media Text. In *Proceedings of the International AAAI Conference on Web and Social Media* (pp. 216-225). PKP Publishing Services Network.

KeswaniV. S. (2020, July 21). *Unimodal and bimodal sentiment analysis of Internet memes*. https://arxiv.org/abs/2007.10822

Mayukh Sharma, I. K. (2022). R2D2 at SemEval-2022 Task 5: Attention is only as good as its Values! A multimodal system for identifying misogynist memes. In *Proceedings of the 16th International Workshop on Semantic Evaluation (SemEval-2022)* (pp. 761–770). Association for Computational Linguistics.

Mokady, R. (n.d.). *Simple image captioning model using CLIP and GPT-2*. Retrieved from https://replicate.com/rmokady/clip_prefix_caption

Pimpalkar, A. &. (2022). Sentiment Identification from Image-Based Memes Using Machine Learning. *International Journal of Innovations in Engineering and Science*, 89-96.

Qu, Y. &. (2023). On the Evolution of (Hateful) Memes by Means of Multimodal Contrastive Learning. In *2023 IEEE Symposium on Security and Privacy (SP)* (pp. 293-310). IEEE Computer Society.

Rohan KashyapV. K. (2022, November 28). *GPT-Neo for commonsense reasoning-a theoretical and practical lens*. https://arxiv.org/abs/2211.15593

Scott, W. (2020). *Kaggle*. Retrieved from Memotion Dataset 7k: https://www.kaggle.com/datasets/williamscott701/memotion-dataset-7k

Chapter 12
Cyberbullying in the Digital Age:
Consequences and Countermeasures

Ayushi Malik
University of Petroleum and Energy Studies, India

Pankaj Dadure
https://orcid.org/0000-0002-8003-9671
University of Petroleum and Energy Studies, India

ABSTRACT

This chapter delves into the pervasive issue of cyberbullying, an alarming phenomenon that has emerged with the advent of digital communication platforms. While the digital age has brought numerous benefits, it has also introduced drawbacks, with cyberbullying significantly affecting the emotional and psychological well-being of individuals, particularly adolescents. The chapter reviews existing approaches to address cyberbullying, including technological interventions, policy measures, and educational initiatives. The chapter also highlights the importance of maintaining an updated and accessible database of cyberbullying incidents to facilitate research, policymaking, and intervention development. Moreover, this chapter underscores the potentially severe consequences of cyberbullying on victims, ranging from anxiety and depression to even self-harm.

DOI: 10.4018/979-8-3693-0728-1.ch012

INTRODUCTION OF CYBERBULLYING

Figure 1. Cyberbullying (Kidshelpline, n.d.)

In an era characterized by the rapid evolution of technology and the ubiquitous presence of the internet, the digital age has ushered in unprecedented opportunities for connectivity, communication, and information sharing. While these advancements have revolutionized the way we interact and access information, they have also given rise to new challenges, one of the most concerning being cyberbullying. Cyberbullying, a form of harassment and aggression that occurs online, has emerged as a pressing social issue with far-reaching consequences. It transcends geographical boundaries and impacts individuals of all ages, making it a pervasive threat in today's interconnected world. This book chapter explores the multifaceted dimensions of cyberbullying, delving into its various forms, consequences, and the strategies developed to counteract this digital menace. As we navigate the intricacies of cyberbullying, we aim to shed light on the emotional, psychological, and even physical toll it can take on victims. Moreover, we will examine the role of technology in facilitating cyberbullying behaviors and the profound impact it has on the mental well-being of those targeted. Beyond merely identifying the problem, we will also explore proactive measures and countermeasures that individuals, educators, parents, policymakers, and technology companies can employ to mitigate the effects of cyberbullying and promote a safer digital environment. Through a comprehensive examination of cyberbullying's complexities, this book chapter seeks to equip readers with a deeper understanding of the issue and the tools necessary to combat it effectively. By addressing both the consequences and countermeasures associated with cyberbullying in the digital age, we hope to contribute to the ongoing efforts to create a more inclusive, respectful, and secure online space for everyone.

Cyberbullying is a form of aggressive and harmful behavior that takes place in the digital realm, typically through electronic devices and online platforms. It involves the deliberate use of technology, such as social media, instant messaging, email, or other digital communication tools, to harass, threaten, or harm individuals or groups. Cyberbullying can manifest in various ways, including but not limited to spreading false information, sharing hurtful messages or images, impersonation, exclusion, and online defamation. It often targets individuals based on their characteristics, such as gender, race, religion, sexual orientation, or physical appearance, and can have severe emotional, psychological, and sometimes physical consequences for the victims (Akhter et al., 2023). Key characteristics of cyberbullying include the use of electronic devices and the internet to perpetrate harm, the potential for anonymity, and the ability to reach a wide audience quickly. Unlike traditional bullying, cyberbullying can occur at any time and in any location, making it challenging for victims to escape. The consequences of cyberbullying can be severe, with victims often experiencing emotional distress, anxiety, depression, and a sense of isolation. In extreme cases, cyberbullying has been linked to self-harm and suicide. Addressing cyberbullying involves a multifaceted approach, including education, awareness, reporting mechanisms, legal measures, and mental health support.

Evolution of Bullying to Cyberbullying

Figure 2. Evolution of bullying to cyberbullying (Kapersky, n.d.)

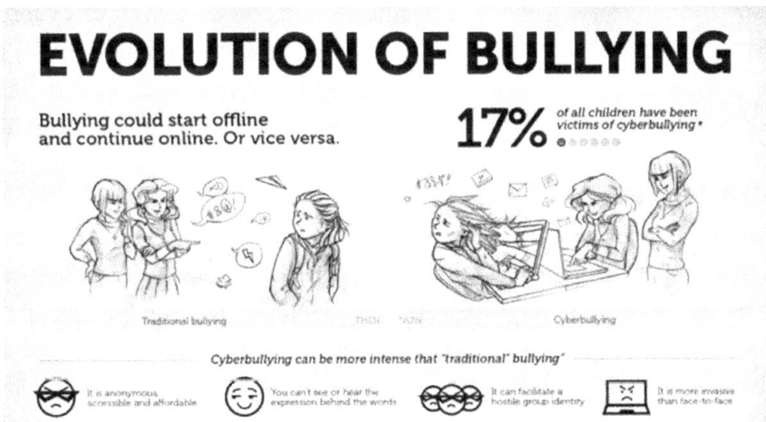

Bullying has been a social issue for centuries, rooted in the dynamics of power, aggression, and human interaction. Traditionally, bullying primarily occurred in physical spaces, such as schools, neighborhoods, and workplaces (Nair et al., 2023).

The advent of the digital age has brought about a profound transformation in the landscape of bullying, giving rise to a new and concerning phenomenon known as cyberbullying. In contrast to traditional bullying, which typically involves face-to-face interactions and physical aggression, cyberbullying represents a paradigm shift in the realm of harassment and victimization. Traditional bullying encompassed behaviors such as physical violence, verbal taunts, social exclusion, and intimidation, and it was often constrained by physical proximity, which allowed authorities in schools or other settings to monitor and intervene. However, with the emergence of technology as an integral part of modern life, the nature of bullying began to change dramatically. The proliferation of the internet and the widespread use of smartphones provided individuals with powerful tools for communication and social interaction. This technological shift brought about new opportunities for bullying to manifest in the digital realm, leading to the natural evolution known as cyberbullying. Cyberbullying involves the use of electronic devices and online platforms to harass, intimidate, or harm others. The key distinction is that cyberbullying transcends physical boundaries, allowing perpetrators to target victims anywhere, at any time. This anonymity and physical distance have emboldened some individuals to engage in aggressive behaviors they might not have attempted in face-to-face interactions. Cyberbullying encompasses a wide range of behaviors, including sending hurtful messages via social media, sharing private or embarrassing information online, impersonating others, spreading false rumors, and even engaging in online hate speech. The anonymity afforded by the internet can amplify the intensity and frequency of cyberbullying incidents, as individuals may feel emboldened to act cruelly when they believe they can do so without consequences. The impact and consequences of cyberbullying can be severe and lasting. Victims often experience emotional distress, anxiety, depression, and a profound sense of isolation. In extreme cases, cyberbullying has been tragically linked to self-harm and suicide. Additionally, cyberbullying leaves a digital footprint that can persist indefinitely, making it challenging for victims to escape the trauma and move forward. Recognizing the unique challenges posed by cyberbullying, various countermeasures and prevention strategies have been developed. These include educational programs aimed at raising awareness about the issue, legal measures to hold perpetrators accountable, technological safeguards to protect potential victims, and initiatives by social media platforms to combat online harassment. As the digital landscape continues to evolve, addressing cyberbullying remains a critical societal concern, requiring ongoing research, education, and intervention efforts to protect individuals from the harms of this pervasive and insidious form of harassment.

Importance of Addressing Cyberbullying

Figure 3. Effects of cyberbullying (Verywellfamily, n.d.)

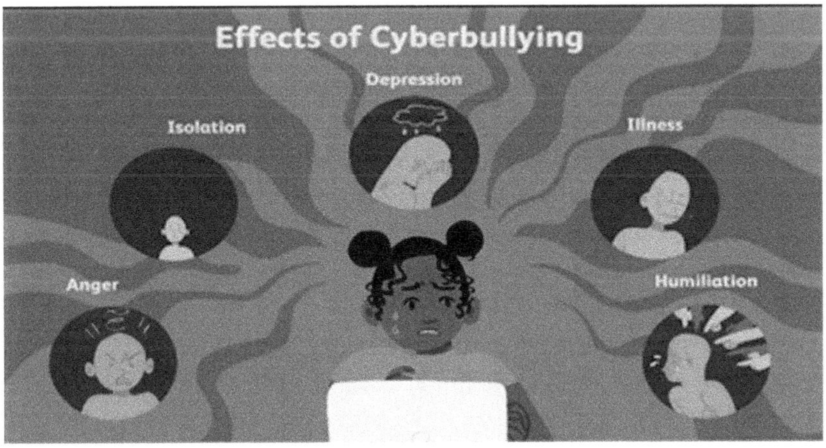

In the rapidly evolving digital age, addressing cyberbullying has become a matter of utmost importance due to its far-reaching implications for individuals, communities, and society as a whole. The significance of addressing cyberbullying can be understood through several key factors (Fredrick et al., 2023):

Psychological and Emotional Well-Being: Cyberbullying inflicts emotional and psychological harm on its victims. The constant fear, anxiety, and distress experienced by individuals targeted by cyberbullies can lead to long-term mental health issues, including depression and even suicidal thoughts. Addressing cyberbullying is vital to safeguard the emotional well-being of those affected.

Physical Safety: In some cases, cyberbullying can escalate to physical harm or threats. Threats of violence made online can have real-world consequences, necessitating intervention to prevent physical harm to victims or others.

Impact on Education: Cyberbullying often spills into educational settings, affecting students' ability to learn and thrive in school. Victims may experience decreased academic performance, absenteeism, and a hostile learning environment. By addressing cyberbullying, educators can create safe and conducive spaces for learning.

Social Isolation: Victims of cyberbullying may withdraw from social interactions, both online and offline, out of fear and humiliation. This isolation can have lasting negative effects on their social development and overall well-being. Addressing cyberbullying helps combat social isolation and promotes healthy social connections.

Digital Citizenship: Fostering responsible digital citizenship is crucial in the digital age. By addressing cyberbullying, we educate individuals, especially young people, about the ethical use of technology, online etiquette, and respectful communication. This, in turn, contributes to a more positive online culture.

Preventing Escalation: Unaddressed cyberbullying can escalate into more serious criminal activities, such as doxing (revealing personal information online), harassment, or even threats of violence. Timely intervention can prevent these escalations and protect both victims and potential perpetrators.

Legal and Ethical Implications: Many countries have enacted laws against cyberbullying, recognizing it as a serious offense. Addressing cyberbullying is essential to ensure that individuals are held accountable for their harmful online actions, promoting legal and ethical standards in digital interactions.

Mental Health Burden: The mental health burden placed on victims of cyberbullying can extend to their families and support networks. Addressing cyberbullying is not only about helping victims but also alleviating the distress experienced by their loved ones.

Digital Society: As our society becomes increasingly digitized, addressing cyberbullying is pivotal for maintaining trust in digital platforms, encouraging responsible online behavior, and ensuring that the internet remains a safe and inclusive space for all users.

Long-Term Impact: The consequences of cyberbullying can be long-lasting, affecting individuals well into adulthood. By addressing cyberbullying comprehensively, we can mitigate its enduring impact on individuals' lives.

Understanding the importance of addressing cyberbullying is the first step toward creating a safer, more empathetic, and digitally responsible society.

Figure 4. Types of cyberbullying

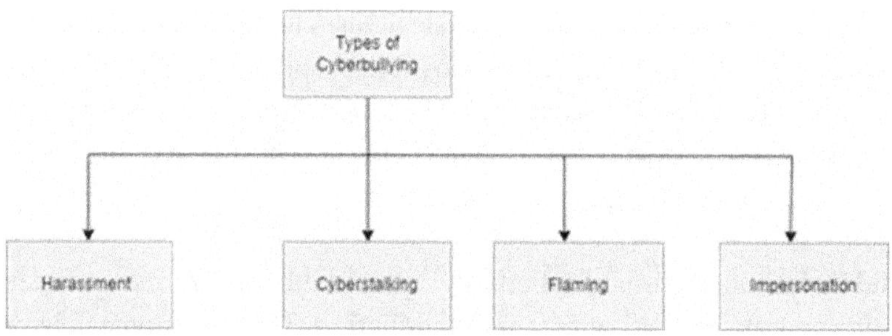

Forms and Types of Cyberbullying

Cyberbullying encompasses a wide range of behaviors and tactics, each designed to harass, harm, or intimidate individuals through digital means (Chiao et al., 2023). Harassment encompasses the disturbing practice of repeatedly sending offensive, threatening, or abusive messages or comments to an individual, which can occur through various digital platforms such as social media, email, or instant messaging. In a similar vein, flaming involves engaging in online arguments, often referred to as "flame wars," with the deliberate intent of provoking and insulting others, often escalating with harsh language and personal attacks. Exclusion or social isolation tactics involve the intentional exclusion of someone from online groups, forums, or social circles, along with the spread of rumors to isolate them socially, causing significant emotional distress. Outing, a particularly damaging form of cyber misconduct, entails the sharing of private or embarrassing information, photos, or videos about an individual without their consent, leading to humiliation and reputational damage. Doxing goes even further, as it involves publishing or distributing someone's personal and private information, such as their home address, phone number, or financial details, often with malicious intent and potential real-world consequences like stalking and harassment. Impersonation involves the creation of fake profiles or accounts to deceive and manipulate others, causing confusion and distress while engaging in harmful behavior under the guise of the victim or others. Trolling, a disruptive practice, entails posting provocative or offensive content online with the aim of generating reactions from others, often creating conflicts and chaos for the troll's amusement. Cyberstalking represents a menacing and persistent online behavior, which may involve sending threatening messages, tracking someone's online activity, or repeatedly contacting them against their will, leading to emotional distress and safety concerns. Catfishing involves the creation of a fake online persona or identity to deceive and manipulate others emotionally or financially, often targeting individuals for fake romantic relationships. Finally, cyberbullying through photos and videos involves the unauthorized sharing of manipulated or embarrassing visual content of individuals, including deep fakes or digitally altered imagery, causing significant harm to the victim's reputation and well-being. These various forms of online misconduct highlight the need for awareness, prevention, and intervention measures to create safer digital spaces. It's important to note that cyberbullying can take many forms and may involve a combination of these tactics. The impact of cyberbullying can be profound, leading to emotional distress, mental health issues, and even physical harm in some cases. Recognizing and addressing these various forms of cyberbullying is crucial for creating a safer digital environment.

Consequences of Cyberbullying

Figure 5. Consequences of cyberbullying

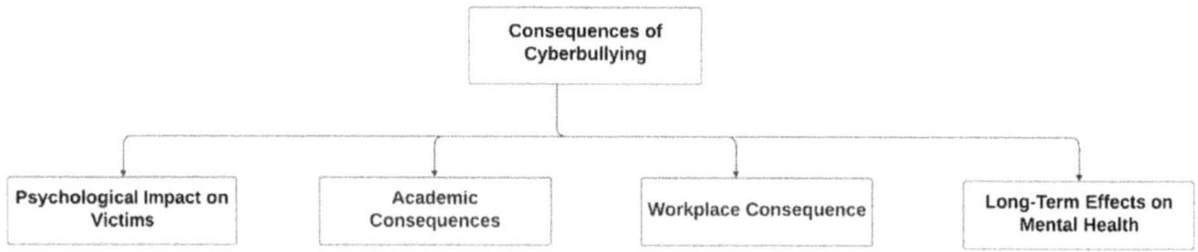

Psychological Impact on Victims

Cyberbullying, a unique and pervasive form of harassment in the digital domain, inflicts a wide spectrum of severe psychological consequences upon its victims. These repercussions are profound, with the potential to cast a long shadow over their mental well-being and overall quality of life. A comprehensive understanding of these psychological effects is essential for effectively addressing the multifaceted challenges posed by cyberbullying. One of the primary psychological consequences of cyberbullying is emotional distress. Victims often find themselves grappling with heightened levels of emotional turmoil, feeling perpetually overwhelmed, anxious, and on edge as they anticipate further instances of harassment or humiliation. Furthermore, the relentless and insidious nature of cyberbullying can lead to depression, with victims experiencing persistent feelings of sadness, hopelessness, and despair. These emotions can significantly compromise their daily functioning, disrupt their relationships, and erode their self-esteem. Anxiety is another prevalent psychological consequence of cyberbullying. Victims may develop significant apprehension about going online or engaging with others, constantly fearing new episodes of harassment. This anxiety can manifest in various forms, including social anxiety, generalized anxiety disorder, or even panic attacks, exacerbating their mental distress. As a coping mechanism, victims of cyberbullying often resort to isolation, withdrawing from social interactions both online and offline to escape the torment. However, this isolation can lead to profound feelings of loneliness and exclusion, further intensifying their emotional turmoil. Cyberbullying has the capacity to significantly erode self-esteem and self-worth. The consistent bombardment of negative messages and humiliation can foster self-doubt, causing victims to question their abilities and intrinsic value as individuals. In the most severe cases, the psychological toll of cyberbullying can drive victims toward self-harming behaviors or suicidal ideation. These individuals may perceive themselves as trapped and hopeless, unable to envision an escape from their torment, making it imperative to address cyberbullying as a life-threatening issue. Some victims of severe cyberbullying may develop symptoms reminiscent of Post-Traumatic Stress Disorder (PTSD). They may experience flashbacks, nightmares, and hypervigilance as they involuntarily relive their traumatic online experiences. Moreover, the emotional distress wrought by cyberbullying can have a direct bearing on a victim's academic pursuits, leading to academic decline. Concentration becomes difficult, assignments go unfinished, and school attendance dwindles, all of which detrimentally affect their educational progress. Cyberbullying's repercussions extend beyond the individual victim, impacting their relationships with friends and family. Victims may withdraw from loved ones or exhibit irritability and emotional distance due to their internal turmoil, straining these vital support networks. Trust, both online and offline, can be profoundly affected by cyberbullying. Victims may develop skepticism about the intentions of others and struggle to form new relationships, perpetuating their sense of isolation. As a distress-coping mechanism, some victims may resort to unhealthy practices, such as substance abuse or self-destructive behaviors, to numb their emotional pain, further exacerbating their mental health struggles. Lastly, it's crucial to acknowledge that the psychological consequences of cyberbullying often persist into adulthood, casting a shadow over victims' mental health and overall well-being long after the bullying episodes have ceased. In light of these profound psychological consequences, addressing cyberbullying is not only a matter of responding to online harassment but a multifaceted endeavor that requires comprehensive support systems, including mental health professionals, educators, and parents, to help victims cope, recover, and regain their emotional well-being. Preventive measures and strategies to combat cyberbullying are equally vital to mitigate the prevalence of these detrimental outcomes in the first place. It is essential to recognize and address these psychological consequences promptly and effectively. Support systems, including mental health professionals, educators, and parents, play a crucial role in helping victims cope with and recover from the trauma of cyberbullying. In the subsequent sections of this chapter, we will explore strategies and countermeasures to mitigate the psychological impact of cyberbullying and promote resilience among victims (Li et al., 2023).

Academic and Workplace Consequences

Cyberbullying, a digital menace that knows no boundaries, inflicts severe consequences not only on the mental well-being of its victims but also on their academic and workplace environments. This insidious form of harassment can disrupt educational and professional pursuits in profound ways, leaving a lasting impact on the lives of those affected. In academic settings, cyberbullying can create a cascade of negative effects, starting with decreased academic performance. The emotional distress caused by online harassment can make it incredibly challenging for victims to concentrate on their studies. As they grapple with anxiety, fear, and humiliation, their grades may suffer, leading to a decline in academic achievement. In some extreme cases, students subjected to severe cyberbullying may even contemplate or execute the drastic step of dropping out of school or college, jeopardizing their educational futures. The fear of encountering cyberbullies can result in increased absenteeism among victims. The mere thought of facing harassment, whether in person or online, can cause students to skip classes or avoid school altogether. This persistent absenteeism disrupts their educational progress, further hindering their ability to keep up with coursework and engage actively in the learning process. Cyberbullying creates a negative impact on the learning environment, transforming what should be a safe and nurturing space into one fraught with tension and anxiety. Students who experience online harassment may feel unsafe, both within the physical school premises and during online classes. This atmosphere of insecurity can severely hinder their ability to focus on their studies, engage with teachers and peers, and thrive academically. The relentless nature of cyberbullying can gradually chip away at a student's self-esteem and confidence. The constant barrage of hurtful messages and humiliation erodes their self-worth, making it increasingly challenging to participate in class, ask questions, or engage in extracurricular activities that are essential for holistic personal development. This decline in self-esteem can hinder their overall growth and hinder their academic progress. Furthermore, cyberbullying often drives victims into a state of isolation and loneliness. To escape the torment, they may withdraw from social interactions, both online and offline. This isolation exacerbates feelings of loneliness and depression, creating an environment in which academic success becomes even more elusive.

In the workplace, cyberbullying can have equally detrimental effects. Victims of workplace cyberbullying may find their job performance reduced significantly. The emotional toll exacted by online harassment can make it difficult to concentrate on tasks, meet deadlines, and maintain the high level of productivity expected by employers. This decline in performance can threaten job security and professional advancement. Cyberbullying can also have a profound impact on career advancement. Victims may see their professional reputation tarnished, with relationships strained both with colleagues and supervisors. As a result, opportunities for career growth and progression may be curtailed, impeding their long-term professional prospects. The stress and emotional distress caused by workplace cyberbullying can lead to increased stress and burnout among victims. Prolonged exposure to such harassment can contribute to burnout, leading to decreased job satisfaction and potentially higher turnover rates. A workplace tainted by cyberbullying creates a hostile work environment, adversely affecting the well-being of all employees. This, in turn, hampers teamwork, collaboration, and overall morale, which can negatively impact organizational performance. Legal and HR issues can also arise as a result of workplace cyberbullying. Employers may face legal complications related to harassment, discrimination, or hostile work environments if they fail to address and prevent cyberbullying incidents. The stress and anxiety caused by workplace cyberbullying can have adverse effects on an individual's physical and mental health, leading to increased sick days and healthcare costs for both employees and employers. In some cases, talented employees who experience workplace cyberbullying may choose to leave their jobs, resulting in a loss of skilled talent for the organization. This talent drain can have a detrimental impact on organizational productivity and competitiveness. In both academic and workplace settings, addressing cyberbullying is imperative not only for the well-being of individuals but also for fostering healthy and productive environments. Strategies to combat cyberbullying, coupled with proactive measures to create safe and inclusive spaces, are essential for mitigating the prevalence and impact of this detrimental behavior. Addressing cyberbullying in academic and workplace settings is essential not only for the well-being of individuals but also for fostering healthy and productive learning and working environments (Weiss, 2022).

Long-Term Effects on Mental Health

Cyberbullying, with its insidious and often relentless nature, inflicts profound and lasting damage on the mental health of its victims. While the immediate emotional toll is evident, the long-term consequences of cyberbullying can be equally devastating (Perwitasari & Wuryaningsih, 2022). The lasting and profound damage inflicted by cyberbullying on the mental health of its victims is a distressing reality that demands our attention. While the immediate emotional toll is evident, the enduring consequences of cyberbullying can be equally devastating, casting a long shadow over the lives of those affected. Depression stands as one of the most prevalent long-term consequences of cyberbullying. Victims are at an elevated risk of developing depression that can persist long after the bullying incidents have ceased. The unrelenting barrage of hurtful messages, derogatory comments, and social exclusion takes a toll on their self-esteem and self-worth, contributing to an overwhelming sense of hopelessness and sadness. Anxiety disorders, including generalized anxiety disorder, social anxiety disorder, and even post-traumatic stress disorder (PTSD), can emerge from the constant fear and anticipation of cyberbullying incidents. Victims often live in a perpetual state of hyper-vigilance, perpetually expecting further harassment. This heightened anxiety can manifest as anxiety attacks or panic disorders, further exacerbating their mental distress. Tragically, the psychological distress inflicted by cyberbullying can lead to suicidal ideation and self-harm among victims. Overwhelmed by their torment, some individuals may feel trapped and hopeless, believing that ending their life is the only escape from the relentless agony they endure. Regrettably, some succumb to these feelings, underscoring the critical importance of addressing cyberbullying as a life-threatening issue. As a coping mechanism to numb the emotional pain and trauma inflicted by cyberbullying, some victims turn to substance abuse. This self-medication can lead to long-term addiction issues, further exacerbating their mental health struggles and compounding the challenges they face in recovering their well-being. Cyberbullying also profoundly affects trust and relationship dynamics. Victims' trust in others becomes eroded, making it arduous to form and sustain healthy relationships. They may become increasingly isolated, intensifying their feelings of loneliness and despair. In conclusion, the long-term consequences of cyberbullying on mental health are far-reaching and deeply distressing. It is incumbent upon us as a society to not only combat cyberbullying itself but also to provide victims with access to the mental health support, counseling, and resources they need to heal and reclaim their emotional well-being. Additionally, preventative measures and strategies aimed at curbing cyberbullying are vital in reducing the prevalence and severity of these detrimental outcomes in the first place. It is imperative that we recognize the enduring consequences of cyberbullying on mental health. To mitigate these long-term effects, it is essential to not only address and intervene in ongoing cyberbullying incidents but also provide victims with access to mental health support, counselling, and resources to help them heal and regain their emotional well-being. Additionally, preventive measures and strategies to combat cyberbullying are crucial to reducing the prevalence of these detrimental outcomes in the first place.

CASE STUDIES ILLUSTRATING THE CONSEQUENCES

Case Study 1: The Tragic Impact on a Teenager's Life

In 2017, a 15-year-old girl from Mumbai became the victim of severe cyberbullying. Her classmates created a fake Facebook profile in her name and posted derogatory comments, humiliating photos, and false allegations. The relentless harassment led to a deep sense of shame and depression in the young girl. She struggled with anxiety and became socially withdrawn. The consequences of cyberbullying can be profoundly distressing, as exemplified by a real-life scenario where a victim's life took a distressing turn. In this case, the victim experienced a series of devastating outcomes: Firstly, the victim's academic performance declined significantly. The relentless torment of cyberbullying created an environment where concentrating on studies became an arduous task. The emotional distress and anxiety induced by the harassment hindered her ability to focus, resulting in lower grades and a notable decline in her academic achievements. Secondly, the victim developed severe depression and anxiety disorders. The constant barrage of hurtful messages, derogatory comments, and exclusionary behavior took a toll on her mental health. These traumatic experiences left her overwhelmed with feelings of sadness, hopelessness, and despair, and she began experiencing anxiety attacks and persistent fear. These debilitating conditions became a part of her daily life, further complicating her journey toward recovery. Thirdly, the family had to seek professional counseling and therapy for her. The profound emotional trauma inflicted by cyberbullying necessitated the intervention of mental health professionals. Therapy became a lifeline, offering her a chance to heal, regain her self-esteem, and rebuild her emotional well-being. Her family, too, faced the emotional toll of watching their loved one suffer, emphasizing the ripple effect of cyberbullying on an individual's support network. Lastly, this distressing incident served as a stark reminder of the urgent need for schools to implement comprehensive anti-cyberbullying policies and prioritize educating students about responsible digital behavior. The victim's harrowing experience underscored the devastating consequences of online harassment, prompting a call to action within the educational community. It became evident that fostering a safe and inclusive digital environment and equipping students with the skills to combat cyberbullying were essential steps in preventing such tragedies from recurring. This real-life account serves as a poignant illustration of how cyberbullying can disrupt lives, leaving a lasting impact not only on the victim but also on their families and the broader educational community. It underscores the critical importance of proactive measures to address and prevent cyberbullying, thereby safeguarding the well-being and futures of those at risk.

Case Study 2: Targeted Cyberbullying Campaign Against a Celebrity

In 2019, a famous Bollywood actress was the target of a relentless online hate campaign. Trolls flooded her social media accounts with derogatory comments, threats, and false rumors. The sustained cyberbullying took a toll on her mental health and well-being. The consequences of the cyberbullying incident against the actress were both immediate and far-reaching. First and foremost, she experienced severe stress and anxiety as a direct result of the relentless online harassment. The continuous onslaught of negative messages, derogatory comments, and personal attacks took a toll on her mental well-being, causing her significant emotional distress. In response to this overwhelming situation, the actress found it necessary to take breaks from social media and public appearances. These hiatuses were crucial for her to regain her emotional balance and shield herself from further harassment. Stepping away from the constant scrutiny of the online world became a means of self-preservation and a way to protect her mental health. Moreover, the incident involving the actress drew significant attention to a pervasive issue: the rampant culture of online harassment against celebrities. Her experience served as a stark reminder that even individuals in the public eye are not immune to the harmful effects of cyberbullying. It highlighted the urgent need for stricter regulations on social media platforms to combat online harassment effectively. The incident spurred discussions about improving safety measures, reporting mechanisms, and holding perpetrators accountable for their actions in the digital realm.

Case Study 3: Cyberbullying in Educational Institutions

In 2020, a high school in New Delhi faced a cyberbullying crisis when a group of students started a WhatsApp group to target and bully their peers. Hurtful messages, personal insults, and false rumors were circulated within the group, causing immense emotional distress to the victims. The consequences of cyberbullying can be stark and distressing, with real and lasting impacts on the lives of those affected. In the context of a school environment, these consequences become particularly concerning. Several students who fell victim to cyberbullying began to grapple with anxiety and depression. The incessant barrage of hurtful messages, derogatory comments, and the emotional distress inflicted by online harassment took a toll on their mental well-being. The resulting anxiety and depression cast shadows over their daily lives, affecting their ability to learn, interact, and thrive within the school community. In response to the torment they endured, some victims took the drastic step of skipping school to avoid their tormentors. The fear and anxiety associated with encountering cyberbullies, whether online or in person, became so overwhelming that they felt compelled to stay away from school to safeguard their emotional well-being. This absenteeism not only disrupted their educational progress but also perpetuated a cycle of isolation and anxiety. Recognizing the urgent need to address these distressing consequences, the school took proactive measures to tackle the issue head-on. They initiated a comprehensive anti-cyberbullying program aimed at raising awareness and providing crucial support to affected students. This program serves as a beacon of hope, fostering a safe and inclusive environment where students can not only learn and grow but also find solace and assistance in navigating the complex challenges posed by cyberbullying. In such instances, it becomes evident that proactive and decisive actions, like implementing anti-cyberbullying programs, are indispensable in safeguarding the well-being of students and ensuring that schools remain places of learning, growth, and emotional support.

Case Study 4: The Tragic Suicide of a Cyberbullying Victim

In 2018, a 17-year-old boy from Bangalore took his own life after enduring relentless cyberbullying on a popular social media platform. Anonymous users posted hurtful comments and encouraged the victim to harm himself. The tragedy shocked the nation and sparked a conversation on the urgent need to address cyberbullying. The consequences of a recent high-profile cyberbullying case reverberated throughout the nation, sparking a nationwide outcry and prompting urgent discussions on the need to strengthen cyberbullying laws and regulations. The shocking and tragic events that unfolded in the wake of this case brought into sharp focus the dire need for more comprehensive legal measures to combat this insidious form of harassment. Mental health organizations, too, witnessed a significant surge in requests for support from victims and their families. The case served as a stark reminder of the profound and lasting damage that cyberbullying can inflict on mental well-being. The overwhelming emotional distress experienced by victims necessitated a heightened level of mental health support and resources to help them cope with and recover from the trauma. Most poignantly, the case underscored the life-threatening consequences of unchecked cyberbullying. It served as a heartbreaking reminder that cyberbullying is not merely a digital nuisance but a grave threat to individuals' lives and well-being. This tragic incident has galvanized efforts to address cyberbullying comprehensively, from legal and regulatory reforms to bolstering mental health services and raising awareness about the profound impact of online harassment on victims. These case studies from India highlight the diverse and severe consequences of cyberbullying, ranging from mental health issues to tragic outcomes. They emphasize the need for robust legal measures, awareness campaigns, and mental health support systems to combat cyberbullying effectively and protect individuals from its devastating effects.

CYBERBULLYING VS. TRADITIONAL BULLYING

Cyberbullying and traditional bullying share the common denominator of causing harm to individuals, but they diverge significantly in their methods, reach, and consequences. Cyberbullying, a product of the digital age, unfolds in the virtual realm using electronic devices and online platforms. In contrast, traditional bullying occurs in physical spaces such as schools, neighborhoods, or workplaces. The distinction in the medium is pivotal. Traditional bullying's limitations are defined by physical proximity, whereas cyberbullying transcends geographical boundaries, making it more pervasive and challenging for victims to escape. One of the most striking disparities is the role of anonymity and disinhibition in cyberbullying. Online platforms frequently offer users the option to create anonymous profiles or hide their real identities. This cloak of anonymity emboldens cyberbullies, as it shields them from immediate consequences, allowing them to target victims without immediate fear of retaliation. Furthermore, the absence of face-to-face interaction in online communication fosters a greater degree of disinhibition, making perpetrators less accountable for their actions and more prone to engage in extreme and hurtful behaviors. Audience reach and speed further distinguish cyberbullying from its traditional counterpart. In the digital landscape, cyberbullying possesses the potential for a vast audience reach. Hurtful content can rapidly go viral, reaching acquaintances, strangers, and even potential employers. This amplifies the humiliation and distress experienced by victims. Moreover, the speed at which cyberbullying incidents unfold is unparalleled. A few clicks can lead to the swift sharing, commenting, or reposting of hurtful content within seconds, leaving victims little time to react or seek help. While both forms of bullying have severe psychological and emotional consequences for victims, cyberbullying's unique characteristics can exacerbate these effects. Victims of both cyberbullying and traditional bullying experience anxiety, depression, low self-esteem, and isolation. However, the constant connectivity of the digital age can make cyberbullying more relentless, intensifying victims' emotional distress (Kowalski et al., 2022).In conclusion, cyberbullying and traditional bullying may share the same goal of harming others, but they operate in distinct domains with varying methods and consequences. Understanding these differences is essential for crafting effective prevention and intervention strategies to combat the evolving challenges posed by bullying in the digital age (Li et al., 2022).

Figure 6. Cyberbullying vs. traditional bullying (Developmentaid, 2022)

Factors Contributing to Cyberbullying

1. **Anonymity and Disinhibition:**

Online anonymity allows individuals to hide their identities, making it easier for them to engage in cyberbullying without fear of immediate consequences.

Disinhibition in online communication occurs when people feel less constrained by social norms and empathy due to the absence of face-to-face interaction. This can lead to more aggressive and hurtful behavior.

2. **Accessibility to Technology:**

The widespread availability of smartphones, computers, and internet access has made it easier for individuals, including young people, to engage in cyberbullying. The convenience of technology means that cyberbullying can occur at any time and from any location, amplifying its prevalence.

3. **Lack of Supervision**: In some cases, children and adolescents may have access to digital devices and social media without proper supervision or guidance from parents or caregivers. This can increase the likelihood of cyberbullying.
4. **Social Media Platforms**:

Social media platforms, while offering many benefits, also provide opportunities for cyberbullying. These platforms enable users to share content widely and communicate with others, making it easier for bullies to target victims.

5. **Peer Pressure and Group Dynamics**:

Cyberbullying can escalate when a group of individuals collectively targets a victim. Peer pressure and group dynamics may encourage participants to engage in harmful behavior they might not do individually (Olckers & Hattingh, 2022).

Role of Technology and Social Media

In the digital age, technology, and social media play a dual role in the landscape of cyberbullying. While these platforms offer numerous benefits in terms of connectivity and communication, they also provide the infrastructure for cyberbullying to thrive. The advent of technology and the proliferation of social media platforms have fundamentally transformed the landscape of bullying, giving rise to the phenomenon known as cyberbullying. The role of technology and social media in cyberbullying is multifaceted and presents both opportunities for positive interaction and challenges for addressing online harassment (Ohara, 2023).

Amplified Reach: Technology and social media provide individuals with powerful tools for communication and social interaction. While this has enabled positive connections and global communication, it has also amplified the reach of cyberbullying. Perpetrators can target victims anywhere, at any time, transcending physical boundaries. The viral nature of online content means that hurtful messages, images, or videos can spread rapidly, reaching a vast audience and intensifying the humiliation experienced by victims.

Anonymity and Disinhibition: The online environment often allows users to create anonymous profiles or conceal their real identities. This anonymity can embolden cyberbullies, making them feel shielded from immediate consequences and allowing them to target victims without fear of retaliation. Additionally, the absence of face-to-face interaction in online communication can lead to disinhibition, with individuals feeling less restrained by social norms and consequences. This can result in cyberbullies engaging in more extreme and hurtful behaviors than they might in traditional bullying scenarios.

Persistent Digital Footprint: Unlike traditional bullying, which often leaves no lasting evidence, cyberbullying leaves a persistent digital footprint. Hurtful messages, images, or rumors can linger online indefinitely, making it challenging for victims to escape the trauma and for authorities to intervene effectively. This digital permanence can exacerbate the psychological impact on victims.

Online Hate Speech: Social media platforms have become breeding grounds for hate speech and extremist ideologies. Cyberbullies may engage in online hate campaigns, targeting individuals based on their race, ethnicity, gender, or other characteristics. Such behaviors not only harm individual victims but also contribute to a toxic online culture.

Countermeasures and Prevention: Recognizing the unique challenges posed by cyberbullying, various countermeasures and prevention strategies have been developed. These include educational programs to promote digital literacy and responsible online behavior, legal measures aimed at holding cyberbullies accountable, and technology safeguards that empower users to protect themselves online. Social media platforms have also taken steps to combat online harassment by implementing reporting mechanisms and policies against hate speech and cyberbullying. The role of technology and social media in cyberbullying is complex, offering both opportunities for positive connection and challenges in addressing online harassment. Understanding these dynamics is crucial for developing comprehensive strategies to combat cyberbullying and foster a safer and more inclusive online environment for all users.

Legal and Ethical Considerations

Cyberbullying raises complex legal and ethical questions that vary across jurisdictions and cultures. Addressing this issue requires a delicate balance between safeguarding individuals from harm and respecting principles of free speech and online expression.

Laws Addressing Cyberbullying in Different Jurisdictions

The legal landscape surrounding cyberbullying varies considerably across different jurisdictions, reflecting the unique approaches and challenges that each region faces in addressing this digital phenomenon.

United States: In the United States, there is no federal law specifically dedicated to cyberbullying. Instead, the legal framework for addressing cyberbullying largely relies on state laws, which can vary significantly. Some states have enacted legislation explicitly defining and criminalizing cyberbullying, while others rely on existing laws related to harassment, stalking, or bullying to prosecute cyberbullying cases. This decentralized approach means that the legal response to cyberbullying can vary from one state to another.

United Kingdom: The UK has taken a more proactive stance in combatting cyberbullying. The Communications Act of 2003, for instance, makes it illegal to send grossly offensive or menacing messages online. Additionally, UK schools are required to have anti-bullying policies that encompass cyberbullying, reflecting a commitment to address this issue comprehensively.

Canada: Canada's legal framework includes provisions related to cyberbullying within its Criminal Code. Offenses such as criminal harassment and uttering threats can be applied to cyberbullying cases. In 2015, Canada passed the "Protecting Canadians from Online Crime Act" (Bill C-13), which specifically addresses cyberbullying and the non-consensual distribution of intimate images, demonstrating the country's commitment to combatting online harassment.

European Union: The European Union (EU) has enacted data protection regulations, including the General Data Protection Regulation (GDPR), which include provisions related to online harassment and personal data protection. Member states within the EU also have their own legal frameworks addressing cyberbullying, which may vary in their approach and scope.

The absence of a uniform international standard for addressing cyberbullying highlights the complexity of this issue and the need for nuanced, context-specific legal responses. While some jurisdictions have taken proactive steps to define and combat cyberbullying, others rely on broader laws related to harassment and online behaviour. As the digital landscape continues to evolve, it is likely that legal frameworks in various jurisdictions will adapt to address the unique challenges posed by cyberbullying comprehensively (Azumah et al., 2023).

Challenges in Enforcing Cyberbullying Laws

Enforcing cyberbullying laws is a complex task, marked by several significant challenges that law enforcement and legal systems must contend with in the digital age.

Jurisdictional Challenges: The borderless nature of the internet means that cyberbullying incidents can transcend national boundaries. When perpetrators and victims are in different jurisdictions, enforcing cyberbullying laws becomes intricate. International legal cooperation and coordination between countries are essential to address this issue effectively. Harmonizing laws and extradition treaties can facilitate the prosecution of cyberbullies operating across borders.

Anonymity: Perpetrators of cyberbullying often exploit the anonymity provided by online platforms. They hide behind pseudonyms or create fake profiles, making it exceedingly difficult to identify and prosecute them. The cloak of anonymity can embolden cyberbullies, as they may believe they can act without consequences. Law enforcement agencies face the daunting task of unmasking these anonymous wrongdoers, which can require substantial time and resources.

Evidentiary Challenges: Collecting evidence for cyberbullying cases poses unique challenges. Digital communications can be transient, and perpetrators may quickly delete harmful messages or content. This creates difficulties in preserving evidence and establishing a clear trail of online harassment. Additionally, the use of encrypted messaging apps can further complicate efforts to gather evidence, as these platforms prioritize user privacy.

Reporting and Victim Reluctance: A significant portion of cyberbullying incidents goes unreported. Victims often hesitate to come forward due to fear of retaliation, shame, or a lack of awareness about the legal avenues available for redress. This reluctance can hinder law enforcement's ability to investigate and prosecute cases effectively. Encouraging victims to report cyberbullying and providing them with the necessary support and protection is a critical aspect of addressing this issue.

Addressing these challenges necessitates a multi-pronged approach that includes international cooperation, technological advancements in digital forensics, public awareness campaigns, and legal reforms to adapt to the evolving nature of cyberbullying. Law enforcement agencies and legal systems must continuously evolve to keep pace with the complexities of the digital world and ensure that cyberbullies are held accountable for their actions (Mantri, 2023).

Ethical Considerations in Addressing Cyberbullying

Efforts to combat cyberbullying are laden with ethical considerations that touch upon fundamental principles like freedom of expression, content moderation, and the importance of education and awareness.

Freedom of Expression: Protecting freedom of expression is a cornerstone of democratic societies, and it's essential to strike a balance between this right and the imperative to prevent harm caused by cyberbullying. The ethical challenge lies in defining the boundaries where free expression transforms into harmful conduct online. Policymakers and legal systems must navigate this delicate balance, ensuring that legitimate speech is protected while harmful online behaviors are appropriately addressed.

Content Moderation: Social media platforms and online communities grapple with content moderation challenges daily. These platforms must establish and enforce community guidelines that address various forms of online harassment and hate speech. Ethical considerations emerge when determining what content should be removed or restricted, as the line between free expression and harm is not always clear-cut. Consistency in enforcing these guidelines and addressing concerns about potential biases in content moderation algorithms is an ongoing ethical concern.

Education and Awareness: Promoting ethical behavior online includes educating individuals about the consequences of their actions. Ethical considerations extend to fostering digital literacy and responsible online behavior. Educational initiatives should not only focus on preventing victims from becoming targets of cyberbullying but also emphasize the importance of empathy, kindness, and respectful communication in digital spaces. This ethical dimension highlights the proactive role that individuals, educators, and communities can play in preventing cyberbullying and creating a more inclusive online environment.

Ultimately, addressing cyberbullying requires a nuanced and ethical approach that respects the principles of free expression while safeguarding individuals from harm. Balancing these considerations in the digital age is an ongoing challenge, requiring collaboration between policymakers, technology companies, educators, and society at large to create a safer and more ethical online environment (Gawu & Mensah, 2022).

Prevention and Intervention Strategies

Cyberbullying is a pervasive issue in the digital age, but effective prevention and intervention strategies can mitigate its impact and foster a safer online environment. Addressing the pervasive issue of cyberbullying necessitates a multi-pronged approach that involves not only policymakers and law enforcement but also educational institutions, parents, and the community at large. Addressing cyberbullying effectively requires a multifaceted approach that combines prevention and intervention strategies aimed at creating a safer and more respectful online environment. Education and awareness are key aspects of prevention, with schools incorporating cyberbullying awareness programs into their curricula. These programs teach students about responsible online behavior, the consequences of cyberbullying, and how to seek help if they are targeted. Additionally, fostering empathy, digital citizenship, and the importance of promptly reporting cyberbullying incidents is crucial. Parents should play an active role by participating in workshops and seminars that educate them about recognizing signs of cyberbullying, understanding the platforms their children use, and encouraging open communication. Digital literacy is fundamental, with educators teaching critical thinking skills to evaluate online content and identify potential risks. Anonymous reporting systems should be established in schools and online platforms to provide a secure means for victims and witnesses to report incidents. Peer support programs can encourage students to look out for each other, report cyberbullying, and provide emotional support to victims (Tozzo et al., 2022). Responding swiftly to reports and enforcing consequences for perpetrators sends a strong message that cyberbullying will not be tolerated. Schools should also provide counseling and mental health support for victims, acknowledging the psychological impact of cyberbullying. Legal measures, including the enactment and enforcement of cyberbullying laws, are essential. Lastly, community engagement involving local authorities, organizations, and social media platforms can lead to more comprehensive prevention and intervention efforts. Together, these strategies contribute to a safer online environment where individuals can interact respectfully and without fear of harassment or harm. Cyberbullying prevention and intervention should remain an ongoing priority for educational institutions, parents, policymakers, and society as a whole (Burlet & Panahon, 2022).

Supporting Cyberbullying Victims

Cyberbullying can have severe emotional and psychological consequences for victims. Providing support and resources is essential to help them cope with the trauma and regain their well-being (Sanchez, 2023). Supporting cyberbullying victims is of paramount importance in mitigating the negative consequences of online harassment. Victims often experience emotional distress, anxiety, and a sense of isolation. To provide effective support, it is essential to foster an open and empathetic environment where victims feel comfortable sharing their experiences. Encouraging them to confide in a trusted friend, family member, or counselor can help alleviate their emotional burden. Schools and online platforms should have mechanisms in place for anonymous reporting, ensuring that victims can seek help without fear of retaliation. Counseling and mental health resources are crucial for helping victims cope with the psychological impact of cyberbullying. These resources can assist victims in processing their emotions, building resilience, and recovering from the trauma. Legal measures, such as reporting cyberbullying incidents to authorities, should also be an option when necessary. Above all, offering unwavering emotional support and reminding victims that they are not alone in their struggle can make a significant difference in their healing process. By addressing their emotional needs and providing resources, we can help victims regain their confidence and well-being in the face of cyberbullying.

FUTURE CHALLENGES AND TRENDS

As we look ahead, several future challenges and trends in the realm of cyberbullying are emerging. One significant challenge is the evolution of technology itself (Marr, 2022). With new communication platforms, social media features, and online spaces constantly emerging, cyberbullies have more opportunities to exploit vulnerabilities. Additionally, the issue of anonymity on the internet remains a challenge, as it empowers perpetrators to engage in hurtful behaviours without immediate consequences. As technology continues to advance, so does the sophistication of cyberbullying tactics, making it even more critical to stay vigilant and adapt prevention and intervention strategies accordingly. Another trend to watch is the intersection of cyberbullying with other forms of online harm, such as online harassment, hate speech, and doxing (revealing personal information online). These interconnected issues create complex challenges for policymakers, online platforms, and society as a whole, demanding a holistic approach to tackle the broader spectrum of online harm effectively. Moreover, the mental health impact of cyberbullying is gaining increased attention. As our understanding of the psychological consequences deepens, mental health support and counselling services must be readily available to victims. The long-term effects of cyberbullying on individuals' well-being, even into adulthood, underscore the need for comprehensive and sustained support systems. In terms of trends, the role of artificial intelligence (AI) and machine learning in combating cyberbullying is on the horizon. AI algorithms can be employed to detect and mitigate cyberbullying incidents more swiftly and accurately, potentially reducing the harm inflicted on victims. However, the ethical implications and potential biases in AI-powered solutions also require careful consideration. Furthermore, legislation and regulation surrounding cyberbullying are expected to evolve, with more jurisdictions addressing this issue with specific laws and policies. The responsibility of online platforms to moderate and police harmful content will likely continue to be a focal point, with increasing pressure for platforms to take proactive measures against cyberbullying.

As technology evolves and our understanding of cyberbullying deepens, we face both new challenges and opportunities in addressing this pervasive issue. Vigilance, adaptability, and a commitment to providing comprehensive support for victims will be key in shaping the future response to cyberbullying.

CONCLUSION

In conclusion, the chapter on "Cyberbullying in the Digital Age: Consequences and Countermeasures" underscores the critical importance of addressing this pervasive issue that has evolved alongside the rapid growth of technology and the internet. Cyberbullying, with its unique characteristics in the digital realm, inflicts severe psychological, emotional, and even physical harm on its victims. The consequences of cyberbullying are far-reaching, impacting individuals, families, communities, and society as a whole. This chapter has highlighted the profound psychological consequences of cyberbullying, including emotional distress, depression, anxiety, isolation, and even thoughts of self-harm and suicide. It has emphasized the impact on academic and workplace performance, as well as the strain on relationships and trust. Moreover, the enduring nature of these consequences, extending into adulthood, underscores the urgency of addressing cyberbullying comprehensively. Countermeasures and prevention strategies are essential in mitigating the harm caused by cyberbullying. Education, awareness programs, and responsible digital citizenship play a vital role in prevention. Reporting mechanisms, peer support, and swift intervention are critical for addressing ongoing incidents effectively. Legal measures and community engagement further contribute to a holistic approach in combating cyberbullying. Looking forward, the chapter has also discussed the challenges and trends on the horizon, including evolving technology, AI-powered solutions, the intersection of cyberbullying with other online harms, and the continued development of legislation and regulation. As we navigate these challenges, it is imperative that we remain committed to creating a safe and inclusive digital space for all users. In essence, the battle against cyberbullying is ongoing, and it requires a collaborative effort from educators, parents, policymakers, online platforms, mental health professionals, and society as a whole. By recognizing the consequences of cyberbullying, implementing effective countermeasures, and staying attuned to emerging trends, we can work together to combat cyberbullying and create a more compassionate and secure digital world for everyone.

REFERENCES

Akhter, A., Acharjee, U. K., Talukder, M. A., Islam, M. M., & Uddin, M. A. (2023). A robust hybrid machine learning model for Bengali cyberbullying detection in social media. *Natural Language Processing Journal*, 100027.

Azumah, S. W., Adewopo, V., & ElSayed, Z. (2023). A Secure Open-Source Intelligence Framework For Cyberbullying Investigation. *arXiv preprint arXiv:2307.15225.*

Burlet, R. E., & Panahon, C. J. (2022). Cyberbullying Prevention and Intervention: Current Practices in Schools. *Journal of Prevention and Health Promotion*, *3*(2), 258–267. doi:10.1177/26320770221087454

Chiao, Alimu, Yang, & Kang. (2023). What you think is a joke is actually cyberbullying: The effects of ethical dissonance, event judgment and humor style on cyberbullying behavior. *Computers in Human Behavior, 142*. doi:10.1016/j.chb.2023.107670

Developmentaid. (2022). https://www.developmentaid.org/api/frontend/cms/file/2022/03/Cyberbullying-vs-traditional-bullying-1.jpg

Fredrick, S. S., Coyle, S., & King, J. A. (2023). Middle and high school teachers' perceptions of cyberbullying prevention and digital citizenship. *Psychology in the Schools*, *60*(6), 1958–1978. doi:10.1002/pits.22844

Gawu, D. A., & Mensah, R. O. (2022). Balancing the Freedom of Expression, Right to Information and Use of Social Media in Ghana. In *Democratic Governance, Law, and Development in Africa: Pragmatism, Experiments, and Prospects* (pp. 121–145). Springer International Publishing. doi:10.1007/978-3-031-15397-6_5

Kapersky. (n.d.). https://www.google.com/url?sa=i&url=https%3A%2F%2Fwww.kaspersky.com%2Fabout%2Fpress-releases%2F2015_the-evolution-of-bullying-from-schoolyard-to-smartphone-24-7&psig=AOvVaw0n4x_8rs6k1K-jiaZYRnOp&ust=1694603771838000&source=images&cd=vfe&opi=89978449&ved=0CBAQjRxqFwoTCKi1rZD5pIEDFQAAAAAdAAAAABAE

Kidshelpline. (n.d.). https://kidshelpline.com.au/sites/default/files/bdl_image/Teen%20girl%20being%20cyberbullied_2.png

Kowalski, R. M., Giumetti, G. W., & Feinn, R. S. (2022). Is cyberbullying an extension of traditional bullying or a unique phenomenon? A longitudinal investigation among college students. *International Journal of Bullying Prevention : an Official Publication of the International Bullying Prevention Association*, 1–18.

Li, C., Wang, P., Martin-Moratinos, M., Bella-Fernández, M., & Blasco-Fontecilla, H. (2022). Traditional bullying and cyberbullying in the digital age and its associated mental health problems in children and adolescents: A meta-analysis. *European Child & Adolescent Psychiatry*, 1–15. doi:10.1007/s00787-021-01763-0 PMID:36585978

Li, J., Wu, Y., & Hesketh, T. (2023). Internet use and cyberbullying: Impacts on psychosocial and psychosomatic wellbeing among Chinese adolescents. *Computers in Human Behavior, 138*, 107461. doi:10.1016/j.chb.2022.107461

Mantri, G. R. (2023). *Channelization of social media through cyber law and its enforcement challenges in India*. Academic Press.

Marr, B. (2022). *Future skills: The 20 skills and competencies everyone needs to succeed in a digital world*. John Wiley & Sons.

Nair, M. M., Fernandez, T. F., & Tyagi, A. K. (2023, January). Cyberbullying in Digital Era: History, Trends, Limitations, Recommended Solutions for Future. In *2023 International Conference on Computer Communication and Informatics (ICCCI)* (pp. 1-10). IEEE. 10.1109/ICCCI56745.2023.10128624

Ohara, M. R. (2023). The Role of Social Media in Educational Communication Management. *Journal of Contemporary Administration and Management, 1*(2), 70–76. doi:10.61100/adman.v1i2.25

Olckers, C., & Hattingh, M. J. M. (2022). *The dark side of social media-cyberbullying, catfishing and trolling: a systematic literature review*. Academic Press.

Perwitasari, D. R., & Wuryaningsih, E. W. (2022). Why did you do that to me?: A systematic review of cyberbullying impact on mental health and suicide among adolescents. *NurseLine Journal, 7*(1), 35–47. doi:10.19184/nlj.v7i1.27311

Sanchez, M. (2023). Interventions to support young cyberbullying victims: A scoping review. *AGPE The Royal Gondwana Research Journal of History, Science, Economic, Political and Social Science, 4*(4), 24–33.

Tozzo, P., Cuman, O., Moratto, E., & Caenazzo, L. (2022). Family and educational strategies for cyberbullying prevention: A systematic review. *International Journal of Environmental Research and Public Health, 19*(16), 10452. doi:10.3390/ijerph191610452 PMID:36012084

Verywellfamily. (n.d.). https://www.verywellfamily.com/thmb/wRCDeFcZDIfnqMGGSfCMmxuKTiA=/1500x0/filters:no_upscale():max_bytes(150000):strip_icc()/what-are-the-effects-of-cyberbullying-460558_color1-5b50c42946e0fb0037b84d00.png

Weiss, A. (2022). Professor and victim: Cyberbullying targeting professors in the higher education workplace. In *Research Anthology on Combating Cyber-Aggression and Online Negativity* (pp. 1516–1532). IGI Global. doi:10.4018/978-1-6684-5594-4.ch077

Compilation of References

Aadhavan SadasivamK. G. (2020, April 30). *memeBot: Towards Automatic Image Meme Generation.* https://arxiv.org/abs/2004.14571

Abacha, A. B., & Zweigenbaum, P. (2011, June). Medical entity recognition: a comparaison of semantic and statistical methods. In *Proceedings of BioNLP 2011 workshop* (pp. 56-64). Academic Press.

Abed, S. A., Tiun, S., & Omar, N. (2016). Word sense disambiguation in evolutionary manner. *Connection Science*, *28*(3), 226–241. doi:10.1080/09540091.2016.1141874

Agarwal, A., Xie, B., Vovsha, I., Rambow, O., & Passonneau, R. (2011). Sentiment analysis of Twitter data. *Proceedings of the Workshop on Languages in Social Media.*

Ah-Pine, J., & Jacquet, G. (2009, March). Clique-based clustering for improving named entity recognition systems. In *Proceedings of the 12th Conference of the European Chapter of the ACL (EACL 2009)* (pp. 51-59). 10.3115/1609067.1609072

Ajay, S., Srikanth, M., Kumar, M. A., & Soman, K. (2016). Word embedding models for finding semantic relationship between words in tamil language. *Indian Journal of Science and Technology*, *9*(45), 1–5. doi:10.17485/ijst/2016/v9i45/106478

Akhtar, M. S., Kumar, A., Ekbal, A., & Bhattacharyya, P. (2016). A hybrid deep learning architecture for sentiment analysis. *Proceedings of COLING 2016, the 26th International Conference on Computational Linguistics: Technical Papers.*

Akhter, A., Acharjee, U. K., Talukder, M. A., Islam, M. M., & Uddin, M. A. (2023). A robust hybrid machine learning model for Bengali cyberbullying detection in social media. *Natural Language Processing Journal*, 100027.

Alexandre, L. (2017). *La guerre des intelligences: Intelligence artificielle versus Intelligence humaine*. JCLattès.

Ali, M. N. Y., Rahman, M. L., Chaki, J., Dey, N., & Santosh, K. C. (2021). Machine translation using deep learning for universal networking language based on their structure. *International Journal of Machine Learning and Cybernetics*, *12*(8), 2365–2376. doi:10.1007/s13042-021-01317-5

Amarappa, S., & Sathyanarayana, S. (2013). Named entity recognition and classification in kannada language. *International Journal of Electronics and Computer Science Engineering*, *2*(1), 281–289.

Amarappa, S., & Sathyanarayana, S. (2015). Kannada named entity recognition and classification using conditional random fields. *2015 International Conference on Emerging Research in Electronics, Computer Science and Technology (ICERECT)*. 10.1109/ERECT.2015.7499010

Ambati, V., Vogel, S., & Carbonell, J. G. (2011). Multi-strategy approaches to active learning for statistical machine translation. *Proceedings of Machine Translation Summit XIII: Papers*.

Ameta, J., Joshi, N., & Mathur, I. (2012). *A lightweight stemmer for Gujarati*. arXiv preprint arXiv:1210.5486.

Amit Pimpalkar, J. R. (2020)). Influence of Pre-processing Strategies on the Performance of ML Classifiers Exploiting TF-IDF and BOW Features. *Advances in Distributed Computing and Artificial Intelligence Journal*, 49-68.

Anand Kumar, M., Dhanalakshmi, V., Soman, K., & Rajendran, S. (2010). A sequence labeling approach to morphological analyzer for tamil language. *International Journal on Computer Science and Engineering*, *2*(06), 1944–1951.

Anandika, A., & Mishra, S. P. (2019, May). A study on machine learning approaches for named entity recognition. In *2019 International Conference on Applied Machine Learning (ICAML)* (pp. 153-159). IEEE. 10.1109/ICAML48257.2019.00037

Anbukkarasi, S., Varadhaganapathy, S., Jeevapriya, S., Kaaviyaa, A., Lawvanyapriya, T., & Monisha, S. (2022). *Named entity recognition for Tamil text using deep learning*. Institute of Electrical and Electronics Engineers Inc. doi:10.1109/ICCCI54379.2022.9740745

Anita, R., & Subalalitha, C. (2019a). An approach to cluster Tamil literatures using dis- course connectives. In *2019 IEEE 1st International Conference on Energy, Systems and Information Processing (ICESIP)* (pp. 1–4). IEEE.

Anita, R., & Subalalitha, C. (2019b). Building discourse parser for Thirukkural. *Proceedings of the 16th International Conference on Natural Language Processing*, 18–25.

Antony, P., & Soman, K. (2010). Kernel based part of speech tagger for kannada. *2010 International conference on machine learning and cybernetics*.

Antony, P., Ajith, V., & Soman, K. (2010b). Statistical method for English to Kannada transliteration. *Information Processing and Management: International Conference on Recent Trends in Business Administration and Information Processing, BAIP 2010, Trivandrum, Kerala, India, March 26-27, 2010. Proceedings*. 10.1007/978-3-642-12214-9_57

Antony, P., Ajith, V., & Soman, K. (2010a). Kernel method for English to Kannada transliteration. *2010 International Conference on Recent Trends in Information, Telecommunication and Computing*.

Appelt, D. (1995). *SRI International Fastus System MUC-6 Test Results and Analysis*. SRI International. doi:10.21236/ADA460970

Arivazhagan, N., Bapna, A., Firat, O., Lepikhin, D., Johnson, M., Krikun, M., Chen, M. X., Cao, Y., Foster, G., & Cherry, C. (2019). Massively multilingual neural machine translation in the wild: Findings and challenges. *arXiv preprint arXiv:1907.05019.*

Arul Deepa, K., & Deisy, C. (2012). A rule based converter of formal tamil to colloquial tamil (ft2ct). *11th International Tamil Internet Conference.*

Asopa, S., Asopa, P., Mathur, I., & Joshi, N. (2016). Rule based chunker for hindi. In *2016 2nd international conference on contemporary computing and informatics (ic3i)* (pp. 442–445). 10.1109/IC3I.2016.7918005

Avinesh, P., & Karthik, G. (2007). Part-of-speech tagging and chunking using conditional random fields and transformation based learning. *Shallow Parsing for South Asian Languages*, *21*, 21–24.

Azumah, S. W., Adewopo, V., & ElSayed, Z. (2023). A Secure Open-Source Intelligence Framework For Cyberbullying Investigation. *arXiv preprint arXiv:2307.15225.*

Baby, A., NL, N., Thomas, A. L., & Murthy, H. A. (2016). A unified parser for developing Indian language text to speech synthesizers. *Text, Speech, and Dialogue: 19th International Conference, TSD 2016, Brno, Czech Republic, September 12-16, 2016, Proceedings.*

Babych, B., & Hartley, A. (2003). Improving machine translation quality with automatic named entity recognition. *Proceedings of the 7th International EAMT workshop on MT and other language technology tools, Improving MT through other language technology tools, Resource and tools for building MT at EACL 2003*. 10.3115/1609822.1609823

Bahdanau, D., Cho, K., & Bengio, Y. (2014). Neural machine translation by jointly learning to align and translate. *arXiv preprint arXiv:1409.0473.*

Baker, P., Hardie, A., McEnery, T., Cunningham, H., & Gaizauskas, R. J. (2002). *67-Million Word Corpus of Indic Languages: Data Collection, Mark-up and Harmonisation*. LREC.

Baksa, K., Golović, D., Glavaš, G., & Šnajder, J. (2016). Tagging named entities in Croatian tweets. *Slovenščina 2.0: Empirical, Applied and Interdisciplinary Research, 4*(1), 20-41.

Bala Das, S., Panda, D., Mishra, T. K., & Patra, B. K. (2023). Statistical Machine Translation for Indic Languages. *arXiv e-prints*, arXiv: 2301.00539.

Balaji, J., Geetha, T., Parthasarathi, R., & Karky, M. (2011). Morpho-semantic features for rule-based tamil enconversion. *International Journal of Computer Applications*, *26*(6), 11–18. doi:10.5120/3109-4269

Balaji, J., Ranjani, P., & Geetha, T. (2016). Unsupervised learning of semantic relations of a morphologically rich language. *International Journal of Information and Communication Technology*, *8*(4), 344–356.

Balamurali, A., Joshi, A., & Bhattacharyya, P. (2012). Cross-lingual sentiment analysis for indian languages using linked wordnets. *Proceedings of COLING 2012: Posters, Banane, M., & Erraissi, A. (2022). A comprehensive study of Natural Language processing techniques Based on Big Data. 2022 International Conference on Decision Aid Sciences and Applications (DASA).*

Banday, T. A., Panzoo, O., Lone, F. A., Nazir, S., Malik, K. A., Rasoool, S., & .... (2009). Developing A Trilingual (English-Hindi-Kashmiri) E-Dictionary: Issues And Solutions. *Interdisciplinary Journal of Linguistics.*, *2*(1), 295–304.

Banerjee, S., & Lavie, A. (2005). METEOR: An automatic metric for MT evaluation with improved correlation with human judgments. *Proceedings of the acl workshop on intrinsic and extrinsic evaluation measures for machine translation and/or summarization.*

Banerjee, S., Choudhury, M., Chakma, K., Naskar, S. K., Das, A., Bandyopadhyay, S., & Rosso, P. (2020). MSIR@FIRE: A Comprehensive Report from 2013 to 2016. *SN Computer Science*, *1*(1), 55. Advance online publication. doi:10.1007/s42979-019-0058-0

Banik, D., Ekbal, A., & Bhattacharyya, P. (2018). Machine learning based optimized pruning approach for decoding in statistical machine translation. *IEEE Access : Practical Innovations, Open Solutions*, *7*, 1736–1751. doi:10.1109/ACCESS.2018.2883738

Barba, E., Procopio, L., Campolungo, N., Pasini, T., & Navigli, R. (2020). Mulan: Multilingual label propagation for word sense disambiguation. In *Proceedings of the Twenty-Ninth International Joint Conference on Artificial Intelligence* (pp. 3837-3844). 10.24963/ijcai.2020/531

Barbosa, L., & Feng, J. (2010). *Robust Sentiment Detection on Twitter from Biased and Noisy Data*. AT&T Labs - Research.

Batra, S., & Rao, D. (2009). *Entity Based Sentiment Analysis on Twitter*. Department of Computer Science, Stanford University.

Behera, B. K. (2017). Language Endangerment and Maintenance: A Study of the HO Language. *Journal of Applied Linguistics and Language Research*, *4*(3), 1–11.

Ben Abacha, A., & Zweigenbaum, P. (2011). Automatic extraction of semantic relations between medical entities: A rule based approach. *Journal of Biomedical Semantics*, *2*(5), 1–11. doi:10.1186/2041-1480-2-S5-S4 PMID:22166723

Bender, O., Och, F. J., & Ney, H. (2003). Maximum entropy models for named entity recognition. In *Proceedings of the seventh conference on Natural language learning at HLT-NAACL 2003* (pp. 148-151). 10.3115/1119176.1119196

Bharati, A., Chaitanya, V., Kulkarni, A. P., & Sangal, R. (2003). Anusaaraka: machine translation in Stages. *arXiv preprint cs/0306130.*

Bhargava, R., Arora, S., & Sharma, Y. (2019). Neural network-based architecture for sentiment analysis in Indian languages. *Journal of Intelligent Systems*, *28*(3), 361–375. doi:10.1515/jisys-2017-0398

Bidirectional LSTMS. (n.d.). https://intellipaat.com/blog/what-is-lstm/

Bifet, A., & Frank, E. (2010). Sentiment knowledge discovery in Twitter streaming data. *Proceedings of the Fourth International Workshop on Knowledge Discovery from Sensor Data.*

Bikel, D. M., Miller, S., Schwartz, R., & Weischedel, R. (1998). Nymble: a high-performance learning name-finder. *arXiv preprint cmp-lg/9803003.*

Boateng, E. Y., Otoo, J., & Abaye, D. A. (2020). Basic tenets of classifica- tion algorithms k-nearest-neighbor, support vector machine, random forest and neural network: A review. *Journal of Data Analysis and Information Processing*, *8*(4), 341–357. doi:10.4236/jdaip.2020.84020

Bogers, T. (2004). *Dutch named entity recognition: Optimizing features, algorithms, and output* [Unpublished MS Thesis]. University of Van Tilburg.

Bojanowski, P., Grave, E., Joulin, A., & Mikolov, T. (2017). Enriching word vectors with subword information. *Transactions of the Association for Computational Linguistics*, *5*, 135–146. doi:10.1162/tacl_a_00051

Borthwick, A., Sterling, J., Agichtein, E., & Grishman, R. (1998). NYU: Description of the MENE named entity system as used in MUC-7. *Seventh Message Understanding Conference (MUC-7): Proceedings of a Conference Held in Fairfax, Virginia, April 29-May 1, 1998.*

BR, S., & Kumar, R. (2012). Kannada part-of-speech tagging with probabilistic classifiers. *International Journal of Computer Applications, 48*(17), 26-30.

Bulusu, A., & Sucharita, V. (2019). Research on machine learning techniques for pos tagging in nlp. *International Journal of Recent Technology and Engineering, 8*(1S4).

Burlet, R. E., & Panahon, C. J. (2022). Cyberbullying Prevention and Intervention: Current Practices in Schools. *Journal of Prevention and Health Promotion*, *3*(2), 258–267. doi:10.1177/26320770221087454

Buvet, A. P., & Crezka, A. (2009). Les dictionnaires électroniques du modèle de classes d'objets. *Langages*, 176.

Chakravarthi, A., & Raja, B. (2020). *Leveraging orthographic information to improve machine translation of under-resourced languages*. NUI Galway.

Chakravarthi, B. R., Priyadharshini, R., Muralidaran, V., Jose, N., Suryawanshi, S., Sherly, E., & McCrae, J. P. (2022). DravidianCodeMix: Sentiment analysis and offensive language identification dataset for Dravidian languages in code-mixed text. *Language Resources and Evaluation*, *56*(3), 765–806. doi:10.1007/s10579-022-09583-7 PMID:35996566

Chakravarthi, B. R., Priyadharshini, R., Thavareesan, S., Chinnappa, D., Thenmozhi, D., Sherly, E., McCrae, J. P., Hande, A., Ponnusamy, R., Banerjee, S., & Vasantharajan, C. (2021). Findings of the Sentiment Analysis of Dravidian Languages in Code-Mixed Text. *CEUR Workshop Proceedings*, *3159*, 872–886.

Chen, H. H., Ding, Y. W., & Tsai, S. C. (1998). Named entity extraction for information retrieval. *Computer Processing of Oriental Languages*, *12*(1), 75–85.

Chen, J., Zhong, L., & Cai, C. (2016). Using exponential kernel for semi-supervised word sense disambiguation. *Journal of Computational and Theoretical Nanoscience*, *13*(10), 6929–6934. doi:10.1166/jctn.2016.5649

Chen, S., Pei, Y., Ke, Z., & Silamu, W. (2021). Low-resource named entity recognition via the pre-training model. *Symmetry*, *13*(5), 786. doi:10.3390/sym13050786

Chen, X., Liu, X., & Wang, J. (2021). Cross-lingual transfer learning in NLP: A survey. *Journal of Artificial Intelligence Research*, *72*, 101–126.

Chiao, Alimu, Yang, & Kang. (2023). What you think is a joke is actually cyberbullying: The effects of ethical dissonance, event judgment and humor style on cyberbullying behavior. *Computers in Human Behavior, 142*. doi:10.1016/j.chb.2023.107670

Cho, K., Van Merriënboer, B., Bahdanau, D., & Bengio, Y. (2014). On the properties of neural machine translation: Encoder-decoder approaches. *arXiv preprint arXiv:1409.1259*. doi:10.3115/v1/W14-4012

Chollet, F., (2015). *Keras*. GitHub. Retrieved from https://github.com/ fchollet/keras

Chorowski, J. K., Bahdanau, D., Serdyuk, D., Cho, K., & Bengio, Y. (2015). Attention-based models for speech recognition. *Advances in Neural Information Processing Systems*, 28.

Choudhary, N., Singh, R., Bindlish, I., & Shrivastava, M. (2018). Emotions are universal: Learning sentiment based representations of resource-poor languages using siamese networks. *International Conference on Computational Linguistics and Intelligent Text Processing*.

Chowdhary, K., & Chowdhary, K. R. (2020). Natural language processing. *Fundamentals of Artificial Intelligence*, 603-649.

Chun-Xiang, Z., Yan-Chen, S., Xue-Yao, G., & Zhi-Mao, L. (2015). Chinese Word Sense Disambiguation Based on Hidden Markov Model. *International Journal of Database Theory and Application*, *8*(6), 263–270. doi:10.14257/ijdta.2015.8.6.24

Church, K. W. (2017). Word2Vec. *Natural Language Engineering*, *23*(1), 155–162. doi:10.1017/S1351324916000334

Code-switching | Linguistic Benefits & Challenges | Britannica. (n.d.). Retrieved September 16, 2023, from https://www.britannica.com/topic/code-switching

Collins, M. (2002, July). Ranking algorithms for named entity extraction: Boosting and the votedperceptron. In *Proceedings of the 40th Annual Meeting of the Association for Computational Linguistics* (pp. 489-496). Academic Press.

Computational Linguistic Research Group (CLRG), AU-KBC Research Centre, MIT Campus of Anna University. (2016). *Aukbc-pos-corpus*. Available at www.au-kbc.org/nlp/corpusrelease.html

Cui, J., Kingsbury, B., Ramabhadran, B., Sethy, A., Audhkhasi, K., Cui, X., Kislal, E., Mangu, L., Nussbaum-Thom, M., & Picheny, M. (2015). *Multilingual representations for low resource speech recognition and keyword search. In 2015 IEEE workshop on automatic speech recognition and understanding*. ASRU.

Dalal, A., Nagaraj, K., Sawant, U., & Shelke, S. (2006). Hindi part-of-speech tagging and chunking: A maximum entropy approach. *Proceeding of the NLPAI Machine Learning Competition.*

Dandapat, S., Sarkar, S., & Basu, A. (2007). Automatic part-of-speech tagging for Bengali: An approach for morphologically rich languages in a poor resource scenario. *Proceedings of the 45th Annual Meeting of the Association for Computational Linguistics Companion Volume Proceedings of the Demo and Poster Sessions*. 10.3115/1557769.1557833

Das, A., & Bandyopadhyay, S. (2010). Topic-based Bengali opinion summarization. *arXiv preprint arXiv:2301.00539.*

Das, D., & Bandyopadhyay, S. (2010). Developing bengali wordnet affect for analyzing emotion. In *International Conference on the Computer Processing of Oriental Languages* (pp. 35-40). Academic Press.

Dasgupta, S., & Ng, V. (2006). Unsupervised morphological parsing of Bengali. *Language Resources and Evaluation*, *40*(3-4), 311–330. doi:10.1007/s10579-007-9031-y

Das, N. K. (2015). The Social Organization of the HO Tribe. *International Journal of Social Science and Humanities Research*, *3*(3), 198–205.

Das, S. K. (2021). The HO Tribe of Jharkhand: A Study of their Language, Culture and Social Organization. *International Journal of Humanities and Social Science Research*, *2*(1), 1–11.

Das, S., & Mandal, S. (2020). POS Tagging and Named Entity Recognition in HO Language. In *Proceedings of the 3rd International Conference on Intelligent Computing and Control Systems (ICICCS)* (pp. 1779-1785). IEEE.

Datta, A., Ramabhadran, B., Emond, J., Kannan, A., & Roark, B. (2020). Language-agnostic multilingual modeling. *ICASSP 2020-2020 IEEE International Conference on Acoustics, Speech and Signal Processing (ICASSP)*. 10.1109/ICASSP40776.2020.9053443

Dave, S., Parikh, J., & Bhattacharyya, P. (2001). Interlingua-based English–Hindi machine translation and language divergence. *Machine Translation*, *16*(4), 251–304. doi:10.1023/A:1021902704523

David, M., & Beskow, S. K. (2020). The evolution of political memes: Detecting and characterizing internet memes with multi-modal deep learning. *Information Processing & Management*, 1–13.

Decision tree . (n.d.). https://www.ibm.com/in-en/topics/decision-trees#:~:text=A\%20decision\%20tree\%20is\%20a,internal\%20nodes\%20and\%20leaf\%20nodes

Derczynski, L., Maynard, D., Rizzo, G., Van Erp, M., Gorrell, G., Troncy, R., Petrak, J., & Bontcheva, K. (2015). Analysis of named entity recognition and linking for tweets. *Information Processing & Management*, *51*(2), 32–49. doi:10.1016/j.ipm.2014.10.006

Developmentaid. (2022). https://www.developmentaid.org/api/frontend/cms/file/2022/03/Cyberbullying-vs-traditional-bullying-1.jpg

Devlin, J., Chang, M. W., Lee, K., & Toutanova, K. (2018). BERT: Bidirectional Encoder Representations from Transformers. *arXiv preprint arXiv:1810.04805.*

Devlin, J., Chang, M. W., Lee, K., & Toutanova, K. (2018). *Bert: Pre-training of deep bidirectional transformers for language understanding.* arXiv preprint arXiv:1810.04805.

Dew, K. N., Turner, A. M., Choi, Y. K., Bosold, A., & Kirchhoff, K. (2018). Development of machine translation technology for assisting health communication: A systematic review. *Journal of Biomedical Informatics*, *85*, 56–67. doi:10.1016/j.jbi.2018.07.018 PMID:30031857

Dhanalakshmi, V., Kumar, A., Shivapratap, G., Soman, K., & Rajendran, S. (2009). Tamil pos tagging using linear programming. *International Journal of Recent Trends in Engineering*, *1*(2), 166.

Dhanalakshmi, V., Kumar, A., Shivapratap, G., Soman, K., & Rajendran, S. (2009). Tamil POS tagging using linear programming. *International Journal of Recent Trends in Engineering*, *1*(2), 166.

Dimitrov, M., Bontcheva, K., Cunningham, H., & Maynard, D. (2005). A lightweight approach to coreference resolution for named entities in text. *Anaphora Processing: Linguistic, Cognitive and Computational Modelling, 263*, 97.

Diwan, A., Vaideeswaran, R., Shah, S., Singh, A., Raghavan, S., Khare, S., Unni, V., Vyas, S., Rajpuria, A., & Yarra, C. (2021). Multilingual and code-switching ASR challenges for low resource Indian languages. *arXiv preprint arXiv:2104.00235.*

Doddapaneni, S., Aralikatte, R., Ramesh, G., Goyal, S., Khapra, M. M., Kunchukuttan, A., & Kumar, P. (2023). Towards Leaving No Indic Language Behind: Building Monolingual Corpora, Benchmark and Models for Indic Languages. *Proceedings of the 61st Annual Meeting of the Association for Computational Linguistics (*Volume 1*: Long Papers).* 10.18653/v1/2023.acl-long.693

Dong, Z., & Dong, Q. (2003, October). HowNet-a hybrid language and knowledge resource. *International conference on natural language processing and knowledge engineering Proceedings, 2003*, 820–824.

Dowling, M., Lynn, T., Graham, Y., & Judge, J. (2016). *English to Irish machine translation with automatic post-editing*. Academic Press.

Du, Y., Li, C., Guo, R., Yin, X., Liu, W., Zhou, J., Bai, Y., Yu, Z., Yang, Y., Dang, Q., & Wang, H. 2020. Ppocr: A practical ultra lightweight ocr system. *ArXiv*, abs/2009.09941.

Eaglman, D. (2016). *Les vies secrètes de cerveau*. Academic Press.

Edunov, S., Ott, M., Auli, M., & Grangier, D. (2018). Understanding back-translation at scale. *arXiv preprint arXiv:1808.09381*. doi:10.18653/v1/D18-1045

Eisenstein, J. (2019). *Introduction to natural language processing*. MIT Press.

Ekbal, A., & Bandyopadhyay, S. (2009). A conditional random field approach for named entity recognition in Bengali and Hindi. *Linguistic Issues in Language Technology*, *2*, 2. doi:10.33011/lilt.v2i.1203

Ekbal, A., & Bandyopadhyay, S. (2010). Named entity recognition using appropriate unlabeled data, post-processing and voting. *Informatica (Vilnius)*, *34*(1).

Ekbal, A., Haque, R., & Bandyopadhyay, S. (2007). Bengali part of speech tagging using conditional random field. *Proceedings of seventh international symposium on natural language processing (SNLP2007).*

El Hannach, M. (1990). Esquisse d'une théorie informatico-linguistique de construction des dictionnaires électroniques de l'arabe. *Linguistica – communicatio, 2*(2), 1990.

Elkateb, S., Black, W. J., Vossen, P., Farwell, D., Rodríguez, H., Pease, A., Alkhalifa, M., & Fellbaum, C. (2006). Arabic WordNet and the challenges of Arabic. *Proceedings of the International Conference on the Challenge of Arabic for NLP/MT.*

Ezhilarasi, S., & Maheswari, P. U. (2021). Depicting a neural model for lemmatization and POS tagging of words from palaeographic stone inscriptions. *Proceedings - 5th International Conference on Intelligent Computing and Control Systems, ICICCS 2021*, 1879–1884. 10.1109/ICICCS51141.2021.9432315

Fanni, S. C., Febi, M., Aghakhanyan, G., & Neri, E. (2023). Natural language processing. In *Introduction to Artificial Intelligence* (pp. 87–99). Springer International Publishing. doi:10.1007/978-3-031-25928-9_5

Farmakiotou, D., Karkaletsis, V., Koutsias, J., Sigletos, G., Spyropoulos, C. D., & Stamatopoulos, P. (2000, September). Rule-based named entity recognition for Greek financial texts. In *Proceedings of the Workshop on Computational lexicography and Multimedia Dictionaries (COMLEX 2000)* (pp. 75-78). Academic Press.

Fillmore, C. J., Baker, C. F., & Sato, H. (2002). *The FrameNet Database and Software Tools.* LREC.

Fredrick, S. S., Coyle, S., & King, J. A. (2023). Middle and high school teachers' perceptions of cyberbullying prevention and digital citizenship. *Psychology in the Schools*, *60*(6), 1958–1978. doi:10.1002/pits.22844

Friburger, N., Maurel, D., & Giacometti, A. (2002, August). Textual similarity based on proper names. In *Proc. of the workshop Mathematical/Formal Methods in Information Retrieval* (pp. 155-167). Academic Press.

Gamon, M. (2004). *Sentiment classification on customer feedback data: noisy data, large feature vectors, and the role of linguistic analysis.* Microsoft Research.

Gated Recurrent Unit . (n.d.). https://towardsdatascience.com/understanding-gru-networks-2ef37df6c9be

Gawu, D. A., & Mensah, R. O. (2022). Balancing the Freedom of Expression, Right to Information and Use of Social Media in Ghana. In *Democratic Governance, Law, and Development in Africa: Pragmatism, Experiments, and Prospects* (pp. 121–145). Springer International Publishing. doi:10.1007/978-3-031-15397-6_5

Ghanghor, N. K., Krishnamurthy, P., Thavareesan, S., Priyadarshini, R., & Chakravarthi, B. R. (2021). IIITK@DravidianLangTech-EACL2021: Offensive Language Identification and Meme Classification in Tamil, Malayalam and Kannada. *Proceedings of the 1st Workshop on Speech and Language Technologies for Dravidian Languages, DravidianLangTech 2021 at 16th Conference of the European Chapter of the Association for Computational Linguistics, EACL 2021*, 222–229.

Ghasemi, A., & Zahediasl, S. (2012). Normality tests for statistical analysis: A guide for non-statisticians. *International Journal of Endocrinology and Metabolism*, *10*(2), 486–489. doi:10.5812/ijem.3505 PMID:23843808

Gheini, M., & May, J. (2019). A universal parent model for low-resource neural machine translation transfer. *arXiv preprint arXiv:1909.06516.*

Girden, E. R. (1992). ANOVA: Repeated measures. *Sage (Atlanta, Ga.).*

Go, A., Bhayani, R., & Huang, L. (2009). Twitter sentiment classification using distant supervision. CS224N Project Report, 1(12).

Gogoi, A., Baruah, N., & Sarma, S. K. (2020, December). Assamese word sense disambiguation using genetic algorithm. In *Proceedings of the 17th International Conference on Natural Language Processing (ICON)* (pp. 303-307). Academic Press.

Goldsmith, J. (2001). Unsupervised learning of the morphology of a natural language. *Computational Linguistics*, *27*(2), 153–198. doi:10.1162/089120101750300490

Gonsalves, R. A. (2021, June 3). *towardsdatascience*. Retrieved from TowardsDataScience: https://towardsdatascience.com/ai-memer-using-machine-learning-to-create-funny-memes-12fc1fe543e4

Gonsalves, R. A. (2022, September 18). *AI-Memer: Using Machine Learning to Create Funny Memes*. Retrieved from AI-Memer: https://colab.research.google.com/github/robgon-art/ai-memer/blob/main/AI_Memer.ipynb

Goyal, V., & Lehal, G. (2011). N-Grams Based Word Sense Disambiguation: A Case Study of Hindi to Punjabi Machine Translation System. *International Journal of Translation*, *23*(1), 99–113.

Goyal, V., & Lehal, G. S. (2011). Hindi to Punjabi machine translation system. International Conference on Information Systems for Indian Languages. *Journal of King Saud University. Computer and Information Sciences*, *33*(5), 497–507.

Gross, G. (2012). *Manuel d'analyse linguistique: approche sémantico-syntaxique du lexique*. Presses universitaires.

Gross, M. (1986). Grammaire transformationnelle du Français: syntaxe du verbe cantilène. Academic Press.

Gross, M. (1989). La construction de dictionnaires électroniques. *Télécommunication, 44*(1-2).

Gross, M. (1975). *Méthodes en syntaxe: Régimes des constructions complétives.* Hermann.

Gross, M. (1981). Les bases empiriques de la notion de prédicat sémantique. *Langages*, 63.

Guillet, A. (1986). Représentation des distributions dans un lexique–grammaire. *Langue française, 69.*

Gujjar, V., Mago, N., Kumari, R., Patel, S., Chintalapudi, N., & Battineni, G. (2023). A Literature Survey on Word Sense Disambiguation for the Hindi Language. *Information (Basel), 14*(9), 495. doi:10.3390/info14090495

Guo, H., Zhu, H., Guo, Z., Zhang, X., Wu, X., & Su, Z. (2009, June). Domain adaptation with latent semantic association for named entity recognition. In *Proceedings of Human Language Technologies: The 2009 Annual Conference of the North American Chapter of the Association for Computational Linguistics* (pp. 281-289). 10.3115/1620754.1620795

Gupta, V., & Lehal, G. S. (2011). Named entity recognition for Punjabi language text summarization. *International Journal of Computer Applications, 33*(3), 28-32.

Gupta, J. P., Tayal, D. K., & Gupta, A. (2011). A TENGRAM method based part-of-speech tagging of multi-category words in Hindi language. *Expert Systems with Applications, 38*(12), 15084–15093. doi:10.1016/j.eswa.2011.05.036

Gupta, V., & Lehal, G. S. (2011). Named entity recognition for Punjabi language text summarization. *International Journal of Computer Applications, 33*(3), 28–32.

Haddow, B., & Kirefu, F. (2020). PMIndia—A Collection of Parallel Corpora of Languages of India. *arXiv preprint arXiv:2001.09907.*

Han, S., & Shirai, K. (2021, February). Unsupervised Word Sense Disambiguation based on Word Embedding and Collocation. ICAART, (2), 1218-1225. doi:10.5220/0010380112181225

Han, X., & Zhao, J. (2010, July). Structural semantic relatedness: a knowledge-based method to named entity disambiguation. In *Proceedings of the 48th Annual Meeting of the Association for Computational Linguistics* (pp. 50-59). Academic Press.

Han, A. L. F., Zeng, X., Wong, D. F., & Chao, L. S. (2015, July). Chinese named entity recognition with graph-based semi-supervised learning model. In *Proceedings of the Eighth SIGHAN Workshop on Chinese Language Processing* (pp. 15-20). 10.18653/v1/W15-3103

Harish, B., & Rangan, R. K. (2020). A comprehensive survey on Indian regional language processing. *SN Applied Sciences, 2*(7), 1204. doi:10.1007/s42452-020-2983-x

Harissh, V. S., Vignesh, M., Kodaikkaavirinaadan, U., & Geetha, T. V. (2018). Unsupervised domain ontology learning from text. *Polibits, 57*, 59–66. doi:10.17562/PB-57-6

Harris, Z. S. (1971). *Structures mathématiques du langage.* Dunod.

Hedderich, M. A., Lange, L., Adel, H., Strötgen, J., & Klakow, D. (2020). A survey on recent approaches for natural language processing in low-resource scenarios. *arXiv preprint arXiv:2010.12309.*

Heitzman, J., & Worden, R. L. (1995). A country study. Academic Press.

Hou, B., Qi, F., Zang, Y., Zhang, X., Liu, Z., & Sun, M. (2020, December). Try to substitute: An unsupervised chinese word sense disambiguation method based on hownet. In *Proceedings of the 28th International Conference on Computational Linguistics* (pp. 1752-1757). 10.18653/v1/2020.coling-main.155

Hutchins, J. (1997). Evaluation of machine translation and translation tools. *Iš: Survey of the State of the Art in Human Language Technology*, 418-419.

Hutchins, J. (2005). The first public demonstration of machine translation: the Georgetown-IBM system, 7th January 1954. *noviembre de.*

Hutchins, W. J. (1996). The state of machine translation in Europe. *Conference of the Association for Machine Translation in the Americas.*

Hutto, C. &. (2014). VADER: A Parsimonious Rule-Based Model for Sentiment Analysis of Social Media Text. In *Proceedings of the International AAAI Conference on Web and Social Media* (pp. 216-225). PKP Publishing Services Network.

Ibrahim, A. H., & Gross, M. (2002). Une refondation de la linguistique au crible de l'analyse automatique. Taln 2002, Nancy.

Jagan, B., Geetha, T., & Parthasarathi, R. (2012). Semantic parsing of Tamil sentences. *Proceedings of the Workshop on Machine Translation and Parsing in Indian Languages*, 15–22.

Jagan, B., Parthasarathi, R., & Geetha, T. V. (2019). Bootstrapping of semantic relation extraction for a morphologically rich language: Semi-supervised learning of semantic relations. *International Journal on Semantic Web and Information Systems*, *15*, 119–149. doi:10.4018/IJSWIS.2019010106

Jain, A. (2019). *Named Entity Recognition for Hindi Language Using NLP Techniques*. Academic Press.

Jain, A., & Arora, A. (2018). Named entity system for tweets in Hindi language. *International Journal of Intelligent Information Technologies*, *14*(4), 55–76. doi:10.4018/IJIIT.2018100104

Jain, A., Tayal, D. K., & Arora, A. (2018). OntoHindi NER—An ontology based novel approach for Hindi named entity recognition. *Int J Artif Intell*, *16*(2), 106–135.

Jain, M., Punia, R., & Hooda, I. (2020). Neural machine translation for Tamil to English. *Journal of Statistics and Management Systems*, *23*(7), 1251–1264. doi:10.1080/09720510.2020.1799582

Janz, A., & Piasecki, M. (2019). A weakly supervised word sense disambiguation for Polish using rich lexical resources. *Poznán Studies in Contemporary Linguistics*, *55*(2), 339–365. doi:10.1515/psicl-2019-0013

Japkowicz, N., & Shah, M. (2011). *Evaluating learning algorithms: A classification perspective*. Cambridge University Press. doi:10.1017/CBO9780511921803

Jayan, J. P., Rajeev, R. R., & Sherly, E. (2013, October). A hybrid statistical approach for named entity recognition for malayalam language. In *Proceedings of the 11th Workshop on Asian Language Resources* (pp. 58-63). Academic Press.

Jha, G. N. (2010). *The TDIL Program and the Indian Langauge Corpora Intitiative (ILCI)*. LREC.

Jha, P., Agarwal, S., Abbas, A., & Siddiqui, T. J. (2023). A Novel Unsupervised Graph-Based Algorithm for Hindi Word Sense Disambiguation. *SN Computer Science*, *4*(5), 675. doi:10.1007/s42979-023-02116-1

Jiang, M., Chen, Y., Liu, M., Rosenbloom, S. T., Mani, S., Denny, J. C., & Xu, H. (2011). A study of machine-learning-based approaches to extract clinical entities and their assertions from discharge summaries. *Journal of the American Medical Informatics Association : JAMIA*, *18*(5), 601–606. doi:10.1136/amiajnl-2011-000163 PMID:21508414

Joksimoski, B., Zdravevski, E., Lameski, P., Pires, I. M., Melero, F. J., Martinez, T. P., Garcia, N. M., Mihajlov, M., Chorbev, I., & Trajkovik, V. (2022). Technological solutions for sign language recognition: A scoping review of research trends, challenges, and opportunities. *IEEE Access : Practical Innovations, Open Solutions*, *10*, 40979–40998. doi:10.1109/ACCESS.2022.3161440

Joshi, A., Prabhu, A., Shrivastava, M., & Varma, V. (2016). Towards sub-word level compositions for sentiment analysis of hindi-english code mixed text. *Proceedings of COLING 2016, the 26th International Conference on Computational Linguistics: Technical Papers*.

Joty, S., Guzmán, F., Màrquez, L., & Nakov, P. (2019). DiscoTK: Using discourse structure for machine translation evaluation. *arXiv preprint arXiv:1911.12547*.

Jung, J. J. (2012). Online named entity recognition method for microtexts in social networking services: A case study of twitter. *Expert Systems with Applications*, *39*(9), 8066–8070. doi:10.1016/j.eswa.2012.01.136

Jyrwa, M. B. (1989). *A descriptive study of the noun phrase in Khasi. Academic Press.*

Kachru, B. B. (2016). Kashmiri and other Dardic Languages'. *Current Trends in Linguistics*, *5*, 284–306.

Kahane, S. (2001). Grammaires de dépendance formelles et théorie Sens-Texte. TALN 2001, Tours.

Kak, A. A., Ahmad, F., Mehdi, N., Farooq, M., & Hakim, M. (2017). Challenges, Problems, and Issues Faced in Language-Specific Synset Creation and Linkage in the Kashmiri WordNet. *The WordNet in Indian Languages*, 209-220.

Kak, A. A. (2005). Globalization of English and its Reflection on Kashmiri. *South Asian Language Review, 15*(1), 37–50.

Kak, A. A., Mehdi, N., & Lawaye, A. (2009). What should be and What should not be? Developing a POS tagset for Kashmiri. *Interdisciplinary Journal of Linguistics, 2*, 185–196.

Kalaivani, A., Thenmozhi, D., & Aravindan, C. (2021). TOLD: Tamil Offensive Language Detection in Code-Mixed Social Media Comments using MBERT with Features based Selection. *CEUR Workshop Proceedings, 3159*, 667–679.

Kanakaraddi, S. G., & Nandyal, S. S. (2018). Survey on parts of speech tagger techniques. In 2018 International Conference on Current Trends Towards Converging Technologies (ICCTCT).

Kandimalla, A., Lohar, P., Maji, S. K., & Way, A. (2022). Improving English-to-Indian language neural machine translation systems. *Information (Basel), 13*(5), 245. doi:10.3390/info13050245

Kannan, R. R., Rajalakshmi, R., & Kumar, L. (2021). IndicBERT based approach for Sentiment Analysis on Code-Mixed Tamil Tweets. *CEUR Workshop Proceedings, 3159*, 729–736.

Kapersky. (n.d.). https://www.google.com/url?sa=i&url=https%3A%2F%2Fwww.kaspersky.com%2Fabout%2Fpress-releases%2F2015_the-evolution-of-bullying-from-schoolyard-to-smartphone-24-7&psig=AOvVaw0n4x_8rs6k1K-jiaZYRnOp&ust=1694603771838000&source=images&cd=vfe&opi=89978449&ved=0CBAQjRxqFwoTCKi1rZD5pIEDFQAAAAAdAAAAABAE

Karuppaiah, D., & Vincent, P. D. R. (2021a). Hybrid approach for semantic similarity calculation between Tamil words. *International Journal of Innovative Computing and Applications, 12*(1), 13–23. doi:10.1504/IJICA.2021.113609

Karuppaiah, D., & Vincent, P. D. R. (2021b). Word sense disambiguation in tamil using indo-wordnet and cross-language semantic similarity. *International Journal of Intelligent Enterprise, 8*(1), 62–73. doi:10.1504/IJIE.2021.112320

Kathiravan, P., & Haridoss, N. (2018). Preprocessing for Mining the Textual data-A Review. *International Journal of Scientific Research in Computer Science Applications and Management Studies IJSRCSAMS, 7*(5). www.ijsrcsams.com

Kaur, B., & Veer, D. (2016). Translation challenges and universal networking language. *International Journal of Computer Applications, 133*(15), 36-40.

Kawakami, K. (2008). *Supervised sequence labelling with recurrent neural networks* [Unpublished doctoral dissertation]. Technical University of Munich.

KeswaniV. S. (2020, July 21). *Unimodal and bimodal sentiment analysis of Internet memes.* https://arxiv.org/abs/2007.10822

Khan, N. J., Anwar, W., & Durrani, N. (2017). Machine translation approaches and survey for Indian languages. *arXiv preprint arXiv:1701.04290.*

Khanam, M. H. (2016). *Named Entity Recognition using Machine Learning Techniques for Telugu language*. Academic Press.

Kidshelpline. (n.d.). https://kidshelpline.com.au/sites/default/files/bdl_image/Teen%20girl%20being%20cyberbullied_2.png

Kim, J. H., Kang, I. H., & Choi, K. S. (2002). Unsupervised named entity classification models and their ensembles. In *COLING 2002: The 19th International Conference on Computational Linguistics*. 10.3115/1072228.1072316

Kim, H., & Lee, S. (2019). Comparative analysis of cross-lingual sentiment analysis techniques. *Journal of Computational Linguistics*, *32*(2), 99–115.

Knopp, J. (2011). *Extending a multilingual lexical resource by bootstrapping named entity classification using Wikipedia's category system*. Academic Press.

Koehn, P., & Knowles, R. (2017). Six challenges for neural machine translation. *arXiv preprint arXiv:1706.03872*. doi:10.18653/v1/W17-3204

Kohli, G., Kaur, P., & Bedi, J. (2021). ARGUABLY at ComMA@ICON: Detection of Multilingual Aggressive, Gender Biased, and Communally Charged Tweets Using Ensemble and Fine-Tuned IndicBERT. *Proceedings of the 18th International Conference on Natural Language Processing: Shared Task on Multilingual Gender Biased and Communal Language Identification*, 46–52. https://aclanthology.org/2021.icon-multigen.7

Kokane, C., Babar, S., & Mahalle, P. (2023, March). An Adaptive Algorithm for Polysemous Words in Natural Language Processing. In *Proceedings of Third International Conference on Advances in Computer Engineering and Communication Systems: ICACECS 2022* (pp. 163-172). Singapore: Springer Nature Singapore. 10.1007/978-981-19-9228-5_15

Konkol, M., Brychcín, T., & Konopík, M. (2015). Latent semantics in named entity recognition. *Expert Systems with Applications*, *42*(7), 3470–3479. doi:10.1016/j.eswa.2014.12.015

Koul, O. N. (1996). On the standardisation of Kashmiri Script. *Standardisation and Modernisation Dynamics of Language Planning*.

Kowalski, R. M., Giumetti, G. W., & Feinn, R. S. (2022). Is cyberbullying an extension of traditional bullying or a unique phenomenon? A longitudinal investigation among college students. *International Journal of Bullying Prevention : an Official Publication of the International Bullying Prevention Association*, 1–18.

Krishnan, P., Sankaran, N., Singh, A. K., & Jawahar, C. V. 2014. Towards a robust ocr system for indic scripts. *2014 11th IAPR International Workshop on Document Analysis Systems*, 141–145. 10.1109/DAS.2014.74

Küçük, D., & Yazıcı, A. (2012). A hybrid named entity recognizer for Turkish. *Expert Systems with Applications*, *39*(3), 2733–2742. doi:10.1016/j.eswa.2011.08.131

Kugler, M., Ahmad, K., & Thurmair, G. (2013). *Translator's workbench: Tools and terminology for translation and text processing* (Vol. 1). Springer Science & Business Media.

Kumar, G. K., Gehlot, A. S., Mullappilly, S. S., & Nandakumar, K. (2022). MuCoT: Multilingual Contrastive Training for Question Answering in Low-resource Languages. *DravidianLangTech 2022 - 2nd Workshop on Speech and Language Technologies for Dravidian Languages, Proceedings of the Workshop, 1*, 15–24. 10.18653/v1/2022.dravidianlangtech-1.3

Kumar, A., Kohail, S., Ekbal, A., & Biemann, C. (2015). IIT-TUDA: System for sentiment analysis in Indian languages using lexical acquisition. *Mining Intelligence and Knowledge Exploration: Third International Conference, MIKE 2015,* Hyderabad, India, December 9-11, 2015, *Proceedings*, 3.

Kumaresan, P. K., Premjith, Sakuntharaj, R., Thavareesan, S., Navaneethakrishnan, S., Madasamy, A. K., Chakravarthi, B. R., & McCrae, J. P. (2021). Findings of Shared Task on Offensive Language Identification in Tamil and Malayalam. *ACM International Conference Proceeding Series*, 16–18. 10.1145/3503162.3503179

Kumari, A., & Goyal, V. (2012). Font convertors for Indian languages—A survey. *Computer Science*, *1*(12).

Kumari, R., Ashok, N., Ghosal, T., & Ekbal, A. (2021). Misinformation detection using multitask learning with mutual learning for novelty detection and emotion recognition. *Information Processing & Management*, *58*(5), 102631. doi:10.1016/j.ipm.2021.102631

Kumar, P., Kumar Goel, R., & Sagar Sharma, P. (2014). Domain Specific Named Entity Recognition (DSNER) from Web Documents. *International Journal of Computer Applications*, *86*(18), 24–29. doi:10.5120/15087-3360

Kumar, S., & Kumar, M. (2019). Named Entity Recognition in HO Language Using Conditional Random Fields. *International Journal of Computer Science and Mobile Computing*, *8*(7), 227–237.

Kumawat, S., & Chandra, N. (2014). Distance-based Reordering in English to Hindi Statistical Machine Translation. *International Journal of Computer Applications, 975*, 8887.

Kunchukuttan, A., Mehta, P., & Bhattacharyya, P. (2017). The iit bombay english-hindi parallel corpus. *arXiv preprint arXiv:1710.02855.*

Lafferty, J., McCallum, A., & Pereira, F. C. (2001). *Conditional random fields: Probabilistic models for segmenting and labeling sequence data.* Academic Press.

Lakshmana Pandian, S., & Geetha, T. (2008). Morpheme based language model for tamil part-of-speech tagging. *Polibits*, *38*, 19–25. doi:10.17562/PB-38-2

Lample, G., Ballesteros, M., Subramanian, S., Kawakami, K., & Dyer, C. (2016). Neural architectures for named entity recognition. *arXiv preprint arXiv:1603.01360.* doi:10.18653/v1/N16-1030

Laskar, S. R., Khilji, A. F. U. R., Pakray, P., & Bandyopadhyay, S. (2020). Hindi-Marathi cross lingual model. *Proceedings of the Fifth Conference on Machine Translation.*

Lawaye, A. A., & Purkayastha, B. S. (2013). Towards Developing a Hierarchical Part of Speech Tagger for Kashmiri: Hybrid Approach. In *Proceedings of the 2nd National Conference on Advancement in the Era of Multidisciplinary Systems* (pp. 187-192). Academic Press.

Lawaye, A. A., & Purkayastha, B. S. (2014). Kashmir part of speech tagger using CRF. *Computer Science, 3*(3), 3.

Leaman, R., & Gonzalez, G. (2008). BANNER: an executable survey of advances in biomedical named entity recognition. In Biocomputing 2008 (pp. 652-663). Academic Press.

Leaman, R., & Lu, Z. (2016). TaggerOne: Joint named entity recognition and normalization with semi-Markov Models. *Bioinformatics (Oxford, England), 32*(18), 2839–2846. doi:10.1093/bioinformatics/btw343 PMID:27283952

Leidner, J. L., Sinclair, G., & Webber, B. (2003). Grounding spatial named entities for information extraction and question answering. In *Proceedings of the HLT-NAACL 2003 workshop on Analysis of geographic references* (pp. 31-38). 10.3115/1119394.1119399

Lei, J., Tang, B., Lu, X., Gao, K., Jiang, M., & Xu, H. (2014). A comprehensive study of named entity recognition in Chinese clinical text. *Journal of the American Medical Informatics Association : JAMIA, 21*(5), 808–814. doi:10.1136/amiajnl-2013-002381 PMID:24347408

Li, C., Wang, P., Martin-Moratinos, M., Bella-Fernández, M., & Blasco-Fontecilla, H. (2022). Traditional bullying and cyberbullying in the digital age and its associated mental health problems in children and adolescents: A meta-analysis. *European Child & Adolescent Psychiatry*, 1–15. doi:10.1007/s00787-021-01763-0 PMID:36585978

Li, J., Wu, Y., & Hesketh, T. (2023). Internet use and cyberbullying: Impacts on psychosocial and psychosomatic wellbeing among Chinese adolescents. *Computers in Human Behavior, 138*, 107461. doi:10.1016/j.chb.2022.107461

Liu, H., Simonyan, K., & Yang, Y. (2018). Darts: Differentiable architecture search. *arXiv preprint arXiv:1806.09055.*

Lone, N. A., Giri, K. J., & Bashir, R. (2022b). Machine intelligence for language translation from Kashmiri to English. *Journal of Information & Knowledge Management*, 2250074.

Lone, N. A., Giri, K. J., & Bashir, R. (2022a). Natural Language Processing Resources for the Kashmiri Language. *Indian Journal of Science and Technology, 15*(43), 2275–2281. doi:10.17485/IJST/v15i43.1964

Long Short-Term Memory (LSTM). (n.d.). https://www.ibm.com/cloud/learn/ recurrent-neural-networks#toc-variant-rn-2xvhbyi.

Lopez, C., Partalas, I., Balikas, G., Derbas, N., Martin, A., Reutenauer, C., . . . Amini, M. R. (2017). Cap 2017 challenge: Twitter named entity recognition. *arXiv preprint arXiv:1707.07568.*

Lucas, S. M. 1995. High performance ocr with syntactic neural networks. In *1995 Fourth International Conference on Artificial Neural Networks* (pp. 133–138). IET. 10.1049/cp:19950542

Magueresse, A., Carles, V., & Heetderks, E. (2020). Low-resource languages: A review of past work and future challenges. *arXiv preprint arXiv:2006.07264*.

MagueresseA.CarlesV.HeetderksE. (2020). *Low-resource Languages: A Review of Past Work and Future Challenges*. http://arxiv.org/abs/2006.07264

Mahmud, T., Ptaszynski, M., Eronen, J., & Masui, F. (2023). Cyberbullying detection for low-resource languages and dialects: Review of the state of the art. *Information Processing & Management*, *60*(5), 103454. doi:10.1016/j.ipm.2023.103454

Mai, K., Pham, T. H., Nguyen, M. T., Nguyen, T. D., Bollegala, D., Sasano, R., & Sekine, S. (2018, August). An empirical study on fine-grained named entity recognition. In *Proceedings of the 27th International Conference on Computational Linguistics* (pp. 711-722). Academic Press.

Malik, A. B., & Bansal, K. (2015). Named Entity Recognition for Kashmiri Language using Noun Identification and NER Identification Algorithm. *International Journal on Computer Science and Engineering*, *3*(9), 193–197.

Manning, C. D., Surdeanu, M., Bauer, J., Finkel, J., Bethard, S. J., & McClosky, D. (2014). The Stanford CoreNLP natural language processing toolkit. In *ACL* (pp. 55–60). System Demonstrations. doi:10.3115/v1/P14-5010

Mantri, G. R. (2023). *Channelization of social media through cyber law and its enforcement challenges in India*. Academic Press.

Marr, B. (2022). *Future skills: The 20 skills and competencies everyone needs to succeed in a digital world*. John Wiley & Sons.

Marrero, M., Urbano, J., Sánchez-Cuadrado, S., Morato, J., & Gómez-Berbís, J. M. (2013). Named entity recognition: Fallacies, challenges and opportunities. *Computer Standards & Interfaces*, *35*(5), 482–489. doi:10.1016/j.csi.2012.09.004

Mayukh Sharma, I. K. (2022). R2D2 at SemEval-2022 Task 5: Attention is only as good as its Values! A multimodal system for identifying misogynist memes. In *Proceedings of the 16th International Workshop on Semantic Evaluation (SemEval-2022)* (pp. 761–770). Association for Computational Linguistics.

McCallum, A., Freitag, D., & Pereira, F. C. (2000, June). Maximum entropy Markov models for information extraction and segmentation. In Icml (Vol. 17, No. 2000, pp. 591-598). Academic Press.

Mejri, S. (2011). *Constructions à verbes supports, collocations et locutions verbales*. Academic Press.

Melamud, O., Goldberger, J., & Dagan, I. (2016, August). context2vec: Learning generic context embedding with bidirectional lstm. In *Proceedings of the 20th SIGNLL conference on computational natural language learning* (pp. 51-61). 10.18653/v1/K16-1006

Meng, F. (2022). Word Sense Disambiguation Based on Graph and Knowledge Base. In *4th EAI International Conference on Robotic Sensor Networks* (pp. 31-41). Springer International Publishing. 10.1007/978-3-030-70451-3_3

Menon, V. K., Rajendran, S., Anandkumar, M., & Soman, K. (2017). Dependency resolution and semantic mining using tree adjoining grammars for tamil language. *arXiv preprint arXiv:1704.05611.*

Meselhi, M. A., Bakr, H. M. A., Ziedan, I., & Shaalan, K. (2014, December). Hybrid named entity recognition-application to Arabic language. In *2014 9th International Conference on Computer Engineering & Systems (ICCES)* (pp. 80-85). IEEE. 10.1109/ICCES.2014.7030933

Mesfar, S. (2008). *Analyse morpho-syntaxique automatique et reconnaissance des entités nommées en arabe standard* [Thèse de doctorat]. Université de Franche-Comté, France.

Miao, Y., Blunsom, P., & Specia, L. (2021). A generative framework for simultaneous machine translation. *Proceedings of the 2021 Conference on Empirical Methods in Natural Language Processing*. 10.18653/v1/2021.emnlp-main.536

Miller, G. A., Leacock, C., Tengi, R., & Bunker, R. T. (1993). A semantic concordance. *Human Language Technology: Proceedings of a Workshop Held at Plainsboro, New Jersey, March 21-24, 1993.*

Miller, G. A. (1995). WordNet: A lexical database for English. *Communications of the ACM, 38*(11), 39–41. doi:10.1145/219717.219748

Mir, T. A., Lawaye, A. A., Rana, P., & Ahmed, G. (2023). Building Kashmiri Sense Annotated Corpus and its Usage in Supervised Word Sense Disambiguation. *Indian Journal of Science and Technology, 16*(13), 1021–1029. doi:10.17485/IJST/v16i13.2396

Mithe, Indalkar, & Divekar. (2013). Optical character recognition. *International Journal of Recent Technology and Engineering, 2*(1), 72–75.

Mohanty, R. K. (2008). The HO Language. *Linguistic Survey of India, 11*(1), 29–52.

Mokady, R. (n.d.). *Simple image captioning model using CLIP and GPT-2*. Retrieved from https://replicate.com/rmokady/clip_prefix_caption

Mokanarangan, T., Pranavan, T., Megala, U., Nilusija, N., Dias, G., Jayasena, S., & Ranathunga, S. (2016). Tamil morphological analyzer using support vector machines. *Natural Language Processing and Information Systems: 21st International Conference on Applications of Natural Language to Information Systems, NLDB 2016, Salford, UK, June 22-24, 2016 Proceedings, 21*, 15–23.

Molina, A., Pla, F., & Segarra, E. (2002, November). A hidden markov model approach to word sense disambiguation. In *Ibero-American Conference on Artificial Intelligence* (pp. 655-663). Springer Berlin Heidelberg. 10.1007/3-540-36131-6_67

Moore, R. C. (2002). Fast and accurate sentence alignment of bilingual corpora. *Conference of the Association for Machine Translation in the Americas.*

Morgan, R. G., Garigliano, R., Callaghan, P., Poria, S., Smith, M. H., Urbanowicz, A., . . ., the LOLITA Group. (1995). University of Durham: Description of the LOLITA System as Used in MUC-6. *Sixth Message Understanding Conference (MUC-6): Proceedings of a Conference Held in Columbia, Maryland, November 6-8, 1995.*

Moro, A., Raganato, A., & Navigli, R. (2014). Entity linking meets word sense disambiguation: A unified approach. *Transactions of the Association for Computational Linguistics*, *2*, 231–244. doi:10.1162/tacl_a_00179

Morwal, S., Jahan, N., & Chopra, D. (2012). *Named entity recognition using hidden markov model (hmm). International Journal on Natural Language Computing* (Vol. 1). IJNLC.

Nadeau, D., & Sekine, S. (2007). A survey of named entity recognition and classification. *Lingvisticae Investigationes*, *30*(1), 3–26. doi:10.1075/li.30.1.03nad

Nair, M. M., Fernandez, T. F., & Tyagi, A. K. (2023, January). Cyberbullying in Digital Era: History, Trends, Limitations, Recommended Solutions for Future. In *2023 International Conference on Computer Communication and Informatics (ICCCI)* (pp. 1-10). IEEE. 10.1109/ICCCI56745.2023.10128624

Nakazawa, T., Nakayama, H., Ding, C., Dabre, R., Higashiyama, S., Mino, H., Goto, I., Pa, W. P., Kunchukuttan, A., & Parida, S. (2021). Overview of the 8th workshop on Asian translation. *Proceedings of the 8th Workshop on Asian Translation (WAT2021).*

Névéol, A., Robert, A., Anderson, R., Cohen, K. B., Grouin, C., Lavergne, T., & Zweigenbaum, P. (2017, September). CLEF eHealth 2017 Multilingual Information Extraction task Overview: ICD10 Coding of Death Certificates in English and French. In *CLEF* (pp. 1–17). Working Notes.

Nivre, J., De Marneffe, M.-C., Ginter, F., Goldberg, Y., Hajic, J., & Manning, C. D. (2016). Universal dependencies v1: A multilingual treebank collection. *Proceedings of the Tenth International Conference on Language Resources and Evaluation (LREC'16)*, 1659–1666.

Nothman, J., Ringland, N., Radford, W., Murphy, T., & Curran, J. R. (2013). Learning multilingual named entity recognition from Wikipedia. *Artificial Intelligence*, *194*, 151–175. doi:10.1016/j.artint.2012.03.006

Och, F. J., & Ney, H. (2004). The alignment template approach to statistical machine translation. *Computational Linguistics*, *30*(4), 417–449. doi:10.1162/0891201042544884

Ohara, M. R. (2023). The Role of Social Media in Educational Communication Management. *Journal of Contemporary Administration and Management*, *1*(2), 70–76. doi:10.61100/adman.v1i2.25

Okuda, T., Tanaka, E., & Kasai, T. (1976). A method for the correction of garbled words based on the Levenshtein metric. *IEEE Transactions on Computers*, *100*(2), 172–178. doi:10.1109/TC.1976.5009232

Olckers, C., & Hattingh, M. J. M. (2022). *The dark side of social media-cyberbullying, catfishing and trolling: a systematic literature review*. Academic Press.

Osborne, M. (2000). Shallow parsing as part-of-speech tagging. *Fourth Conference on Computational Natural Language Learning and the Second Learning Language in Logic Workshop.* 10.3115/1117601.1117636

Pak, A., & Paroubek, P. (2010). Twitter as a corpus for sentiment analysis and opinion mining. *Proceedings of the Seventh International Conference on Language Resources and Evaluation (LREC'10).*

Pal, A. R., Saha, D., Dash, N. S., Naskar, S. K., & Pal, A. (2019). A novel approach to word sense disambiguation in Bengali language using supervised methodology. *Sadhana*, *44*(8), 1–12. doi:10.1007/s12046-019-1165-2

Palomino, N. (2018). The Role of Approximate Negators in Modeling the Automatic Detection of Negation in Tweets. *ProQuest Dissertations and Theses, May*, 203. https://search.proquest.com/docview/2065161701?accountid=49007%0Ahttp://www.yidu.edu.cn/educhina/educhina.do?artifact=&svalue=The+Role+of+Approximate+Negators+in+Modeling+the+Automatic+Detection+of+Negation+in+Tweets&stype=2&s=on%0Ahttp://sfx.cceu.org.cn doi:10.1201/9781003319887-8

Panda, N. (2018). Language Use and Attitudes Among the HO Tribal Community in Odisha. *Indian Journal of Applied Linguistics*, *44*(2), 179–195.

Pandey, A. K., & Siddiqui, T. J. (2008). An unsupervised Hindi stemmer with heuristic improvements. *Proceedings of the second workshop on Analytics for noisy unstructured text data.* 10.1145/1390749.1390765

Pandey, A., Srivastava, B. M. L., & Gangashetty, S. V. (2017). Adapting monolingual resources for code-mixed hindi-english speech recognition. *2017 International Conference on Asian Language Processing (IALP).* 10.1109/IALP.2017.8300583

Pandian, S. L., Devakumar, J., & Geetha, T. (2008). Semantic information extraction from tamil documents. *International Journal of Metadata, Semantics and Ontologies*, *3*(3), 226–232. doi:10.1504/IJMSO.2008.023570

Pang, B., Lee, L., & Vaithyanathan, S. (2002). Thumbs up? Sentiment classification using machine learning techniques. In *Proceedings of the ACL-02 conference on Empirical methods in natural language processing-Volume 10* (pp. 79-86). 10.3115/1118693.1118704

Pan, S., & Saha, D. (2019). An automatic identification of function words in TDIL tagged Bengali corpus. *International Journal on Computer Science and Engineering*, *7*(1), 20–27.

Papineni, K., Roukos, S., Ward, T., & Zhu, W. J. (2002). BLEU: A method for automatic evaluation of machine translation. In *Proceedings of the 40th annual meeting on association for computational linguistics* (pp. 311-318). Academic Press.

Papineni, K., Roukos, S., Ward, T., & Zhu, W.-J. (2002). Bleu: a method for automatic evaluation of machine translation. *Proceedings of the 40th annual meeting of the Association for Computational Linguistics.*

Parikh, R., & Movassate, M. (2009). Sentiment Analysis of User-Generated Twitter Updates using Various Classification Techniques. Academic Press.

Patel, P., Popat, K., & Bhattacharyya, P. (2010). Hybrid stemmer for Gujarati. *Proceedings of the 1st Workshop on South and Southeast Asian Natural Language Processing.*

Patil, N., Patil, A. S., & Pawar, B. V. (2016). Survey of named entity recognition systems with respect to Indian and foreign languages. *International Journal of Computer Applications, 134*(16), 21–26. doi:10.5120/ijca2016908197

Patra, B. G., Das, D., Das, A., & Prasath, R. (2015). Shared task on sentiment analysis in indian languages (sail) tweets-an overview. *Mining Intelligence and Knowledge Exploration: Third International Conference, MIKE 2015,* Hyderabad, India, December 9-11, 2015, *Proceedings,* 3.

Pattabhi, R., Rao, T., Ram, R. V. S., Vijayakrishna, R., & Sobha, L. (2007). A text chunker and hybrid pos tagger for indian languages. *Proceedings of International Joint Conference on Artificial Intelligence Workshop on Shallow Parsing for South Asian Languages, IIIT Hyderabad, Hyderabad, India.*

Paul, S., Tandon, M., Joshi, N., & Mathur, I. (2013). Design of a rule based Hindi lemmatizer. *Proceedings of Third International Workshop on Artificial Intelligence, Soft Computing and Applications.* 10.5121/csit.2013.3408

Pedregosa, F., Varoquaux, G., Gramfort, A., Michel, V., Thirion, B., & Grisel, O. (2011). Scikit-learn: Machine learning in python. *Journal of Machine Learning Research, 12,* 2825–2830.

Pennington, J., Socher, R., & Manning, C. (2014, October). GloVe: Global vectors for word representation. In *Proceedings of the 2014 conference on empirical methods in natural language processing (EMNLP)* (pp. 1532–1543). Association for Computational Linguistics. doi:10.3115/v1/D14-1162

Perwitasari, D. R., & Wuryaningsih, E. W. (2022). Why did you do that to me?: A systematic review of cyberbullying impact on mental health and suicide among adolescents. *NurseLine Journal, 7*(1), 35–47. doi:10.19184/nlj.v7i1.27311

Pham, H., Guan, M., Zoph, B., Le, Q., & Dean, J. (2018, July). Efficient neural architecture search via parameters sharing. In *International conference on machine learning* (pp. 4095-4104). PMLR.

Pimpalkar, A. &. (2022). Sentiment Identification from Image-Based Memes Using Machine Learning. *International Journal of Innovations in Engineering and Science*, 89-96.

Plu, J., Rizzo, G., & Troncy, R. (2015). A hybrid approach for entity recognition and linking. In *Semantic Web Evaluation Challenges: Second SemWebEval Challenge at ESWC 2015, Portorož, Slovenia, May 31-June 4, 2015, Revised Selected Papers* (pp. 28-39). Springer International Publishing. 10.1007/978-3-319-25518-7_3

Poornima, C., Dhanalakshmi, V., Anand, K., & Soman, K. (2011). Rule based sentence simplification for english to tamil machine translation system. *International Journal of Computer Applications, 25*(8), 38-42.

Post, M., Callison-Burch, C., & Osborne, M. (2012). Constructing parallel corpora for six indian languages via crowdsourcing. *Proceedings of the seventh workshop on statistical machine translation.*

Prahallad, K., Kumar, E. N., Keri, V., Rajendran, S., & Black, A. W. (2012). The IIIT-H Indic speech databases. *Thirteenth annual conference of the international speech communication association.* 10.21437/Interspeech.2012-659

Prakash, M. (2011). Natural language processing: An introduction. *Journal of the American Medical Informatics Association, 18*(5), 544–551. doi:10.1136/amiajnl-2011-000464 PMID:21846786

Premjith, B., & Soman, K. P. (2021). Deep learning approach for the morphological synthesis in malayalam and tamil at the character level. *ACM Transactions on Asian and Low-Resource Language Information Processing*, 20.

Premjith, B., Kumar, M. A., & Soman, K. P. (2019). Neural machine translation system for english to indian language translation using mtil parallel corpus. *Journal of Intelligent Systems, 28*(3), 387–398. doi:10.1515/jisys-2019-2510

Qi, P., Zhang, Y., Zhang, Y., Bolton, J., & Manning, C. D. (2020). Stanza: A python natural language processing toolkit for many human languages. *arXiv preprint arXiv:2003.07082.* doi:10.18653/v1/2020.acl-demos.14

Qu, Y. &. (2023). On the Evolution of (Hateful) Memes by Means of Multimodal Contrastive Learning. In *2023 IEEE Symposium on Security and Privacy (SP)* (pp. 293-310). IEEE Computer Society.

Rabiner, L. R. (1989). A tutorial on hidden Markov models and selected applications in speech recognition. *Proceedings of the IEEE, 77*(2), 257–286. doi:10.1109/5.18626

Raganato, A., Bovi, C. D., & Navigli, R. (2017, September). Neural sequence learning models for word sense disambiguation. In *Proceedings of the 2017 conference on empirical methods in natural language processing* (pp. 1156-1167). 10.18653/v1/D17-1120

Rahman, N., & Borah, B. (2022). An unsupervised method for word sense disambiguation. *Journal of King Saud University. Computer and Information Sciences, 34*(9), 6643–6651. doi:10.1016/j.jksuci.2021.07.022

Rajan, K., Ramalingam, V., Ganesan, M., Palanivel, S., & Palaniappan, B. (2009). Automatic classification of Tamil documents using vector space model and artificial neural network. *Expert Systems with Applications, 36*(8), 10914–10918. doi:10.1016/j.eswa.2009.02.010

Rajasekar, M., & Geetha, A. (2021). Machine learning algorithm for information extraction from gynaecological domain in tamil. *J. Math. Comput. Sci., 11*(6), 7140–7153.

Rajasekar, M., & Geetha, A. (2022). Comparison of machine learning methods for tamil morphological analyzer. In *Intelligent Sustainable Systems Proceedings of ICISS, 2021*, 385–399.

Rajkumar, N., Subashini, T. S., Rajan, K., & Ramalingam, V. (2020). Tamil Stopword Removal Based on Term Frequency. In K. S. Raju, R. Senkerik, S. P. Lanka, & V. Rajagopal (Eds.), *Data Engineering and Communication Technology* (pp. 21–30). Springer Singapore. doi:10.1007/978-981-15-1097-7_3

Ramachandran, V. A., & Krishnamurthi, I. (2012). An iterative stemmer for Tamil language. *Intelligent Information and Database Systems: 4th Asian Conference, ACIIDS 2012, Kaohsiung, Taiwan, March 19-21, 2012, Proceedings*, 4.

Ramalingam, A., & Navaneethakrishnan, S. C. (2021). A discourse-based information retrieval for tamil literary texts. *Journal of Information and Communication Technology*, *20*, 353–389. doi:10.32890/jict2021.20.3.4

Ramanathan, A., & Rao, D. D. (2003). A lightweight stemmer for Hindi. *The Proceedings of EACL.*

Ramanathan, A., Hegde, J., Shah, R., Bhattacharyya, P., & Sasikumar, M. (2008). Simple syntactic and morphological processing can help English-Hindi statistical machine translation. *Proceedings of the Third International Joint Conference on Natural Language Processing: Volume-I.*

Ramanathan, A., & Rao, D. D. (2003). A lightweight stemmer for Hindi. *Proceedings of EACL.*

Ramani, B., Christina, S. L., Rachel, G. A., Solomi, V. S., Nandwana, M. K., Prakash, A., Aswin Shanmugam, S., & Raghava Krishnan, S. P. (n.d.). A Common Attribute based Unified HTS framework for Speech Synthesis in Indian Languages. *8th ISCA Speech Synthesis Workshop.*

Ramasamy, L., & Zˇabokrtsky´, Z. (2015). *Ud tamil ttb.* Available at https://universaldependencies.org/treebanks/tattb/index.html

Ramasamy, L., Bojar, O., & Žabokrtský, Z. (2012). Morphological processing for English-Tamil statistical machine translation. *Proceedings of the Workshop on Machine Translation and Parsing in Indian Languages.*

Ramesh, G., Doddapaneni, S., Bheemaraj, A., & Jobanputra, M. (2022). Samanantar: The Largest Publicly Available Parallel Corpora Collection for 11 Indic Languages. Transactions of the Association for Computational Linguistics, 10, 145-162. doi:10.1162/tacl_a_00452

Ramshaw, L., & Marcus, M. (1995). Text chunking using transformation- based learning. In *Third workshop on very large corpora.* Retrieved from https://aclanthology.org/W95-0107

Ranathunga, S., Lee, E.-S. A., Prifti Skenduli, M., Shekhar, R., Alam, M., & Kaur, R. (2023). Neural machine translation for low-resource languages: A survey. *ACM Computing Surveys*, *55*(11), 1–37. doi:10.1145/3567592

Randhawa, G., Ferreyra, M., Ahmed, R., Ezzat, O., & Pottie, K. (2013). Using machine translation in clinical practice. *Canadian Family Physician Medecin de Famille Canadien*, *59*(4), 382–383. PMID:23585608

Random forest. (n.d.). https://www.ibm.com/cloud/learn/random-forest

Ranjan, P., & Basu, H. (2003). Part of speech tagging and local word grouping techniques for natural language parsing in Hindi. *Proceedings of the 1st International Conference on Natural Language Processing (ICON 2003).*

Rao, P. R., Malarkodi, C. S., Ram, R. V. S., & Devi, S. L. (2015). ESM-IL: Entity Extraction from Social Media Text for Indian Languages@ FIRE 2015-An Overview. In FIRE workshops (pp. 74-80). Academic Press.

Ravi, K., & Ravi, V. (2016). Sentiment classification of Hinglish text. *2016 3rd International Conference on Recent Advances in Information Technology (RAIT).*

Ravikiran, M., & Annamalai, S. (2021). DOSA: Dravidian Code-Mixed Offensive Span Identification Dataset. *Proceedings of the 1st Workshop on Speech and Language Technologies for Dravidian Languages, DravidianLangTech 2021 at 16th Conference of the European Chapter of the Association for Computational Linguistics, EACL 2021*, 10–17.

Revanuru, K., Turlapaty, K., & Rao, S. (2017). Neural machine translation of indian languages. *Proceedings of the 10th annual ACM India compute conference.* 10.1145/3140107.3140111

Rohan KashyapV. K. (2022, November 28). *GPT-Neo for commonsense reasoning-a theoretical and practical lens.* https://arxiv.org/abs/2211.15593

Rohini, V., Thomas, M., & Latha, C. (2016). Domain based sentiment analysis in regional Language-Kannada using machine learning algorithm. *2016 IEEE International Conference on Recent Trends in Electronics, Information & Communication Technology (RTEICT).* 10.1109/RTEICT.2016.7807872

Roy, P. K., Bhawal, S., & Subalalitha, C. N. (2022). Hate speech and offensive language detection in dravidian languages using deep ensemble framework. *Computer Speech & Language*, *75*, 75. doi:10.1016/j.csl.2022.101386

Sagot, B., & Tolone, E. (2010). *Exploitation des tables du Lexique-Grammaire pour l'analyse syntaxique automatique.* Paris-Rocquencourt / Paris 7, Université Paris-Est.

Saha, S. K., Chatterji, S., Dandapat, S., Sarkar, S., & Mitra, P. (2008, January). A hybrid approach for named entity recognition in indian languages. In *Proceedings of the IJCNLP-08 Workshop on NER for South and South East Asian languages* (pp. 17-24). Academic Press.

Saha, A. K., Mridha, M. F., Rafiq, J. I., & Das, J. K. (2019). *Information extraction from natural language using universal networking language* (Vol. 924). Springer Verlag. doi:10.1007/978-981-13-6861-5_24

Saharia, N., Sharma, U., & Kalita, J. (2012). Analysis and evaluation of stemming algorithms: a case study with Assamese. *Proceedings of the International Conference on Advances in Computing, Communications and Informatics.* 10.1145/2345396.2345533

Sai, A. B., Mohankumar, A. K., & Khapra, M. M. (2022). A survey of evaluation metrics used for NLG systems. *ACM Computing Surveys*, *55*(2), 1–39. doi:10.1145/3485766

Sailor, H. B., & Hain, T. (2020). Multilingual Speech Recognition Using Language-Specific Phoneme Recognition as Auxiliary Task for Indian Languages. *Interspeech*, 4756–4760. doi:10.21437/Interspeech.2020-2739

Sanchez, M. (2023). Interventions to support young cyberbullying victims: A scoping review. *AGPE The Royal Gondwana Research Journal of History, Science, Economic, Political and Social Science*, *4*(4), 24–33.

Sarma, S. K., Bharali, H., Gogoi, A., Deka, R., & Barman, A. (2012, December). A structured approach for building Assamese corpus: insights, applications and challenges. In *Proceedings of the 10th workshop on Asian language resources* (pp. 21-28). Academic Press.

Sarveswaran, K. P., Krishnamurthy, K., & Balasubramani. (2020). *Ud tamil-mwtt*. Available at https://universaldependencies.org/treebanks/ta_mwtt/index.html

Sarveswaran, K., Dias, G., & Butt, M. (2018). Thamizhifst: A morphological analyser and generator for tamil verbs. *2018 3rd International Conference on Information Technology Research (ICITR)*, 1–6. 10.1109/ICITR.2018.8736139

Sarveswaran, K., & Dias, G. (2021). Building a Part of Speech tagger for the Tamil Language. *2021 International Conference on Asian Language Processing, IALP 2021*, 286–291. 10.1109/IALP54817.2021.9675195

Sarveswaran, K., Dias, G., & Butt, M. (2021). Thamizhi morph: A morphological parser for the tamil language. *Machine Translation*, *35*(1), 37–70. doi:10.1007/s10590-021-09261-5

Sarveswaran, K., & Mahesan, S. (2014). Hierarchical tagset for rulebased processing of tamil language. *International Journal of Multidisciplinary Studies*, *1*(2), 67–74. doi:10.4038/ijms.v1i2.53

Sasidhar, B., Yohan, P. M., Babu, A. V., & Govardhan, A. (2011). A survey on named entity recognition in Indian languages with particular reference to Telugu. *International Journal of Computer Science Issues*, *8*(2), 438.

Sathiya, B., & Geetha, T. V. (2018). Automatic ontology learning from multiple knowledge sources of text. *International Journal of Intelligent Information Technologies*, *14*(2), 1–21. doi:10.4018/IJIIT.2018040101

SauravK.SaunackK.KanojiaD.BhattacharyyaP. (2021). *"A Passage to India": Pre-trained Word Embeddings for Indian Languages*. http://arxiv.org/abs/2112.13800

Scott, W. (2020). *Kaggle*. Retrieved from Memotion Dataset 7k: https://www.kaggle.com/datasets/williamscott701/memotion-dataset-7k

Sellam, T., Bapna, A., Camp, J., Mackinnon, D., Parikh, A. P., & Riesa, J. (2023). SQuId: Measuring speech naturalness in many languages. *ICASSP 2023-2023 IEEE International Conference on Acoustics, Speech and Signal Processing (ICASSP).*

Selvam, M. and Natarajan, A. (2009). Improvement of rule based morphological analysis and pos tagging in Tamil language via projection and induction techniques. *International Journal of Computers*, *3*(4), 357–367.

Selvam, M., & Natarajan, A. (2009). Improvement of rule based morphological analysis and pos tagging in tamil language via projection and induction techniques. *International Journal of Computers, 3*(4), 357-367.

Sequiera, R., Choudhury, M., Gupta, P., Rosso, P., Kumar, S., Banerjee, S., . . . Chakma, K. (2015, December). Overview of FIRE-2015 Shared Task on Mixed Script Information Retrieval. In FIRE workshops (Vol. 1587, pp. 19-25). Academic Press.

Sha, F., & Pereira, F. (2003). *Shallow parsing with conditional random fields*. Academic Press.

Shaalan, K., & Raza, H. (2008). Arabic named entity recognition from diverse text types. In *Advances in Natural Language Processing: 6th International Conference, GoTAL 2008 Gothenburg, Sweden, August 25-27, 2008 Proceedings* (pp. 440-451). Springer Berlin Heidelberg. 10.1007/978-3-540-85287-2_42

Shahariar Azad Rabby, A. K. M. (2018). A universal way to collect and process handwritten data for any language. *Procedia Computer Science*, *143*, 502–509. doi:10.1016/j.procs.2018.10.423

Shalini, K., Ravikurnar, A., Reddy, A., & Soman, K. (2018). Sentiment analysis of indian languages using convolutional neural networks. *2018 International Conference on Computer Communication and Informatics (ICCCI).*

Shambhavi, B. R., Kumar, P. R., Srividya, K., Jyothi, B. J., Kundargi, S., & Shastri, G. V. (2011). Kannada morphological analyser and generator using trie. *International Journal of Computer Science and Network Security, 11*(1).

Sharma, P. (2015). *Named entity recognition for a resource poor indo-aryan language* [Doctoral dissertation]. Tezpur University.

Sheshasaayee, A., & Deepa, V. R. A. (2017). *Ascertaining the morphological components of tamil language using unsupervised approach*. Institute of Electrical and Electronics Engineers Inc.

Shorten, C., Khoshgoftaar, T. M., & Furht, B. (2021). Text Data Augmentation for Deep Learning. In Journal of Big Data (Vol. 8, Issue 1). Springer International Publishing. doi:10.1186/s40537-021-00492-0

Shrivastava, M., & Bhattacharyya, P. (2008). *Hindi POS tagger using naive stemming: harnessing morphological information without extensive linguistic knowledge*. International Conference on NLP (ICON08), Pune, India.

Silberztein, M. (1993). *Dictionnaires électroniques et analyse automatique des textes, le système INTEX*. Masson Paris.

Silberztein, M. (2016). *La formalisation des langues, l'approche de NooJ*. Hermann.

Siripragada, S., Philip, J., Namboodiri, V. P., & Jawahar, C. (2020). A multilingual parallel corpora collection effort for Indian languages. *arXiv preprint arXiv:2007.07691.*

Sitender & Bawa, S. (2022). Sanskrit to universal networking language enconverter system based on deep learning and context-free grammar. Springer Science and Business Media Deutschland GmbH.

Sitender, & Bawa, S. (2021). Sansunl: A Sanskrit to unl enconverter system. *Journal of the Institution of Electronics and Telecommunication Engineers*, *67*(1), 117–128. doi:10.1080/03772063.2018.1528187

Smith, J., & Johnson, A. (2022). Building parallel corpora for low-resource languages. *Journal of Natural Language Processing*, *45*(3), 237–254.

Snover, M., Dorr, B., Schwartz, R., Micciulla, L., & Makhoul, J. (2006). A study of translation edit rate with targeted human annotation. In Proceedings of Association for Machine Translation in the Americas (Vol. 2006, pp. 223-231). Academic Press.

Sokolova, M., & Lapalme, G. (2009). A systematic analysis of performance measures for classification tasks. *Information Processing & Management*, *45*(4), 427–437. doi:10.1016/j.ipm.2009.03.002

Sousa, S., Milios, E., & Berton, L. (2020, July). Word sense disambiguation: an evaluation study of semi-supervised approaches with word embeddings. In *2020 International Joint Conference on Neural Networks (IJCNN)* (pp. 1-8). IEEE. 10.1109/IJCNN48605.2020.9207225

Sowmya Lakshmi, B., & Shambhavi, B. (2019). Bidirectional Long Short-Term Memory for Automatic English to Kannada Back-Transliteration. *Emerging Research in Computing, Information, Communication and Applications: ERCICA 2018,* 1.

Sridhar, R., Sethuraman, P., & Krishnakumar, K. (2016). English to tamil machine trans- lation system using universal networking language. *Sadhana - Academy Proceedings in Engineering Sciences*, *41*, 607–620.

Sridhar, A., Ganesan, R. G., Kumar, P., & Khapra, M. (2020). Include: A large scale dataset for indian sign language recognition. *Proceedings of the 28th ACM international conference on multimedia.* 10.1145/3394171.3413528

Srinidhi Skanda, V., Anand Kumar, M., & Soman, K. P. (2017). Detecting stance in kannada social media code-mixed text using sentence embedding. *2017 International Conference on Advances in Computing, Communications and Informatics, ICACCI 2017,* 964–969. 10.1109/ICACCI.2017.8125966

Srinivasan, R., & Subalalitha, C. (2019). Automated named entity recognition from tamil documents. *2019 IEEE 1st international conference on energy, systems and information processing (ICESIP)*, 1–5. 10.1109/ICESIP46348.2019.8938383

Subalalitha, C. (2019). Information extraction framework for kurunthogai. *Sadhana*, *44*(7), 156. doi:10.1007/s12046-019-1140-y

Subalalitha, C. N., & Poovammal, E. (2018). Automatic bilingual dictionary construction for tirukural. *Applied Artificial Intelligence*, *32*(6), 558–567. doi:10.1080/08839514.2018.1481590

Subhashini, R., & Kumar, V. J. S. (2010). Shallow nlp techniques for noun phrase extraction. In Trendz in information sciences & computing (tisc2010) (pp. 73–77). doi:10.1109/TISC.2010.5714612

Support vector machine . (n.d.). https://www.analyticsvidhya.com/blog/ 2017/09/understaing-support-vector-machine-example-code/

Suriyah, M., Anandan, A., Narasimhan, A., & Karky, M. (2020). Piripori: morphological analyser for tamil. In *Proceedings of International Conference on Artificial Intelligence, Smart Grid and Smart City Applications: AISGSC 2019* (pp. 801–809). Springer. 10.1007/978-3-030-24051-6_75

Suryawanshi, S., Chakravarthi, B. R., Verma, P., Arcan, M., McCrae, J. P., & Buitelaar, P. (2020). A Dataset for Troll Classification of TamilMemes. *Proceedings of the WILDRE5– 5th Workshop on Indian Language Data: Resources and Evaluation, 1*(May), 7–13. https://www.aclweb.org/anthology/2020.wildre-1.2

Taghipour, K., & Ng, H. T. (2015, July). One million sense-tagged instances for word sense disambiguation and induction. In *Proceedings of the nineteenth conference on computational natural language learning* (pp. 338-344). 10.18653/v1/K15-1037

Tanabe, L., Xie, N., Thom, L. H., Matten, W., & Wilbur, W. J. (2005). GENETAG: A tagged corpus for gene/protein named entity recognition. *BMC Bioinformatics*, *6*(S1), 1–7. doi:10.1186/1471-2105-6-S1-S3 PMID:15960837

Tan, Z., Wang, S., Yang, Z., Chen, G., Huang, X., Sun, M., & Liu, Y. (2020). Neural machine translation: A review of methods, resources, and tools. *AI Open*, *1*, 5–21. doi:10.1016/j.aiopen.2020.11.001

Thabah, N. D. J., Mitri, A. M., Saha, G., Maji, A. K., & Purkayastha, B. S. (2022). A deep connection to khasi language through pre-trained embedding. *Innovations in Systems and Software Engineering*, 1–15. doi:10.1007/s11334-022-00497-9

Tham, M. (2020). Nlp tools for khasi, a low resource language. In *Proceedings of the 17th international conference on natural language processing (icon): System demonstrations* (pp. 26–27). Academic Press.

Tham, M. J. (2018a). Challenges and issues in developing an annotated corpus and hmm pos tagger for khasi. *The 15th international conference on natural language processing.*

Tham, M. J. (2018b). Khasi shallow parser. In *Proceedings of the 15th interna- tional conference on natural language processing (icon 2018). patiala, punjab, india* (pp. 43–49). Academic Press.

Tham, M. J. (2022). *Tham khasi annotated corpus.* https://catalog.elra.info/en- us/repository/browse/ELRA-W0321/

Tham, M. J. (2020). Bidirectional gated recurrent unit for shallow parsing. *Indian Journal of Computer Science and Engineering*, *11*(5), 517–521. doi:10.21817/indjcse/2020/v11i5/201105167

ThangarasuM.ManavalanR. (2013). *A Literature Review: Stemming Algorithms for Indian Languages*. *4*(8), 2582–2584. http://arxiv.org/abs/1308.5423

Thara, S., & Poornachandran, P. (2018). Code-Mixing: A Brief Survey. *2018 International Conference on Advances in Computing, Communications and Informatics, ICACCI 2018*, 2382–2388. 10.1109/ICACCI.2018.8554413

Thavareesan, S., & Mahesan, S. (2020). Sentiment Lexicon Expansion using Word2vec and fastText for Sentiment Prediction in Tamil texts. *MERCon 2020 - 6th International Multidisciplinary Moratuwa Engineering Research Conference, Proceedings*, 272–276. 10.1109/MERCon50084.2020.9185369

Thavareesan, S., & Mahesan, S. (2020). Word embedding-based part of speech tagging in tamil texts. In *2020 IEEE 15th International conference on industrial and information systems (ICIIS)* (pp. 478–482). IEEE. 10.1109/ICIIS51140.2020.9342640

Thenmozhi, D., & Aravindan, C. (2018). Ontology-based tamil-english cross-lingual information retrieval system. *Sadhana*, 43.

Thenmozhi, D., Kumar, B. S., & Aravindan, C. (2018). Deep learning approach to English- Tamil and Hindi-Tamil verb phrase translations. In *FIRE* (pp. 323–331). Working Notes.

Todi, K. K., Mishra, P., & Sharma, D. M. (2018). Building a kannada pos tagger using machine learning and neural network models. *arXiv preprint arXiv:1808.03175*.

Tomori, S., Ninomiya, T., & Mori, S. (2016, August). Domain specific named entity recognition referring to the real world by deep neural networks. In *Proceedings of the 54th Annual Meeting of the Association for Computational Linguistics (*Volume 2*: Short Papers)* (pp. 236-242). 10.18653/v1/P16-2039

Tozzo, P., Cuman, O., Moratto, E., & Caenazzo, L. (2022). Family and educational strategies for cyberbullying prevention: A systematic review. *International Journal of Environmental Research and Public Health*, *19*(16), 10452. doi:10.3390/ijerph191610452 PMID:36012084

Tribal Language Development Authority. (n.d.). *Government of Jharkhand*. Retrieved May 4, 2023, from https://tlda.jharkhand.gov.in/

Tribal Research Institute. (n.d.). *Government of Odisha*. Retrieved May 4, 2023, from http://tri.scdl.gov.in/Default.aspx

Tsapatsoulis, N., & Djouvas, C. (2017). Feature extraction for tweet classification: Do the humans perform better? *Proceedings - 12th International Workshop on Semantic and Social Media Adaptation and Personalization, SMAP 2017*, 53–58. 10.1109/SMAP.2017.8022667

Tummalapalli, M., & Mamidi, R. (2018). Syllables for sentence classification in morphologically rich languages. *Proceedings of the 32nd Pacific Asia conference on language, information and computation.*

Unnikrishnan, P., Antony, P., & Soman, K. (2010). A novel approach for English to South Dravidian language statistical machine translation system. *International Journal on Computer Science and Engineering*, *2*(08), 2749–2759.

Usié, A., Cruz, J., Comas, J., Solsona, F., & Alves, R. (2015). CheNER: A tool for the identification of chemical entities and their classes in biomedical literature. *Journal of Cheminformatics*, *7*(1), 1–8. doi:10.1186/1758-2946-7-S1-S15 PMID:25810772

Van NguyenM.LaiV. D.VeysehA. P. B.NguyenT. H. (2021).Trankit: A light-weight transformer-based toolkit for multilingual natural language processing. *arXivpreprint arXiv:2101.03289.* doi:10.18653/v1/2021.eacl-demos.10

Vaswani, A., Shazeer, N., Parmar, N., Uszkoreit, J., Jones, L., Gomez, A. N., . . . Polosukhin, I. (2017). Attention is all you need. In Advances in neural information processing systems (pp. 30-31). Academic Press.

Vens, C., Struyf, J., Schietgat, L., Džeroski, S., & Blockeel, H. (2008). Decision trees for hierarchical multi-label classification. *Machine Learning*, *73*(2), 185–214. doi:10.1007/s10994-008-5077-3

Verbeke, S. (2018). Some linguistic features of the Old Kashmiri language of the Bāṇāsurakathā. *Acta Orientalia Academiae Scientiarum Hungaricae*, *71*(3), 351–367. doi:10.1556/062.2018.71.3.7

Verywellfamily. (n.d.). https://www.verywellfamily.com/thmb/wRCDeFcZDIfnqMGGSfCMmxuKTiA=/1500x0/filters:no_upscale():max_bytes(150000):strip_icc()/what-are-the-effects-of-cyberbullying-460558_color1-5b50c42946e0fb0037b84d00.png

Vial, L., Lecouteux, B., & Schwab, D. (2019). *Sense vocabulary compression through the semantic knowledge of wordnet for neural word sense disambiguation.* arXiv preprint arXiv:1905.05677.

Vijayakrishna, R., & Sobha, L. (2008). Domain focused named entity recognizer for tamil using conditional random fields. *Proceedings of the IJCNLP-08 workshop on named entity recognition for South and South East Asian Languages.*

Vishwakarma, S. K., Lakhtaria, K. I., Bhatnagar, D., & Sharma, A. K. (2015). Monolingual Information Retrieval using Terrier: FIRE 2010 Experiments based on n-gram indexing. *Procedia Computer Science*, *57*, 815–820. doi:10.1016/j.procs.2015.07.484

Vlachos, A., & Gasperin, C. (2006, June). Bootstrapping and evaluating named entity recognition in the biomedical domain. In *Proceedings of the HLT-NAACL BioNLP Workshop on Linking Natural Language and Biology* (pp. 138-145). 10.3115/1654415.1654448

Walia, H., Rana, A., & Kansal, V. (2017, September). A Naïve Bayes Approach for working on Gurmukhi Word Sense Disambiguation. In *2017 6th International Conference on Reliability, Infocom Technologies and Optimization (Trends and Future Directions) (ICRITO)* (pp. 432-435). IEEE. 10.1109/ICRITO.2017.8342465

Wali, K., & Koul, O. N. (1997). *Kashmiri: A cognitive-descriptive grammar*. Psychology Press.

Wang, F., Wu, W., Li, Z., & Zhou, M. (2017). Named entity disambiguation for questions in community question answering. *Knowledge-Based Systems*, *126*, 68–77. doi:10.1016/j.knosys.2017.03.017

Wang, M., & Wang, Y. (2021, August). Word sense disambiguation: Towards interactive context exploitation from both word and sense perspectives. In *Proceedings of the 59th Annual Meeting of the Association for Computational Linguistics and the 11th International Joint Conference on Natural Language Processing (*Volume 1*: Long Papers)* (pp. 5218-5229). 10.18653/v1/2021.acl-long.406

Wang, Y., & Smith, L. (2020). Evaluation metrics for named entity recognition in low-resource languages. *Proceedings of the International Conference on Computational Linguistics, 67*(1), 142-149.

Wani, S. H. (2014). Divergence patterns in kashmiri-english machine translation: A view from translation of tenses. *Interdisciplinary Journal of Linguistics*, 6.

Wani, S. H. (2021). Kashmiri to English machine translation: A study in translation divergence issues of personal and possessive pronouns. *Indian J Multiling Res Dev*, *2*(1), 1–9. doi:10.34256/ijmrd2111

Warjri, S., Pakray, P., Lyngdoh, S. A., & Maji, A. K. (2021). Part-of-speech (pos) tagging using conditional random field (crf) model for khasi corpora. *International Journal of Speech Technology*, *24*(4), 853–864. doi:10.1007/s10772-021-09860-w

Warjri, S., Pakray, P., Lyngdoh, S., & Kumar Maji, A. (2018). Khasi language as dominant part-of-speech (pos) ascendant in nlp. *International Journal of Computational Intelligence & IoT*, *1*(1).

Weiss, A. (2022). Professor and victim: Cyberbullying targeting professors in the higher education workplace. In *Research Anthology on Combating Cyber-Aggression and Online Negativity* (pp. 1516–1532). IGI Global. doi:10.4018/978-1-6684-5594-4.ch077

Willett, P. (2006). The Porter stemming algorithm: Then and now. *Program*, *40*(3), 219–223. doi:10.1108/00330330610681295

Wołk, K., & Marasek, K. (2015). Enhanced bilingual evaluation understudy. *arXiv preprint arXiv:1509.09088.*

Xian-Yi, C., Ling-ling, Z., Qian, Z., & Jin, W. (2010). The framework of network public opinion monitoring and analyzing system based on semantic content identification. *Journal of Convergence Information Technology, 5*(10), 1-5.

Xiao, Y., Wu, L., Guo, J., Li, J., Zhang, M., Qin, T., & Liu, T.-y. (2023). A survey on non-autoregressive generation for neural machine translation and beyond. *IEEE Transactions on Pattern Analysis and Machine Intelligence*, 1–20. doi:10.1109/TPAMI.2023.3277122 PMID:37200120

Xie, L., & Yuille, A. (2017). Genetic cnn. In *Proceedings of the IEEE international conference on computer vision* (pp. 1379-1388). IEEE.

Xu, Y., Wang, Y., Liu, T., Liu, J., Fan, Y., Qian, Y., Tsujii, J., & Chang, E. I. (2014). Joint segmentation and named entity recognition using dual decomposition in Chinese discharge summaries. *Journal of the American Medical Informatics Association : JAMIA*, *21*(e1), e84–e92. doi:10.1136/amiajnl-2013-001806 PMID:23934949

Yadav, R. K., Jiao, L., Granmo, O. C., & Goodwin, M. (2021, February). Interpretability in Word Sense Disambiguation using Tsetlin Machine. ICAART, (2), 402-409. doi:10.5220/0010382104020409

Yuan, D., Richardson, J., Doherty, R., Evans, C., & Altendorf, E. (2016). *Semi-supervised word sense disambiguation with neural models.* arXiv preprint arXiv:1603.07012.

Zhang, C. X., Liu, R., Gao, X. Y., & Yu, B. (2021). Graph convolutional network for word sense disambiguation. *Discrete Dynamics in Nature and Society*, *2021*, 1–12. doi:10.1155/2021/2822126

Zhang, X., Su, J., Qin, Y., Liu, Y., Ji, R., & Wang, H. (2018). Asynchronous bidirectional decoding for neural machine translation. *Proceedings of the AAAI conference on artificial intelligence.* 10.1609/aaai.v32i1.11984

Zhou, G., & Su, J. (2002, July). Named entity recognition using an HMM-based chunk tagger. In *Proceedings of the 40th annual meeting of the association for computational linguistics* (pp. 473-480). Academic Press.

Zoph, B., & Le, Q. V. (2016). Neural architecture search with reinforcement learning. *arXiv preprint arXiv:1611.01578.*

Zoph, B., Yuret, D., May, J., & Knight, K. (2016). Transfer learning for low-resource neural machine translation. *arXiv preprint arXiv:1604.02201*. doi:10.18653/v1/D16-1163

About the Contributors

Partha Pakray is an Assistant Professor at National Institute of Technology, Silchar, India since August 2018. He worked as an Assistant Professor at National Institute of Technology, Mizoram, India from 2015 to 2018. He received his B.E. degree in Computer Science and Engineering from Jalpaiguri Govt. Engineering College, West Bengal, India; and M.E. and Ph.D. degrees from Jadavpur University, West Bengal, India. He received dual post-doctoral fellowships, one from Norwegian University of Science & Technology, Norway, funded by ERCIM (European Union) and another from Masaryk University, Czech Republic, funded by ERCIM & MU (European Union). His areas of research interest and specialization include natural language processing (machine translation, semantic textual similarity, text entailment, question answering, information retrieval, image captioning, summarization), machine learning, deep learning, and machine intelligence. He has published more than 150 papers in reputed journals, conferences and workshops proceedings, and 5 patents. He received 5 research funded projects from various funding agencies like DST, SERB, CEFIPRA, DAAD, ASEAN, MEITY.

Pankaj Dadure is working as an Assistant Professor in the School of Computer Science at the University of Petroleum and Energy Studies Dehradun. He has received his B. Tech and M. Tech degrees in Computer Science and Engineering. He has received his Ph. D in the domain of NLP from the National Institute of Technology Silchar. Dr. Dadure is enthusiastic and dynamic in the field of research with a significant number of publications and research articles in the field of Information Retrieval, Recommendation Systems and NLP with a focus on low resource languages. He pursues and manifests growth in work and in life that helps him achieve his goals to lay a significant impact and encourages young and naive researchers to pursue the domain.

* * *

Anuraj Bose, a dedicated and innovative M.Tech. student at Vellore Institute of Technology, is passionate about the intersection of computer science and statistical approaches. Born and raised in Naihati, India, Anuraj laid the foundation of his academic journey with a bachelor's from Maulana Abul Kalam Azad University of Technology. During his undergraduate years, Anuraj demonstrated his commitment to academia by presenting conference papers at the university level. Anuraj's dedication to his craft is underscored by his participation in the Science, Engineering, and Technology (SET) Conference in Vellore, India, where his paper was selected as a standalone work in SCOPE school.

Ali Boulaalam is an Associate Professor of Arabic Linguistics at Moulay Ismail University in Meknes, He holds a PhD in Computational Linguistics, He participated in several international and National academic events. He also supervised the management of the Regional Observatory for Territorial Intelligence and Development Modelling. Ali Boulaalam is interested in a number of fields related to computational Linguistics such as Linguistic engineering, technology of education, in addition to Machine translation. He is a member in the International Agency for natural Languages Engineering.

Satya Ranjan Dash is an Associate Professor in School of Computer Applications, KIIT University, Bhubaneswar, India. He received his MCA degree from Jorhat Engineering College, Dibrugarh University, Assam and M.Tech. degree in Computer Science from Utkal University, Odisha. He received his Ph.D. in Computer Science from Utkal University, Bhubaneswar, Odisha in 2015. His research interest includes Machine Learning, Bioinformatics and Cloud Computing(.09d1d6f1-d7dd-40d2-aa64-e09e074bccb6)

Debabrata Datta is presently an Assistant Professor in the Department of Computer Science, St. Xavier's College (Autonomous),Kolkata. He has teaching experience of more than 15 years at both the undergraduate level as well as the postgraduate level of Computer Science and Applications. He also has a research experience of about 10 years and his research interest is mainly in the domain of data analytics. He has published more than 30 research papers in different international peer reviewed journals as well as conferences. He has also contributed in 6 different book chapters so far. He is a life member of IETE.

Nisrine El Hannach is an Assistant Professor of English Linguistics at Nador Polydisciplinary Faculty- Mohammed 1st University of Oujda / Morocco Prof. Nisrine El Hannach is an Assistant Professor of English Linguistics. She is a Moroccan Professor and Researcher. She is the director of an educational institute in charge of empowering nonspeaking Arabic communities and helping them learn Arabic using creative approaches, she has also been involved in developing and designing a platform for online Arabic language assessment e-lang. Throughout her career as a professor, she has been teaching a number of subjects related to FLT and ESP in a number of private and public institutions. Along with her interest in linguistics, education, and communication Nisrine El Hannach is interested in Gender issues in relation to communication and migration.

P. Kathiravan received the M.Sc. and M.Phil degrees in Computer Science from Bharathidasan University in 2011 and 2012, respectively. He is pursuing a Ph.D. in computer science at the Central University of Tamil Nadu. His research interests include Social Computation, Natural Language Processing, Machine Learning, and Social Media Data Analytics. He is currently working on knowledge discovery from electronic word-of-mouth.

Arnab Kumar Maji received B.E. degree in Information Science and Engineering from Visvesvaraya Technological University (VTU) and M.Tech in Information Technology from Bengal Engineering and Science University, Shibpur (Currently IIEST, Shibpur). He received his Ph.D. from Assam University Silchar (A Central University of India) in the year. He has approximately 19 years of professional experience. He is currently working as Associate Professor in the Department of Information Technology, North Eastern Hill University, Shillong (A Central University of India). He has published around 39 nos. of research papers in several reputed internationally indexed journals. He has also published around 35 nos. of book chapter with several international publishers like Springer, IGI global. Around 15 papers he authored in several Conference proceedings. 03 edited books is published by him. 03 national patents is filed and 01 international patent and 01 copyright is granted to him as a co-inventor. He has so-far produced 04 Ph.D. scholars as main supervisor and 04 Ph.D. scholars as joint supervisor. His Research interests include Machine Learning, Image Processing, and Natural Language Processing. He is a senior member of IEEE.

Aadil Ahmad Lawaye received a master's degree in Computer Applications from the University of Kashmir, Jammu and Kashmir, India and a Ph.D. Degree in Computer Sciences from the Assam University, Silchar, Assam, India, in 2015. He has worked as "Computer Scientist" in the Department of Linguistics, University of Kashmir for the Projects Entitled "Development of Language Tools and Linguistics Resources for Kashmiri" and "Development of Indradhanush: An Integrated WordNet for Bengali, Gujarati, Konkani, Kashmiri, Oriya, Punjabi and Urdu" sanctioned and funded by "Ministry of Communications & Information Technology" and

"Department of Information Technology", Government of India, New Delhi. He is presently working as Assistant Professor in the Department of Computer Sciences, Baba Ghulam Shah Badshah University, Rajouri, J&K from September 21, 2017. His research interests are Natural Language Processing, Speech Processing, Cross Lingual Information Extraction and Retrieval. He has authored many research articles in the reputed journals and conferences.

Goutam Majumder holds a Ph.D. in Computer Science & Engineering from the National Institute of Technology Mizoram. His dissertation, completed in 2021, focused on "Interpretable Semantic Textual Similarity using Alignment of Chunks with Classification and Regression," demonstrating his expertise in NLP and semantic analysis. His educational qualifications also include a Master of Technology in Computer Science & Engineering from Tripura University, where he achieved the top rank in the Science & Technology Department. He also holds a Postgraduate Diploma in Advanced Computing from C-DAC Pune, and a Bachelor of Engineering (B.E.) in Computer Science & Engineering from the National Institute of Technology Agartala. Dr. Majumder has a strong research background with a total of 25 publications, including journal articles, conference papers, and book chapters. His research interests encompass topics such as semantic textual similarity, machine translation, and natural language processing.

Mahmood Hussain Mir has received his PhD. in Computer Science from the Department of Computer Sciences, Baba Ghulam Shah Badshah University, Rajouri, Jammu and Kashmir, India and he has received MPhil. Computer Science from St. Joseph's College, Bharathidasan University, Trichy, Tamil Nadu, India. Apart from above research, he has received his Master's in Computer Applications (MCA) from Baba Ghulam Shah Badshah University, Rajouri, Jammu and Kashmir, India and Bachelor's in Computer Applications (BCA) from Islamia College of Science and Commerce, University of Kashmir, Srinagar, Jammu and Kashmir India. His primary research interests are Internet of Things, Machine Learning, Edge Computing, and Healthcare Data Analytics.

Matan P. is a Computer Science Ph.D. scholar at College of Engineering Guindy, Anna University, specializing in Natural Language Processing. He received his Bachelor's degree in Computer Science and Engineering from Anna University in 2019 and a Master's degree in Computer Science and Engineering from Anna University in 2021. Matan's research interests include developing algorithms and models for improving machine understanding of natural language, with a focus on multilingual and cross-lingual language understanding. He has published research articles in many international journals. After graduation, he hopes to continue his research in academia and contribute to advancing the field of Natural Language Processing.

Velvizhy P. is a highly accomplished academician with over 13 years of experience in the field of Computer Science. She holds a Ph.D. degree in Computer Science from Anna University. She received her Bachelor's degree in Computer Science and Engineering from Pondicherry University in 2001 and a Master's degree in Computer Science and Engineering from Annamalai University in 2006. Her research interests focus on Recommendation Systems, Object Oriented System Development. She has published numerous research papers in leading engineering journals. Dr. P Velvizhy is currently working as Assistant Professor(Sl. Gr.) at Department of Computer Science and Engineering, College of Engineering Guindy, Anna University, Chennai. She is also a mentor and advisor to several graduate students and research scholars in the field of Computer Science.

Saranya Rajiakodi is currently working as an Assistant Professor at Department of Computer Science, Central University of Tamilnadu, Thiruvarur, India. She has completed her PhD in the area of Software Engineering in Madurai Kamaraj University, Tamilnadu, India during the year 2015. She has pursued her M.E and B.E in the Computer Science and Engineering at Anna University, Chennai, India. She has more than 10 years of teaching experience in postgraduate and undergraduate courses. She is a member of various academic bodies such as CSI, IEEE and IE. She has presented more than 15 research papers in International / National conferences and also published more than 10 research articles in peer reviewed journals (Scopus/SCI) and book chapters. She is also a reviewer of many international journals and conferences. Her area of interest includes Software Engineering, Social Media Data Analytics and IoT.

Goutam Saha received B.E. (Electrical Engineering) from University of Calcutta, India, M.E. (Electronics and Telecommunication Engineering) from University of Calcutta, India, Ph.D. (Engineering) from IIT Kharagpur, India, and P.D.F. from Ben Gurion University, Israel in the field of Bioprocess Engineering and Bioinformatics. He is a Professor in the Department of Information Technology, Dean, School of Technology, North Eastern Hill University, Shillong. Dr. Saha has 29 years of teaching and research experience. He works in the field of Systems Biology, Computational Biology and Bioinformatics, and Bioprocess Controller. He has guided 11 PhD Scholars. He has published one book, more than 25 papers in conference proceedings and various national and international journals, and also has one patent.

Index

A

AI4Bharat 53, 71
Ambiguity 89, 101, 106, 115, 119, 126-127, 135, 140
Arabic language 25-27, 29-31, 33-34, 36-40, 45-47, 125
Artificial Intelligence 2, 30-32, 87, 106, 114, 136, 165, 269
Austroasiatic Language 157-158
automatic processing 25, 39, 41, 46

B

Bambara Language 187, 190-191, 196
Baseline Methods 183, 192
Bi-LSTM 88, 103
BIO tagging 141
BLEU 64, 69, 91, 103

C

Centralized Hub 1, 3
Comparative Analysis 64, 73, 137, 151, 153, 183, 192
compositional grammar 40
Context-Window 135
cross-lingual applications 20-21
Cross-lingual transfer 14, 183-186, 192
Cross-Lingual Transfer Learning 14, 183-186, 192
Cross-Validation 126, 130, 135
CTL approach 184, 187, 193, 195
CTL Classifier 183, 187-190
CTL model 188, 191-194, 196
Cyberbullying 247, 249-270

D

Data acquisition 15, 20-21
Data Annotation 16
Data Collaboration 2
DataSets 1-6, 8-10, 14, 16, 20, 52, 64, 67, 69, 72, 99-100, 103, 117-118, 120, 123, 162, 186, 206, 209, 236, 239, 243
Datraw 1, 3, 5, 7-10
Decision Trees 118, 137, 147
Deconverter 89
deep learning 2-4, 17, 31, 64, 88, 90, 94, 97, 101-103, 105-106, 137, 200, 234-235
Digital India 52

E

electronic dictionaries 26, 31-32
Enconverter 89

F

Feature Selection 64, 126, 202, 207-209, 212-213
Finite State Transducer 94-95

G

Gated Recurrent Units 94, 137, 145, 148, 150, 153

H

Harassment 248, 250, 252-261, 264-269
Ho Language 157-159, 170, 173, 175

I

Indian languages 12, 17, 52-54, 58-60, 63-64, 67, 70-73, 115-116, 121-122, 138-139, 161-163, 168-170
Indian Languages Corpora Initiative 53
Information Extraction 87, 90, 92, 98, 102, 115, 138, 160, 164-165, 192
Information Retrieval 2, 17, 86-88, 93, 96-97, 107, 116, 160-164

K

Khasi language 137-141, 151, 153

L

language-related applications 93, 97
Linguistic Analyzers 25-26, 32, 46
Logistic Regression 137, 145-146, 150, 153
Long short-term memory (LSTM) 145, 148, 150, 153
Low Resource Language 1, 10, 20, 53, 59, 86, 139, 158

M

Machine Learning 2-3, 14, 16, 18, 31, 33, 45, 53, 57, 64, 93-94, 97, 102, 106, 113, 117-118, 123, 126, 130, 135-137, 139-140, 146, 150, 153, 162-163, 166, 185, 198-200, 205, 208-209, 212, 269
machine learning models 136, 140, 150, 209
Machine Translation 8, 17-21, 32, 47, 51-52, 54, 56, 58-60, 62-64, 67-68, 71, 73-74, 86-88, 90-91, 93, 96-98, 101, 103, 106, 115-116, 123, 160, 165, 186-187, 189, 191, 193-194
media marketing 235, 244-245
Meme Generator 233-234
Mental Health 13, 249, 251-253, 255, 257-259, 261, 268-270
Morphological Analysis 17, 61, 86-87, 89, 93, 97, 103, 107
Morphological Analyzer 33, 86, 91-94, 96, 101, 105, 107
Morphological study 87
Multinomial Naive Bayes 137, 146, 150, 153, 202

N

Naive Bayes Classifier 201
Named Entity Recognition 18, 103, 123, 157-159, 161, 163-166, 192
National Language Translation Mission 53, 70-71
Natural Language Processing (NLP) 2, 8, 11-13, 15-19, 21, 27, 31, 45-46, 51, 53-54, 57-58, 63-64, 74, 86-87, 93, 97-98, 105, 107, 113-114, 125, 136-138, 146, 159-160, 165, 183-185, 198-200, 207
NER techniques 158, 167-169, 175
Neural Machine Translation 60, 63-64, 68, 101, 103

O

Optical Character Recognition (OCR) 4-5, 235

P

Parsing 88, 93, 96-98, 100, 119, 137-141, 151, 153
Part-of-Speech 17-18, 120, 123, 137, 162, 167, 191

Q

question-answering systems 98, 105, 117, 160

R

Random Forest 137, 145, 147, 150, 153

S

Semantic Analysis 18, 86-87, 98, 106-107, 168, 192
Sense-Inventory 136
Sentiment Analysis 2, 8, 13, 15, 17-19, 64, 87, 98, 107, 115, 117, 186, 191, 193-194, 199-202, 205-207, 212, 214, 226-231, 233, 235-237, 239, 242
Social Media 11-16, 18, 160-161, 163, 170, 235-236, 244-245, 249-250, 253, 259-261, 263-264, 267-269
Support Vector Machines 87, 137, 153, 200-201

T

Tag Set 123, 139
Tamil Language 12, 17-18, 86, 93-97, 101, 103, 106-107
Text Mining 13
translation systems 20-21, 57, 59, 71, 93
Twitter 12, 15, 163, 172, 198-207, 229, 235

U

Unitex 25, 42, 46
Universal Networking Language 86-92, 100-101, 107

V

VADAR 233, 243
Vanilla RNN 145, 148, 150, 153
virtual assistants 93, 107

W

Warang Chiti 157-158, 164
Word Sense Disambiguation 98, 104, 113, 115, 136, 160

Ensure Quality Research is Introduced to the Academic Community

Become a Reviewer for IGI Global Authored Book Projects

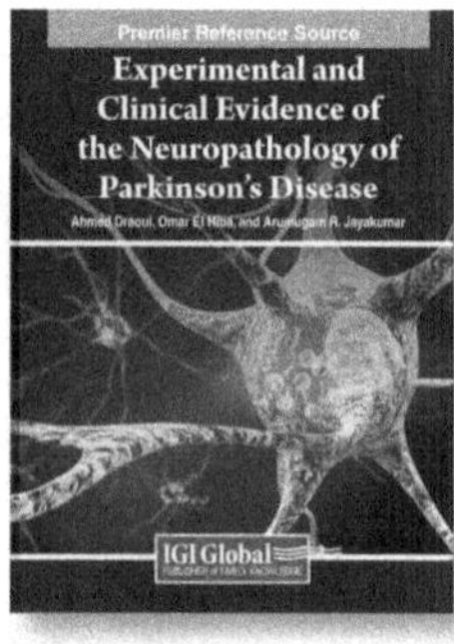

The overall success of an authored book project is dependent on quality and timely manuscript evaluations.

Applications and Inquiries may be sent to:

development@igi-global.com

Applicants must have a doctorate (or equivalent degree) as well as publishing, research, and reviewing experience. Authored Book Evaluators are appointed for one-year terms and are expected to complete at least three evaluations per term. Upon successful completion of this term, evaluators can be considered for an additional term.

If you have a colleague that may be interested in this opportunity, we encourage you to share this information with them.

www.ingramcontent.com/pod-product-compliance
Lightning Source LLC
LaVergne TN
LVHW080640011026
849160LV00014B/1275